STRATEGY FOR THE WEALTHY FAMILY

Seven Principles to Assure Riches to Riches Across Generations

STRATEGY FOR THE WEALTHY FAMILY

Seven Principles to Assure Riches
to Riches Across Generations

MARK HAYNES DANIELL

WILEY

John Wiley & Sons (Asia) Pte. Ltd.

This publication is designed to provide accurate and authoritative information in regard
to the subject matter covered. It is sold with the understanding that the publisher is not
engaged in rendering professional services. If professional advice or other expert assistance is required, the services of a competent professional person should be sought.

Other Wiley Editorial Offices

John Wiley & Sons, 111 River Street, Hoboken, NJ 07030, USA

John Wiley & Sons, The Atrium Southern Gate, Chichester P019 8SQ, England

John Wiley & Sons (Canada), Ltd., 5353 Dundas Street West, Suite 400, Toronto,
Ontario M9B 6H8, Canada

John Wiley & Sons Australia Ltd., 42 McDougall Street, Milton, Queensland 4064,
Australia

Wiley-VCH, Boschstrasse 12, D-69469 Weinheim, Germany

Library of Congress Cataloging-in-Publication Data

ISBN   978-0-470-82370-5

Typeset in 11/13 point, Minion by C&M Digitals (P) Ltd.
Printed in Singapore by Markono Print Media Pte. Ltd.
10   9   8   7   6   5   4   3   2   1

"Money, as money, is power in repose.
Set in motion, it may fall like dew or rush like a whirlwind;
it may be light to irradiate, or lightning to destroy…
The conditions of stewardship are not the terms of bargain and hire,
but of promise and grace."

Rev. Thomas Binney

Money: A Popular Exposition (1865)

TABLE OF CONTENTS

DEDICATION

This book is dedicated to
Anne-Catherine Sophie Alexandra Daniell,
the most recent addition to our own family.

About Family Office Exchange

Celebrating its 20th anniversary, Family Office Exchange (FOX) remains true to its founding mission of shared knowledge, owner education and peer exchange across a sophisticated, global network of wealth-owning families and their advisors. FOX is a membership-based advisory firm that serves as the definitive source of insight and best practices about managing and transferring family wealth. FOX is recognized as a leading provider of advice and consulting services for its member group of 500+ families and advisors in 23 countries, as shown below.

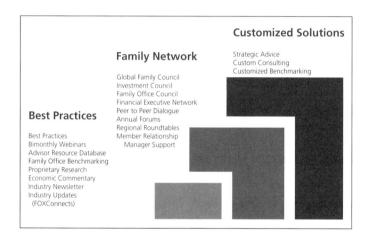

During the past 20 years, FOX has made significant contributions to the private wealth management industry, including the following "firsts":

- The first global community for idea exchange for wealthy families
- Strategic Councils for multi-generational and multi-national families
- Peer group benchmarking for family offices since 1991
- A carefully screened Directory of Leading Wealth Advisors
- An Educational Toolkit designed to prepare individuals to be responsible wealth owners
- Comprehensive studies on Family Office Compensation, Technology and Best Practices
- Thought Leadership forums on a variety of topics including The Role of the Family Office as Risk Manager and Identifying Conflicts of Interest

Information about Family Office Exchange and its global network of families and advisors can be found at www.familyoffice.com.

FOREWORD

Special FOX 20th Edition

Family Office Exchange (FOX) has been an advocate for hundreds of families around the world for the past 20 years, sharing the processes and practices that have helped the most enduring financial families survive and thrive. The challenge for the family is to develop a wealth management strategy to grow and preserve the family's assets (its financial and human treasures). Owners must appreciate the complexities of shared family wealth and the challenges involved in preserving the family's financial and human capital. An early FOX client very clearly summed up this challenge:

> "Help me make this wealth a source of satisfaction
> and reward for the family and not a source of stress."

"Strategy for the Wealthy Family" outlines a framework for the effective management of the complexities of the family enterprise, from the intricacies of sustaining a family business to the challenges of preparing the next generation to continue and strengthen the family's legacy. Mark Daniell's personal experience as a wealth inheritor and business consultant brings real insight to the work of effective family wealth management. His wealth management process and sample documents bring structure to the challenging work of transforming ideas and goals into practices designed to preserve family legacy and family wealth.

We hope that you will enjoy the compelling messages provided by *"Strategy for the Wealthy Family."* It is the perfect guide for any family on the journey to living a truly wealthy life. Enjoy the journey!

Sara Hamilton
Founder & CEO
Family Office Exchange

PREFACE

The Daniell family's economic fortunes have traversed many cycles over the nearly four centuries since we first came to America, in 1635, from East Anglia in the United Kingdom. The most significant Daniell family business in past generations was built by my great-great-great grandfather, Warren Fisher Daniell. Born on June 26, 1826, Warren Daniell was a hardworking entrepreneur in New England's nineteenth-century industrial era, building a healthy, privately owned business in and around the city of Franklin, New Hampshire. In addition to the core business of paper manufacturing, the family made brief forays into publishing, which included early versions of *The Farmers' Almanack* and a *Polyglott Bible*, published by Peabody & Daniell in the mid-nineteenth century.

According to New Hampshire state histories, the Daniell family business, known as J.F. Daniell & Son after the family's acquisition of the Peabody interests in 1854, became "one of the largest and best-known private manufacturing establishments in the state."

I am pleased to note that these same historical records are fulsome in their praise of the virtues and values of my forebears and their colleagues who led the nineteenth-century industrialization of New England. As one contemporary chronologist recorded in his description of Warren F. Daniell:

> [men like Warren Daniell] established their factories without the expectation that they were changing worthless plains and forests into cities or plain mechanics into millionaires. They aimed only to create productive industries and win a fair reward for their labor. But they were skilful workmen and under their inspiration and direction their enterprises have grown into great proportions, which have made the fortunes of their owners and called into being communities that are models of the best that skill and thrift can produce.[1]

The same author noted: "While compassing his own success, Mr. Daniell has contributed much to that of others, and in his struggle upward has pulled no one down."[2]

Would that all family patriarchs receive such heartfelt post-mortem praise and leave behind such an honorable and enduring legacy.

Mark Haynes Daniell
Singapore, 2007

---

[1] *History of Merrimack and Belknap Counties, New Hampshire*, D. Hamilton Hird (ed.), 1885.
[2] Ibid.

ACKNOWLEDGMENTS

In writing any book, an author will always benefit enormously from the experiences, insights, wisdom, and contributions of others.

The experts on strategy and family wealth in its many forms who made very valuable contributions to this particular book include: Stephen George, CIO of Capricorn Investment Group LLC; Robin Tomlin, Vice Chairman of UBS Asia; Christopher Wilson and Lane P. Pendleton of The Family Office Trust; TJ and Peggy Ng of Kwan Hua Art Gallery; Michael Haughey of RISQ Asia; Andreas Baer of Baer and Karrer in Zurich; Jimmy Hsu of TIF Ventures; R. "Jaya" Jayachandran; Prince Philipp von und zu Liechtenstein and colleagues at the LGT Bank; Michael Willcox of Willcox & Lewis; the private wealth management team at Goldman Sachs; the team at Private Banker International and VRL KnowledgeBank; Campden Publishing; Stan Miranda of Partners Capital Investment Group; Robert Chiu, Chief Executive of EFG Bank (Asia); and Dr. Randel Carlock, Berghmans Lhoist Professor and Director of the Wendel International Center for Family Enterprise at the INSEAD business school.

The manuscript itself benefited from the very expert attentions of Hilary Galea, editor at The Cuscaden Group, who did an exceptional job and made a great contribution to the quality, content, and style of the book. Mandy Young, also of Cuscaden, helped to ensure that the manuscript was properly completed and that all of us were fully supported along the way. I would like to thank Jeeta K'inan in London; Bruce Ross-Larsen at Communications Development Inc., in Georgetown; Nick Wallwork, Patricia Lee, Janis Soo, and Joel Balbin at John Wiley & Sons (Asia) Pte. Ltd; and editor John Owen. Their thoughtful suggestions made *Strategy for the Wealthy Family* a far better effort than it otherwise might have been.

I would also like to single out for thanks Asif Rangoonwala, who provided years of friendship, along with a network of contacts and a depth of experience that helped to shape the ideas and form the substance of this book.

Above all, I am grateful to a quiet friend, a vastly successful entrepreneur, investor, and family man who has been a constant and intelligent companion on the journey that this book became.

A final word of thanks goes to my own family, and in particular to my beloved wife Karin, whose patience, love, support, and understanding provide the greatest source of true wealth any man could ever hope for.

INTRODUCTION

There is a discreet world of the respected super-rich, where family legacies, high-return portfolio investments, successful family businesses, philanthropic endeavors, and protective trust practices have been refined and have evolved to reach the highest levels of excellence in private wealth management. These practices and strategies have been employed to build and protect great family fortunes across generations in many countries around the world.

Until today, the benefits and wisdom of that world have been inaccessible to most of us.

Drawing on the closely guarded knowledge of this inner sanctum, *Strategy for the Wealthy Family* brings to you the wisdom and practical knowledge from some of the world's wealthiest and most successful families about how to become—and remain—wealthy across generations.

Strategy for the Wealthy Family provides a clear framework for highly informed strategic management of the family, the family business, the family's financial assets, the family's approach to trust and tax management, philanthropic activities, risk factors, and the family's surrounding eco-system of institutions, advisors, friends, and influencers. It also provides insights, and an approach, to ensure that the important individuality of all family members is fully reflected in every aspect of strategy for the greater family.

Defining true family wealth as far more than pure financial capital, *Strategy for the Wealthy Family* sets out insights and information to help you to grow, protect, transfer, and share all aspects of your own family wealth successfully across future generations.

Ultimately, this is a book for those who wish to understand and manage their own family wealth, and to join the club of the world's best-managed wealthy families—and stay there.

It is indeed possible to beat the proverbial curse of "riches to rags in three generations." Whether you have $1 million, $1 billion, or even more, this book shows you how it can be done.

MASTERING THE CHALLENGE OF FAMILY WEALTH

A variation of the sad aphorism "from riches to rags in three generations" can be found in nearly every major civilization on earth, serving as a reminder of the permanent eclipse of many of the world's wealthiest family dynasties.

Two thousand years ago, in China, the proverb "*fu bu guo san dai*" ("wealth never survives three generations") was born. In thirteenth-century Europe, the adage translated into "clogs to clogs in three generations." In the United States, the saying became "shirtsleeves to shirtsleeves" and, in Asia, "paddy field to paddy field" in the same three generations.

More specifically, it is traditionally the first generation that makes the family wealth, the second generation that maintains the family fortune and the third generation that loses it.

History is littered with the names of once-wealthy families whose tumbles from financial grace are testament to the fact that beating the odds against family wealth preservation, and overcoming the gravitational forces of history, is no easy task.

LEARNING FROM "SUCCESSFULLY WEALTHY" FAMILIES

Yet, despite the universal presence of this repetitive three-generational pattern, there are wealthy families who have managed to identify and pursue strategies which have allowed great fortunes to be built—and to remain intact—across many succeeding generations.

The enduring prosperity of a select few "successfully wealthy" families across many generations proves that the age-old pattern of riches to rags can be mastered; family wealth can indeed be protected and wealthy families can prosper and grow across far more than three generations.

The history and practices demonstrated by these winning families show us that it is indeed possible for a family to build, preserve, and enjoy its wealth in a harmonious and supportive family environment.

By harnessing the experiences, approaches, and insights of the world's most successful and respected ultra-high-net-worth families, it is possible to provide leaders of other wealthy families with the tools they need to design and implement the best possible strategies to keep their own wealth intact, and flourishing, in an uncertain future.

Importantly, one of the most common insights from the world's most successfully wealthy families is that family wealth is far more than the sum of the financial assets of the family as a whole. Although often associated with great financial fortunes, true family wealth includes, but also goes far beyond, pecuniary or other material resources.

TRUE FAMILY WEALTH MORE THAN MONEY

True family wealth encompasses financial resources, but also includes family harmony, physical wellbeing, a broader sense of legacy and reputation, integrity, spiritual growth, intellectual capital, and the personal happiness of each family member. Not only do these intrinsic states of being determine the quality of family wealth in the broader sense, they also provide the platform from which continuing financial prosperity can best be pursued.

> True family wealth can thus be defined as what is most important to you.

True family wealth can thus be defined as what is most important to you. To that end, a family strategy is, at its essence, about identifying and preserving that which you hold most dear through time and across generations.

With popular magazines and research reports now counting 8.7 million identified millionaires in the world,[1] and nearly 1,000 billionaires,[2] the number of wealthy families in the world who could benefit from a more strategic approach to their family's future fortunes is large, and increases daily.

---

[1] Merrill Lynch–Capgemini *World Wealth Report 2006*, Figure A, "HNWI Ranks Show 10 Years of Steady Expansion," p.3. www.us.capgemini.com/worldwealthreport/

[2] *Forbes Magazine* Special Report: "The World's Richest People", edited by Luisa Kroll and Allison Fass, 8 March, 2007. http://www.forbes.com/2007/03/07/billionaires-worlds-richest_07billionaires_cz_lk_af_0308billie_land.html

THE "HAVES AND THE HAVE YACHTS"

The total value of financial assets in the hands of families with wealth exceeding US$1 million is now estimated to be over US$37.2 trillion.[3] We are living in an era of unprecedented concentrations of wealth, with the richest 1% of the population now owning 40% of the world's financial resources.[4]

This accumulation of so much financial capital in the hands of such a limited population has given rise to a new term highlighting the difference between the ordinary affluent population and the truly wealthy.

For many years, economists have spoken about the poverty gap looming between "the haves and the have nots." More recently, another phrase has been coined to describe a new gap emerging at the highest end of the economic spectrum, whimsically referred to as the gap between "the haves and the have yachts."

It is these "have yachts" who may possess the greatest fortunes, but who also face the greatest challenges in preserving and growing their family wealth.

> ...another phrase has been coined to describe a new gap emerging at the highest end of the economic spectrum, whimsically referred to as the gap between "the haves and the have yachts."

WEALTH CREATION AND DESTRUCTION

The first decade of the new millennium was an era of great wealth creation and prosperity. For many wealthy families, it was the greatest time ever to create, grow—or lose—a family fortune. Not only were there more wealthy individuals and families created than ever before, there were also more fortunes lost than ever expected during the good times.

---

[3] Merrill Lynch–Capgemini, op. cit.
[4] World Institute for Development Economics Research of the United Nations UNU-WIDER study on "The World Distribution of Household Wealth," 5 December, 2006, p.26. http://www.wider.unu.edu/research/2006-2007/2006-2007-1/wider-wdhw-launch-5-12-2006/wider-wdhw-report-5-12-2006.pdf

World economic turbulence, rising capital market volatility, a property boom and bust in many countries, mergers and acquisitions of unprecedented proportion, the rise and fall of alternative asset classes, changes in geographic markets and industrial sectors, skyrocketing—and then plummeting—annual and retirement compensation packages for highly paid CEOs, investment bankers, hedge fund managers, private equity partners, cagey investors and a host of other individuals, families, and corporations have all created wealth challenges of an extraordinary magnitude.

It may come as a surprise to those who associate family wealth with established legacy fortunes to discover that, through thick and thin, the vast majority of the wealthiest families and individuals made their fortunes themselves. According to the Merrill Lynch–Capgemini *World Wealth Report 2006*, less than 20% of wealthy families received their wealth through inheritance; the remaining 80% earned their fortunes through career-related compensation, investment, or the ownership or sale of operating businesses.[5]

In many ways, wealth creates more wealth. The rise of private equity funds and hedge funds, for example, created a circle of newly wealthy families in four related areas: those who sold their businesses to private equity and hedge funds; families of the partners and managers of those funds; families of the investors who backed the funds; and finally, but far from least, families of the investment bankers who arranged the deals and who took home annual multi-million-dollar compensation packages.

In 2006, three hedge fund managers took home earnings exceeding US$1 billion.[6] In the United Kingdom, 12 partners from Goldman Sachs alone were reported to have achieved a net worth exceeding US$160 million.[7] Sound strategies can preserve many of these recent fortunes.

In addition, CEOs and other employees are receiving compensation packages unprecedented in the history of business. The CEO of Occidental Petroleum, Dr. Ray R. Irani, took home a US$400-million reward in 2006,[8] joining such celebrity CEOs as Jack Welch of GE,

---

[5] Merrill Lynch–Capgemini, op. cit., Figure 12, "Sources of HNWI Wealth, 2005", p.19.
[6] Jenny Anderson and Julie Cresswell, "Top Hedge Fund Managers Earn Over $240 Million," *New York Times*, 24 April, 2007.
[7] The Sunday Times Rich List 2007, *The Sunday Times*, London, April 2007, p.45
[8] Reuters Limited, *USA Today*, www.usatoday.com/money/industries/energy/2007-04-08-oxy-pay_N.htm

Michael Eisner of Disney, and Lee Raymond of Exxon, to become a centimillionaire through job-related compensation and options schemes.

The boom in capital and property markets, accompanied by the emergence of new geographic markets—notably the BRIC markets of Brazil, Russia, India, and China—have created a whole new crop of families rising swiftly in the ranks of the world's wealthy.

Fame and fortune: Artistic and athletic endeavor can now pave the way to great riches as well as to great fame. Michael Schumacher, seven times world Formula One champion, Swiss resident and savvy investor, is reputed to be nearing (and maybe even surpassing) US$1 billion in personal net worth—and with years of investment still to come. Tiger Woods may be golf's first billionaire. He is joined by multi-million-dollar sports stars such as David Beckham, Roger Federer, Maria Sharapova, Shaquille O'Neal, LeBron James, Barry Bonds, Alex Rodriguez, Roger Clemens, and other famous stars who are building large financial fortunes as rapidly as they build careers of great athletic accomplishment.

Oprah Winfrey, David Geffen, Arnold Schwarzenegger, Madonna, and a whole galaxy of media magnates and Hollywood stars have also built enormous financial fortunes to match their global fame and celebrity status.

Even writing, historically associated with struggling artists in cold attics, can today be a pathway to a golden future. Earnings from Dan Brown's blockbuster *The Da Vinci Code* were reported to have mounted to US$88 million between 2005 and 2006.[9] The Harry Potter series made J. K. Rowling one of only five self-made female billionaires by 2006, and the first billion-dollar author.[10] Rising to the top levels of global wealth for the first time, successful authors are generating fortunes far beyond those which even their own fertile imaginations could have created a few short years ago.

RICHES TO RICHES: A MULTI-GENERATIONAL CHALLENGE

Wealth creation is a great accomplishment and a giant step toward the establishment of a multi-generational legacy of wealth, stature, and influence.

---

[9] *Forbes Magazine*, "The Top 100 Celebrities," 2006, www.forbes.com/lists/2006/53/T5P9.html

[10] James Burleigh, "JK Rowling conjures up $1 billion fortune," *The Telegraph*, 10 March, 2007, http://www.telegraph.co.uk/news/main.jhtml?xml=/news/2007/03/09/nrich09.xml

Yet it is only the first step of a much longer journey to maintain and grow that wealth across multiple generations, a journey that requires the application of a different set of insights, the development of a different set of skills, and the development and execution of a different kind of family wealth strategy from that which created the wealth in the first place.

An unfamiliar challenge: Nearly US$40 trillion of family wealth is expected to be transferred across generational lines in the next 50 years, in the United States alone.[11] According to some experts, nearly 70% of cross-generational transfers of wealth in the past have failed to achieve their desired objectives.[12]

Despite the enormous wealth built with extraordinary speed and capability in so many areas, the creators of these large "have yacht" fortunes all share one common characteristic: they all face the challenge of maintaining their new fortunes and, later, of transferring that wealth successfully to future generations.

For many wealthy families, and for all families creating wealth in a first generation, there is no precedent or model within their experience for the preservation and transfer of that wealth. This lack of experience can present many challenges, because only those capable of developing a forward strategy that stretches out across multiple generations are the most likely to preserve and enhance their family wealth across those same generations.

THE IMPORTANCE OF A STRATEGIC FRAMEWORK

Ironically, despite such an enormous amount of money being at stake, and with such daunting odds against success, there has been little guidance or information available on how to respond effectively to the many demands created by this phenomenon of growing wealth, and the need to transfer that wealth intact to future generations. One of the reasons that so few families are sufficiently prepared in the most vital areas of family wealth strategy is that relevant frameworks have been missing, and information has been diffuse, evolving by the year, and hard to pull together into any coherent and useable model.

---

[11] Boston College Social Welfare Research Institute, "Millionaires and the Millennium: New Estimates of the Forthcoming Wealth Transfer and the Prospects for a Golden Age of Philanthropy," John J. Havens and Paul G. Schervish, October 1999, introduction.
[12] Roy Williams and Vic Preisser, *Preparing Heirs: Five Steps to a Successful Transition of Family Wealth and Values*, 2003, Robert D. Reed Publishers, p.17.

While the costs and efforts required can be higher than expected, particularly for the newly rich, the returns on such an investment in family strategy can be enormous in both financial and non-financial terms, and the costs of failure to make the same investment can be truly catastrophic.

THE SEVEN PRINCIPLES OF STRATEGY FOR THE WEALTHY FAMILY

Strategy for the Wealthy Family provides a comprehensive strategic framework, and a set of proven approaches within each element of that framework, to guide the wealthy family successfully across multiple generations.

Although each strategy will be as different as the family that creates it, there are a number of consistent principles, derived from the most successful family strategies, which can be extracted, analyzed and employed to further the plans of any wealthy family.

The elements of strategy to be integrated into one common strategic framework embrace all seven principles and combine to form a coherent, unified approach to a family's future. Strategies for each of these elements will need to be developed separately, and then adapted as necessary, to fit into an overall framework which can lead to a fully integrated and aligned approach to family wealth strategy.

Like a chemical compound, these individual elements can be bonded together, over time and with the application of energy, to

---

The Seven Principles of *Strategy for the Wealthy Family*

Principle 1: Set a family strategy with an objective of multi-generational preservation and growth of family wealth

Principle 2: Organize the family and manage the surrounding eco-system

Principle 3: Structure asset holdings and adopt practices for long-term asset preservation

Principle 4: Diversify assets and access the best investments and investment managers through a formal process of asset allocation and wealth management

(continued)

(continued)

Principle 5:   Clarify and integrate family business strategy with long-term family wealth plans

Principle 6:   Share wealth in a manner that unites the family and gives it meaning

Principle 7:   Remember the unique nature of individual family members—including yourself

create a new and unified structure which will be stronger and more enduring than any individual element on its own.

In addition to embracing these seven principles, a consistent characteristic of successfully wealthy families is that they consciously invest time, thought, effort, and funds to define and execute an integrated strategy to create the greatest likelihood of their wealth surviving long into the future.

A UNIQUE FORM OF STRATEGY

Family wealth strategy is different from any other kind of strategy. There are complex and interrelated issues to consider. Even the time frame for the strategy is unique. Family strategy requires a long-term view that extends forward across three generations (at least), at a time when business, technology, and other strategies are often getting shorter in cycle.

> "The solution to a problem never arises at the same level as the problem itself."

There is not a clearly defined competitor with whom to compete, or against whom one can measure relative success or performance; the strategic foe are more likely to be found in the volatility and vicissitudes of financial markets, the risks of substantial tax obligations, the weight of history, the burden of great potential, and the many human problems that can arise within the family itself.

Finding solutions: As Albert Einstein once famously stated, "The solution to a problem never arises at the same level as the problem itself." To resolve the problem of wealth dissipation in a later generation, the best solution may well lie in addressing the full set of challenges now, before the problem of wealth dissipation even arises. Good family strategy needs to look deeply and honestly into family history, but also needs to gaze forward with intelligence and realism into the future.

Structure, organization, and integrity are also important components of an overall solution. A family with a strong set of values and a shared sense of family unity and purpose is far more likely to retain its financial wealth than a dissolute and disorganized family lacking the fundamental insights, wisdom, and disciplines necessary to protect and enhance its future financial status.

By seeking intelligent solutions to future problems at the various levels and times where they are most likely to be found, family leaders will be employing a more measured and more effective response to the historic challenges of the preservation of family wealth.

FAMILY SPIRIT AND INDIVIDUAL FULFILLMENT

In the pursuit of the goal of a happier and more substantial future, one cannot lose sight of the fact that a family is both an entity in itself and a collection of unique individual members.

No one person is ever the same as another, even in a family with a strong sense of shared identity and a common set of values. Each member of a family possesses a unique character with differing skills, capabilities, interests, and limitations. Each has a private destiny. All of our children are born to lead individual lives, which may or may not be based upon an interest in making money or managing a business in the traditional context of a wealthy family.

Great family strategy will need to consider and facilitate the diverse achievements and aspirations of all of its individual members. Fostering a sense of individual purpose and meaningful accomplishment can be a powerful contributor to the successful future of any privileged family, significantly increasing the likelihood of the family remaining together and prospering through time and across generations.

A FRAMEWORK FOR FAMILY STRATEGY

Set a family strategy with an objective of multi-generational preservation and growth of family wealth

1. THE ELEMENTS OF STRATEGY

While each family strategy will be unique in its content and execution, there are four characteristics that are common to all good family strategies. They should all:

- address the full set of elements illustrated in the framework below
- address all elements on both an individual and integrated basis
- take a long-term, multi-generational forward view
- be practical and capable of being implemented.

There is obviously no "right" answer that can be easily imported from other successfully wealthy families. Each family will need to design and implement its own practical approach with regard to its organization, leadership, eco-system, family businesses, wealth preservation, wealth management, philanthropy, and its individual members.

> All elements of strategy for a wealthy family need to be developed from a multi-generational forward perspective.

PLANNING ACROSS GENERATIONS

It is ironic that, in a business world where strategic cycles are getting shorter and shorter, family strategy needs to be extended well beyond the time horizon of most individuals' thinking. It is simply impossible to master a multi-generational challenge with only a short-term plan or limited set of immediate actions in hand. All elements of strategy for a wealthy family need to be developed from a multi-generational forward perspective.

Effective family wealth strategy requires a forward view across three generations, with each generation addressing its own issues while, at the same time, anticipating those of its children and grandchildren. Only in this way can families make the most lasting and valuable contribution to their own family and financial legacies.

> "Don't stop, thinking about tomorrow. Don't stop, it'll soon be here."

Although such long-term thinking may not yield immediate benefit, there is indeed valuable wisdom in the words of the popular Fleetwood Mac song: "Don't stop, thinking about tomorrow. Don't stop, it'll soon be here."

The essential elements of family strategy, as outlined in Figure 1.1, are defined and described below.

Figure 1.1 An Integrated Framework for Family Wealth Strategy

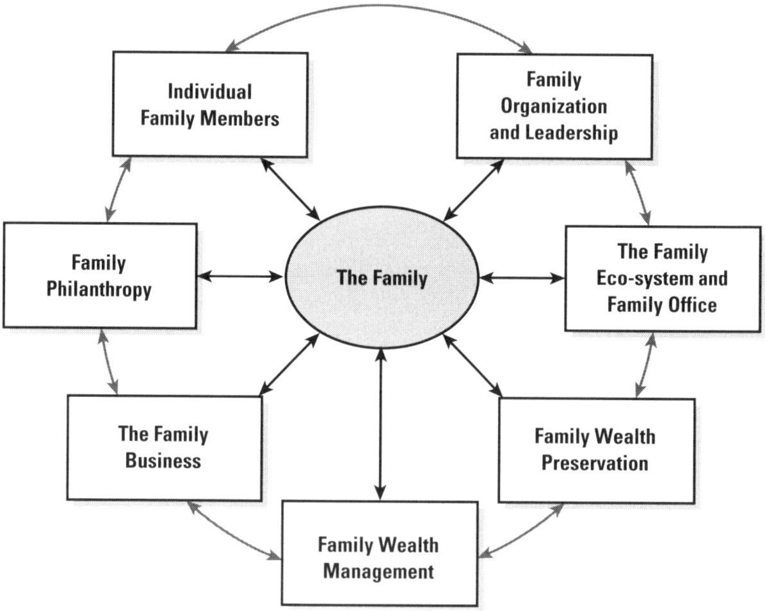

THE FAMILY

At the centre of the integrated framework lies the family itself, providing the *raison d'être* of the strategy and exerting gravitational influence on all constituent elements of that strategy. The family is defined by bloodlines, history, traditions, values, and relationships developed over time. It is both the sum of its members, family units, family generations, and informal family groupings, and a complete unit unto itself.

A good family wealth strategy will need to consider the family as a whole, and to reflect the importance of all of its various internal dynamics. Further, it will need to take into account the full merits, aspirations and limitations of each individual family member.

Family legacy—a major concern: In a 2007 survey carried out by the Family Office Exchange,[1] a group dedicated to serving the needs of wealthy families, the top three concerns cited by the 40 ultra-high-net-worth families surveyed were:

1. Family legacy
2. Family governance and decision-making
3. Family relationships

In setting out a strategy for any wealthy family, these concerns need to be given the prominence they deserve. Only by identifying and addressing family issues can related issues—such as wealth preservation, investment performance, and family business strategy—develop in a sustainable context. Without an agreed approach to the family itself, or in a situation where a negative family dynamic overwhelms an agreed approach, issues of family wealth are very difficult to address and optimize.

In designing and implementing strategy, addressing the priority issues within the family may be one of the greatest contributors to the reduction of risk, and to the realization of opportunity, that family leaders can offer.

FAMILY ORGANIZATION AND LEADERSHIP

A first critical element in developing a multi-generational family wealth strategy is an organized approach to the family and to family structures. The family business, wealth management and philanthropic activities, and even the greater family itself, can all benefit

---

[1] Sara Hamilton, "Families at Risk", *Worth* (April 2007) Vol.16, No.4, pp.46–8.

from a cohesive and organized approach to family roles, governance, and leadership.

Perhaps captured in a formal family constitution for a large family, an organized approach will create a solid platform upon which successful strategies can be built.

That robust platform can serve to increase engagement and harmony, reduce conflict, improve ties, and address, with better information and decision-making, the key concepts of a family's true wealth—financial, intellectual, spiritual, and emotional.

THE FAMILY "ECO-SYSTEM" AND FAMILY OFFICE

None of the strategic elements can be pursued successfully without the support of external resources and influencers surrounding a family. That interconnected eco-system, consisting of individuals, institutions and communities surrounding and connected to the family, plays a very important role in shaping the values and characters of the family, and in preserving its fortunes over time.

All of the active participants making up that eco-system need to be reviewed and managed as potential sources of influence, good and bad, in a family's future. One key part of the eco-system may be a dedicated Family Office—an organization set up to look after many of the family's interests, including tax and estate planning, wealth management, business issues, philanthropic initiatives, and the more personal aspects of family management.

The Family Office is usually staffed by outside professionals, reporting to a senior member of the family or, in the first generation, to the founder of the family fortune.

FAMILY WEALTH PRESERVATION

Beating the odds of history and remaining rich across more than three generations requires a specific strategy to protect family wealth from the greatest risks and sources of potential loss.

Everything from estate planning, scenario planning, historical awareness, tax management, investment disciplines, spending and distribution patterns, family values, and other elements of a forward-thinking approach to risk management needs to be considered in developing a structured approach to wealth preservation.

FAMILY WEALTH MANAGEMENT

Every wealthy family, by definition, has a substantial amount of financial wealth. Assets can be tied up in an illiquid and concentrated family business or property holding, or may already be fully liquid and managed as a diversified portfolio of global financial investments. Many of the wealthiest families have, in fact, a combination of both.

No matter how the wealth is held, each family will need to determine its investment profile, set its investment objectives and define a disciplined and high-quality investment process in order to make the most of its current assets and future opportunities.

Suddenly wealthy: Many families and individuals who have become suddenly wealthy, or find themselves holding substantial liquid wealth for the first time, are discovering that wealth management is a separate discipline from operating a business; it requires separate skills, a separate knowledge base, and a different approach to business analysis and fund management than does operating a manufacturing or service business.

All too often, wealthy families believe that because they have run an operating business successfully for generations they can swing smoothly and quickly into the management of a complex international investment portfolio. Avoiding this classic error, and moving swiftly to a new best-practice approach to wealth management on a portfolio basis, is a key factor in preserving the fortunes of many wealthy families facing the transition from "business family" to "investing family."

THE FAMILY BUSINESS

A family business, if one exists, may play a central role in a family's history and future economic fortunes. That business can be a major contributor to the family's stature in the various communities to which it belongs. A family business can also play a dominant role in the individual careers, personal aspirations, and lifestyles of family members.

As well as addressing the full set of considerations applicable to any business strategy, such as customer analysis, channel evolution, cost position, service levels, and competitive situation, a family business carries with it a separate set of challenges related to the family's role in ownership and management. These may be particularly sensitive in areas of finance, brand, HR management, leadership, and other elements of organizational and commercial strategy.

Role in wealth management: In addition to playing a central role in family history and family members' careers, a family business may play a major *de facto* role in wealth management, as the holding can create a major source of value, and brings with it both risks and opportunities in the context of a family's total wealth calculation.

A family business, which can generate the bulk of a family's income, and may constitute the bulk of its assets, may require offsetting portfolio management actions including, but not limited to, diversification, exposure reduction, and hedging single-stock concentration risk.

FAMILY PHILANTHROPY

Many wealthy families, of all scales and categories of wealth, will share some of their accumulated wealth by supporting a charitable organization or philanthropic cause. Some may even create their own philanthropic foundations and related organizational entities. Philanthropy can also play a major role in a family's history, current identity, and future unity. Sharing wealth effectively, and with a clear sense of value and purpose, is an essential element of the strategic framework for any wealthy family.

Defining the vision, objectives, practices, organization, and target results of a successful wealth-sharing program requires a dedicated effort, a substantial amount of thought and an application of the same kind of discipline and intensity brought to bear on a family business or a program of wealth management and preservation.

INDIVIDUAL FAMILY MEMBERS

The consideration of individual family members, each distinctive and unique as well as an indissoluble part of the collective family entity, is essential to any successful wealth strategy. The sum of individual strengths and weaknesses, values, aspirations, and actions will ultimately determine the future of the greater family.

Family strategies which fully contemplate the individual are inherently more stable, and far more likely to succeed, than those which attempt to impose a similar life pattern on every family member.

INTERDEPENDENT ELEMENTS

The first reason to consider all elements of strategy on an integrated basis is that they are all inextricably intertwined. Trust structures and strictures can have an influence on estate plans and wealth management. Philanthropic objectives can have an influence on wealth management and family infrastructure. The family eco-system can play a major role in all aspects of family strategy.

A second reason is that the interaction of the elements can create an even better outcome in any one area of strategy than would an isolated approach. By considering each element on a standalone basis, family leaders and strategists will be able to create a series of focused strategies targeted at the achievement of specific objectives in each critical area of family strategy. By integrating these individual strategies into a coherent whole, they will contribute to overall results which are far greater than the sum of the individual parts.

The third reason to proceed on a coordinated basis is to ensure that all elements of strategy are aimed at achieving the same overarching goal; alignment of activities is far more likely to lead to the achievement of the desired outcome. Throughout the process, it should be remembered that the ultimate goal of a strategy for the wealthy family is to achieve the greatest possible harmony, happiness, and prosperity for the family across many succeeding generations.

2. DEFINING TRUE FAMILY WEALTH

Financial wealth is an obvious and important component of family wealth, but it is only a part of a much larger concept. Any strategy for a wealthy family begins with an understanding of what family wealth means for that particular family.

True wealth is about having an abundance of those things we cherish most in life. In identifying and focusing on those things, families can set out with a clear sense of purpose to establish and implement strategies which will assist them in increasing, as much as possible, the quantum of true family wealth in this broader and more valuable definition.

As noted family counselor Jeffrey Murrah remarked: "The challenging question is, 'What is true wealth?' Definitions of wealth which consider only bank accounts, possessions and property are wholly inadequate. Limiting the definition of wealth to those things only identifies people who are miserly. Ironically, the root word for 'miser' and 'miserable' are the same." [1]

The notion of a broader and deeper definition of wealth is not new. For many centuries terms such as a "wealth of ideas" and a "commonwealth of nations" have been used to indicate abundance, connection, sharing, and value beyond the purely financial or commercial. The word "commonwealth" carries with it many levels of meaning, including reference to those things which bind countries together, such as a common culture, a shared set of values, perhaps a common language and, most importantly, a common set of interests for the future.

> "Definitions of wealth which consider only bank accounts, possessions and property are wholly inadequate."

THE LOST MEANING OF WEALTH

Somehow, over the years, the original and more comprehensive definition of wealth has been lost. In recent times, a definition limiting the concept of wealth to the material, or to items with a specific financial or

---

[1] Jeffrey D. Murrah, from his essay "The True Meaning of Wealth," in *Pasadena ISD Parent University* magazine, www.pasadenaisd.org/ParentUniversity/parent42.htm.

trading value, has become common. This is unfortunate, since it replaces a more comprehensive, and more meaningful, historic definition.

At its essence, wealth is a broad concept of plenty. The true definition of family wealth extends to embrace non-financial aspects of life which include family harmony, individual happiness and a positive contribution to the world beyond the family.

"Wealth" is described in the Merriam-Webster dictionary as deriving from the obsolete word "weal," a Middle English word which, in turn, comes from the Old English word "wela." "Weal" means "a sound, healthy or prosperous state" and is akin to the modern words "well" and "wellbeing," meaning "in a good overall state".

True wealth, in its original English meaning, thus encompasses both tangible and intangible, and material and non-material, attributes of life. Family wealth is thus all about improving the overall state of affairs for a family and creating an abundance of goodwill, good fortune, and prosperity across all aspects of family life.

In other linguistic systems, the notion of wealth also has deeper meaning than the purely economic. In Chinese calligraphy, there is a fascinating character which represents the broader idea of family wealth. The character, which is read as *fu*, is best defined as family happiness and cohesion, combined with business prosperity and good fortune. The character is extraordinarily robust: unlike almost all other characters, it can be written in hundreds of different ways—and can even be read correctly when written upside down.

Definition and action: For all wealthy families of all nations and cultures, defining family wealth, and pursuing it through conscious strategies and tangible actions, is an individual choice that will vary in form, content, objective, and impact from one family to another.

But in all cases, the challenge of family wealth is not mastered merely by preserving financial wealth across multiple generations. This would be stale consolation indeed if all other aspects of a family are in disarray. The desired goal of any full family wealth strategy is to protect and grow financial wealth while fostering all aspects of a unique family's history, heritage, happiness, and future legacy.

THE CONTENT OF TRUE FAMILY WEALTH

While there is no prescribed taxonomy of family wealth which can help to define a common structure for every family, there are seven frequently recurring aspects which merit consideration in any definition of family wealth.

The Content of True Family Wealth

- Financial wealth
- Integrity
- Accomplishment
- Physical security, health, and fitness
- Knowledge, wisdom, and spiritual growth
- Family harmony
- Individual happiness

The content of true family wealth is made up of a series of individual, yet interdependent, parts. These common elements can combine to create a concept of family wealth which is far greater than the sum of its individual parts.

FINANCIAL WEALTH

Money, for many entrepreneurs and business-focused families, can be a way of keeping score; it can be a measure of success and a major source of identity and stature for a family.

Money is also a tool and a kind of energy—a means to an end, not an end in itself. Financial wealth, when used appropriately, is a means by which a family can achieve greater success in all aspects of true family wealth. Money is a great enabler and financial wealth, properly managed, is a key that can open the door to a far wider world of opportunity for many generations to come. The very word "money" carries with it a sense of great power and potential. Its etymology traces its roots back to Juno Moneta, a Roman goddess within whose Capitoline temple was located the official mint.

Financial wealth can create security for future generations, providing a home, healthcare, and an education commensurate with the abilities and ambitions of each family member. It can also provide families and individuals with the freedom necessary to pursue a broader array of opportunities and life choices without worrying about earned income, daily expenses, or the need to squirrel away reserves for future emergencies.

Financial wealth also makes it possible to contribute toward bettering the lives of those less fortunate. Donations and trusts can be established to support educational or religious institutions, environmental organizations, community services, and community or international health programs.

INTEGRITY

Integrity is perhaps even more important than financial wealth, which can rise and fall with time. A family's ethical and moral foundations are an essential part of what a family is—and is not.

Integrity has meaning at many levels, combining such worthy attributes as incorruptibility, unity, soundness, and completeness. It is both a stabilizing point of reference in turbulent times and an aspiration and desired state of being at all times. It is neither relative nor situational.

> "I cannot and will not cut my conscience to fit this year's fashion."

The enduring value of integrity is well captured in the words of the actress Lillian Hellman during the McCarthy Era hearings: "I cannot and will not cut my conscience to fit this year's fashion."[2]

The development and maintenance of an immutable sense of integrity, family values, work ethic, humility, and a respect for others all contribute fundamentally to true family wealth and the long-term success of the family. These attributes are both benefits in themselves and the foundation upon which a family's future financial fortune can best be preserved.

Conversely, a lack of integrity is a great risk to a family's future, both in its potential impact on the family's financial assets and its threat to the broader qualities and values of family members. Boundaries need to be set, and disciplines observed, on what a family is and what it stands for.

---

[2] Quoted in Ellen Schrecker, *The Age of McCarthyism: A Brief History with Documents* (Boston: Bedford Books of St. Martin's Press), 1994, pp.201–2.

ACCOMPLISHMENT

To a great extent we are what we do; or, at the very least, our actions (and lack of actions) reflect who and what we are.

Our efforts, our accomplishments, our failures and our dreams all make up a substantial part of our family's history and its current sense of self; this past and present set of efforts and accomplishments will also go a long way toward defining the family's future legacy.

PHYSICAL SECURITY, HEALTH, AND FITNESS

The old adage "healthy, wealthy, and wise" begins with the notion of physical health. There is no price for the gift of health and safety for our loved ones, and no way to set a value on an existence free from danger, pain, suffering, and illness.

Taking care of our physical welfare and the health of other family members is a key part of family wealth today and an essential step toward continuing family progress into the future.

Perhaps the ancient classical civilizations best summarized the value of physical and mental health as linked objectives in the saying *mens sana in corpore sano*: a healthy mind in a healthy body.

KNOWLEDGE, WISDOM, AND SPIRITUAL GROWTH

Developing a healthy and well-educated mind, a deeper understanding of the world, and a spiritual dimension to life are also important parts of family wealth.

While knowledge can be defined relatively simply as an accumulation of facts, principles, and observations regarding the world around us, wisdom is a more complex word. As a result, wisdom has many more definitions but they are less precise. It has been defined as the "use of knowledge" or a "framework of understanding to give depth and meaning to isolated facts."

Wisdom has also been defined as that which helps us to understand what we know, and, perhaps even more importantly, of knowing what we don't know.

Nicholas Maxwell gives his definition of wisdom as follows: "Wisdom is taken to be the capacity to realise what is of value in life, for oneself and others. It includes knowledge, understanding and technological know-how, and much else besides."[3]

> "Wisdom is taken to be the capacity to realise what is of value in life, for oneself and others. It includes knowledge, understanding and technological know-how, and much else besides."

In many civilizations and religions around the world, the pursuit of spiritual development or the adherence to religious practice is of the highest priority—a goal far more important than the pursuit of money or other tangible possessions in the temporal world. Spiritual insight and practice are considered to be the highest form of human wisdom and knowledge.

For millennia, spiritual or religious affiliations have shaped and defined families. They have had an enormous impact on family identity, the development of family values, and on family decisions regarding geographical location, business practices, marriage, the education of children, traditions, and many of the most important family standards and objectives.

Increasingly, members of many families, including the wealthy, are embarking on personal quests to seek a deeper and more individualized meaning to life, to discover more about spirituality and their personal relationship to the divine beyond the confines of an established religion. The paths they explore and the answers they find in these personal quests can reshape family beliefs and recast the definition of a family's true wealth, as well as influencing, in great measure, how they, and their children, manage their personal lives and material wealth going forward.

FAMILY HARMONY

Our greatest happiness, and therefore the greatest source of family wealth in a broader sense, can come from the love found in the context of a supportive, harmonious, and united family. Similarly, family conflict and division can be the cause of our greatest unhappiness, and one of the most common sources of wealth destruction.

---

[3] Nicholas Maxwell, *From Knowledge to Wisdom*, Blackwell, Oxford, 1984.

Ironically, as we observe the histories of families who have fallen from financial grace, their decline is not always due to problems associated with purely financial or business decisions. The real reason many family fortunes fall apart can be related to family issues and failures in family value systems.

By addressing carefully the important components of family harmony within every generation, financial wealth is far more likely to be maintained and improved upon, now and into the future.

INDIVIDUAL HAPPINESS

Ultimately, human happiness cannot be fully quantified, nor can it ever be presumed to be the same for different individuals. While there are common factors, such as the existence of love within a family, the discovery of aesthetically pleasing experiences, emotional satisfaction, loving and being loved in a marriage, and enjoying a sense of individual purpose and accomplishment, the final determination of what makes us happy is based upon an entirely individual set of emotions, needs, desires, experiences, attitudes, and objectives.

The pursuit of happiness, an idea from the Age of Enlightenment so powerful it was enshrined in the American Declaration of Independence and in other fundamental national documents of the time, is also an essential element of a family's wealth strategy.

Unhappy family members are unlikely to find the will, or the understanding, to contribute to the successful future happiness, harmony and prosperity of the greater family.

FAMILY WEALTH AND FAMILY LEGACY

It is the pursuit of this broader definition of family wealth which creates a family's legacy; one which can vary enormously, from the exalted to the ignominious.

Each wealthy family carries with it the burden of great potential; those who leave behind only shallow and meandering footprints on the sands of time stand as a testament to a lost opportunity for substantive contribution to the world in which they lived.

The worst of legacies leave only an indelible stain on the fabric of history, reflecting an unnecessary loss of wealth and stature, or an uninspiring level of individual and collective accomplishment. This

> "For of all sad words of tongue or pen, The saddest are these: 'It might have been!'"

sense of lost potential is perhaps best captured in the words often attributed to Kipling, but actually penned by John Greenleaf Whittier: "For of all sad words of tongue or pen, The saddest are these: 'It might have been!'"[4]

On the other hand, the best of family legacies will stand as a testament to accomplishment and the realization of our full human potential. These legacies are perhaps as described by the poet Stephen Spender, setting out in the most luminous of terms the highest standards of aspiration and attainment for which a family can strive:

> *I think continually of those who were truly great . . .*
> *The names of those who in their lives fought for life,*
> *Who wore at their hearts the fire's centre.*
> *Born of the Sun they travelled a short while towards the sun,*
> *And left the vivid air signed with their honour.*[5]

---

[4] From *Maud Muller*, Stanza 53 (1856), in John Bartlett, *Familiar Quotations*, 14th edition, Little, Brown and Company (1968), p.626.
[5] Stephen Spender, "I think continually of those who were truly great," *Oxford Anthology of English Literature*, Kermode and Hollander, eds., Oxford University Press, 1973.

3. CATEGORIES OF FINANCIAL WEALTH AND THEIR IMPLICATIONS

The scale of wealth required to be considered a "wealthy family" is rising all the time. It was recently proposed by the United States government that the threshold level of liquid wealth required in order to be considered sufficiently wealthy to invest in certain types of asset classes and transactions be raised from US$1 million to US$2.5 million, and even to US$5 million in certain high-risk areas.[1]

In another analysis of what it takes to be a millionaire, a team of economists looked at the purchasing power of US$1 million in the 1960s, when the "millionaire" concept and label became popular. Their conclusion: it takes US$10 million today to achieve the same level of economic standing as a "millionaire" as defined a half-century ago.

While, for some, being wealthy may be a state of mind independent of financial assets, for our purposes, substantial financial assets are a major consideration in the forward strategy for the family.

Although there are many definitions and segments of "high-net-worth," "ultra-high-net-worth," "rich" and "super-rich" families, the four broad categories of wealth outlined in the table below capture groups with similar opportunities with regard to family wealth strategy.

Needless to say, the value of good strategy and the scale of potential positive change rise with each level of wealth.

Wealth Category	Description	Family Investible Assets (in US Dollars)
I	Substantial family wealth	$1–10 million
II	Significant family wealth	$10–100 million
III	Legacy wealth	$100 million–1 billion
IV	Super-rich	$1–100+ billion

---

[1] Federal Register/Vol.72, No.2/Thursday, 4 January, 2007/Proposed Rules. *Part III Securities and Exchange Commission, 17 CFR Parts 230 and 275*, pp.405–6.

While these categories provide convenient segments to think about the various strategic options open to a family with wealth of the magnitude indicated, there is no magic or defined cut-off at any of these levels of family wealth; strategies for a Category II family may well have a high degree of sharing with approaches taken by a Category III family, and vice versa.

Combining resources, achieving scale. The consolidation of resources, whether within one family or when combined with other families, can be critical to long-term investment success. There is great value in combining strengths, particularly in the various alternative asset classes, where scale counts in gaining access to scarce world-class investment managers. For first-time investors, in particular, gaining access to a top-quality manager with a small pool of family funds may be an impossible task.

One family with US$100 million to invest will have far more presence in the minds of fund managers than, say, a group of four families with US$25 million each. At a lower level, the same economics of consolidation could benefit a group of like-minded siblings each with US$250,000 to invest, allowing them to jointly achieve a "fund" of US$1 million for investment.

The issue of access to fund managers and other strategic issues relating to the four categories of wealth are spelled out in more detail below.

CATEGORY I: $1–10 MILLION

This category of wealth, with its families holding an average investible net worth (excluding residential property and net of all debt, including mortgage debt) of US$5.5 million, may have been built from a successful professional career, business development, inheritance, or investment.

Wealth of this first level can provide a luxury lifestyle, a broad-based domestic or international investment portfolio and access to a wide range of retail investment products and advisors. Primary, and possibly secondary, residences may make up a part of the total net worth, but still leave a comfortable seven-figure sum for investment.

For many in this wealth bracket, the main family focus may be on a single family unit, with, as yet, no aspirations to broader inclusion, no need of a broader, formal family structure, and no opportunity to establish a Family Office or access the services of a high-level Multi-Family Office (MFO).

If there is a family business involved, it is usually of a small to medium size with little, if any, international presence. Many German *mittelstand*, and similar Asian companies, established after the Second World War, would fall into this category.

Wealth management in this first category may be pursued on an *ad hoc* asset allocation basis, with a network of local brokers and other advisors providing recommendations on a product-by-product basis, including all traditional asset class products and some alternative asset funds, funds of funds and small direct investments. Alternative assets at this level of wealth usually make up a relatively small portion of the investment portfolio, represented only by highly selective participations, if any, and may be entered more logically via a fund of funds.

The usual asset structuring approach to a Category I fortune is a single domestic trust, or master trust with associated sub-trusts for children of the settler sharing on an equal basis. In some cases, partnerships and corporations may also be used. Inheritance tax issues may be addressed through a large life insurance policy rather than complex off-shore trust structures.

Local charities, schools and colleges, church and community healthcare projects make up the bulk of philanthropic activity for most individuals and families in this bracket.

Supporting resources are usually made up of a network of brokers, bankers, accountants, family lawyers, "mass" private banks with entry-level account requirements below those of the more selective elite banks, and the smaller MFOs. Clients of this wealth level are pursued by investment and private banks, which may employ a limited set of standard wealth management tools and off-the-shelf allocation models, with limited exposure to most alternative asset classes. If not employing a central private advisor, broker or private banker, many Category I individuals and families manage their own asset allocation models within a single currency context.

If advised by one of the "mass" private banks, the investor has probably been advised to pursue one of the following standard asset allocation models, along with some cash holdings: high risk (70% equities/30% fixed income), medium risk (50%/50%) or low risk (30% equities/70% fixed income). In addition, the investor may have been persuaded to place a substantial amount of money in the bank's proprietary products or in structured products, which are great fee earners for the banks, bankers, or brokers, but perhaps do not represent best-in-class investments for the client.

Although the infrastructural and investment options available may be more limited than for the wealthiest families, the strategic approach required is the same for all families: wealth preservation will justify asset structuring, careful tax management and estate planning; wealth management will merit the development of a personalized asset allocation model and management of costs and risks in a portfolio; and family members will need to prepare for the inheritance of what is, by any realistic definition, a substantial amount of money.

CATEGORY II: $10–100 MILLION

In this category of significant family wealth, those with an average of US$55 million of investible assets, are families with the potential for a luxury lifestyle in almost every jurisdiction, often with multiple residences and a significant investment portfolio. Unless tied up almost exclusively in a single business or illiquid asset, a Category II portfolio is usually of sufficient scale to merit global asset allocation and to seek direct access to selected high-alpha investment managers who provide financial returns well above their peer group benchmarks.

The family business, if there is one, may be publicly listed, and may also have been professionalized, in whole or in part, at a management level.

The approach to wealth management can be very sophisticated, employing a global asset allocation model with various currency positions and a range of higher yielding (and higher risk) alternative asset products. There is an opportunity for the more sophisticated or better advised client to enter a balanced portfolio of all asset classes directly and via selected funds of funds.

Category II wealth may be protected by a series of independent trusts, many of which are offshore for non-U.S. residents. Issues of manager concentration, trust jurisdiction, and trustee diversification become relevant.

Philanthropic endeavors can achieve significant scale, with some families in this category preferring (and able) to establish a substantial dedicated charitable presence or separate foundation in their communities.

The supporting resources are made up of high-level advisors, possibly one or more MFOs, and, at the higher end of the category, a small Family Office which may be integrated with a family business headquarters.

Wealth of this level opens the door to the more selective private banks and most high-level private wealth advisors. There may be a dedicated (but not exclusive) team at a leading private bank with access to interesting investments, a philosophy of "open architecture" which allows the sale of third-party products and a consolidating approach to achieve the scale necessary to access the more selective fund managers.

Many private banks and wealth services create a separate sub-category within Category II of ultra-high-net-worth families, which begins at US$30 million. This threshold level is seen by some banks and wealth advisors as creating a sufficient sum of money to take care of all lifestyle and family needs and still leave sufficient funds for longer term, more sophisticated investment.

CATEGORY III: $100 MILLION–1 BILLION

At this level of wealth, enjoyed by only about 15,000 families around the world, all reasonable personal spending can be taken care of for many lifetimes, with a substantial amount of money left over for structuring, investment, and management.

One unique feature of the US$100 million level of wealth is that it may justify the establishment of a dedicated Family Office. Such an institution, usually set up initially to provide tax and estate planning advice, trust management and family services, investment manage-ment, and oversight of philanthropic foundations, can ensure that all aspects of a family wealth strategy are clear, organized, and executed.

Since the costs of even a small Family Office can amount to a minimum of US$1 million, wealth of at least US$100 million is required to cover the expense at a maximum of 1% of assets under management. Below this level, the potential benefits available do not often justify the expense of such a dedicated office when compared to the higher quality alternatives available.

The starter Family Office is usually led by a competent profes-sional, perhaps the family's trusted accountant, banker or lawyer, whose salary and bonus may make up the bulk of a small Family Office's expense.

Wealth of this magnitude allows the individuals who create or inherit it to begin to access many best-in-class fund managers, to gain access to virtually all investment products, and to share information with the world's financial elite, both individual and institutional. Individuals and families of this financial stature also have the potential to make a substantial contribution to the greater philanthropic world.

Individuals and families with Category III wealth and above should also be thinking in terms of an approach to wealth management which is global in scope and scale. Sophisticated currency models and asset allocation approaches can be adopted which reflect this global scale of wealth.

Multiple trusts and other asset structures, with multiple layers in multiple jurisdictions with multiple trustees, may be employed to manage taxes of all kinds. These trusts may be run with or without a consolidating master trust or parent holding company or corporate entity. A trust, trustee, and trust jurisdiction diversification policy may be adopted to ensure that a great proportion of a family fortune cannot be lost due to the failures of any one asset structure, investment decision or professional relationship.

The same diversification policy can apply to investment managers as well, with wealth of this category providing sufficient scale to create a number of investment portfolios which will be of interest to even the most selective of managers.

At the higher end of this category, and increasingly at the low end as well, the expense to set up a private trust company may be justified and a custom-tailored approach taken to trust operations and administration.

The family eco-system can be of the highest quality, including those important institutions and influencers which can affect the family and the individuals within it. Some of these influencing institutions such as schools, communities, or organizations may be able to be influenced themselves, or even created, by wealth of this magnitude.

Risk management, including physical security for family members in some countries, can become an important issue at this level of family wealth. All aspects of risk need to be taken into account for individuals whose wealth is, in itself, sufficient reason for the media and others to take an interest in the private lives of the members of the family, whether or not they seek such attention.

CATEGORY IV: $1–100+ BILLION

A billion dollars is a massive amount of money by any definition at any time in history. There are only an estimated 1,000 individuals with wealth of this scale in the world today.

The Category IV, or "super-rich," families can benefit from the most sophisticated asset allocation models and investment knowledge. They can enjoy access to fund managers usually available only to the largest investing institutions of the world—university endowments, pension funds, insurance companies, and the like—which have large staffs of financial professionals and benefit from knowledge and access to all asset classes and to the top managers of the world.

> Being "inside the velvet rope" does not mean everyone gets to the head of the queue…

However, even a billion dollars of capital may be insufficient to access all the best opportunities in a world awash with liquidity. Being "inside the velvet rope" does not mean everyone gets to the head of the queue when it comes to accessing the most attractive venture capital, private equity, property, and hedge fund opportunities.

The supporting resources found in the eco-systems of this highest tier of private wealth, which can help to identify and secure the best investment opportunities, may include a private Family Office, or perhaps even a strategic network of dedicated Family Offices and creative strategic platforms, along with access to high-level Family Office networks.

At this top end, the amount of funds available may require individuals and families to consider changes of nationality, domicile, and residence to optimize their long-term aggregate tax and wealth position.

Philanthropy on a grand scale can be undertaken, with an enormous impact felt for many generations by many thousands, if not millions, of beneficiaries.

At this very top end, which could be described as encompassing all those who have wealth from US$1 billion through to the wealth of Bill Gates, virtually all strategic approaches across all elements in the strategic framework will differ from those of a Category I individual or family.

THE NATURE OF GREAT WEALTH

In one fabled conversation, F. Scott Fitzgerald, elegant author of *The Great Gatsby* and a man fascinated with the lives of the super-rich, said to fellow author Ernest Hemingway: "The rich are different from you and me." "Yes," replied Hemingway, "they have more money."

In this exchange can be seen two views on the challenges facing the wealthy family as it ascends the various categories of financial wealth. Hemingway recognizes that, at a minimum, these families just have more money to consider, more financial decisions to make and greater material opportunities to pursue in otherwise normal human lives.

From a Fitzgeraldian perspective, the vaunted wealthy live in a state so different, and face issues so unique, that the fundamental nature of their lives is altered.

Whatever your own category of wealth, and whatever your own family history and situation, a thoughtful and comprehensive approach to all of the unchanging elements of strategy is far more likely to help you to defeat the odds of history, preserving the benefits and freedoms created by your own family wealth across many future generations.

4. EVOLUTION ACROSS GENERATIONS

Wealthy families do not stand still—they continually develop and evolve over time and across generations. A successfully wealthy family is one that manages that evolution well, addressing all aspects of family wealth and pursuing strategies that keep family wealth, in all of its forms, intact and flourishing across generations.

As wealthy families grow and extend across generations, the challenge—and therefore the skills required to be successful—changes in scale and content.

WEALTH CREATION IN THE FIRST GENERATION

Wealthy families are usually created by an entrepreneurial individual, a savvy investor, or by the joint efforts of a group of entrepreneurial individuals within the same family.

Creating wealth often requires an intense focus of effort and attention in one area of business or investment. The strengths of the entrepreneur are usually his or her business decision-making abilities, a preparedness to take high levels of risk, and a willingness to put in the effort to drive forward and create a new enterprise or a liquid pool of assets of substantial economic proportion.

The dominant wealth-creating personality, often characterized by an independent nature with little need of outside affirmation or advice, usually concentrates all aspects of family, family business ownership, family business management, wealth management, and philanthropic donation under his or her direct control.

In many cases, that same personality may not be as well adapted to develop complex tax-effective inheritance and estate structures, to think forward across multiple generations, and to develop an inclusive family model which will provide stability in the future as well as dynamism in the present. As a result, addressing the requirements of a successful evolution for a wealthy family—if they are addressed at all—may be left to the following generations.

As the original family wealth devolves from one generation to the next, each passing generation is less likely to reflect the concentration of power that characterized the original wealth creators.

In order to understand the best path forward from this original wealth-creating generation, identifying the most common evolutionary patterns can be instructive.

CLASSICAL MODEL OF EVOLUTION OF THE FAMILY AND THE FAMILY BUSINESS

In 1982, Professors R. Tagiuri and J. A. Davis published a working paper at the Harvard Business School which analyzed the patterns of ownership, management, and family activity within families owning private enterprises.[1] Their pioneering work demonstrated conclusively that there were indeed common and predictable patterns in the way that most business families evolved over the first three generations.

The evolutionary model they propounded showed that the three areas of the family, family business ownership, and family business management visibly diverged over time and across generations.

In the founder's generation, these three elements are usually dominated by an individual, and operate as one integrated system, with all aspects coming together at a single source of strategic decision-making and implementation responsibility.

This single, merged approach in the first generation is illustrated in Figure 1.2.

Figure 1.2   Family Model Generation I

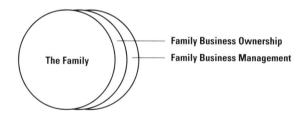

In the second generation, the three elements begin to diverge, with some outsiders perhaps brought in to join and lead management teams, with some family members pursuing careers outside the family business and, perhaps, with some outside shareholders or

---

[1] R. Tagiuri and J. A. Davis, "Bivalent attributes of the family form," Working Paper, Harvard Business School (1982).

partners in the business. This second stage of development is illustrated in Figure 1.3.

Figure 1.3   Family Model Generation II

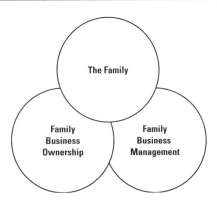

In a third and final stage of development, often found in the
third or later generation of a business family, the three areas operate
independently. This diverged set of responsibilities and activities is
illustrated in Figure 1.4.

Figure 1.4   Family Model Generation III

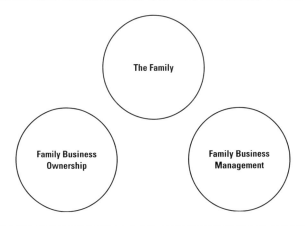

The implications of this normative pattern are significant
because the roles created are different for each generation; any family that wishes merely to replicate the roles and responsibilities of a

preceding generation may not be focused on the correct roles or areas of greatest relevance and potential for value addition in a new and different paradigm.

Families that navigate only with a rear-view mirror will not be preparing adequately for the future. They may even fall prey to the old adage that "today's generals are always fully prepared to fight yesterday's battles."

By seeing clearly the underlying patterns of change, leaders of more successful families will be able to think through the best strategies, roles, responsibilities, and responses within the context of a predictably evolving family model.

Although the work of Professors Tagiuri and Davis was ground-breaking in 1982, and is still relevant as a contribution to general understanding, a more complex view of a modern family's evolution may illuminate a broader set of challenges and opportunities for today's wealthy family.

A VERY MODERN MODEL

As an understanding of family wealth has evolved, a more advanced family model has emerged, resulting from the expansion of the three-element model to one with six interrelated elements. This modern model can provide more relevant guidance for the development of family strategies, and can help to prepare family members to take up a larger and more specialized role or responsibility.

In addition to the three original elements, family leaders would now be well advised to add the elements of business governance, wealth management, and philanthropic activities to the planning and management of family affairs.

In developing this richer model, there is still a very high overlap of activity in the first, wealth-founding generation. This first stage of the development of a wealthy family, with a more complete set of variables than the original 1982 model, is shown in Figure 1.5.

In a second phase, particularly for large families in the higher wealth categories, these six elements begin to diverge, just as they did in the Tagiuri–Davis model. Some family members may be involved only in governance (sitting on boards or committees) and others may focus only on wealth management or philanthropic activities. In other cases, a senior family member may still retain a role in all

Figure 1.5   Family Model Generation I—Wealth Creation

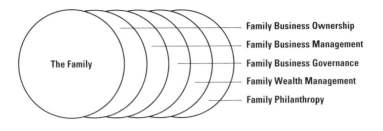

family activities. This second phase of development is illustrated in Figure 1.6.

Figure 1.6   Family Model Generation II—The Direct Heirs

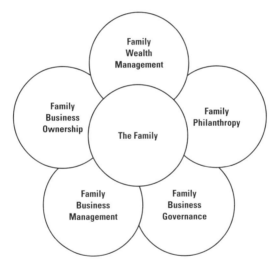

By the third generation, or in a subsequent generation which follows the sale of the family business, many different configurations may emerge which cannot adequately be represented in the simpler three-element model. If confined to the elements of the 1982 model, a family which has sold its primary operating business has no visible operating activities to bind it together. A more detailed model, however, shows the number of opportunities for commercial, investment, and philanthropic activity by the family which can provide a bonding platform to endure beyond the sale of the business.

Some family members may sit on boards, participating in governance activities but eschewing management responsibilities. Others may participate in wealth management activities, a business in its own right, but not manage operating businesses in any direct fashion. Still others may remain involved in family matters and philanthropic initiatives, but prefer to avoid commercial activities in either an operating business or wealth management role.

This extended range of possibilities can be represented using the six elements which make up this more complex model, with two such variations illustrated in Figures 1.7 and 1.8.

Figure 1.7   Family Model—"Post-Management Generation"

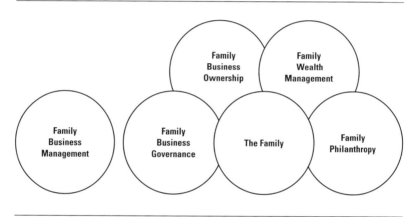

Figure 1.8   Family Model—"Post-sale Generation"

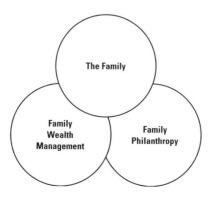

POST-SALE FAMILY MODELS

One of the reasons why a wealthy family may want to consider employing a more sophisticated model in the second, third, or following generation is that, following the sale of a family business, the roles and responsibilities which can bind a family together are fewer.

As demonstrated in Figure 1.8, however, there are still roles available for family members to consider in family life after the sale of the family business; the earlier three-element model set out in Figure 1.3 would not illustrate these opportunities and could leave many members adrift on a sea of liquidity, with little consideration of unifying opportunities in the areas of family wealth management and family philanthropy.

However the family evolves, the same challenges and elements of multi-generational wealth preservation and enhancement strategy need to be addressed in every generation.

There is, of course, no obligation or expectation that a particular family will follow the typical evolutionary patterns described above. For example, the Wiley family, controlling shareholders of the privately controlled and publicly listed company publishing this book, are now in the seventh generation of business leadership, a long and unbroken 200-year history, in which family members continue to play leading roles in management, governance, ownership, and other family business matters.

5. PROCESS AND CONTENT OF FAMILY STRATEGY

One of the great advantages of drawing on the past experiences of other successfully wealthy families is that the content and process of strategy can be clarified, and valuable lessons extracted and applied, for the benefit of a family undertaking its first strategic exercise.

THE DECISION TO BEGIN

There is no single answer to the question "When is it best to begin a family strategy?"

At any stage in a family's history, family leaders may act upon an opportunity to design and implement a new strategy, or renew or revise an existing strategy. However, there are three common trigger points which have, historically, caused many families to undertake such an initiative.

The first impetus for setting out on such a strategic exercise is related to a major wealth-creating or liquidity event, such as the sale of a family business. With consolidating global industries and private equity and hedge funds completing more—and larger—acquisitions, the number of realizations of this type is increasing every year.

A second trigger event for many families is a generational change. This could be a transition in leadership from the first or second generation to a larger set of inheritors with a more diverse set of skills or interests in a following generation, or could be from a new generation of leadership emerging in a later generation in a multi-generational family.

The third common trigger is the result of a number of factors moving together at the same time, creating a kind of internal "tipping point" where the confluence of a rising scale of financial wealth, the occurrence of a major liquidity event, the emergence of a major risk factor, changes in the family or family leadership, the desire to create a philanthropic foundation, and a host of other relevant and interrelated factors can evolve and coalesce to bring about the need for a comprehensive strategic review.

FAMILY WEALTH CHECK

In order to understand whether the time is right for you and your family to undertake a strategy exercise, a simple wealth check may help to clarify where you are, and what the best next steps might be.

Unlike a health check, which may involve complicated tests and analyses, a wealth check to see whether or not your family could benefit from an investment in family strategy is simple, easy, and painless. All that is required, no matter how wealthy your family, is a "yes" or "no" answer to three basic questions:

- Do you have a clear and documented strategy to preserve and enhance your family wealth—in all its dimensions—across future generations?
- Do all relevant members of the family understand and support that strategy?
- Are you implementing that strategy successfully?

If your answer to these three questions is in the affirmative, you are among the very small minority of families who have addressed this important family issue properly, and should be firmly congratulated for having an effective family wealth strategy in place.

If your answer to any of these questions is in the negative, then it could be instructive to carry out a more thorough check of your vital wealth signs by asking yourself some more specific questions:

- Do you understand who you are as a family—your history, values, and principles—and share a perspective of what makes you unique with all family members? Do you know how you define family wealth in the broader sense of the term?
- Have you thought through how best to organize the family as a unit and how to manage your family's surrounding eco-system of individuals, institutions, advisors, schools, friends, family office resources, and other influences on the current and future state of your family?
- Do you have a specific plan to protect and transfer your family's financial wealth across generations, as efficiently and as effectively as possible? Are members of the next generations fully prepared to be good inheritors?

- Have you paid sufficient attention to the mechanisms—trusts, wills, family business principles, investment philosophy, and others—which protect the wealth of your family and the current (and future) individuals within it?

- Do you, as a family, have a thoughtful approach to identify and manage, in advance, the major risks to your wealth and happiness?

- Do you have a clear wealth management plan with the correct team, objectives, and processes in place, which performs well against relevant benchmarks?

- Does your family business have a clear and effective business strategy? Are that business and business strategy fully aligned and integrated with your financial wealth management strategy?

- Have you developed a policy with regard to the desired focus, amount of time, and amount of money you wish to dedicate to philanthropic activities?

- Does your family wealth strategy fully and accurately reflect and accommodate the full aspirations and realistic capabilities of the individual members of your family?

If your answer to any, or even all, of these specific questions is in the negative, then it is hoped that the insights and ideas captured in the following pages can help to improve your family wealth strategy for the benefit of current and future generations.

THE LENGTH OF THE EFFORT

The length of a family's strategic exercise will vary by the scale of family wealth, the number of generations involved and the complexity of the family's affairs, within each of the seven elements of strategy.

In order to determine the most appropriate timeframe, there needs to be sufficient time allotted to each part of a three-phase process addressing diagnosis, design, and implementation of a family wealth strategy.

The actual timeframes necessary may vary substantially between families. Some well-prepared families in less complicated situations may be able to complete the initial phases in a few short months and move swiftly to implementation.

In other cases, there may be a substantial change required in business ownership, family organization, or trust structuring. There may be an element of learning about new areas of relevance—for example, offshore trust and tax law, or scientific asset allocation approaches—which may extend the overall timeframe.

Other strategies can require the investment, or reinvestment, of substantial assets; a process that may take between 12 and 18 months to complete on a fully invested basis.

THE SCALE OF EFFORT

It is important to "right-size" the strategic effort to avoid undue expenditure when a faster, simpler, and more cost-effective solution may be better suited for a particular wealthy family's situation. But it is also important to invest enough to ensure that the best possible strategy is in place for the future.

While there may be some risk of over-investment (especially for a family with Category I wealth), there is an opposite situation at the other end of the scale: some very wealthy families under-invest in a strategy to address all elements of family wealth, avoiding the costs and efforts of an integrated strategic review, but missing the potential benefits that could justify the investment many times over.

Perhaps due to inexperience or preoccupation, many newly wealthy families, in particular, invest far too little in defining their own pathway forward, thus dramatically increasing the odds of a fall from fortune to misfortune in three generations—or even fewer.

INCLUSIVITY AND REPRESENTATION

Wealthy families that have evolved through many generations can include hundreds of members with an economic and personal interest in the family's affairs. This increase in the number of beneficiaries and potential members in a family business or other family activity is exacerbated in cultures where large families over many generations are the norm.

The continuing prosperity of one of the largest and wealthiest northern European families shows that a highly structured approach, with special consideration given to the requirements of the larger family, can lead to a successful integration of family issues and the achievement of high standards of family wealth management across generations.

To guide this family, operating procedures are very clearly spelled out in a series of manuals which specify who is allowed into the family business, and what family members of various categories can expect in terms of income and capital inheritance. In great part, the continuing success of this one, very large, successfully wealthy family is due to a very high entry barrier to the family business and a very clear and forward-thinking approach to all matters related to the family, family wealth, and family business.

Process is especially critical in a strategy where implementation of an agreed approach requires the approval and participation of many family members with differing interests, spread across different generations.

While the process of strategy may not involve all members in the large and successful family enterprise, there needs to be tacit support and respect for decisions made. This assent is required to avoid conflict and to give legitimacy and effectiveness to policies which apply equally across family groupings and generations, and to all individual members.

DOCUMENTATION

There are three reasons to document a family strategy. The first is to be absolutely clear about the content of the strategy. The process of crafting a carefully worded document will both increase the quality of thought and reduce the risk of misinterpretation or disagreement.

A second reason for capturing the strategy in a written document is to facilitate communication in a consistent manner. Many families today are widely spread and constantly on the move. By providing access to a written document, each member of each generation of the family can read and review the content of the family strategy as and when necessary.

Another reason for the strategy to be documented is that it allows subsequent revisions to the strategy to be made in a clear manner. Only with a written record of the past can a new plan for the future be drafted on a fully informed and high-quality basis.

At the end of the exercise it may be beneficial to draft a summary strategy document, capturing the essential elements in a concise but comprehensive fashion.

Such a document—both in complete and summary forms—can be extremely valuable in clarifying thought, in ensuring that all bases have been covered, and that all parties share the same clear understanding of the elements and implications of the approach selected. Any required communications can thus be made with a common simple understanding of the messages and action requirements of the chosen strategy.

Implementation of the chosen strategy is also much more likely to be successful if all of these bases have been covered.

IMPLEMENTATION AND CONTROL

Good corporate strategy was once described by 1980s strategy guru Ralph Willard as "an inexorable flow of logic from insight to action."[1] That same definition can be applied to strategies aimed at preserving and enhancing family wealth across multiple generations.

Only with full implementation of agreed plans, enabled by tight controls over priority actions and achievements, can a family leader ensure that the family is placed, and kept, firmly on the pathway to many generations of wealth and happiness.

Review and control during the implementation process should be neither an overly narrow exercise in accounting nor an overly broad discussion of progress without consequence. Specific performance against objectives and a review of the more qualitative aspects of strategy should be assessed and the appropriate conclusions drawn. The regular strategic reviews need to lead to corrective actions, if necessary, to ensure that the strategy stays in line with its original objectives and is consistent with all family values.

As with any dynamic system, frequent, small, corrective interventions are vastly more efficient in keeping a strategy on track than massive intervention once it is dramatically off course.

Like a missile flying toward a specific destination, frequent, small corrections increase the quality of the flight, reduce the amount of energy needed to provide the change in direction, reduce the risk of ill-timed intervention, and substantially increase the likelihood of the missile arriving at its chosen target.

---

[1] Ralph Willard, one of the founders of Bain & Company, in conversation with the author.

ADAPTATION AND EVOLUTIONARY SUCCESS

Once set, strategies will need to adapt both to reflect changes within the family and in the external environment. Our entire world is in a constant state of flux; nothing, other than constant change, is fixed. The perspective that best captures the ever-flowing, ever-changing nature of all things is the Hindu observation that "you never cross the same river twice."

Similarly, no wealthy family remains subject to the same pressures, risks, opportunities, and influences over time. In this flow of constant change, a family must stay its chosen course, but must also evolve and adapt its strategy in order to survive and prosper.

Darwinian wisdom: Perhaps one of the best-known quotes attributed to the natural scientist Charles Darwin's Theory of Evolution is "survival of the fittest." However, this "quote" is neither a fully accurate summary of his theories, nor a phrase originally used by Darwin himself. These words were actually first penned by Herbert Spencer, the English biologist, philosopher, and author of *Principles of Biology*, when describing Darwin's ideas.

In fact, Darwin's real theory was that species which best adapted themselves to changes in their environment had a better chance of survival; an observation both more complex and more useful when considering strategy for the wealthy family.

Just as evolution is all about the survival of different species through adaptation to change, successful family wealth preservation can best be pursued through an approach which responds well to changes in the family and its external environment.

RESULTS—THE ULTIMATE TEST

In the end, the only strategies that have any value are those which create tangible results. For a multi-generational family wealth strategy, those results will be the realization of the family's vision, the honoring of its values, and the achievement of its financial and other family wealth goals.

For a wealthy family to reap these benefits, it will need to make the investment—in time, resources, discipline, and emotional courage—to create a strategy that will endure across many generations and ensure the survival and the continued prosperity of its deserving members.

PRINCIPLE 2

FAMILY ORGANIZATION AND LEADERSHIP

*Organize the family and manage
the surrounding eco-system*

6. FAMILY IDENTITY, VISION, AND VALUES

A comprehensive strategy for any wealthy family needs to begin with a clear understanding and awareness of the family itself.

In the Family Office Exchange study cited earlier, the ultra-high-net-worth families surveyed highlighted the fact that managing a family is not just about such "hard issues" as asset allocation or investment policy.

> "these so-called soft issues, aren't 'soft' issues at all. Maybe we should call them the 'even harder' issues."

The real concerns were the "softer" issues regarding a family's legacy and sense of identity, its organization and governance, and, finally, the human interactions of the individuals who make up the family itself.

Mastering these social, organizational, and human issues is not easy. As one observer summarized: "these people issues, these so-called soft issues, aren't 'soft' issues at all. Maybe we should call them the 'even harder' issues."

STRATEGY AND STRUCTURE

In order to identify and respond to these "soft" but challenging elements of family leadership, consensus must be reached on a number of fundamental approaches. These include:

- defining the family vision, values, and goals
- clarifying the rights and responsibilities of family members, with particular focus on drawing up a Family Constitution
- preparing future generations for their role as stewards of family wealth and avoiding the pitfalls of "the dark side of wealth"
- creating and managing an eco-system of advisors to support the family
- setting up and maintaining a Family Office
- establishing a model of strong leadership and engagement.

But even before moving into these fertile areas for family governance and development, it is important to define who is, and who is not, a member of the family.

FAMILY IDENTITY

What qualifies someone to be a member of the family? At a practical level, family definition is essential in order to formalize membership for the purposes of inheritance and other rights and responsibilities. At a more esoteric level, definition and identity is important to keep the family together, fostering its uniqueness and ensuring the importance of its common history and shared values.

Although the classical "bloodline" definition still holds for most families, the modern world of frequent divorce and remarriage can force families to ask themselves more probing questions about who is, and who is not, part of the family.

Does the family include stepchildren? Does it include children born out of wedlock? (In Austria today, for example, almost 40% of children are born to couples who are not married.[1]) Does the family recognize same-sex marriages or unmarried life partners? Does it include adopted children or adopted adults? In some countries, inheritance tax varies enormously according to whether the inheritance is bestowed upon the child (including an adopted child) of the benefactor, or a more distantly related family member or non-family member, and according to the size of the estate.

In other families, a noble title can only be transferred to a son or daughter of the family. Childless aristocratic couples may have no alternative other than to adopt in order to maintain their lineage.

And what about defending against family members who create schisms and damage family wealth and reputation? Can a family member be expelled and, if so, under which circumstances? How does a family go about extinguishing family rights and freeing up an individual, voluntarily or involuntarily, from his or her responsibilities in the family?

---

[1] Figures from Statistik Austria, Geborene seit 1998 nach ausgewählten demografischen und medizinischen Merkmalen, www.statistik.at/web_de/statistiken/bevoelkerung/geburten/022899.html.

ROLES, RIGHTS, AND RESPONSIBILITIES

As well as defining who is included, family definitions may also need to clarify the differing roles, inheritance rights, and attendant responsibilities of family members.

Many royal families and other aristocratic lineages adhere to the right of primogeniture, whereby the oldest son benefits from a principal inheritance of title, lands, financial assets, and role as head of the family. Primogeniture ensures that a family fortune and attendant political power and social standing remain intact, an approach which has kept many fortunes together across generations.

On the negative side, primogeniture historically excluded females and diminished the inheritance rights of younger male siblings, who were far less fortunate economically, purely by accident of birth order.

The recent and very public concerns over the production of a male heir to follow Crown Prince Akihito's tenure on Japan's imperial Chrysanthemum Throne reflects the fact that this very old tradition is alive and well in modern Japan.

Even in more modern wealthy families, different classes of membership may exist within the same generation, with some members selected to inherit far more wealth than others. In the recent restructuring of the Oetker family fortune in Germany, for example, only eight descendants out of a far larger pool were chosen to be shareholders in the multi-billion-dollar family business.

In another European family, a Family Council selects those few members of the family they believe to be capable of preserving and adding to the family fortune and, as a result, stand to inherit the lion's share of a multi-billion-dollar family fortune. The remaining family members are shunted aside with a fixed, and much smaller, US$20 million inheritance settlement.

FAMILY HISTORY

Family history gives its members a sense of place and uniqueness; a link to the past which can provide a firm foundation for the present and future. A family's history and beliefs can explain a great deal about its members' ethics, behavior, and attitudes toward wealth, inheritance, and family legacy.

A family history is more than a family tree showing births, deaths, and marriages. It is a rich flow of events, individual histories, shared ethics, and collective accomplishments. Just as the history of a nation is about far more than a simple time line, a more complete history of a wealthy family will cover far more territory from the past—and offer many more useful insights to guide the future.

National origins, religious affiliations, associations with groups or places, educational standards, and economic progress are all parts of the fabric of understanding who a family is and what it stands for.

For example, the famous eighteenth-century English banking families the Lloyds, the Barclays, and the Gurneys were all Quaker families, known for their probity. Many prominent English families of the day, and their inheritors, entrusted their money to these Quaker bankers, whose own family fortunes grew as a result of their founders' reliable values and staunch religious beliefs.

Similarly, the erratic Howard Hughes, developer of one of America's most unusual and famous family fortunes, preferred to hire Mormons because he trusted that their religious values would protect his wealth from dishonesty and fraud.

Some Swiss family fortunes, particularly in and around Geneva, have been built on the back of timepiece businesses influenced very directly, at their origins, by religious belief. With the rise of Calvinism, and its simple philosophies and dislike of materialism and ostentation, many skilled craftsmen in Switzerland turned away from a declining jewelry industry and shifted their attention to the development of more practical, and less gaudy, timepieces.

Family stories and icons: Many families carry forward their traditions and values through oral histories, passed down from one generation to another. This storytelling ensures that all members of the family remember what makes them unique and what binds them together. The more organized families actually research their histories, creating an archive of relevant historical data and documenting a family tree with roots extending as far back as documents can verify.

In old family homes, a position of prominence is often given to a large oil painting of the family patriarch, or founder of the family business. This painting serves as a constant reminder of the importance and influence of the august individual, even if long departed. The painting may guide future behavior as well, serving as an icon and reminder of the value system which created the family's privileged position.

By building an understanding of history, and using values, experience and understanding to support growth in future generations, family leaders will be putting in place one of the fundamental elements of strategy.

Sara Hamilton, founder and CEO of The Family Office Exchange, described the importance of family integrity and family legacy in *Worth* magazine: "When wealth inheritance comprises one of a family's goals, a strong family legacy can provide the emotional glue that keeps the generations motivated to work together. Many families believe in instilling this legacy even in young children, so that they grow up understanding their history and who they are."[2]

> "When wealth inheritance comprises one of a family's goals, a strong family legacy can provide the emotional glue that keeps the generations motivated to work together."

FAMILY VISION

Having defined what a family is and where it has come from, the next important objectives are to agree upon a vision which will define where the family would like to go, and to reaffirm the values family members will live by as they navigate toward that agreed destination.

There is no easy way to set a vision for a family, just as there is no easy way to establish a corporate vision for a family business. Sometimes the most simple and brief of statements are the most difficult to get right.

Defining a family vision is as much art as science, requiring that the drafters combine a subtle blend of historical insight, precise language, and broad aspirational ideals. Finding the right content, the right tone, the right words, and even the right process by which a family defines a common goal, are as important as the actual words themselves.

A vision is not a strategy. A vision can inspire or define the limits on strategy, and will set the overarching goal for many strategies, but the two are very different indeed.

---

[2] Sara Hamilton, "Families at Risk," *Worth* (April 2007) Vol.16, No.4, pp.46–8.

Military theory neatly sums up the difference. Conquering a continent or freeing an independent country from a colonial empire is a vision. Doing it through a series of political alliances and military encounters is a strategy. Pursuing this strategy by moving as quickly as possible, under the cover of night, is tactics.

> A vision statement can make a powerful contribution to all elements of strategy for a wealthy family.

In addition to clarifying goals, a vision statement can make a powerful contribution to all elements of strategy for a wealthy family.

The highly respected family wealth management expert Stephen George, co-founder and CIO of Capricorn LLC, underscored the critical role of an overall family vision in family wealth management when he stated: "Lack of a vision is often the root cause of failure in family wealth management. The creation of a clear family vision carries into the best process for laying out a tailored approach to the portfolio itself, followed on by a supporting statement of values and a resulting philosophy for investment."[3]

The content of a family vision statement: In order to give some real-world flavor to the idea of a vision statement, and an overall family strategy, a full example of a Family Constitution, complete with vision and values statements is included as Example 2 at the end of this book. That document forms part of the wealth strategy documentation for the (entirely fictitious) Cuscaden family. Their vision reads:

> The Cuscaden Family will strive to become one of the world's most highly respected business families, constantly setting and achieving new standards of excellence in business results, sustainable wealth management, community engagement, philanthropic contribution, and family harmony across generations.

> Throughout all of our endeavors we shall respect the highest standards of business ethics and family integrity—building on our historic reputation as "capitalists with a conscience."

---

[3] Private conversation between Stephen George and the author.

A broader description outlining the benefits that will be brought about by the realization of the family vision statement could read as follows:

> The achievement of this vision will allow us:
>
> 1. to secure the health, education, and financial welfare of members of the Cuscaden Family indefinitely.
>
> 2. to make a valuable contribution in selected areas of philanthropy and principled investment.
>
> 3. to create a process to protect, enhance, distribute, and share Cuscaden Family capital—financial and human—across generations in a manner which increases the available life choices and enhances the quality of life of all bloodline descendents of James and Catriona Cuscaden.
>
> In the pursuit of this vision we will adhere at all times to the highest standards of business and personal ethics, create honest businesses based on hard work and entrepreneurial risk-taking and ensure that each and every family member and business colleague understands and respects the values of the founder of our family business.

Families may wish to address other aspects of the integrated strategy framework, which, to continue our example, may include:

Financial Wealth Management: We will preserve and enhance family wealth so that each generation doubles the capital it receives in real terms to pass to the next generation.

Wealth Protection and Transfer: The Cuscaden Family will establish a coherent and state-of-the-art set of investment, ownership, and distribution vehicles to ensure that the family wealth is protected and transferred as effectively as possible across all future generations.

Family Eco-system: We will strive to surround ourselves with individuals, institutions, and advisors of the highest integrity and capability. In so doing, we will expose members of the Cuscaden Family to the highest standards of excellence and benefit from that proximity and association.

Effective Philanthropy: We will establish a global network of orphanages and schools for girls in emerging markets. These institutions will be funded by an allocation of 20% of all Cuscaden Family income and capital gains from the liquid and operating assets of the family.

The Family Office: We will set up and maintain a Cuscaden Family Office to support the family in its achievement of all elements of its vision and strategy across generations. The members of that Family Office will be of the highest capability and integrity and conduct themselves as ambassadors of the Cuscaden Family at all times.

The Family Business: So long as the Cuscaden Family own, manage, and decide governance for our family business(es), we will pursue the highest standards of accomplishment. At all times, we will involve the family only in areas where that family involvement will improve the accomplishments of the business and the professionalism of all those that serve within it.

Risk Management: We will be attentive to the full set of risks that threaten our family and family wealth in the broadest sense of the term. By understanding and acting to anticipate and reduce risk we will contribute to the achievement of our broader goals.

Individual Choice and Support: We hereby commit that each and every member of the Cuscaden Family will understand and contribute to this vision to the best of his or her ability.

FAMILY VALUES

A family vision will establish what a family wants to be and where it wants to go.

Family values will establish how the family will act on the way toward that long-term goal. As life is as much a journey as a destiny or destination, the principles we live by contribute substantially toward the determination of our value as individuals and as members of a greater family.

Family values establish the limits, standards, and rules its members live by. In great part, the people they are, the families they create, and the legacy they leave behind are deeply influenced by the values they adopt in their personal and business lives.

Family values will, of course, be unique to each and every family, but many have adopted such statements as:

In pursuing the family vision, we will adhere to a set of values which lie at the core of the Cuscaden Family's history and our unique identity. These values are to be honored in our family and in our business ventures:

Unity: The family will remain united and strong through all environments and events, no matter how adverse or challenging. This may require individual sacrifice to ensure that the family's interests are maintained and that the harmonious integrity of the Cuscaden Family is preserved.

Perseverance and Adaptability: We will foster a strong work ethic in every individual, in every generation, and build a culture which recognizes that life changes, and that we must change with it. Adaptability is the essence of survival and our approach to the family and business matters will reflect this understanding.

Discretion: Our family values and corporate activities require that individual family members avoid excessive personal and corporate coverage in the media. To that end, all external communications should be made consistent with the policies and parameters determined by the relevant family entities.

Social Responsibility: We will always remember the privileges that result from our commercial efforts and endeavor to share the benefits of our activities with those less fortunate than we. We will pursue extraordinary opportunities to make a substantial and positive impact on the lives of the many colleagues and individuals who engage with our business systems, especially in the emerging markets in which we pursue our business interests.

In our approach to business we will be sensitive to the appropriate standards of socially responsible behavior; in the pursuit of our philanthropic objectives we will be generous and thoughtful in improving the lives of other citizens whose needs are far greater than ours.

BELIEF AND ACTION

A mere statement of aspirational values does not fulfill any strategic purpose; each family will need to define the appropriate actions and communications to ensure that its own value statements become a real operating value system.

Younger members of the family will constantly be looking at the behavior of their elders in coming to an understanding of true family values and how to apply them. From these observations they will draw their own conclusions, which will no doubt resonate with the old aphorism "your actions speak so loud I cannot hear your words."

7. ORGANIZATION, GOVERNANCE, AND THE FAMILY CONSTITUTION

Every social entity needs some degree of governance, structure, and organization to function effectively as a unit. The wealthy family is no exception to this rule.

Bringing order to a family can contribute to the identity and efficiency of the group. It can create a platform for interaction and bonding, making it easier to develop and share a sense of common purpose. It can bring family units together on an equal footing and, if necessary, act swiftly and effectively to address any potential family risk or dispute. Thoughtful structuring and organization can strengthen and unify a family in deep and lasting ways across many generations and through many challenges.

Throughout the founding and second generations, many wealthy families can work effectively without the requirement of formal documentation and procedures. The influence of the patriarch or matriarch is often sufficient to hold the family together and keep its values intact.

Yet within one more generation, the family may have grown in size and complexity to the point that a more formal approach to organizational structure becomes necessary in order to offset the increased risk of fragmentation, division, and conflict. By the third generation, there will be multiple sets of children who have been brought up with different parents and been exposed to different value systems. It is in this high-risk generation that the benefits of a clear strategy may be greatest.

The objectives of organizing a family's structure and operating principles are related to all of the elements of the strategy described throughout this book. When built upon a sound and well-structured foundation, family wealth can be better managed; trusts and other wealth-preservation approaches can be vetted and approved; family businesses and philanthropic endeavors can be more fully integrated with the family; salient risks can be well managed; and individual life plans followed through in a reliable and transparent fashion.

Different approaches by wealth category: The structures and procedures required to organize and govern the wealthy family will vary according to the size of the family, the amount of family wealth, and each family's preferences and needs.

For some families with wealth at a Category I or II level, the establishment of regular Family Meetings and a single family representational group, the Family Council, may be sufficient to address all aspects of organization and strategy. However, most families in the higher categories of wealth may benefit from the establishment of additional organizational entities, including a Family Funds Board, a Family Business Board, a Wealth Management Board, a Philanthropic Board, and a Family Office.

The purpose and goals of each of these bodies, together with membership criteria, may be clearly set out in a formal Family Constitution. In all governing documents and structures, there needs to be a complete alignment of family vision, values, definition, and structure.

FAMILY

The issues related to the definition of a family are spelled out in some detail above and do not require further elaboration here. It is worth noting, however, that while "the family" and the Family Meeting may include all related members, not all families will give equal rights to all family members. In some families, its members, or the children of its members, who have sold their shares in a family enterprise are no longer included in any family affairs.

FAMILY MEETING

The Family Meeting will include all members of the family, as defined in the Family Constitution. The objectives of the Family Meeting, are two-fold: first, to foster a single family ethos by providing every member of the family with a sense of belonging and an opportunity for family bonding; and second, to provide guidance and legitimacy to the various policies, decisions, and bodies responsible for protecting and furthering the family's collective interests.

Family Meetings for larger, well-established families may be major events spanning several days and held every year or two. Smaller families may hold much lower-key meetings lasting only a few hours which take place on a much more frequent schedule.

The agenda will usually include high-level summaries of past, current, or planned activity across all areas of family wealth (see Figure 2.1).

Figure 2.1 Sample Family Meeting Agenda

1. Matters arising from previous Family Meetings
2. Objectives of the current meeting
3. Year in review: objectives and accomplishments
   - Family business
   - Financial wealth management
   - Wealth preservation and transfer
   - Eco-system
   - Philanthropy
   - The Family Office
   - Risk management
   - Family progress
   - Individual accomplishments
   - Other issues arising
4. Coming year
   - Economic environment
   - Family transitions
   - Key objectives of family strategy:
     - Family business
     - Financial wealth management
     - Wealth preservation and transfer
     - Eco-system
     - Philanthropy
     - The Family Office
     - Risk management
     - Individual plans
5. Long-term plans (multi-generational context)
   - Family and individual development (Next Generation preparation)
   - Key areas of strategy
   - Changes in Family Constitution (every three years)
6. Other issues arising

In some tough-minded families, failure to attend a Family Meeting without advance approval from the Meeting Chair can result in a penalty of 10% of personal dividends being forfeited by the offending member, and perhaps contributed to a selected charity or to the Family Foundation.

During the course of the Family Meetings, separate meetings are often arranged for different generational groups within the larger family. The purpose of these meetings is often as much social as formal. By setting aside time for older or younger generations to meet and discuss items of mutual interest, family leaders will be advancing the causes of family harmony and common purpose as well as addressing any specific issues arising.

Council of Elders: Some Family Meetings may include a meeting of a Council of Elders, consisting of all—or an elected sub-set of—family members over some august age (usually 60 or 65) after which these individuals are no longer eligible for positions of active leadership or management of the family or family business. Some families, in order to make room for the next generation, have even reduced the age limit on active roles to 55.

The role of the Council of Elders, or "Family Wise Men and Women," is to provide historical perspective and sage guidance in resolving the personal, factional, generational, or family-wide issues that could erupt into major family disputes if not addressed by a sufficiently revered and experienced group.

Next Generation Group: Separate, generation-specific groups may also be set up in larger wealthy families to develop teamwork and prepare younger family members for leadership of the family in the future. This is particularly important when geographical distance, or simply the large number of individuals involved, mean that opportunities for same-generation members to come together are few and far between.

FAMILY COUNCIL

The role of the Family Council is similar to that of a corporate board of directors, but in this instance the "corporation" is the wealthy family itself, and the "shareholders" are the individual family members.

The broad responsibilities of the Family Council may include oversight and responsibility for all areas relevant to a family's long-term strategy and annual operations. In most cases, due to the size, low frequency of meeting and diversity of representation at a Family Meeting, most major policies and issues are raised and resolved within the Family Council or the supporting boards. The authority for decision-making will vary substantially between family structures as each family chooses.

The Family Council may also determine matters related to trust establishment and oversight, corporate structures and tax planning, business ownership, membership of the family boards (Business, Wealth Management, and Philanthropy), the appointment of non-family members to family boards, the promotion of family members within family businesses, and strategies for wealth management. The Family Council may also operate as a *de facto* supervisory board for a family business.

The Family Council, made up only of family members selected according to the family's informal procedures or governing documents, usually uses Family Meetings more to communicate than to debate or decide family matters of substance. One of the Council's most important roles is to provide input to trustees or other decision-makers to set the timing, level, and method of distribution of family capital or income to family members and to selected philanthropic activities.

FAMILY FUNDS BOARD

Under the management of the Family Council, a set of special purpose funds may be established to provide financial support to the overall unity, security, and objectives of the family.

Actual examples of special purpose funds include the following:

- *Family Contingency Fund*: to cover the costs of unanticipated emergencies and hardship such as uninsured medical emergencies and medical insurance.

- *Family Development Fund*: to cover the costs of all levels of family education and training, including continuing executive education programs for family members serving in the family business.

- *One Family Fund*: to cover reasonable expenses associated with Family Meetings, family socials, holidays and other pre-approved activities which strengthen family bonds.

- *Family Venture Capital Fund or "Family Bank"*: to stimulate an entrepreneurial spirit and broaden the future business base, many families will establish an internal institution to provide capital, as equity or loans, to family members wishing to develop new business initiatives outside existing operating business lines.

Addressing the unexpected: Not all aspects of a family's activities will be predictable. The Family Council may often retain the role of taking the lead in unexpected family crises, or delegate the powers of decision-making to a smaller group of its members, or solely to a selected leader of the family.

FAMILY BUSINESS BOARD

In many families where a single business is of great importance, the Family Council and Family Business Board may be the same entity. In others, where the family business or portfolio of businesses is of great magnitude, there may be a need for two separate entities, with one focused on non-business family affairs and an integrated approach to family strategy, and another focused exclusively upon business operations. There is usually some overlap in membership of the two, especially in the earlier generations of a wealthy family.

In most cases, the Family Council will take precedence over the Family Business Board in deciding on family, and family business, matters.

The Family Business Board usually addresses and decides on most business ownership, strategic, and operating matters. In particular, it will need to address the career paths, succession plans, and the development of both family members and professional non-family managers within the business.

Although the Family Business Board is charged to decide upon most business-related issues, some may be of such significance that they are referred to the Family Council for debate and resolution. These issues could include the sale, acquisition, restructuring, or alliance of the family business, or address issues relating to key business opportunities and the career paths of family members.

WEALTH MANAGEMENT BOARD

The role of a Wealth Management Board is to invest the family's non-operating business funds in line with selected risk/return guidelines and investment parameters. Non-operating business funds can be defined as publicly quoted investments, fixed income instruments, alternative assets, liquid funds, securities, property, equity stakes and other passive financial investments representing an ownership interest of less than 10% of any business, and any other financial investments which the Family Council may allocate to this category.

The Board will specify the risk appetite, liquidity preference, investment horizon, and fund manager selection criteria, with a plan submitted to the Family Council for approval on an annual basis.

In the most advanced family wealth strategies, the Wealth Management Board will stipulate a desired performance, aimed at an absolute return target for each asset class and for the total investment portfolio. A detailed strategy will be worked out and followed for each asset class.

The portfolio will be set to balance, as appropriate, the family's risk/return profile across its entire set of financial and commercial activities. Asset management performance will be compared to peer performance benchmarks on a transparent annual basis and reported upon as part of the Family Meeting agenda.

The Wealth Management Board may meet quarterly to set strategy and to review performance against strategic targets.

Investment Committee: Operating under the Wealth Management Board, there is often an Investment Committee made up of some Board members and selected professional managers and advisors.

The tactical investment decisions and implementation of strategy are usually within the purview of this Investment Committee, which meets far more frequently and has a more detailed and tactical agenda than does the Board itself. The members of the Investment Committee may be drawn from the family, the Inner Circle (as described below), the Family Office and, particularly for higher-category families, from among professionals not included within these three groups.

For all categories of family wealth, an operating Investment Committee should be established and meet regularly to review the selected asset allocation model, revise investment strategy, and make tactical investment decisions.

Both the higher level Wealth Management Board and operational Investment Committee usually provide guidance on the investment of funds for the family and family philanthropic organizations, and may do the same for the family business or individual family members as well.

FAMILY PHILANTHROPIC BOARD

The role of a Family Philanthropic Board is to determine a forward vision and approach to sharing family wealth. That vision should lead to a set of target areas for philanthropic activity and to the allocation of funds to approved charities in accordance with the philanthropic terms of reference and consistent with family policies, values, trust conditions, and any specific reference in a Family Constitution.

FAMILY OFFICE

In order to facilitate the family's operations and activities, a Family Office may be established, particularly by families in the higher two categories of wealth, with a staff and location selected by the Family Council.

Most Family Offices have a wealth management agenda, along with the responsibility for managing, or supporting the family to manage, the seven elements of family wealth strategy set out earlier.

The Family Office will also assist individual family members with the day-to-day management and organization of the family's affairs including, but not limited to, supporting corporate functions, wealth management, trust and estate planning, share administration, risk management, development needs, health and family services, personal tax filing, and other aspects of family financial planning and administration.

FAMILY ORGANIZATIONAL STRUCTURE

The actual bodies of governance required for each family will vary according to its size, complexity, and wealth category. For example, a Family Office or Family Funds Board may not be necessary for a smaller family in the lower wealth categories, and a Next Generation Group may not be necessary for a smaller family group with very young children.

Figure 2.2 sets out the organizational structure of an actual Category III Family, showing sample membership of each body of family governance, in a model that has proved successful over time. This model assumes that the family owns an operating business, and therefore includes a Family Business Board within the structure.

Figure 2.2 Category III Family Organization Structure

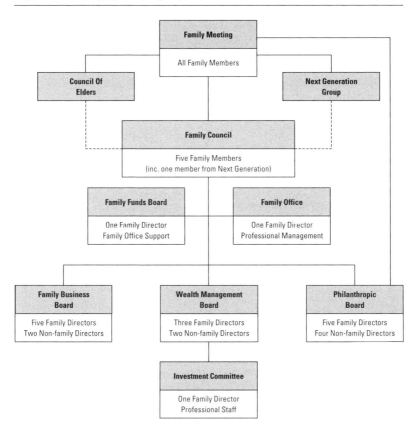

THE FAMILY CONSTITUTION

Just as the Constitution of the United States set out a practical approach to the organization, governance, and advancement of the new American nation, a carefully crafted Family Constitution can set out an equitable approach to guide and structure the future of the wealthy family. This document can provide a common reference on family vision and values, as well as defining the bodies of family governance and organization. In addition, the content of the document can ensure that a system of checks and balances is in place to curb any arbitrary exercise of power.

A Family Constitution can capture family definition, identity, vision, values, and its members' rights and responsibilities in a single master document, and thereby help to ensure that the family policies and strategies are fully aligned in support of a single and well-thought-out multi-generational approach to family vision, harmony, integrity, and prosperity.

Long-term value: A Family Constitution should always be drafted with a multi-generational approach in mind. This will require that drafters take into account how family membership will be determined, how voting and economic rights will work, and which bodies will be responsible for which area of activity. In a longer-term approach, a fair and transparent process (rather than nomination by an individual or tightly knit founding group) may need to be set out to decide on membership and key roles in a family organization.

In setting out a constitutional approach that can endure across generations, specific names (except for the initial members of governing bodies) should be replaced with defined processes for election, perhaps requiring a balancing of membership to ensure the appropriate representation is assured from different family units, groups, or generations.

In addition to fair processes and balanced representation, processes of amendment, of checks and balances, and of dispute resolution need to be built in anticipation of the flexibility required to manage a family across different generations.

Constitution, Compact, Agreement, or Protocol? Although traditionally known as a Family Constitution, this important foundation document can also be called an Agreement, Protocol, or Compact.

Historically, compacts were used by small groups to set out a binding commitment to pursue an overall goal with a shared set of values and a common approach. The Mayflower Compact, for example, named after the ship which brought the first pilgrim settlers to America in 1620, was a very brief document which set out the commitment of the members of the new community to pursue their vision of a new life in a new land, based on an agreement to work together as a single democratic body to further their common goals.

The Mayflower Compact

We whose names are underwritten, the loyal subjects of our dread Sovereign Lord King James, by the Grace of God of Great Britain, France and Ireland, King, Defender of the Faith, etc.

Having undertaken, for the Glory of God and advancement of the Christian Faith and Honour of our King and Country, a Voyage to plant the First Colony in the Northern Parts of Virginia, do by these presents solemnly and mutually in the presence of God and one of another, Covenant and Combine ourselves together into a Civil Body Politic, for our better ordering and preservation and furtherance of the ends aforesaid; and by virtue hereof to enact, constitute and frame such just and equal Laws, Ordinances, Acts, Constitutions and Offices, from time to time, as shall be thought most meet and convenient for the general good of the Colony, unto which we promise all due submission and obedience. In witness whereof we have hereunder subscribed our names at Cape Cod, the 11th of November, in the year of the reign of our Sovereign Lord King James, of England, France and Ireland the eighteenth, and of Scotland the fifty-fourth. Anno Domini 1620.

That brief document, only 200 words long, stood for more than a century as the chief governing pact that guided the new American nation.

Although the Mayflower Compact is laudable in its brevity, most modern families prefer to spell out the functions of their various governing bodies in rather more detail, specifying membership and leadership-selection procedures in a structure more reminiscent of the more specific American Constitution of 1789.

DRAFTING PROCESS

The procedure for drafting a Family Constitution can be as important as the final content of the document itself in ensuring acceptance and durability. Each person's rights and responsibilities may be affected by what is ultimately adopted by the larger family and each member deserves an opportunity to contribute to the development of the document.

By carefully defining the process, ensuring that all generations and relevant family units and members are represented, and that the final document is both fair in content and the result of a fair and open process, family leaders will improve the odds of a high-quality document being produced which achieves high levels of understanding and support into the future.

While it is important to involve as many individuals and generations as possible, it may not be in the best interests of all parties concerned to have too lengthy a drafting process. Excessive time can allow small issues to creep into discussions which should remain focused on the more substantial and high-level elements of family organization. Excessive time dedicated to the drafting can also be unnecessarily expensive if outside advisors are involved.

PROCESS OF APPROVAL

For any form of family governance to be legitimate, it requires the assent of the governed: the family will need to validate the chosen structure and approach. It should be clear from the outset whether the ultimate ratification will be determined by a single family member, by a defined set of family members, by all family members, or by some other process of family consent.

PROCESS OF AMENDMENT

A document which can be changed at whim or by a small percentage of voting members will soon have little meaning or value. Conversely, raising too high a barrier to change can be equally counter-productive. It is therefore important to establish the level of votes required and the correct process of amendment for proposed changes to the Family Constitution.

It should also be noted that a change in one document could well require complementary or collateral changes in other documents. A change in the Family Constitution, for example, could require subsequent changes in wills, trust documents, letters of wishes and documents pertaining to family philanthropies, lending activities, and educational policies.

CONTENT

A full example of a Family Constitution is included on page 403. For immediate reference, see the sample table of contents provided in Figure 2.3. While most of these items have been addressed above, the three items in point XV are explained more fully below as a key part of ensuring that individual members of the family understand the full nature and extent of their rights, responsibilities, and required commitment.

Figure 2.3 Sample Family Constitution Table of Contents

I.	Statement of Purpose
II.	Family Membership
III.	Vision
IV.	Family Values
V.	Family Structures and Processes
VI.	The Family Meeting
VII.	The Family Council
VIII.	Family Business Board
IX.	Cuscaden Venture Capital Fund
X.	Asset Management Board
XI.	Foundation Board
XII.	Family Office
XIII.	Family Funds
XIV.	Cuscaden Group Business Ownership
XV.	Family Member Rights, Responsibilities, and Individual Commitment

BILL OF RIGHTS

Based on an appreciation for the robust structure and enduring success of the United States Constitution, a Bill of Rights which sets out the benefits and perquisites of family membership can be appended to a Family Constitution, an approach which has already been adopted in more than one wealthy family.

BILL OF RESPONSIBILITIES

A Bill of Responsibilities may also be necessary so that family members, young and old, understand that the very substantial rights endowed upon them do not come free, nor are rights granted on a one-sided basis—family members need to give as well as receive.

By specifying responsibilities as well as rights, and by creating enforcement mechanisms to ensure the responsibilities are met, a family will both create a more robust *esprit de corps*, and establish, from an early age, the fundamental notion that wealth carries obligations as well as benefits.

INDIVIDUAL COMMITMENT

A final creative addendum to the Family Constitution is the obligation for each family member reaching a specified age to make a personal affirmation and commitment to the Family Constitution before acceding to any rights, including the distribution of dividends or voting in Family Meetings.

By setting out the vision, values, rights and responsibilities, operating procedures, and governance principles of its formal structures, the wealthy family can ensure that its approaches to each and every family member across each and every generation is fair, correct, even-handed, and more likely to create a strong sense of family unity which is respected by all members of each succeeding generation.

8. "HEIR CONDITIONING": PREPARING THE NEXT GENERATION

The privileges of great financial wealth are obvious for all to see: financial security; social standing and influence; luxury travel; access to the best medical care; the finest clothing, foods, and wines; grand homes; greater investment opportunities and access to the best investment advice; and the ability to make profound and far-reaching philanthropic gestures. When used wisely, wealth creates the potential for greater personal choice, greater personal impact, and the potential for greater personal happiness for all members of a wealthy family.

On the other hand, the expression "to whomsoever much is given, of him shall much be required" captures but one of the pressures placed on the shoulders of wealthy individuals, and of their successors. Many wealthy heirs grow up in an environment where much is expected of them, but where that same environment may deprive them of the hardships, knocks, challenges, and potential achievements that can shape ambition, build a sound work ethic, or hone the skills necessary to meet those high levels of expectation.

Perhaps even greater than the physical and financial risks to the family touched on in Principle 3 (Chapter 18, "Risks to Family Wealth and Wellbeing") are the psychological risks and challenges facing the individual members of a wealthy family.

THE DARK SIDE OF WEALTH

In a recent conversation I had with one of the wealthiest self-made men in Europe, an exceptionally thoughtful individual, he observed that he was actually becoming a little afraid of the enormous wealth he had amassed. Pausing to reflect on the impact of his success, he summarized his concerns about what he called "the money monster," in a succinct and caring manner:

The Negative Impact of Wealth

"You know, I think every entrepreneur, when he gets to a certain stage in his life, wonders about the impact that his wealth will have on his children's lives. We work so hard for so many decades making money, and are so focused on making money, that sometimes we don't stop to think that it can create big problems for our kids.

For instance, my daughter is never sure why people want to get to know her, or if they really appreciate her for who she is, or why someone may really want to marry her. We have created an extra angle of fear and uncertainty in our children's lives that I never had time to think about while I was making the money.

Sometimes, after a life of building this level of wealth, I think I may have created something that won't make anyone happy."

On another occasion, an equally successful friend of this billionaire added his own concern over the effect his money might have on his own four children. As he considered how to structure his children's inheritance, his concerns were summarized in the striking words: "I don't want to poison my children."

Although hard to conceive for the billions of individuals in the world struggling along on one or two dollars a day, very few of the world's rich fully enjoy the wealth and abundance they have inherited or created for themselves without some deep (and well-founded) concerns and misgivings about the impact their wealth can have on the lives of family members. For many, great wealth is a double-edged sword—as much a burden and source of stress as a source of pleasure and fulfillment.

"I don't want to poison my children."

Research suggests that many of the problems facing wealthy families would appear to stem not from having too much money, but from not knowing what to do with the wealth they build or inherit. With so many options and possibilities open to the wealthy, it is very easy to stray from the path which leads to personal and family happiness and fulfillment.

Suicide of a Scion

It has long been said that there is "no heavier burden than great potential." Unless carefully managed, the great potential of substantial wealth can become an unbearable burden.

Even among the most celebrated of wealthy families, with histories of wealth and success that span centuries, the weight of history and expectation can be overwhelming. Amschel Rothschild, scion of a family whose name has been synonymous with family wealth for centuries, committed suicide in Paris in 1996, at the age of 41.

Following his death, it was suggested that the burden of expectation and the pressures of his position were such that they led to a very talented young man ending his own life rather than face the full challenges of the life of privilege he had been granted.

Without deeply held values, the members of a wealthy family can lose sight of how money can be used as a tool to create meaning, fulfillment, and purpose in their lives. Without a guiding vision, money and its privileges can be pursued as goals in themselves, or to open the door to a path in life which is troubled, and, in the worst circumstances, even self-destructive.

SHARED SET OF ISSUES

According to psychologists and counselors, the psychological issues facing many of today's wealthy, particularly second- and third-generation family members, may include:

- lack of self-esteem, and a feeling of inadequacy
- laziness, apathy, lack of ambition, distribution dependence, and a false sense of entitlement
- "inhibition deprivation" (reflecting a lack of normal behavioral borders)
- lack of personal fulfillment, sense of purpose, and independent identity
- lack of trust within the family and a sense of emotional abandonment

- naivety and a lack of worldly experience (financial and personal)
- lack of empathy and a misplaced sense of superiority
- cynicism and a mistaken belief that money can solve all problems
- guilt, unworthiness and religious or ethical dissonance
- abusive overcompensation.

The Witch of Wall Street

Hetty Green, reputedly the wealthiest woman in America in her era, was a notorious miser of extraordinary magnitude and a leading example of abusive overcompensation in her lifestyle.

Raised in an austere Quaker family in New England, she left a fortune valued at over US$100 million on her death in 1916.

Although an astute investor and wealthy for her entire life, Henrietta Howland Robinson Green was best known for her miserly ways: she reportedly lived in a small apartment in Hoboken, New Jersey, appeared in shabby dress, lunched on a handful of dry oatmeal in an unheated office, attended charity clinics for her medical needs and, famously, refused to pay for high-quality private medical treatment for her son's leg problems, which created the need for a subsequent amputation.

Reportedly, shortly after her death, her son spent millions of dollars of his inheritance on a collection of postage stamps.

IN THE FOOTSTEPS OF THE PATRIARCH

It can be particularly difficult, at a psychological level, for a son or daughter to follow in the footsteps of a founding entrepreneurial father or mother. The time allocations, priorities, and personality of the hyper-successful entrepreneur are not always those of an ideal father. Such issues as narcissism, workaholic characteristics, extended and frequent absences for business travel, a clear priority given to economic accomplishments and values, and a compulsive or obsessive personality without a sense of limits or altruism can all contribute to a difficult father-child or mother-child relationship.

Many children of founding entrepreneurs with strong personalities may be left with a lifelong sense of inadequacy, created by their own lack of relative accomplishment and by the actions and words of a parent for whom nothing that the child can do is ever enough.

In order to relieve this sense of inadequacy and lack of self-esteem, family expectations must be realistic and in line with the personal qualities and strengths of each individual within the family.

Family leaders and parents are often advised by family counselors to discuss expectations—both their own and the child's—openly, and offer guidance on how these expectations might be achieved. Heirs, in turn, must understand their opportunities, rights, and responsibilities, as set out in the Family Constitution.

> Ultimately, self-esteem will be achieved by mastering the challenges of life; it cannot be inherited.

Ultimately, self-esteem will be achieved by mastering the challenges of life; it cannot be inherited.

DEVELOPMENT IMPERATIVES FOR THE NEXT GENERATION

While each family is unique, there are certain development imperatives which can contribute to the preparation of any member of the next generation.

Development Imperatives for the Next Generation

- Build a foundation of values
- Build a foundation of knowledge and understanding
- Build a foundation of experience
- Communicate openly
- Instill a sense of individual purpose and responsibility
- Provide love and discipline
- Build trust
- Create time for the family

BUILD A FOUNDATION OF VALUES

A set of values related specifically to the development and preparation of heirs and heiresses can supplement the core family values spelled out in the Family Constitution. Some of the supplementary values chosen by wealthy families across three continents have included:

Education: The benefits of an educated, well-furnished mind last a life-time—indeed, education is a lifelong process in itself. Ensuring that the maximum benefit is extracted from every educational experience and opportunity throughout life, particularly during school and college years, is a great investment and one that will reap rewards for individual family members and for the family as a whole.

Ambition and excellence: It is laudable for a family to strive for a culture of continuous excellence in every context, but achieving excellence may be more difficult for a wealthy family.

The explanation for this is simple: It has been proven in studies on the psychology of world-class athletes that the real reason so many men and women push themselves to such high levels of effort and accomplishment is not a desire to win, but a deep-seated fear of failure.

In many wealthy families, financial wealth provides such a comfortable safety net that there is no motivation to develop either a survival instinct or a motivating fear of failure in any real sense of the word.

> "The price of accomplishment is effort, and the Gods have ordained that we must pay in advance."

Family leaders will therefore need to focus particular energy in encouraging the development of both ambition and drive in the next generation, without instilling an excessive fear of failure.

Industry and accomplishment: Almost all family fortunes have been built and preserved through a history of hard work and related accomplishment. As the poet Hesiod wrote in the seventh century BC: "The price of accomplishment is effort, and the Gods have ordained that we must pay in advance."

Responsibility: Many wealthy European families have prospered across generations by inculcating the value of responsible stewardship of family assets and by ensuring that the younger members of the family pursue a responsible and low-profile lifestyle in their private lives.

More recently, the notion of responsibility has been extended to embrace philanthropy and corporate social responsibility as well as individual responsibility, opening up a new array of opportunities for wealthy families to play a leading role in societal progress.

Stewardship and ownership: Learning and applying the difference between these two concepts is essential for both younger and older family members. This idea is not new. In 1865, Reverend Thomas Binney wrote: "money is a trust, and…it must be dealt with on the principle of stewardship…it is one of the most serious and influential of those diversified elements which go to make up the sum total of that for which men are to be called to give account."[1]

This entails accepting that while some family assets are owned outright by an individual, and can be dealt with as that individual sees fit, others are merely held in stewardship for future generations.

Integrity: This encompasses many other important moral values, including honesty, fairness, and loyalty, but can be summed up as striving always to do what is right.

Humility and respect: Particularly emphasized within the teachings of most Asian religions, humility and respect for others, developed at an early age, are fundamental values from which stem many other benefits such as curiosity, modesty, sympathy, empathy, and generosity.

BUILD A FOUNDATION OF KNOWLEDGE AND UNDERSTANDING

Values alone, while necessary, are not enough for any individual's development. There is a need for a broader understanding of the world to determine how and when those values can best be applied. Armed with a deeper level of knowledge and understanding, intelligent actions can be pursued which can support the achievement of family goals and the realization of a family vision.

It is obviously not only family leaders who can give the necessary instruction to the next generation. Universities are the traditional sources of education to build family knowledge and the requisite understanding at all levels of the family. Schools and religious institutions can also provide a substantial experience, as can more focused institutions such as business schools, at a later date.

---

[1] Thomas Binney, *Money: A Popular Exposition*, Jackson, Walford, and Hodder, pp.307–8 (1865).

Established institutions such as Wharton Business School, and newer institutions such as The Wealth Management Institute in Singapore, offer specific courses in wealth management. Some of the larger private banks offer courses (now called "wealth camps") generation of wealthy families to the broad set of investment issues they will face.

Self-education and development throughout an entire lifetime through reading, attending conferences and lectures, and participating in debate on relevant ideas can add to a base core of knowledge.

Mentors: In addition to the formal mechanisms found in family businesses and in the network of family advisors, it may be particularly valuable to consider appointing informal mentors to all Next Generation family members. Mentors can be exceptionally helpful when members of a new generation are taking on senior roles within the family business, or in the family hierarchy.

It may also be important to appoint such mentors to family members who are experiencing personal problems or difficulties, or are adjusting to a new chapter in their lives. Such adjustments might include going away to boarding school or university for the first time, taking up a first job, changing jobs, getting married, or undergoing the trauma of divorce, separation, or the death of a spouse, parent, sibling, or child.

Wisdom as well: In addition to the specific knowledge and understanding of the professional skills required to manage a family business and family wealth, a deeper general wisdom, which gives context, meaning, and perspective to the acquired knowledge, should also be sought. Making a list of what the members of the next generation need to know, and then ensuring that the opportunities to learn these most important lessons are provided, is one of the greatest challenges—and accomplishments—of family leadership.

Wisdom is not just a collection of facts, histories, and principles for application. A broader and wiser understanding of all elements of family wealth, including ethical, spiritual, and personal development, is also essential learning for any individual life, wealthy or not.

A sense of curiosity and a realistic sense of what is known—and what is not—are an important part of wisdom. "Knowing what you don't know" is as much about real wisdom as it is about humility and perspective.

Another perspective on wisdom worthy of communication and discussion is the notion that there is no end to obtaining and applying what we know. The greater the knowledge and true wisdom, the greater the awareness that there is even more to know; or, as quoted by educator Dr. Henry Ploegstra: "As the flames of knowledge reach higher, and as the circle of light grows, thus also increases the circumference of the darkness."[2]

BUILD A FOUNDATION OF EXPERIENCE

As mentioned earlier, many wealthy children grow up in an environment where, because of their privileged position, much is expected of them, but where that same position deprives them of the difficult and challenging experiences that can fuel their ambition, deepen character, or hone the skills that enable them to meet those high levels of expectation.

> "As the flames of knowledge reach higher, and as the circle of light grows, thus also increases the circumference of the darkness."

One American patriarch of a multibillion-dollar fortune that had been well preserved over many generations described the risks of working in a family foundation or charitable organization as dangerously limiting:

> Working all the time on the buy side, where people bow and scrape to convince you to give them money, gives kids a wrong sense of the world. Kids need to learn to work and succeed in a real environment, not bury themselves in a life where they can't do anything wrong, where their bad jokes are funny and where they don't learn anything except that they are the center of the world, which they are not...[3]

Many parents and family patriarchs believe that it is their responsibility to provide an ideal life for their children or grandchildren, protecting them from painful or difficult experiences, even when it is exactly these types of experiences that gave the founders and leaders of the family the strength to succeed.

---

[2] Private conversation between Dr. Henry Ploegstra and the author
[3] Private conversation with the author.

Cutting the cocoon

The result of excessive protection from necessary experience can perhaps best be described in the story of a passer-by who saw a butterfly struggling to escape from its chrysalis. Noting that the insect was emerging only with great difficulty, the well-intentioned man cut open the casing with a pen knife, freeing the butterfly with one quick stroke.

Unfortunately, as a result of avoiding its painful but necessary struggle, the butterfly's wings were not fully formed and its airways were never squeezed free of fluid. After surviving briefly in its stunted form, the butterfly died early, unable ever to fly or to have a fully normal life.

It has been said that we learn little from our most positive experiences; they only reinforce what we already know. It is our most painful and "negative" experiences which provide the greatest positive value, and contribute the most to our learning and personal growth. The great American author Nathaniel Hawthorne captured this sentiment in the words of a character in his novel *The Marble Faun*: "You cannot suffer deeply; therefore you can but half enjoy."[4]

Great financial wealth can attract attention from a multitude of self-interested and manipulative, but seemingly genuine, characters. It is easy to trust people who appear to be pleasant and concerned, but those who trust too quickly can become the victims of the deceitful and the unprincipled. Excessive trust or naivety, often stemming from a lack of worldly experience, can lead to a very unhappy outcome and a very negative impact on all forms of family wealth.

Part of the response to a lack of experience and the buffering protection of wealth lies in the careful management of the eco-system around the family. Ensuring that individuals are exposed to a number of high-quality people who can help to provide the necessary perspective and experience can contribute greatly to the development of a privileged generation.

By exposing children to the rigors of a full life—social, academic, commercial, athletic, and even military—family leaders can partially counterbalance the inevitable cushioning provided by family wealth.

---

[4] Nathaniel Hawthorne, *The Marble Faun*, (Penguin Books, 1990. First published 1860) Ch.5.

COMMUNICATE OPENLY

Virtually every family counselor will emphasize the importance of open and honest communication to maintain a happy family environment. Without communication, there is little opportunity for sharing, learning, and resolving the inevitable tensions that can arise in any family.

Clear and open communication is perhaps Rule No.1 for family leaders. The Latin origin of the word communicate is *communicare*, meaning "to share" on a communal basis; communication must be a two-way process if it is to be effective. Family leaders must be prepared to listen to, and learn from, their fellow family members, just as those family members must be willing to listen to, and learn from, family leaders and elders.

Communicate about money: It has also been shown to be important for families to discuss the issues surrounding family financial wealth from an early age, even if the actual sums and investment issues only come at a much later stage.

Such discussions can be counter-cultural for many families, particularly those, such as Protestant Christian families, where modesty and probity are inculcated as great virtues; a concentration of effort on managing or making money is considered by some to be an unseemly objective—and certainly an unacceptable topic of discussion at the dinner table.

Many wealthy parents have found that giving children a monthly allowance which they must manage for themselves from an early age can be a beneficial first step towards money management and a safe source of discussion on the value of money. One practical approach to this is to give the allowance only upon the completion of pre-set chores.

A second example of using an allowance as a vehicle for training is to divide it into three equal portions: one-third is allocated to charity, one-third to saving, and one-third to the child's discretionary spending. Some families also encourage their children to record their transactions in an accounts book to teach them the value of tracking and controlling money as well.

Additional options for learning about money in the next generation could include:

- an internship or employment in an asset management firm
- a prescribed program of reading and involvement in family investment discussions

- a "carve out" portfolio: a small, discrete sum of money to be treated as a standalone fund and managed by a single member or group of family members. This management could include selecting advisors, establishing an asset allocation model and undertaking all aspects of portfolio review and reporting, including tax and regulatory filing
- direct business experience, backed by a family venture fund
- requiring each member of the family to set up a small charitable trust, selecting the jurisdiction, preparing the trust deeds, and identifying the beneficiaries of the trust.

Timing of full disclosure: There is no single right moment to provide full disclosure regarding the extent of a family's wealth, just as there is no single way to set the right time to transfer ownership and control over those assets.

Although there is no consensus over timing, there is agreement that some degree of maturity needs to have been attained before "opening the kimono" on the full scale and complexity of family affairs. Some families set an age of between 21 and 30 for such conversations. Others begin such discussions at the end of formal education or upon attainment of full participating rights in the affairs of the family.

While timing varies, most advisors counsel that a full discussion of family affairs take place in a structured and well-prepared situation, where there is adequate time to outline the full picture, to describe the implications and challenges inherent in the family's overall situation, and to respond to queries, comments, or observations about the family's financial activities. That discussion might also include a brief review of the family history, a review of the Family Constitution, and a discussion of the principles and structures of the approach to wealth preservation and wealth management.

If there is a family strategy in place, that strategy may provide an important contribution to both the understanding and engagement in family affairs.

A particularly well-structured approach might include, for example, the defining of a specific activity in the context of the family strategy in which the newly informed members can participate with immediate effect, bringing them into an active role from the initial discussions onward.

From mushroom strategy to mushroom cloud: Although many advisors say that communication about money matters is important from an early age, others more cynical (or worldly) may advise an approach known as "mushroom management." This keeps people in the dark for as long as possible, with occasional deposits of organic fertilizer as needed from senior family members and their advisors to keep them going.

There is, of course, a substantial longer-term risk in this approach. Without communication, family members can fail to develop the necessary expertise with regard to their own wealth management, and may become frustrated, confused, and resentful about having information regarding their true financial situation kept from them.

The risks of litigation, family disruption, and alienation are substantial if the forward course is not charted very carefully. The "mushroom strategy" may lead to an explosion at a later date, leaving only a mushroom cloud where better communication could have created a smooth transition.

INSTILL A SENSE OF INDIVIDUAL PURPOSE AND RESPONSIBILITY

When there is no financial pressure to earn a living, the ambition and determination necessary to build a successful career may also be lacking. After all, as one new heir proclaimed, why should he "bust a gut" to make a million dollars over a number of years when he was set to inherit several times that amount within a few years, no matter how hard he worked elsewhere?

Distribution dependence, a psychological dependence upon the passive receipt of trust fund distributions, creates, in the scornful words of one American multi-billionaire, a set of "early pensioners" with nothing but time on their hands and a sense of entitlement that stifles both ambition and accomplishment.

In order to reduce the risk of dependency, or lack of ambition, tackling the Next Generation Development Imperatives listed above can provide an array of positive and fulfilling opportunities. In addition, trust documentation or a letter of wishes can require that a beneficiary hold down a full-time productive job, or maintain a "work-ethic lifestyle," before any distributions are made.

A large inheritance can, unfortunately, lead to far greater problems for the children of affluence than just lack of ambition. Alcoholism, drug dependency, food and sex addictions, depression, alienation, self-destructive behavior, and even suicide can result in those who lack a sense of purpose or self-worth. A world of wealth and financial abundance can seem ideal from the outside, but can feel deeply lonely and lacking from the inside. The ease with which funds can be had to purchase the agents and instruments of addiction can make such addictions a greater risk at an early age for the child of an affluent family.

Helping family members to set individual goals, whether or not related to financial accomplishment, and providing emotional rewards for their accomplishment, are essential steps in the development of an effective response to the challenges of wealth dependence and entitlement-driven attitudes.

Guilt, unworthiness, and religious or ethical dissonance: Financial worth can also lead to a feeling of unworthiness and guilt on the part of individuals struggling with the blessings and burdens of wealth. In her book on the psychology of affluence, Jessie H. O'Neill cites the example of a woman whose affluence created deep religious concerns:

> Her family heritage was based upon a traditional Midwest work ethic that said people had to earn what they received in life. She felt shame and unworthiness in the face of this unearned wealth…made worse by the church considering it "holy" to live in poverty.[5]

"She felt shame and unworthiness in the face of this unearned wealth…made worse by the church considering it 'holy' to live in poverty."

Another view on this same issue suggests that by giving children too much, too early, parents can deprive them of the joys of anticipation, effort and reward, as expressed in the anonymous saying "Sometimes the poorest man leaves his children the richest inheritance."

PROVIDE LOVE AND DISCIPLINE

Numerous family counselors and therapists have told us that children need only two major items of inheritance from their parents to

---

[5] Jessie H. O'Neill, *The Golden Ghetto: The Psychology of Affluence*, (The Affluenza Project, 1997) p.149.

be happy: love and discipline. Children need to know that they are loved unconditionally, and to know where the borders of behavior lie. In finding that love, and in understanding those limits, they can find a sense of security, orientation, and belonging.

Without behavioral boundaries, some wealthy individuals equate their relatively strong financial position, possibly obtained through no effort of their own, as a sign of moral superiority. This misplaced belief can lead to a wide range of anti-social and destructive behaviors, including a psychological condition known as "inhibition deprivation," in which individuals feel exempt from the normal rules of society because they believe that the privileges and stature conferred by a wealthy background make everything they do acceptable.

Harking back in some ways to Nietzsche's thesis of man and superman, those suffering from inhibition deprivation can become victims of their own attitudes as they seek to distance themselves from the greater human family of which they are a part.

As has long been known, the penalty for wanting the wrong things in life is getting them.

A dangerous belief can also develop when money is presented as the solution to all problems and to compensate for any inappropriate behavior. The payment of "hush money" to the media to keep bad behavior out of the press, or the purchase of a replacement car immediately after a teenager destroys a vehicle in a reckless accident, are just two examples of the easy substitution of cash for a more valuable sense of proportion and limitations on behavior. Such attitudes can lead to a lack of personal or emotional development and a cynical view of the human condition.

> … the penalty for wanting the wrong things in life is getting them.

Reducing all human interaction to a set of commercial transactions can deprive some affluent children of the experiences and insights that can be the most sustaining to them at the deepest human level.

BUILD TRUST

Trust needs to be built on all sides of a family relationship, and with individuals and institutions outside the family.

Not everything in the future lives of Next Generation members can be known in advance or controlled through observation and selected intervention. For a great part of their lives, older family members will not be around to provide control, guidance, or information to their progeny and other younger members of the family. At some point, older family members will need to let go and trust in the members of the Next Generation.

Similarly, members of a Next Generation will need to earn that trust through sharing in the responsibility for their development, embracing the values and obligations of family membership, and pursuing lives which reflect their own positive set of values and efforts.

CREATE TIME FOR THE FAMILY

Very often, the busy lifestyle of a wealthy parent can create a sense of emotional abandonment among children and lead to a breakdown of trust within the family. For example, a father who repeatedly promises to attend an important family event or school meeting, but fails to turn up because of business demands, will erode the trust and respect of his offspring. Under the cover of an expensive infrastructure, surrogates in the form of nannies, tutors, au pairs, maids, and even boarding schools may be used to replace the far more valuable and appreciated assets of parental love and attention.

One recent study in Hong Kong reported that Chinese fathers with young children spent, on average, only seven minutes per week alone with their children. Many an English aristocrat or scion of a wealthy family remembers with painful clarity the day he was left on the steps of his boarding school, at the tender age of seven or eight, watching his parents' car drive away and leaving him behind, alone, afraid and unhappy.

To compound this particular issue, many modern parents, regardless of their level of wealth, fall prey to a convenient belief in the surrogacy of purchased goods for real investment of the self and the sharing of time together.

In a recent interview in the journal *More Than Money*, the dangers of giving of the "wrong" kinds of gifts were discussed:

> The problems found among affluent adolescents are caused neither by the affluence itself, nor by giving our children too much…[they] occur

because we do not give enough. We need to give our children more of three things: more time, more limits, and more care. What children want most from adults is their presence, not their presents.[6]

> "What children want most from adults is their presence, not their presents."

Many studies have captured the central insight that children need love and discipline from their parents.[7] One such study of happy families coming from backgrounds of economic privilege pointed out a few very simple characteristics which separated them from their less-happy peers. The first was a requirement for children to tidy up their own rooms. The second was that the happy families regularly took their meals together.

By learning from these simple insights, and spending quality time together, respect, trust, and happiness can be developed that can last across many decades and generations of a wealthy family.

NO SIMPLE SOLUTIONS

Neither managing nor growing up in a wealthy family is as simple as it may seem from the outside. Managing, teaching, and learning to preserve that wealth within and across generations are extremely challenging tasks for both older and younger generations.

There is no guarantee of a successful result from any family's efforts at preparing their Next Generation, no matter how well intentioned or well structured. Yet by learning and applying the most successful principles and approaches from the past, a family's efforts are far more likely to achieve the desired results in their own time and in their own families.

---

[6] Bob Kenny, "Giving to Children. When Is Too Much Not Enough?," *More Than Money*, Issue 34. www.morethanmoney.org/magazine/back_issues/mtm34/mtm34_kenny.htm

[7] See, for example, Becky A. Bailey, *Easy to Love, Difficult to Discipline: The 7 Basic Skills for Turning Conflict into Cooperation*, HarperCollins 1st Quill edition (2002); and Thomas Phelan, *1-2-3 Magic: Effective Discipline for Children 2–12*, Child Management Inc., 3rd rev. ed. (2003).

9. THE FAMILY "ECO-SYSTEM"

In today's interconnected and dynamic world, no family is an island. Like all social organizations, a wealthy family is a dynamic system shaped by a host of factors, both internal and external, which contribute to the survival, failure, or long-term prosperity of the family. Many of the internal factors and approaches which shape a family's future have been addressed above.

At the same time, a set of external factors also combine to influence the family, creating a kind of living and ever-changing eco-system, interconnected with the family and its members and inextricably intertwined with its current state of affairs and future development.

As renowned MIT professor Peter Senge notes:

> The world is becoming more interconnected and interdependent … All of which means we have to change the way we think about learning and interacting with each other at all levels. We have to develop a sense of interconnectedness, a sense of working together as part of a system, where each part of the system is affecting and being affected by the others, and where the whole is greater than the sum of the parts.[1]

A NETWORK OF NETWORKS

This new world has been described by more than one observer as an interconnected network of networks, all developing on their own, but all connected in a whole, and sometimes seemingly chaotic, new world order. In Internet speak, this is a world of "social networks," new forms of communities which grow, develop, interact, evolve, and dissolve, together and separately.

Although present in the larger interconnected world as well, each wealthy family is particularly strongly connected to its own eco-system, the small system of entities and activities that revolves around, and interacts with, a given family. A family eco-system is made up of a collection of individuals, institutions, influencers, practices, and

---

[1] Peter M. Senge, *The Fifth Discipline: The Art and Practice of the Learning Organisation*, (Currency Doubleday, 1994).

principles which nourish and shape it—and which it shapes—through short- and long-term interactions.

The breadth, structure, and complexity of an eco-system will vary enormously from one family to another and from one category of wealth to another.

In a first-generation family with Category I wealth, containing a single, geographically concentrated business, deriving its wealth from one major source of income and operating its wealth preservation and management activities under a single domestic trust, the resulting eco-system is likely to be relatively tight and easy to define and control.

In a fifth-generation family with Category IV wealth, spread across the world and governed by a multi-generational Family Council and coordinated by a set of Family Offices operating in multiple locations, the eco-system will be vast, complex, and much more difficult to define or control.

Developing and managing the family's eco-system, no matter how complex a task, is an important element in every family wealth strategy.

Every family eco-system is different and will change with time. In almost all situations, however, it will include an inner circle of trusted advisors, a network of professional individuals, and a set of independent institutions and individuals which all play a major role in the family's ultimate destiny.

Elements of the Eco-system

- The Family Center
- The Inner Circle of Trusted Advisors
- The Network of Selected Professionals
- Independent Institutions
- Individuals

THE FAMILY CENTER

While it is obvious that the family sits at the center of its own eco-system, the role of family leaders and members as conscious managers of that eco-system may require renewed consideration. Knowingly or not, the family acts as a kind of central sun or powerful gravitational force around which revolve dozens of subsidiary and supporting entities, locked into defined orbits and held in place by the gravitational presence of the family.

Unlike solar systems, where all motion is subject to the laws of physics, a family's eco-system is subject to the conscious (and unconscious) human decisions and personalities of the family, thus a dynamic system is created by will, effort, intervention, values, personal choices, and collective aspirations as well as by the immutable laws of science and nature.

THE INNER CIRCLE OF TRUSTED ADVISORS

Just as every president has a "kitchen cabinet" of trusted friends and advisors outside the formal structures of power, and likewise every CEO has a set of close business advisors, the head of a wealthy family often benefits from the insights and advice of an Inner Circle of Trusted Advisors. This informal set of powerful advisors operates best as a group of peers with whom family leaders can discuss the most sensitive issues regarding the family, its individual members, and issues of central importance to its management. Such conversations can only take place in an atmosphere of full confidence and without any inhibition or fear of disclosure.

Members of the Inner Circle may include lawyers, bankers, the head of a Family Office or family philanthropic foundation, leaders or directors of a family business, tax advisors, trustees, spiritual advisors, and friends. Membership of the Inner Circle is usually based upon a relationship of trust, capability, and shared experience.

While members of an Inner Circle can contribute from their own area of professional expertise, their greatest value may be found in offering informed and impartial advice regarding all aspects of the diverse challenges facing the wealthy family.

The comprehensive advice of a trusted advisor may be particularly valuable at times of a transition in the family's affairs; the potential sale of a family business or other substantial asset, the transition of leadership or ownership of assets from one generation to another, or in a defining business/family crisis.

Issues involving individual family members, trust allocations, tax structures and risks, business performance, Family Office staffing, intergenerational rights and responsibilities, risks, opportunities, and a whole host of other issues can be far better understood, and the best responses developed and implemented, with the benefit of unbiased and trusted advice.

In providing a group of fully informed (and discreet) members operating to an informal set of rules, the Inner Circle must be made up of people with whom the leaders of the family can develop a sense of complete comfort and total trust.

The usual suspects: The Inner Circle of a wealthy family is never large, usually comprising some combination of family members, outside advisors (lawyers, accountants, tax advisors, trustees, private bankers), trusted advisors without a specific supporting role in the family's eco-system, and, in some cases, one or two senior members of the family businesses, Family Office, or philanthropic foundation.

While not all providing representation in the Inner Circle, the following network of professional advisors and friends with whom key family members interact on a regular basis provide the source for most members of the Inner Circle:

- *Lawyers:* Often, a family lawyer is present who can provide answers on numerous issues including tax, trusts, wills, legal agreements, company law, property law, directors' obligations, marriage and divorce, company formation and governance, and even such unwanted subjects as litigation or criminal law, if necessary.

  A vanishing breed, the highly capable legal "General Practitioner" can play many essential roles in the core family group for multiple purposes.

  With the demise of the private client practice group in many of the larger law firms, it is proving difficult for many families, even of the higher categories, to find the quality of advice and experienced people they want in smaller firms. As a result, finding the right legal expert may take more time and effort than it might have in the past.

- *Accountants:* Possibly overlapping with a lawyer in certain areas of expertise, an accountant can provide information on taxes, investments, valuations, balance sheet numbers, accounts, and commercial agreements, where appropriate.

  In addition to providing succinct information on a family business, wealth management and preservation, and the financial situation of any philanthropic activity, a good accountant can also provide creative thoughts in the areas of tax and estate planning, forward budgets, reporting and investment targets, and other elements of a commercial or reporting nature.

- *Tax advisors:* Drawing from the ranks of lawyers, accountants, trust company professionals, and special advisory firms, tax advisors can provide information with regard to asset structuring, wealth preservation, procedural guidance, perspectives on income and capital gains tax, property tax, inheritance tax, and wealth tax. A host of other issues, including residence and domicile, can be well handled by an expert tax advisor.

- *Trustees:* The role of a trustee will range from being fully involved to not present. Depending upon the nature of the trust arrangements, the personality and style of the trustee, and the specific items of relevance, a trustee's presence can be useful, intrusive, or even legally inappropriate.

- *Private bankers:* An old-fashioned private banker, knowledgeable of a family's affairs and members, bringing to bear an understanding of the approaches taken by similarly situated families in similar circumstances, discreet, relationship-oriented and focused on the long-term welfare of the wealthy family, can be worth more than his or her weight in gold.

  With the rise of private wealth management as a lucrative source of corporate profits, however, the old-fashioned private banker who places the clients' longer-term interests above his parent company's quarterly profit goals is a rare breed in a pressure-cooker world of stiff quarterly asset-gathering targets and lucrative commission sales.

  A well-trained and capable private banker can bring expertise to bear on investments, tax, trust, Family Office staffing, family business management and ownership, and would have an experienced view on the development paths of members of the Next Generation. Finding the right private banker, an enlightened individual who can see and act with a family's long-term perspective in mind, may be both the key to financial success for the family and the means to unlock the door to the inner sanctum for that individual banker.

- *Independent chairman or director of family business:* The senior non-family leaders of a family business, along with independent directors, may provide useful perspectives on the commercial and personal affairs of the family.

- *Trusted third-party advisor:* Over the years and across the world, the *comprador, consigliere,* or *homme d'affaires* has played an essential role in the commercial success of many families.

These trusted third-party advisors are not always employees of the family. They may be close friends, business associates, former employees, academics, or strategists who can provide an integrated and objective perspective on all aspects of the family's affairs. A third-party advisor may or may not be paid, depending on the nature of the relationship.

- *Family Office head:* In some families, the head of the Family Office can be a highly respected senior professional who plays a central role in all of the deliberations and decisions taken by the family. In others, the head is relatively junior in experience or stature and is considered to be an administrator or executor of decisions taken by others and is unlikely yet to have earned a seat in the Inner Circle.

- *Close friends:* Whether developed in childhood, at school or university, in military service, or in business or social circles, friends can play a major role in family deliberations.

> Over the years and across the world, the *comprador, consigliere,* or *homme d'affaires* has played an essential role in the commercial success of many families.

Importantly, friends—especially those who have substantial capital and a long personal history with the family—can be rare sources of honest, sometimes painful, advice on strategy, investments, life choices, and other key issues. Giving honest advice is especially difficult for those who "work for" the family. Friends, on the other hand, can deliver tough mes-

---

Seeking Out Values and Dissent

One young, American, multi-billionaire, technology entrepreneur lamented that, as his wealth and stature grew, dissent and disagreement died out. To paraphrase one of his common observations:

> I noticed that people stopped disagreeing with me a long time ago. One of the things I need from my own team is healthy disagreement, perspectives that are different from my own, and a "Deal Prevention" role to keep me from being a victim of my own optimism and past success.

Unlike many newly wealthy individuals, this person was able to see the great risks inherent in a rosy world of constant personal affirmation.

sages, without the fear that their careers may be jeopardized by taking a contrary view.

- *Business associates:* Although most business associates would be excluded from discussions related to mutual business dealings, some such relationships are built upon a broader base of understanding, or can provide a perspective on a sufficiently large number of common interests for it to make sense to include them.

- *Head of Philanthropic Foundation:* Although not every wealthy family will have one, for some the role of a philanthropic entity may lead to the foundation being represented on family matters that go far beyond those directly related to the family's charitable endeavors.

- *PR or lobbyists:* In families of great prominence, it may be useful to have a public relations agent or government liaison representative as part of the Inner Circle. This could be especially true in emerging markets, where a privileged economic relationship with a government and its leaders could be of particular economic importance.

- *Religious advisors:* In some families, it is important that a priest, imam, pastor, rabbi, guru, or other religious or spiritual advisor join in the discussions on the most significant family matters, even if they are not present for all operating or investment discussions. Although of decreasing presence in the Inner Circle of many families, such advisors have had, over the years, a profound influence on the issues discussed, the content of the deliberations, and the final outcome on fundamental family matters.

This list of potential sources of members for an Inner Circle is far longer than indicated by the headings above, but the common nature of the issues discussed and the particular relevance of the expertise of these particular professions and relationships make it more likely than not that some sub-set of these advisors will make up at least part of a family's Inner Circle.

The benefits of creating an Inner Circle: There are many benefits to creating an Inner Circle, and relying on it to understand and select strategies with regard to major family issues, particularly those of a long-term nature. In addition to the various perspectives and experiences that this select group can bring to the debate, the presence of non-family members can provide a less emotional and less personal dimension to the discussion of sensitive family matters.

In some families, typically true of Asian families, important queries, admonitions, and communications may be more effective if passed through a third party. By using non-family members to communicate and resolve major matters between meetings, "face" can be saved and negative personal feelings and unwanted family consequences may be avoided.

An Inner Circle and trusted third-party advisors may be particularly valuable in deciding upon and conveying difficult messages regarding roles in the family business, failure to meet required conditions for a distribution, and unfavorable decisions in a family dispute.

By bringing to bear a dedication to the family's welfare and an impartial view and non-family presence, an Inner Circle can help to make and implement tough decisions with less emotional baggage than that inevitably carried by all of the family members concerned.

Advisory Board: For families in Categories III and IV, with larger and more complex global issues to discuss, it may be advisable to establish a formal (and bigger) Advisory Board to supplement the skills and relationships of a smaller Inner Circle.

Membership of this Advisory Board could include a broader set of outside advisors from various disciplines and geographies. While an Inner Circle can meet frequently and informally to cover either a broad agenda, or to consider a single item on an *ad hoc* basis, an Advisory Board would usually meet on a regular schedule and would address a broader pre-defined agenda at each session.

Characteristics of members: The key to success in putting together, or in being admitted to, an Inner Circle, is very personal. The personality and character of potential members, and their attitude toward working smoothly with the existing team, may be as important as the exact skill sets they can bring to the table.

Many members of these powerful groups would have a common set of personal characteristics, ensuring that all members:

- are discreet and understanding, honest and tough minded, loyal, and are both liked and trusted by key family members
- are experienced in a relevant set of capabilities, are (possibly) expert in at least one important technical area and capable of understanding and integrating multiple perspectives on a single issue

- supplement family capabilities and experiences
- have a good sense of balance and humor.

While opposing views may (and should) be tabled and discussed, an ability to move seamlessly, and without discord, to agreed solutions from a multiplicity of views is one hallmark of an effective Inner Circle member. It goes without saying that assembling the best team of advisors and trusted confidantes is not an easy task. The head of a US$5 billion Family Office in the U.S. described the difficulty in finding even a small handful of such individuals in his American context: "Such top notch, truly enlightened, experienced and trustworthy people are hard to find anywhere in the world."

THE NETWORK OF SELECTED PROFESSIONALS

At a less intimate level of contact with the family than the Inner Circle, in the next level of the eco-system, is found a world of bankers, private bankers, brokers, lawyers, fund managers, trust and administrative service companies, insurance purveyors, risk management service providers, public relations consultants, psychologists, strategic consultants, executive and personal coaches, accountants, tax experts, and other professionals with whom the family may have an extended or one-off transactional relationship.

There is great value to be had in defining and managing this network carefully and effectively, as it can provide investment opportunities, information, ideas, introductions, and perspectives that can contribute substantially to the future financial and personal success of a family and its members.

Although it is relatively easy to sit down and list the advisors, colleagues, individuals, and institutions that have an impact on a wealthy family, it is far more difficult to determine how to go about influencing the interrelated and dynamic eco-system that they become.

Although the network is usually managed on an informal basis, its importance in determining the family's future prosperity may justify the investment of time and thought in a more structured approach.

Review the system objectively: In pursuing the development and efficient functioning of the best possible network of advisors, an arm's-length review of the system and its constituent elements is essential. Objective selection, assessment of performance, and high-quality performance reporting against relevant benchmarks, or a rigorous subjective standard, is critical.

Seven Steps to Obtain an Effective and Efficient Advisor Network

- Decide upon family vision and goals
- Define the "ideally constituted" advisory team
- Avoid the cardinal sin
- Decide on roles and outline selection criteria
- List and interview candidates
- Test and evaluate the selected members of the group
- Manage and refresh the system

The process to get to an effective and efficient advisor network could unfold in seven steps:

Decide upon family vision and goals: Before setting out to define and select a team to serve family purposes, it is always worthwhile to review what the family is trying to achieve. Are the goals primarily financial, or are there issues to address that are personal, educational, psychological, philanthropic, or geographical?

By setting out in advance the overall goals, the most appropriate supporting resources can be identified to support the family, or to supplement its capabilities, to achieve those goals on their own.

Set priorities: Trying to do all things at all times in all places is a recipe for disaster in almost any situation. A few key changes in the eco-system can be far more effective than a blanket coverage of all issues in helping a family to avert disasters and reach a particular destination, perhaps many generations forward.

By addressing only the highest priority issues, family leaders can identify a few changes in the family's eco-system which can lead to the greatest and longest lasting benefits.

With a plethora of vendors and suppliers wanting to make their services available to the wealthy family, it is essential to have an organized approach to the management of the advisor network to avoid wasting time on uninteresting or poor quality advice.

Rather than adopting a haphazard approach to advisor meetings and selection, it might be useful to pursue an approach which may take more time upfront, but which can pay far greater dividends in the long run.

Define the "ideally constituted" advisory team structure: Once the family's needs and aspirations are defined, the structure of the team of advisors can be determined. In some cases the team will be primarily tax, trust, and investment-driven. In other cases, a focus on business strategy, HR, or corporate finance may be appropriate.

Avoid the cardinal sin: One of the most basic mistakes made by many investors, rich and poor, is to use the same investment advisor—the person who selects the funds for an investment portfolio—as a fund manager, the person managing the money. This obvious conflict of interest is most visible in the banking, asset management, private banking, and brokerage worlds. Time and again, "relationship managers" or "personal advisors" push in-house products onto customers, regardless of relative performance, fee levels, or likely return.

> One of the most basic mistakes made by many investors, rich and poor, is to use the same investment advisor—the person who selects the funds for an investment portfolio—as a fund manager, the person managing the money.

Since most bankers and brokers are now rewarded on the profitability of the products they sell to clients, and are indifferent to the client's portfolio performance insofar as their own compensation goes, wealthy families need to understand, and act upon, the real motivations of their advisors and managers.

One former investment banker, now working for a large multi-family office, described the sell-side model as "a kind of buffet of opportunities, most of which are pushed by aggressive brokers indiscriminately (even if they call themselves 'independent wealth advisors')." The approach he prescribes to shopping from this buffet is to "select very carefully and only when it fits the needs of the portfolio vision and objectives. It is important to be part of the fabric of asset management but wisely objective, skeptical, and only aligned with your own clear goals."

Whoever the person appointed as chief investment officer, it is essential to preserve his or her independence from the pressures of advisors' in-house product sale. Many private banks offer a finder's fee to trustees, advisors, CIOs, or other influencers. If such an arrangement exists, it should be made known to the investor. A principled investment advisor should not have any placement fee or reward from any asset or fund manager. Only in this way can the investor be sure to receive truly unbiased advice.

Decide on roles and outline selection criteria: Once the network team's needs have been decided, the specific structure of the team can be decided. How many firms and of which type will need to be included? Will there be a lead advisor in each category? Should a family select a leading group of advisors in each key area? What risk management principles—for example, avoiding concentration risk, security risk, or overdependence on one individual—should be observed?

Most families would not want to confine themselves to a single broker, private banker, or commercial lending bank. Exposure to more than one source of ideas, perspectives, and opportunities has great benefit in these areas.

On the other hand, legal services may be more efficiently procured from a single provider with a full understanding of the family history, business affairs, wealth preservation approach, and other issues.

> Clarifying the roles to be played can stimulate a very healthy competitive dynamic among advisors.

Where the selective use of multiple providers is deemed to be the best approach, some families appoint a lead advisor in each sector and a small group of supporting advisors. These families may also be open to ideas from a broader set of advisors with transactional opportunities or specific points of view which can be usefully applied.

For example, in the area of private banking services, the family may have an established relationship with a "house bank" with which they have a solid and satisfactory relationship. A second tier of preferred suppliers—say, a set of supporting banks of different types from different geographies—can also be established as appropriate. Other private banks can provide specific transaction opportunities and expert advice as and when needed.

Clarifying the roles to be played can stimulate a very healthy competitive dynamic among advisors to reduce the chances of complacency or neglect which can arise if a relationship is taken for granted.

List and interview candidates: After defining the needs, structure, and approach to its advisory network, the family can then list the candidates in each area of need. From this long list of qualified and appropriate advisory firms and individuals will be drawn a shortlist of the most appropriate candidates to be measured against more rigorous selection criteria. These criteria should reflect both the objective needs of the family and any subjective criteria relating to specific family cultural attributes, values, or operating principles.

In defining a family's specific needs, it may be valuable to solicit input from families in similar situations, which may generate general ideas and particular recommendations. This can often serve as a shortcut in an otherwise time-consuming process.

If the family already has advisors in a particular area, the factors which make them successful, or not, can also be factored into the selection criteria.

In the interview process, each member of the selection team should have a score sheet of criteria against which each candidate will be assessed, but assessment should not be based solely on that predefined list, as other important but unexpected elements of the decision may arise during the process.

Many families have found it beneficial to see all candidates for a particular area of support in a compressed timeframe, often seeing as many firms or individuals as possible over the course of a few days. This allows comparisons to be made more easily, before memory fades and subtle details and differences are forgotten.

Having creative criteria and different participants in the process can also be useful. Family advisors who have had experience of the sell side can be very valuable in understanding what to avoid and what may add value.

Test and evaluate the selected members of the group: The successful candidates may be given small pieces of work to confirm their abilities and discretion before being integrated into the broader network. Working together, even briefly, can provide a valuable platform of shared experience for both sides to assess the fit and potential mutual benefits from a longer term relationship.

Manage and refresh the system: As with the hiring and integration of an employee into a family business, the selection and introduction of a professional firm into the network is just the beginning of a much longer journey. Not all employees will rise to the top; nor will they all stay for an extended time period. The same is true for advisors in the broader network.

Many advisors to wealthy families can become complacent as the relationship continues across the years, delivering work which becomes accepted despite its low or declining standard. Seeking out and addressing such underperformance is a key test of effectiveness for family leadership.

By changing or adding advisors from time to time, the remaining players in the system will stay fresh and eager to provide the required level of service.

In most cases, regular and objective reporting on performance against benchmarks, on an after-fees-and-costs basis, is an important part of the management of financial advisors and investment professionals in the network.

Beware of brand-name rapture: In the world of parachuting, there is a phenomenon known as "ground rapture," in which parachutists become entranced with the ground below them and are unable to pull the ripcord to open their canopies and slow their descent. Similarly, some clients of big-name financial institutions become entranced with the name and power of their advisors and fail to manage the relationships properly, even if results are not satisfactory.

> Some clients of big-name financial institutions become entranced with the name and power of their advisors and fail to manage the relationships properly.

In one case in Asia, the private banking arm of a major global powerhouse advised a Category I client to invest heavily in a derivatives portfolio. Lucrative for the bank, the portfolio eventually imploded, erasing millions of dollars of family wealth. Since the banker had been entrusted with the family's entire investment portfolio, this collapse eliminated virtually all of the family's wealth.

No institution is foolproof. Each institution is just a collection of fallible human beings with strengths and weaknesses. Even the most august and respected of financial institutions can make bad investment recommendations.

The Advisors Matrix: One proven tool for the management of a network of advisors is the Advisors Matrix, a simple display which allows family members to see their advisors and evaluate their performance (see Figure 2.4).

Figure 2.4 Advisors and Influencers Matrix

	Negative performance	Positive performance
Long-term Relationship	Imperative: Fix or change	Imperative: Protect and (perhaps) grow
Short-term Relationship	Imperative: Terminate	Imperative: Stay in contact and repeat purchase if services needed again

The matrix simply divides advisors into quadrants based upon two factors. The first factor is the advisor's performance, objectively assessed. This will range from positive to negative. The second factor is whether the relationship with that advisor is short term or long term in nature. Given the costs involved in developing or changing a longer term relationship, the response to an unsatisfactory performance may vary from that in a less involved situation.

For each quadrant there is an implied imperative:

- *Negative performance in a short-term relationship* would usually lead to swift termination of the relationship.
- *Negative performance in a long-term relationship* may initiate a discussion and program to attempt to fix the relationship before termination is considered.

- *Positive long-term relationships* are to be protected, invested in, and, perhaps, grown.
- *Positive short-term relationships* may lead to continuing contact, recommendation, and, at a later date, repeat purchase.

INDEPENDENT INSTITUTIONS

In some wealthy families, a small set of external institutions and communities are integrated into the family's pattern of traditions and identity across many generations. This consistent institutional presence may be particularly true in older families and in the higher categories of wealth, where a substantial fortune may not only assure access, but may create a position of sufficient influence to create or to shape such institutions directly.

Schools: There are, in most families, few institutions that influence and mark its members more than the schools their members attend. Schools can be municipal, private, religious, boarding, international, local, or any other approach which a family selects from the options available.

Schools can determine the standard of education children receive, have a substantial input to the future network of friends and contacts, and can shape the attitudes and expectations of family members in a manner that may even surpass the influence of the immediate or wider family. School experience often does not end with graduation. Alumni activities, advisory boards and trustee positions, financial donations, children's applications, and other continuing contact can underscore the importance of a family's extended relationship with one or more specific institutions.

The traditions linking some elite schools and wealthy families can extend back centuries at famous schools such as Eton, Harrow, and Winchester in the United Kingdom; the Lycee Henri IV in Paris; Le Rosey in Switzerland; and Exeter, Andover, St. Paul's, Lawrenceville, Holderness and others in the United States.

Universities, too, can play a significant role in the development of family members. Harvard, Yale, Princeton, Oxford, Cambridge, the *grandes écoles* in France and similar institutions in other countries, are inextricably intertwined with the histories of many great and wealthy families.

Clubs and Associations: Within these schools, fraternities, secret societies, sporting traditions, departmental majors, and certain scholarships might also play a role in a family's values and development programs.

These traditions are not limited to schools in the United States. In Germany and Austria, an active fraternity system, exclusively male and related to either Catholic or Protestant affiliation, creates a set of elite contacts and traditions which can provide support and opportunity for an entire professional lifetime.

Exclusive dining societies at Oxford and Cambridge also play a role in admitting selected individuals into a boisterous and well-lubricated world of rich and established families.

☠ Skull and Bones ☠

Both George W. Bush and John Kerry were Yale graduates; both were also members of Skull and Bones, a secret society at Yale, of which George H. W. Bush, and many other members of the Eastern Establishment, were also members.

Although increased competition and increased meritocracy make it far harder now to ensure entrance into the leading schools, the leaders of wealthy families may want to think well ahead in developing preferred relations with selected schools. Selected and strategic engagement can increase the likelihood that a family can count on its future generations developing the same useful experiences and values that older members of the family did at the same selective institutions.

Other traditions: There are other institutions that can, for some, play a major role in a family's sense of self and future history: the military, social and sporting clubs, country clubs, hunts, London clubs such as White's and Boodle's, golf, polo, yachting, and other elite institutions and pastimes. Memberships in some clubs or social groups may even be handed down from one generation to the next, with little possibility for new entrants.

In the sporting arena, yachting and polo have always been the sports of kings and industrial princes. Only one of the barriers to full entry to the club has been financial, but the costs of participation are always notoriously high. When Commodore Vanderbilt was once asked how much it cost to acquire and maintain a racing yacht, he replied: "If you have to ask, you can't afford it."

> "If you have to ask, you can't afford it."

In the context of the family's future strategy, the critical question in determining an approach to such institutions and associations is whether they have had, or will have, a significant influence on the family and the extent to which they can, and should, fit into the family's future plans.

Creating institutions: For the higher two wealth categories, it may be possible to create institutions of great and enduring value which will both fill a gap in the global architecture and create a lasting family legacy. Examples of some of the greatest family philanthropic institutions are discussed in more detail in Principle 6 (see Chapter 29, "The History of Generosity.")

INDIVIDUALS

American sage Alexandra Holmes once said that life is a repetition of a limited set of experiences: eating, sleeping, working, talking, listening, loving, raising children, and pursuing other such activities that fill up most of our days. The only differences in meaning between individual lives is determined by the values that are respected, the choices we make in selecting how we do what we do, and the selection of the people with whom we share the available experiences.

Spouses, friends, teachers, business colleagues, religious leaders, gurus, advisors, employees, schoolmates, in-laws, and other individuals can all play a role in a personal network which shapes the life of an individual beyond the family, and hence shapes the future of that family. Of these, a selected marital partner is perhaps the most important by far; some surveys have concluded that 90% of individual happiness is related to the choice of person we marry and with whom we share our lives.

By staying aware of the individuals who are becoming influential in the lives of family members, and in particular those likely to join the family as spouses, leaders can provide the kind of wise counsel that may help to shape the views or actions of younger family members.

One large Asian Category IV family even insists upon potential brides of family members meeting with (a gentle term for an interview process) all other family spouses, who offer advice on the family's operating style, business demands, and family traditions and practices.

MANAGING THE "ECO-SYSTEM"

The overall objective of a program to manage the family eco-system is not to intervene in every aspect of the lives of family members, prohibiting contact or insisting upon imposed outcomes in every situation. Such a heavy-handed approach, inconsistent with the more sophisticated model of family leadership outlined below, would most likely lead to rebellion, no matter how well-intentioned or sagacious the intervention.

The approach which has worked best for some families has been a more subtle approach to "influence the influencers," carefully selecting and managing a few, high-priority issues arising in the critical areas of the eco-system which are most likely to have the largest impact—positive or negative—on a family's wealth and wellbeing.

While not always controllable, the wider personal networks of individual family members may be worth discussing at regular intervals with family leaders and, where possible, shaping for the better. Attracting good advisors, and acting in advance of any major crisis erupting as a result of an inappropriate relationship or influence, can be a major contribution to family stability, unity, and prosperity.

Problems with drugs, alcohol, spendthrift social groups, and religious cults, to name but a few of the risks that can lurk in the penumbra of an individual's evolving network, can all be far more easily addressed if seen and acted upon at an early stage.

Review and respond regularly: By its very nature, a family's eco-system, like any other dynamic system, is constantly evolving, changing, being redirected, and redefined. Thus, it is incumbent upon family leaders to review and adjust their responses to these changes on a regular basis.

By assessing regularly the current state of the family's eco-system, and then acting with a long-term forward view in mind, family leaders may well be capable of pre-empting problems, or strengthening the family to face future challenges, which might otherwise pose a substantial threat to family wealth and wellbeing.

10. THE FAMILY OFFICE

The needs of any family are complex, and the needs of the wealthy multi-generational family are greater in number and more substantial than those of an average family.

For families in wealth Category III and above, the long list of items to be addressed, and the scale of those activities, may justify the establishment of a separate office dedicated to serving the needs of the family. As we have seen, these needs are primarily centered on services to help organize and support the smooth functioning of the family in all of its activities.

The function, structure, and operations of a Family Office vary enormously depending on the family's specific and unique needs. There are, however, some broad areas of commonality between such offices within the same region. In the United States, for example, Family Offices may be more focused on domestic trusts, investment, and philanthropic needs, while in Europe they may be more focused on offshore trusts, tax planning, and family services, along with wealth management and business needs.

In Asia, where family money, family businesses, and family members are still quite closely aligned, the Family Office may also serve as the *de facto* headquarters of the family business enterprise, or, conversely, the actual business headquarters may perform many of the functions of a traditional western Family Office.

THE DEDICATED FAMILY OFFICE

The number of Family Offices in the world may now exceed 10,000,[1] with the numbers going up all the time. Although the numbers and the range of options have grown dramatically in the recent past, the basic functions of a Family Office have not changed.

---

[1] Sue Landau, "The very rich pay family retainers to talk to their bankers," *International Herald Tribune*, Business Section, 20 November, 2006, www.iht.com/ articles/2006/11/19/business/rwmtopbar.php

Research shows that there are a number of consistent activities shared across most Family Offices, with the most important being:

- family services, including family meetings, housing, insurance, travel, payments and account management, educational services and support, security, and healthcare
- wealth preservation, including tax planning, estate planning, insurance, trust and trustee management, risk management, wealth management, financial planning, asset allocation, investment strategy, selection of asset manager, reporting, and negotiation of fees
- family business advice
- accounting and legal advice
- counseling on charitable activities
- performance reporting
- advisor coordination
- integrated strategic advice.

COMPREHENSIVE WEALTH FUNCTION

The main function of most Family Offices, in addition to providing necessary family services, is to support the family's wealth preservation and investment management activities.

Performing this function usually requires defining the approach to asset structuring, setting an investment process, developing an asset allocation model, attracting and reviewing a constant flow of investment offerings that fit the desired portfolio model, selecting investments, investment advisors and fund managers, performing appropriate due diligence, approving investment recommendations, and then following up on each investment.

A Family Office might also develop capabilities in direct equity investment, along with co-investment and investment skills in real assets such as property, commodities, gold, art, and other tangible assets.

SPECIAL FOCUS

In the area of international investment, some far-sighted Family Offices are developing specific expertise in one industrial area, in a set of similar markets, in a particular country, or in one select geographic region. Being selective in identifying the most attractive investment propositions in this way may add an extra dimension to a traditional domestic orientation of the Family Office.

Areas of special focus might include one or more high-growth geographic areas such as Russia, Eastern Europe, India, China, Vietnam, Indonesia, or Brazil. Another area might be in an attractive industrial sector such as energy, education, clean technology, bio-technology, healthcare, or venture capital. Increasingly, families are looking to find a meaningful role in global issues such as sustainable investment, global warming, poverty reduction, or women's rights.

FAMILY SERVICE

In addition to this wealth management priority, most Family Offices will also be tasked with providing a long list of supporting activities to the family's organization (family constitution, meetings, and so on) and staffing needs (staff selection and management, bill paying, residential management, educational programs, cars, drivers, security and travel needs, social events, supplier management, and so on); trust and estate planning services; any required support to a family business; oversight of philanthropic programs; management of the family eco-system; and any special plans for individual family members, from medical treatments to gym memberships to private trainers to religious retreats.

Special activities: In addition to these basic functions, some Family Offices may have a special obligation to develop and oversee training programs for younger family members, or to oversee investment funds to back the commercial ideas of these same members.

Still others may have a specific responsibility to manage an art collection, a set of residences around the world, or yachts and private jets.

Other families may have a specific interest in a major philanthropic foundation or a specific set of global charitable activities. In many Category III and Category IV families, the funds allocated to this purpose may merit the creation and funding of a separate organization. In others, the Family Office will be asked to provide administrative, operating, and other support to the family's philanthropic activities.

ESSENTIAL REPORTING ROLE

With so much going on in so many areas, providing accurate and timely reports on priority investment and family activities on a regular basis is an essential part of the value provided by a well-run Family Office.

One of the biggest gaps in many Family Offices is the lack of concise and usable summary reports on net wealth creation and delivery on the seven key elements of strategy discussed earlier. All too often, even if wealth management objectives are well documented, the other, equally important, elements of strategy, are neglected in the reporting system.

REPOSITORY OF VALUES

One experienced American billionaire, heir to one of the country's great multi-generational fortunes and an articulate spokesman on the role of the Family Office, has argued very strongly in favor of an approach to family infrastructure in which "A Family Office should act primarily as a repository and protector of family values across generations."

> "A Family Office should act primarily as a repository and protector of family values across generations."

From his perspective, building the correct foundation of values in the younger generations is the best response to the risks of financial ruin, family discord, erosion of the family business, or actions likely to bring the family's good name into controversy or disrepute.

While not abnegating the responsibility of family leadership, he sees the enlistment of support from his Family Office in this cross-generational role as an essential part of his approach to long-term family wealth management.

THE TRADITIONAL MODEL

Whether the primary objective of a Family Office is fiscal, financial, philanthropic, values-oriented, or aligned behind some other greater purpose, it is essential to have in mind a clear vision, a supporting set of values and a set of defined priorities (with a definition of success for each priority element) to keep the Family Office focused on the correct set of activities and objectives.

In the traditional model, as illustrated in Figure 2.5, individuals or teams within the Family Office would hold responsibility for all seven of the elements of strategy, and would work together with the family to achieve the overall family vision.

Figure 2.5   Representative Family Office Structure

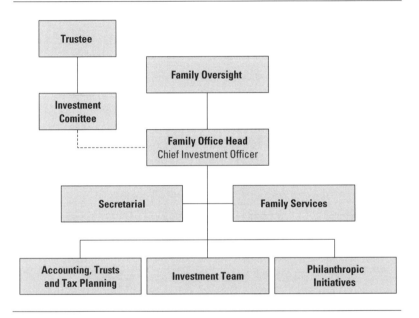

VARIATIONS ON THE THEME

There are many variations on this basic theme and organizational approach. Some offices have scores of employees, while others have less than a handful. Some offices have a high proportion of effort dedicated to philanthropic activity, others none. Some families do their own deals, and hence have a substantial staff processing transactions, while others only invest in funds and indirect transactions, even outsourcing the CIO function to external funds of funds or elite investment advisors capable of making better-informed investment decisions.

Given the amount of money flowing into the Family Office space, it is not surprising that different models are emerging. There are "virtual" offices, with all functions outsourced to best-practice providers of trust, estate, investment, aviation, accounting, and other services. Obviously lacking some of the benefits of security of information and offering risks as well as benefits, this model is emerging as a logical end point to the practice of selective outsourcing.

Sustainable offices, platforms with a constant focus on sustainable investments and ethical business practices, are also being considered.

RANGE OF COSTS

Given the variations available, it is difficult to set a target cost benchmark for a Family Office. In one sample of 10 Family Offices in the United States with family assets ranging from US$120 million to US$1.2 billion, the total cost, as a percentage of assets managed, ranged from 12.5 basis points to 125 basis points—with the highest 1.25% being found in the office of the wealthiest Category IV family surveyed.

Other studies have shown a mean cost level of around 50 to 70 basis points for administrative and accounting services, although even those numbers are hard to use as benchmarks because trust, accounting, administration, investment, and service levels vary substantially between offices of families with similar wealth.

ADVANCED ENTREPRENEURIAL MODEL

An advanced entrepreneurial model, which allows a sponsoring family the luxury (along with the risk) of great freedom, is one in which the Family Office is completely professionalized and left to the professional team to provide wealth management services on a comprehensive and entrepreneurial basis.

In this model, the family gives the head of the Family Office a set of guidelines with regard to governance, vision, values, objectives, rewards (which may include a sharing in the upside of portfolio performance), and expected targets. Within these guidelines, the head of the Family Office is granted the responsibility, authority, and accountability (RAA) to pursue these targets on an entrepreneurial basis without frequent interventions by family members or other advisors.

The RAA rubric can be critical to attracting, retaining, and motivating the best leaders and colleagues. If the role of a Family Office is purely administrative, family members are likely to hire a bureaucrat rather than an intelligent investor or skilled manager. The more advanced Family Offices increasingly want independently-minded professionals who can, with experience and confidence, disagree and debate with the Principal on all sorts of decisions.

Families that want a yes-man in the critical leadership position are doing themselves a great disservice.

Relatively few individuals or advisors disagree with the wealthiest families and their leaders, but it is those who do that gain the most respect and add the most value.

> Relatively few individuals or advisors disagree with the wealthiest families and their leaders, but it is those who do that gain the most respect and add the most value.

THE NETWORK MODEL

One far-sighted billionaire from a European Category IV family recently took an opportunity, triggered by some major liquidity events, to reassess his entire approach to his Family Office infrastructure and wealth management function.

He, along with the head of his existing Family Office and an outside advisor, met with a large set of leading Family Offices, investment and private banks, fund managers, Multi-Family Offices, lawyers, and trust specialists in four countries. The objective was to understand the critical elements of design and the full range of structural options available to prepare his family for the next decade and beyond.

The result of their deliberations was to recommend a new organizational approach which contained the following integrated entities:

Dedicated Family Offices: The original Family Office retained its core oversight and integration role, along with lead responsibility for family service, accounting, and trust activities.

Alongside the original office, two new entities were established. As with the original Family Office, both were entirely owned by the family's various trusts in the appropriate structure. The first was in an offshore wealth management center, set up to uncover and process investment ideas, analysis, and recommendations. The second was a substantial wealth management office set up in Switzerland to manage the bulk of the family trust's money and, eventually, to take on third-party mandates.

Strategic platforms: In addition, a series of partially owned strategic platforms were established. These were owned between 25% and 75% by family trusts, and were small offices with highly qualified local partners in the areas of greatest long-term investment interest to the family. Platforms were set up in three selected countries, with three other platforms established in defined industrial sectors of energy, healthcare, and property.

Outsourced advisory role: Realizing that Family Office resources would not be adequate to assess the full range of investment funds on a global basis, the trustees decided to outsource the indirect investment portfolio to a pair of leading elite family investment managers. The trustee and offshore investment committee developed the overall asset allocation model and participated in discussions on individual fund selection, without having to pay for all of the required resource to process literally thousands of funds, and to assess even more fund managers, in which the family trusts might consider investing.

Private trust company: Keeping some assets under the trusteeship of a commercial trustee with whom the family had enjoyed a good working relationship for over a decade, the existing trustees proposed to put in place a registered private trust company in Bermuda.

The establishment of this trust arrangement was part of a broader approach to wealth protection that also involved a diversification of trust jurisdictions as well as trustees.

Broader network: Surrounding the three core offices and six strategic platforms, a broad network of contacts and friendly institutions (banks, brokers, fund managers, MFOs, business schools, international institutions, and others) was established in order to provide context to priority initiatives, introduce new investment ideas, support transactions and build relationships for the future.

Family capital network: One final element in the creative mix was a network of like-minded Family Offices interested in sharing transaction opportunities and information on emerging fund managers.

Although this highly international family was also interested in developing its own networks, primarily to source transactions that were not lumbered with the usual private equity fees and upside-sharing arrangements, other existing networks of Family Offices and wealthy individuals were also considered for potential inclusion. Family Office Exchange (later joined), Tiger 21, FAME, Club B, and the CCC-Alliance were all identified as groups of potential family interest. For every family, and for every advisor to a wealthy family, there is great value to be had in profiting from the knowledge of others who have gone before along the same pathway.

> In a world of abundant capital, it is learned experience and the identification of opportunity that are the rare commodities.

In formal and informal forums, and through shared advisors, wealthy families are more and more willing to share openly with others—so long as discretion and confidentiality remain as hallmarks of the exchange. Some of the largest families believe that productive exchange is not best done in overly organized, sponsored forums, but in more informal gatherings where like-minded families and their representatives can share ideas, experiences, and opportunities on a one-to-one basis.

In a world of abundant capital, it is learned experience and the identification of opportunity that are the rare commodities.

The resulting approach of this one family is illustrated in Figure 2.6.

Figure 2.6 The Network Model

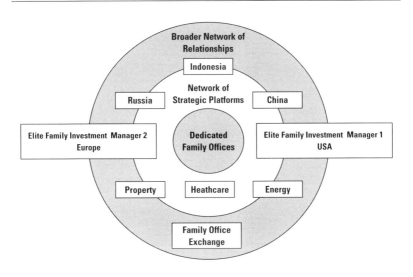

11. PRIVATE BANKS, MFOs, AND ELITE FAMILY INVESTMENT MANAGERS

The banking needs of a wealthy family are different from those of an average financial services customer, extending to sophisticated financial planning, the construction and management of a multi-asset class portfolio, the consideration of trust and estate planning structures, and access to larger scale and more sophisticated products and services.

One of the hallmarks of great wealth is the access that it provides to high-quality institutions dedicated to the servicing the needs of the financial elite. The most notable of these elite institutions are the private banks, for which substantial personal wealth is a *sine qua non*.

DEFINITION OF A PRIVATE BANK

The original private banks were so called because their owners, usually partners with unlimited personal liability, invested their own wealth in the bank and ran their family enterprise much like a partnership with their clients.

Many of the leading private banks were founded in Switzerland, having their origins as commercial banks in the eighteenth and nineteenth centuries. The history of private banking in Geneva, one of the world's leading money management centers, can be traced back even further, to 1387, when Bishop Adhemar Fabri granted the people of Geneva the right to charge interest on loans. This right was, at the time, unique in all of Christendom.

By the seventeenth century, Genevan bankers and their clients had created financial empires that spanned the globe and had long outgrown their small home market. Their celebrated history included financing the Royal Bank of England, the Dutch West Indies Company, the first industrial company in Europe (The Royal Manufacture of Mirrors, later St. Gobain) and the numerous railroads that criss-crossed all major continents and accelerated the onset and expansion of the Industrial Age.

These institutions originally focused on financing trade, commodities, and the various exchanges that flourished in Geneva from the fourteenth century onward. As stock markets evolved, the financing and trading of stock participations grew rapidly. Clients' needs soon drove the Geneva and Zurich private banks to provide increasingly sophisticated financial advisory services to their increasingly wealthy, and increasingly financially savvy, clientele.

Offering financial services from elegant offices in Geneva, Zurich, Basel, and, for Italian families, Lugano, the Swiss private banks set the global standard for discretion, intelligent investment, and wealth preservation; for many generations families managed and passed on enormous sums of money to succeeding generations with the discreet and effective advice of their Swiss banking advisors.

Many of these banks were associated with families that became world famous, and very wealthy themselves, as a result of their successful forays into the private banking world. Julius Baer, Pictet, Lombard Odier Darier Hentsch and other such family names remain on the nameplates of the most prominent private banks in Zurich and Geneva.

A WORLD OF CHANGE

Today, a private bank can be a standalone institution, or a branch or subsidiary of a larger institution, which caters to the financial needs of wealthy clients; that is, broadly of those having liquid wealth (not including a primary residential home, secondary home, company pension, and so on) exceeding US$1 million.

Some high-end private banks such as Goldman Sachs, Citibank, and Deutsche Bank focus on customers with liquid assets exceeding US$10 million. At the other end of the scale, some other "private banking" arms of U.S. brokers can start with an entry-level account as low as US$250,000.

In any event, the old-world institutions that pioneered the art and science of private banking have changed. Today, very few private banks remain as partnerships. The scale needed to compete is enormous, liability and the risk of litigation have forced many banks to corporatize, global capabilities are a must and the family culture may not have survived the mergers, acquisition, integration, or expansion phases.

A NEW CHAPTER IN HISTORY

Recently, the attention of large universal banks has turned once again to the private high-net-worth customer. A combination of declining profitability in corporate banking, an increase in the scale of the market opportunity as private wealth swelled around the world, and an opportunity to pursue a market with attractive profit margins have increased the investment in the private wealth management sector by many of the world's largest financial institutions.

For years, private wealth management and private banking were seen as second-class career paths in the more competitive global banks. Relationship managers were sniffily dismissed by their corporate finance colleagues as "dog walkers" and "gold-bangled bimbos" who performed menial family services or sold on appearance in a world that did not seemingly require much in the way of skill, knowledge, or investment performance.

With the rise in private wealth increasing to more than US$40 trillion, and with an increasingly sophisticated product and service appetite, even the most staid and elite of the world's investment and merchant banks are turning their eye to this large and lucrative market.

No longer a corporate backwater, private wealth management can provide an attractive and lucrative career at almost all large global banks, as well as within the historically elite private banking establishments in the United States and Europe.

The EFG Progression

At a time when many high-growth private banks are becoming populated with inexperienced staff members, and focusing more on asset gathering and product pushing than on client results and true relationships, a few institutions are bucking these trends and developing business models that provide alternative approaches for their high-net-worth clients.

Started only in 1995 with a blank piece of paper, the ambitious vision of Jean Pierre Cuoni and Lonnie Howell, and the backing of the ultra-wealthy Latsis family, the Swiss-based EFG Bank provides an interesting example of creative evolution and a new private banking model.

Global coverage: Although less than a tenth the size of its larger Swiss industry colleagues, by 2007 the EFG Bank operated in more than 30 countries, including many offshore jurisdictions and emerging markets.

(continued)

(continued)

*A **borderless world:*** The professionals working for EFG—the customer relationship officers (CROs)—are allowed the discretion to travel anywhere, to seek any segment of business and to put customers into any investment on the bank's large approved list.

Experienced professionals: Unlike many of its industry colleagues, EFG only hires experienced relationship managers, ensuring that its clients are served by a team with such diverse backgrounds as currency trading or hedge fund management, as well as traditional private banking.

Open architecture: With only 6% of client assets in proprietary products, EFG can claim to be one of the few banks with truly open product architecture.

Low-pressure front: In addition to reduced pressure to push the bank's in-house investment products, there are no stiff quarterly targets for CROs to meet, with individual CROs able to pursue their own targets at an appropriate pace within the bank's overall supportive architecture.

EFG's entrepreneurial model functions in many ways like a professional association, a high-quality partnership of individuals with diverse aspirations, capabilities, and backgrounds, united by a shared set of values, ethics, and professional standards.

With more than 100 billion Swiss francs in assets under management by 2007, after only 12 years of operation, EFG stands as proof that there is exceptional potential for new business models within the old world of banking to the world's financial elite.

STRICTER REGULATION AND SUPERVISORY REGIMES

Although the use of private banks by wealthy families has boomed in recent years, the rise in popularity has been paralleled by an increasing layer of regulation and supervisory regimes.

Even before 9/11, financial regulators around the world were cracking down on many practices which could be abused by criminals, terrorists, tax frauds, and other undesirable elements.

As a result, banks, brokers, fund managers, offshore corporate regulators, credit card companies, property agents, lawyers, accountants, and other conduits for financial transactions have been required to pursue detailed "know your customer" (KYC) and anti-money-laundering (AML) procedures. These procedures can involve every-thing from simple provision of a passport and a current utility bill to more extensive background checks by reputable security companies.

In addition to the burdens placed on private banks and their clients, other regulations which have an impact on private banking clients include a withholding tax on EU citizens' accounts in Switzerland. Through this regulation, account holders need to either disclose their identity and pay appropriate national tax or preserve their anonymity and pay a 15% withholding tax on interest earned to the Swiss government, which will in turn pass on these amounts anonymously to the appropriate host government.

U.S. citizens, regardless of how long they have lived outside the United States, must fill out an annual form which requires disclosure of all bank accounts in which the citizen had an interest or signature authority, or over which he or she exercised control, with severe penalties for non-compliance.

There are other restrictions, obligations, and regulations for cit-izens of different nationalities that may require consideration before opening an account with an overseas private bank. China, Taiwan, and Japan, for example, all have strict regimes with regard to offshore bank accounts that may limit activity or require prior exceptional permission from a central bank regulator.

ROLE OF PRIVATE BANK BY CATEGORY OF WEALTH

As with most financial service providers, private banks will have a different role to play as wealth increases from one category to another. Some of the more exclusive banks will not even consider taking clients until they reach Category II wealth or above.

Across all generations, from the original family wealth creator onward, patriarchs, matriarchs, heirs, and heiresses may prefer to outsource money-management functions to a private bank or an Elite Family Investment Manager (as described below), preferring to pay the fees required in order to offload an obligation for which they do not have sufficient time or to which they do not find themselves well suited.

Roughly, most private banks would play the following roles at the various stages of wealth:

Category I: At this level of wealth, a private bank may act as a "one-stop shop" for many needs, including both products and services. These could include wealth management, basic trust advice and service (usually through a separate trust company subsidiary), pension advice, and financial planning.

The bank could also provide accounting, custody, and other services. In this wealth bracket, the family would rarely have more than one private bank with which it would have an extensive working relationship.

Category II: As wealth increases, the range of products sourced from a private bank may broaden, but the range of services may narrow. Wealthy families may be stepping up to larger investments in alternative assets and other products, but may have grown to a level of sophistication and complexity on trust planning and asset structuring such that they want to use dedicated specialists for advice on more complex structuring tasks.

At this level of wealth, the family may have many banks with which it does business, and may also have a lead bank with a substantially greater share of the family wealth to manage.

As a result, the relationship may focus more on products than on services which can be performed by other specialists.

Categories III and IV: When family wealth exceeds US$100 million, some families will establish a Family Office that performs many of the functions of a private bank. Depending upon the history and nature of the family, these wealthiest families may use their private bankers more for product selection, economic overviews, the identification of investment themes, and for customized services, than for services duplicated by other advisors or provided by their own Family Offices.

PRIVATE BANK VS. PRIVATE BANKER

In all cases, the quality of the individual involved may be more important and valuable to a family than the parent institution itself. Finding a reliable, thoughtful, and effective private banker can be an important step in extracting the full benefit of the relationship with the private bank itself.

In particular, in an era when "open architecture" in private banking means that product offerings from other institutions can be sold and serviced via a private bank relationship manager, a portfolio can move more easily from one bank to another.

With so many relationship managers and senior private bankers changing jobs in the current competitive climate, ensuring that a portfolio is as mobile as possible may add an extra dimension to tactical investment decisions.

CREATIVITY AND CUSTOMIZATION

Wishing to offer as full a range of services to their clients as possible, some private banks and private bankers have developed very creative solutions to individual investment tax and legacy issues. For a while, privately held insurance companies were a vehicle through which clients of private banks could funnel large properties and other assets (paid in as a premium without any gift tax) which could then be received tax free by beneficiaries after the policyholder's death (as a non-taxable insurance policy payout).

This, and countless other schemes and arrangements, have been designed and implemented by banks wishing to support the legal resolution of complex tax and financial issues. By coming up with creative solutions a private bank can establish itself as a favored member of the wealthy family's panoply of preferred advisors.

HOLDING GOLD AND VALUABLES

Private banks can also provide practical and logistical services to the world's wealthiest families. In some conservative portfolios, there is a small allocation of family wealth to assets which are held in a physical form and outside the global financial system.

All of the services related to the acquisition, storage, sale, and auditing of physical gold reserves can be performed by many private banks.

Some older families may remember the devastating impact the 1929 Stock Market Crash and the subsequent Depression had on their wealth. Others may remember that J. P. Morgan himself saved the United States from bankruptcy on two separate occasions.

For some cautious investors, this defensive allocation of a small portion of wealth is seen as a protection against a meltdown of the global financial system as a result of terrorism, national default, implosion in the world's US$410 trillion derivatives market (seven times global GDP), or some other cataclysmic event. Some private banks have vaults from which a client can retrieve physical gold stocks in the event of a financial meltdown, even if the bank is closed.

The same protective services can be offered for art objects, stamps, collections of rare wines and books, jewelry, and other expensive collectibles.

PROPERTY, ART, YACHTS, AND AVIATION

Because of the unique relevance to their wealthy clients' interests, many private banks now offer services related to property acquisition, financing, and management. They may also provide similar services for acquiring, storing, and managing an expensive art collection, as well as services related to the acquisition, financing, storage, lease, and sale of a private jet or yacht.

Some banks may have other specialist services that can be arranged or subcontracted, including business management services, family service needs, security services, and other valuable aspects of support to the lifestyles of the rich and famous.

EDUCATION AND PREPARATION OF THE NEXT GENERATION

In Chapter 8 on the necessary preparation of heirs and heiresses, the value of a proper foundation of knowledge was highlighted, including knowledge of business and wealth management. Private banks may provide part of the solution to that need through four separate avenues: seminars and presentations; specific Next Generation programs; short-term internships; or full-time employment opportunities.

The specific Next Generation programs, offered by both large and small private banks, can provide direct knowledge on asset allocation, investment products, and portfolio management. They can also offer a sharing of experience with children of similar families facing similar issues, offering a valuable network of connections for the future.

COMMERCIAL TRUST SERVICES

Many private banks have large and capable in-house corporate trust companies which offer trust creation, trust administration, custodial, and trustee services. By using corporate trustees in an established private bank, settlers are more likely to ensure their trust is in reliable hands for an extended period of time than with a small or start-up trust company with less financial substance.

DISCRETIONARY ASSET MANAGEMENT

For many years, and across many generations, wealthy families in Europe, and a few in the Middle East, Latin America, the United States, and Asia, used private banks for discretionary asset management (DAM) services. Through DAM mandates, the bank itself made the investment decisions, charged a hefty fee, and left the account holders, beneficiaries (in a trust account), and the settlers out of the decision-making process in managing the money.

Although such services have been a mainstay of European private banking for many decades, this practice is now diminishing, both as a lucrative source of income for private bankers and as a strategy for wealthy families.

The more activist advisory asset management (AAM) mandates, in which account holders, settlers, and beneficiaries take a more engaged role in fund management, have quickly become the preferred manner in which to manage funds in private banking hands. The desire for personal involvement and higher returns than historically offered by DAM accounts, particularly amongst Asians and other newly rich families in growing regions, has led to a substantial rise in advisory accounts. The reasons most usually cited by clients for selecting AAM accounts are numerous. These are, *inter alia*, that such accounts give them:

- greater control over investment choices
- more learning for the client and the family
- faster response to threats and opportunities
- greater alignment with family investment objectives
- lower fees
- reduced risk of high fees on unnecessary investment purchases and sales
- greater response from private banking staff.

While a few old families or unsophisticated clients prefer to delegate all investment decisions to private banks (as do a few untrusting parents), the role of DAM looks set to decline further in the future.

OFFSHORE PRIVATE BANKING

The growth of offshore private banking has much to do with the turbulent history of Europe over the past two centuries. From the second half of the eighteenth century onwards, Europe has been rocked by revolutions, political upheaval, wars, and, perhaps most importantly for many wealthy families in Eastern and Western Europe, confiscatory and heavy tax regimes brought in by communist, socialist, and labor governments. There has been a history of wealth-threatening events in this past century that has created a large market for protective and discreet offshore private banking products and services in multiple currencies and accessed through a range of protective asset structuring vehicles.

It is worth remembering that, only a few short years ago in the United Kingdom, capital gains tax rates were 98% and the highest marginal income tax rate was 83%. Similarly, although perhaps not quite as egregiously, high wealth, property, inheritance, and income tax rates in other European countries contributed to a flow of money into the discreet private banking system, far from the reach of such heavy national tax regimes.

Beginning in the late eighteenth century, many Swiss, French, German, English, and other banks were established in mainland Europe and the United Kingdom to preserve the wealth of Europe's rich families.

As world markets evolved, other centers for offshore banking emerged: Liechtenstein, Monaco, Bermuda, Luxembourg, the Channel Islands, Grand Cayman, Hong Kong, and Singapore have all grown dramatically as centers of private wealth management over recent years.

London, New York, and Miami (for Latin America) have all grown at an extraordinary pace in recent years as both onshore and offshore private wealth management centers for the world's wealthiest families from Europe and America, and are now also serving families from the Middle East, Asia, and other emerging markets.

ONSHORE PRIVATE BANKING

In some countries, most notably the United States, private banking has been primarily a domestic business, based more on high-performance investment, management of single-stock concentration risk, domestic tax management, trust management services, and reporting on financial performance than on preserving and managing cross-border or international flight money.

These onshore banks, while sensitive to trust and tax management concerns, have focused more on financial performance and inward investment than on international tax management for many of their customers.

EMERGING ASIA

Asia is a much more recent growth phenomenon in private banking. While countries such as Japan, Taiwan, and China have strict rules about offshore bank accounts and limits on private bank activity in their domestic markets, Asia is home to two historic centers for regional private banking, Singapore and Hong Kong, which are now becoming global. Asia is now playing a key role as a booking, account, and wealth management center for global clients and providing an investment destination for many seeking high returns from its high-growth economies.

Singapore, for example, was once considered primarily relevant for private bankers as a safe haven for wealthy families resident in other countries in the region, particularly the ethnic Chinese, who are a prosperous minority in Indonesia, Malaysia, Thailand, and other parts of Southeast Asia.

Since 2002, Singapore has become a city of global standing in private banking as a result of its excellent regulation, high-quality infrastructure, newly competitive trust laws, high levels of bank secrecy, a robust and respected legal system, Anglo Saxon-style trust laws, and the presence of most international financial institutions of high standing. Although Hong Kong and other jurisdictions in Asia are competing for private banking business, it is Singapore that has stood out as being particularly effective in contributing to the current global chapter of the history of private banking.

PRIVATE WEALTH MANAGEMENT IN INVESTMENT BANKS

In addition to the private banks, which can play a comprehensive wealth management role for families who cannot afford a full-service

Family Office, investment banks may be valuable in helping to manage wealth and family businesses on an integrated basis. Many of the largest "bulge bracket" investment banks from the United States, and their brethren in other markets, can provide integrated private and corporate banking services, as well as access to the top-quality investment opportunities not available to more mass-market oriented institutions.

Investment banks, in addition to providing access to high-alpha fund managers, may play a key role in the public listings of businesses, taking publicly listed businesses private again, providing financing for family businesses or investment activities, managing single-stock concentration risk, offering financial guidance to operating businesses, offering portfolio management services and fund management for philanthropic foundations, and even, when appropriate, advising on the sale of a long-established family business.

As with private banks, some of the larger investment or universal banks own high-quality trustee companies which can serve as commercial trustees for family trusts.

A PRIVATE BANK RISK

With all of this history, growth, service standard, and attention from the world's leading investment houses, it is interesting that the performance of many portfolios managed by private banks for wealthy families of all categories is, to put it bluntly, uninspiring at best.

One small Geneva-based institution asserts that its aspiration is not to lose any money and then to achieve, "if possible," returns one or two percent above LIBOR, or its equivalent in other markets.

The private bank trap, as it now surfaces in larger banks, is for account holders to receive neither the preferential products they would like nor experienced advice. Far too many clients of private banks, and private banking arms of large banks, now receive only solicitations for a string of in-house products that have a relatively low return for the investor, but a relatively high margin to the bank—and a healthy impact on the relationship manager's asset-gathering and profit-driven bonus.

HOW TO SELECT A PRIVATE BANK

Selecting a private bank, or set of private banks, to take advantage of the opportunities and avoid the risks inherent in a private bank relationship is not an easy process.

Before setting out to shortlist and interview potential service providers, it is important for any family to determine exactly what services and products it wants, and the kind of person it wants as an account executive, to address any specific risks and worries it may have regarding the new arrangements.

If there is any uncertainty on how to proceed or lack of clarity with regard to the respective offerings of the different types of banks, it may be instructive to interview two of the largest private banks, two private banking arms of global banks (possibly branches of larger brokerage houses or commercial or investment banks), and then two smaller, traditional, private banks, to see which style best fits the family's needs.

Once the most appropriate category has been determined, other candidates from within the preferred category can be interviewed. Taking recommendations may also be very valuable in finding the best individual and institution (or institutions) in the shortest possible time.

MANAGING A PRIVATE BANKING RELATIONSHIP

In managing a private banking relationship, a number of rules need to be established in advance: who will oversee the account on a daily basis, how reports will be made, what fees will be charged, and how investment opportunities will be shown to and selected by the client family.

The bank's system for making investment recommendations must be absolutely clear, as must the extent to which it subscribes to the idea of open architecture—providing access to the best possible products regardless of whether they are "manufactured" by the bank. One key question to ask a current or potential private bank is what percentage of assets under management are placed in in-house products; potential clients should not be surprised if the answer is somewhere near, or even exceeding, 75%.

The role of structured products, great earners for the banks but possibly high-risk investments or costly hedges for clients, needs to be clearly described.

Fees need to be clarified and negotiated, both for the overall asset management fees and for charges attached to, or embedded in, the various products offered by the bank.

All private banking relationships need to be managed carefully to ensure that the maximum benefits are obtained and excess costs and risks are avoided. Specialist service providers, such as Novarca in Zurich, focus exclusively on negotiating private banking fees on behalf of large clients in return for a share of the savings.

In every case, it is essential that the primary account holder maintains a current knowledge of market trends, market opportunities, and the respective performances of different fund managers on an independent basis.

> Only through active and informed management is a wealthy family likely to get the results it wants out of any private banking relationship.

Armed with this better understanding of investment opportunity and returns, the wealthy family should set out its own asset allocation model, identify the kinds of investments it wants, and oversee a high-quality program of implementation and post-investment management. Only through active and informed management is a wealthy family likely to get the results it wants out of any private banking relationship.

Divide and conquer: In almost all cases, it is advisable to have more than one private banking relationship because, despite their public statements, very few banks really operate in a truly open fashion. Almost all prefer to sell their own products to the maximum extent possible. Only by seeing more than one bank and more than one bank's products can an investor make an informed choice with regard to the various elements of an investment portfolio.

Working with more than one bank provides the investor with a direct comparison of fees charged, and even the presence of competing rivals can exert a steadying influence on the fees proposed by the individual banks in the portfolio of advisors.

Another good reason to use more than one bank is to diversify management and reduce the risk of being exposed to a single bank's investment committee which might limit the flow of ideas and opportunities or restrict investment within a limited macro-economic perspective.

THE MULTI-FAMILY OFFICE (MFO)

Not everyone will get what they want out of a private bank. Similarly, not every family can afford the luxury of a dedicated Family Office.

In between the two lies the emerging class of Multi-Family Offices which primarily cater to families of Category I and II wealth. The primary focus of most MFOs is asset management mandates, with a clear focus on Category II as the median and average client, although a few of the smaller MFOs will take on clients at the top end of Category I, and a few others may take on, or be established by, a Category III or IV family client.

A Multi-Family Office offers services very similar to those of a dedicated Family Office, often with the same family service, trust, estate and planning capabilities. Many MFOs are based on an office infrastructure once dedicated to a single multi-generational family and thus have years of experience in managing complex estate, trust, tax, philanthropic, and investment arrangements.

Broadly, there are three types of Multi-Family Offices: those which have grown from a single Family Office into an organization capable of taking on more than one client in defined areas of activity; commercial offshoots of an existing private bank or other institution; and start-up MFO businesses, founded and designed *ab initio* to serve the needs of multiple wealthy families.

Found primarily in the United States and Europe, but also beginning to appear in Australia and Asia, MFOs have emerged from prominent families such as the Fleming family in the U.K., the Baer family in Switzerland, the Rockefeller family operations in the United States, and the Myers family in Australia. In fact, one out of every four MFOs in the United States is still owned, in part or in total, by its client families.

In the United States, the operations of MFOs are now growing at a rate exceeding 15% per year and manage funds estimated to exceed US$250 billion. Their scale and growth mean that each year they add more assets than make up the entire MFO unit at US Trust, and double those under management at the MFO arm of Rockefeller & Co.

The average leading American MFO will have assets under advisement in the neighborhood of US$50 million per client family, the median wealth for a Category II family, and bill around US$275,000 per year for asset-based fees. The larger MFOs now manage over US$5 billion for their clients. A larger account of US$100 million would cost, based on industry surveys, around US$475,000 in fees to manage. Minimum accounts tend to be around US$15 million, very similar to that of high-end British MFO.

The rapid growth in assets under advisement is attributed to two unrelated factors. The first is access to alternative investment funds and other opportunities not available to clients of less custom-tailored institutions. With so much of investment portfolio performance being driven over the past year by high-quality alternative asset managers, gaining access to the best-performing managers is a powerful drawing card.

The second element of attraction is the offering of services similar to that of a dedicated Family Office. An MFO provides access to a full set of family services usually provided only to families of a scale large enough to justify a fully-fledged Family Office.

The selection, management, and approach to an MFO is very similar to that of a private bank, with many of the same benefits and opportunities as high-end private banks, but without the risk of account executives and product champions pushing in-house products.

THE ELITE FAMILY INVESTMENT MANAGER

As the scale and complexity of global fortunes has shot up over the past years, new institutions have emerged to serve the demands of the principals and families creating and controlling these vast sums of wealth. In particular, the new fortunes established by young American entrepreneurs, many in the technology sector, have resulted in the creation of a new breed of financial advisor focused entirely on the creation of further family wealth within a fully diversified, disciplined and principled framework.

As such well-known personalities as Bill Gates, Michael Dell, and Jeff Skoll achieved multi-billionaire status at an early age, they brought to the worlds of investment, philanthropy, and financial advisory institutions the same kind of creative energy and drive for accomplishment that they brought to their operating enterprises. In seeking to redefine the way financial assets are managed, they were not limited to established past practices; they were free to pursue new approaches which went well beyond the traditional.

The resulting Elite Family Investment Managers (EFIMs) were originally established to serve the investment needs of families in Categories III and IV, with wealth often counted in the many billions of dollars; a few have become increasingly available to wealthy families of lesser economic means by adapting their business models and setting a minimum long-term investment entry-level portfolio at US$100 million, and even below. These entry points are being met in some cases by families pooling their funds with a common set of objectives and risk parameters to meet a minimum level of funds for the EFIM to manage on a collective basis.

These new institutions have been shaped and developed to focus purely on financial investments for some of the world's largest and most sophisticated family fortunes, leaving the other aspects of traditional Family Office services to independent service providers and less focused MFOs.

DIFFERENTIATING FACTORS

By providing an advanced service to clients of the highest wealth levels, the best of these new EFIMs have been able to achieve performance standards which approach, and in some years exceed, the performance of the leading endowment managers at Harvard, Yale, and Stanford.

As they have grown and evolved, these EFIMs have developed a number of salient characteristics which allow them to stand out from the crowd of traditional investment advisors and fund managers. In addition to their scale of activity, high-quality teams, and high entry-level accounts, EFIMs can be noted for their:

Conflict-free, objective advice: Perhaps the greatest advantage offered by the EFIMs is a full separation of advice and product "manufacturing". There are no in-house products to provide juicy sales margins and incentives for employee advisors to recommend to their clients.

Even in institutions claiming to have adopted an investment model dedicated to "open architecture" which allows relationship managers or brokers to sell third-party products as well as in-house products, there is almost always a high percentage of investment recommendations linked to proprietary products, even in the most selective of large private banks.

By separating advice from any products or investment opportunities, EFIMs can offer truly objective advice to clients across all asset categories.

Disciplined process: As described earlier, there is enormous value in a thorough and disciplined process which presents as many opportunities as possible, evaluates each one thoroughly and objectively, and then selects only the best for investment.

Global coverage: Unlike smaller MFOs, EFIMs provide the scale and quality of resource to find, analyze, select, and monitor investments from Albania to Zimbabwe. In dealing with wealth of a global scale that is often seeking diversification and superior returns, advisors need to be able to provide a seamless service across the major developed regions and emerging markets with a consistently high-quality process and investment team.

Global coverage is not just about geography; there are new opportunities arising in new areas all the time. New markets, new asset classes, new managers, and new opportunities appear and evolve on a daily basis, and need to be included for review and evaluation to ensure that the wealthy family is benefiting from all relevant opportunities on a timely basis.

Expertise in all asset classes: A great part of the superior performance of the larger endowments and family fortunes over past decades has been careful and intelligent exposure to alternative asset classes. Even with the run-up in equity markets in recent years, access to top-quartile private equity and hedge funds has contributed more to the accumulated wealth of many families over the past two decades than public equity markets, many of which had very difficult periods in the early years of the new millennium.

With expert consideration of all alternative asset classes—VC, buyout, secondary funds, distressed debt, hedge funds, derivatives, direct and co-invest, and other similar categories—EFIMs and their wealthy clients can access opportunities to make high-alpha contributions to a well-defined portfolio strategy.

Highest levels of access and alpha: One of the great differentiators in the performance of family investment portfolios is the ability to gain access to the best-performing funds and fund managers. Superior performance above market and benchmark, the highly sought-after "alpha" of managerial performance, is, in today's world, pursued relentlessly by a wave of investment dollars, euros, pounds, yen, and other currencies. Most good funds are heavily oversubscribed; access is only available to a few highly regarded and large investment managers.

By association with high-quality and high-profile investors, such as those underpinning the EFIMs, wealthy families can benefit from access to sought-after funds which an individual family fortune, even of Category I, II or III stature, could not afford.

Performance-driven compensation: One of the other major attractions to the selection of an EFIM over other advisors is the possibility of negotiating an after-cost, performance-driven compensation scheme.

Current fees usually look something like a 50 basis point fee on assets under management, plus 5–10% of profit above an 8–10% hurdle. The costs are a blend of management fee and performance-based incentives which fully align manager and family.

Accordingly, with a 15% net return on the portfolio, the fees would be 1.25% (50 bp + 5% of 15%); and, at 20%, the all-in fee would be 1.5%.

By avoiding a situation where an advisor can profit handsomely as the client loses money, a win/win alignment of interests is created by performance-driven compensation which can serve both parties well.

Custom-tailored joint ventures: A new approach within the EFIM creates a series of relationships, limited in number by the scale of required investment. This has been described by Capricorn LLC CEO Stephen George as a series of "customized joint ventures," established to pursue the wealth management objectives of a unique family with unique risk, asset class, return, asset structuring, and investment style characteristics.

By customizing the approach within a new institutional framework, the EFIM and client can together pursue an overall vision, with all aspects of the journey fully aligned and moving forward as efficiently and effectively as possible.

In some ways this relationship-driven and fully aligned approach to advisory services brings the high-net-worth private banking industry full circle, back to its roots in Geneva 600 years ago, when fully engaged private bankers worked closely with their clients, more as partners than as commission-driven product salesmen, developing their wealth mutually in discreet, highly professional and highly profitable long-term relationships.

Capricorn Rising

Capricorn Investment Group LLC, established in 2003, is one of the world's leading Elite Family Investment Managers and can serve as an example of the new breed of elite advisor available for the world's wealthier families.

Based initially on the multi-billion-dollar fortune created by Jeff Skoll, the first President of eBay, founder of the Skoll Foundation—the prominent philanthropic initiative bearing his name, and founder of Participant Media (a socially focused media company which, among others, helped finance *An Inconvenient Truth*, a successful documentary raising awareness on global climate change), Capricorn is now an independent global advisory firm with coverage and clients that range across North America, Europe, and Asia.

Headquartered in Palo Alto, California, Capricorn managed approximately US$5 billion in total capital in 2007, across a highly diversified, global blend

(continued)

(continued)

of integrated investment funds and, unlike many less entrepreneurial EFIMs, extended its investment success into a carefully selected set of opportunistic direct investment opportunities.

Capricorn's investment approach is to partner with a select group of ultra-high-net-worth families and investing clients to provide consistently superior investment performance and risk management across a multi-strategy portfolio adapted to the needs and wishes of its clients.

Unique characteristics of the Capricorn model include:

- **A principal individual investor** (Jeff Skoll) who provides a scale asset base and personal engagement in all elements to the business.
- **Truly independent and conflict-free investment advisory services** in an environment free of products or product associations.
- **Customized investment strategies** adapted for individuals, families, endowments, and philanthropic bequests. The Skoll Foundation, whose funds are managed by Capricorn to suit an incremental set of objectives from the eponymous founder of the charity, is one of the leaders in the field of social philanthropy.
- **A creative investment approach**, including a forward-looking global multiple-scenario-based approach to asset allocation, risk management, and tactical management of funds and fund managers.
- **An entrepreneurial approach**, extending into carefully selected direct investments under the direction of a dedicated team which add to portfolio performance without incurring traditional "2 and 20" (management and profit sharing) fees for a private equity fund manager.
- **A principled investment approach**, ensuring that the client relationships, people, processes, and underlying investments selected are of uncompromising quality, deeply aligned, ethical, fair, long-term oriented, and not directly harmful to the world or people living in its various communities.
- **A focus on a long-term performance goal**, aligned by performance-based compensation, to use strategy, process and global relationships to generate superior returns over time with limited risk at the portfolio level.

By developing global portfolios along these unique seven dimensions, Capricorn has been able to achieve superior returns across a full range of asset classes and global markets for its highly select, and fortunate, clients.

12. FAMILY LEADERSHIP AND ENGAGEMENT

The exercise of leadership is one of the most important elements of strategy for a wealthy family. While often driven primarily by principles derived from precedent, personality, experience, or intuition, a more structured approach to the development and application of a leadership style may add to natural or learned leadership capabilities.

By setting out a practical framework, leadership may be made more thoughtful, can make more impact and, perhaps, can contribute more to the long-term success of a chosen strategy. Some of the content and principles of a family leadership model are set out below.

Family Leadership Principles

- Aspire to be a great family
- Create the vision
- Live the values
- Engage and motivate
- Master the visible aspect of family leadership
- Master the invisible hand
- Do what needs to be done

ASPIRE TO BE A GREAT FAMILY

Family leaders will never achieve their most ambitious goals if the family aspires only to be conventional in approach or average in result. None of the leaders who created great business success stories, from Henry Ford to Bill Gates, or the leaders of great family legacies, built a winning enterprise using someone else's blueprint or by aiming to achieve the most modest of results: great achievement always arises in an environment of high expectations.

While understanding that the past is always valuable, limiting oneself to that understanding is never the pathway to achieve new standards of excellence and accomplishment. The essence of successful family strategy lies in differentiation, in creativity, and in the art and science of informed action to bring about aspirational change.

CREATE THE VISION

It is essential that a family leader creates and articulates a vision which will provide the long-term goal towards which all supporting decisions and action will be oriented. The vision should be multi-generational in nature and unchanging in context. Like the North Star, it should provide both a long-term direction and navigational assistance "above the horizon" for both senior leaders and junior members of the family, and from any perspective and in any situation or location.

LIVE THE VALUES

In accepting a leadership role, there is a responsibility incumbent upon family leaders to live the values adopted by the family as a whole. Among these values there is none more important than personal integrity. Trust, faith, hope, and many other higher aspects of human emotion are tied up in the complex psychological act of accepting leadership from another individual. Any failure in the personal integrity of a family leader can lead to a loss of faith in that individual and in the set of values by which family members are meant to abide.

ENGAGE AND MOTIVATE

In most families, the vast majority of members want to lead a good life, learn, grow, and contribute to the creation of something special that is greater than any one individual or generation.

By reaching the hearts as well as the minds and financial interests of family members, by responding to their need to contribute to something greater than their individual selves, an effective leader may be able to release new levels of energy to contribute to a family's current and future prosperity.

MASTER THE VISIBLE ASPECT OF FAMILY LEADERSHIP

The best family leaders are constantly mindful of the opportunities inherent in the natural role of leadership from the front. Finding and demonstrating a visible and shared sense of confidence, common purpose, and belief across the family is invaluable.

Often, there is a traditional respect for the selected family leader, but demonstrating clarity of vision and stating with authority the chosen objectives and challenges for the family is still an essential part of confirming that leadership role. Careful and effective communication is critical. Remaining positive is a valuable skill, even if it is personally taxing in many stressful situations.

Disciplining and correcting are also necessary, but need to be done selectively, carefully, constructively—and almost always in private.

MASTER THE INVISIBLE HAND

While mastering the skill of visible leadership from the front, family leaders must also master the more subtle skill of leading from the center, or even from behind the scenes, guiding the family's progress with a less visible hand.

> "You can accomplish almost anything you want, so long as you don't care who gets the credit."

By mastering the art of the invisible hand, and applying that skill to all aspects of a modern family, and within the networks in which it interacts, leaders can influence others to work together toward a desired outcome without overtly driving or dominating the process.

A more subtle approach can create the desired results, along with a pride of ownership and sense of accomplishment in the creation of those results, that a more direct and interventionist approach may never be able to match.

As President Reagan once stated: "You can accomplish almost anything you want, so long as you don't care who gets the credit."

DO WHAT NEEDS TO BE DONE

Many family leaders fail to achieve their goals because they don't address the right issues in the right way to achieve what they set out to accomplish. Avoiding this trap, and getting the job done no matter how challenging the task, is the hallmark of an effective leader.

The attitude necessary to fulfill the role of the head of the family, especially in turbulent times, is aptly summed up in the words of a poem by Stephen K. Hayes:

Admonitions of the Knowing[1]

Do not speak to us
Of that which could have been.
All that was is
All that could have been.
No more.
No less.

Let us level our gaze
and move purposefully into
today.

FAMILY LEADERSHIP IMPERATIVES

In order to pursue these goals, a number of management imperatives and tactical approaches need to be embedded in the family leader's repertoire of skills. These imperatives include forward thinking, dispute resolution, creativity, clear prioritization and effective time allocation.

THINK FORWARD

All elements of family strategy need to be pursued with a multi-generational forward view in mind. Problems and opportunities need to be managed before they arise, and other skills related to the imperative of "seeing the future" need to be built into all aspects of family leadership.

Awareness of potential problems can also lead to anticipatory action. By putting in place solutions to problems before they arise, the essence of effective risk management, problems can be averted at

---

[1] Stephen K. Hayes, *Wisdom from the Ninja Village of the Cold Moon*, (Contemporary Books, Inc., 1984)

relatively low cost and effort. The old adage "an ounce of prevention is worth a pound of cure" would be well heeded in the world of the wealthy family, where the cost of a cure could be expensive in any currency.

DISPUTE RESOLUTION

No one set of structures and organizing principles, no matter how well thought out, carefully crafted and assiduously followed by all members of the family, can foresee all potential disputes and differences of interpretation. Just as the nation state has a judicial branch to resolve disputes in a manner consistent with its basic constitution and relevant regulations and laws, a family should have an approach to dispute resolution which can remove the risk of an isolated dispute escalating to threaten the structure, unity or harmony of the greater family.

Without such a mechanism—which can be as simple as the rule that the eldest parental figure, male or female, will decide in matters of dispute between children or grandchildren—small disputes can blow up to epic proportions in even the most stable of families.

BE CREATIVE

The exercise of creativity in different situations, and the search for answers that are not immediately obvious or linear, is a hallmark of a great family leader. The search for solutions at different levels from those at which the problems arise is another sign of farsighted vision and action.

While the structured approach, as suggested here, can contribute enormously to the long-term success of a wealthy family, only creative thought, coupled with the disciplines of structure, will most likely lead to the best possible strategies.

SET PRIORITIES

Each family is unique and each family strategy will be unique. By defining the priorities and aligning actions with the long-term family vision, family leaders will be able to focus scarce resources on the issues in which there is the greatest need, and from which a family can extract the maximum benefit.

Failure to recognize priority items will significantly reduce the impact of any initiative and detract from the overall strategic effort.

ALLOCATE TIME WISELY

Time allocation for key members of a family is an essential part of planning and the realization of the family vision. It may even be one of the most important resource allocation decisions a family can make. In this regard, family leaders may find it useful to complete the table shown in Figure 2.7 to illustrate the opportunities for more effective use of their time.

Figure 2.7 Family Leader Time Allocation

Area of Activity	Current Time Allocation (%)	Desired Time Allocation (%)	Needed Change
Family Organization			
Family Eco-system			
Wealth Preservation			
Wealth Management			
Family Business Strategy			
Effective Philanthropy			
Individual Family Members			
Personal Development			

The time allocated by family leaders and advisors to selected priority initiatives will vary between families and over time, as will other resources dedicated to the same activities.

With a conscious effort to decide what to do and, even more importantly, what not to do, scarce time and energies can be focused on those areas that will make the biggest difference to the family.

THE PSYCHOLOGY OF LEADERSHIP

Perhaps the most important part of the leadership of a family wealth strategy has nothing to do with the specific content of the strategy itself; nor is it related to the details of time allocation, strategic design, implementation, or review. Without the belief and support of the family, even well-designed and well-documented strategies will fail to have the desired impact. Shaping that belief and mustering the highest level of family support is one of the greatest challenges to family leadership.

Psychologists tell us that behavior is the result of attitudes, which are in turn the product of beliefs. So, if we want to bring the behavior of an entire family into line with that which will best support the preservation of family wealth, the attitudes and beliefs need to change first. The ideal outcome of the wealth strategy process would be as follows:

BELIEFS, ATTITUDES AND BEHAVIOR

Belief: All members of the family believe that the family is special and that each member should act in a manner consistent with the long-term best interests of the greater family. A second beneficial belief is that the approach taken and the content of the family's foundation documents provide a fair and valuable guide to the future family.

Attitude: All attitudes should be supportive of the process and the content of the strategy, and positive about the long-term value of maintaining the family wealth, even at the cost of some short-term individual sacrifice.

Behavior: All behavior needs to be constructive and consistent with the guidelines established, with each individual contributing to the development of the family and the strategy of preserving and enhancing family wealth across generations. Everyone should strive to avoid counter-productive behavior (especially litigation and the creation of divisions within the family) which can both shatter the harmony of the family and lead to substantial reductions in family wealth.

FAMILY SUPPORT

In order to ensure that family beliefs and support are fully in line with the wealth strategy plans, the leaders of the family will need to think carefully about the content and process of strategic and other family communications.

It is important not to move so fast that some members of the family are left behind; early investment in ensuring all parties are on board can have enormous long-term returns.

RENAISSANCE SKILLS REQUIRED

History has many lessons for us all. For today's family leaders, faced with a broad array of complex disciplines to master and integrate, the European Renaissance has much to offer.

In the Renaissance period from 1450 to 1600, a group of extraordinary men emerged in Italy. Leonardo da Vinci, Ludovico Vasari, Leon Battista Alberti, and Andreas Vesalius have remained famous across the centuries as individuals who were extraordinarily learned and capable in many of the arts, sciences, and athletic activities of their time.

These uniquely talented individuals were, at the same time, scientists, theologians, traders, investors, poets, artists, authors, architects, and athletes. Their skills and capabilities, rounding out the definition of *homo universalis*, equipped them to take on a full understanding of all that life had to offer—and to apply that knowledge to live full and accomplished lives.

Family leaders in today's world can learn much from these Renaissance men. By both mastering and integrating the disciplines of our time, combining art and science, and fusing insight and action across many disciplines, today's family leaders can, like their Renaissance counterparts, be held up as great and enduring models of exceptional success and accomplishment.

FAMILY WEALTH PRESERVATION

Structure asset holdings and adopt practices for long-term asset preservation

13. THE LESSONS OF RISK AND HISTORY

Ironically, one of the greatest risks to the multi-generational continuity of a family fortune lies in the simple failure to take up, with sufficient vigor, the interrelated issues of wealth preservation strategy.

Wealth preservation is all about managing risk, and structuring asset ownership and control in the current generation, across generations, and through the turbulence of history and the cataclysmic events that can be visited upon any family, wealthy or otherwise. By learning and applying the lessons learned by other families over time, a wealthy family can prepare itself to protect and preserve its own wealth far better than if left entirely to the confines of its own limited experience.

> Those who cannot remember the past are doomed to repeat it.
>
> George Santayana

ALL ABOUT RISK

In almost all historic cases, the events which had a negative impact on a family's fortunes could have been foreseen and, to some extent and in most cases, remedial action taken in advance to reduce or prevent the breakdown in the family's affairs.

When seen in its full complexity, the challenge of wealth preservation for a wealthy family is, in fact, a three-tier challenge:

Three Stages of Family Wealth Preservation

- Preservation of capital in the first (or current) generation
- Preservation of capital into the next generation
- Preservation of capital across multiple future generations

Within each succeeding stage of wealth preservation, there is less certainty with regard to the individuals concerned, less understanding of the overall family dynamic at the time, and less precise knowledge as to the future risks and opportunities defined by the surrounding tax, economic, financial, and legal environments.

As a result, the solutions to the problems posed at each stage become less concrete, more general, and more focused on family values and principles of the future approach than upon concrete prescriptions for precise and present action.

PRESERVATION OF CAPITAL IN THE FIRST GENERATION

The first test of wealth preservation is not to lose the money in the same generation in which it was made. First generation wealth creators are often risk-takers, fully capable of losing their money in an attempt to "double up"—or even more—on the initial fortune they have made.

Many "boom to bust" entrepreneurs in the early dot-com bubble and participants in the emerging market euphoria which preceded the Asian Economic Crisis, along with countless athletes, film stars, musicians, writers, and ordinary businessmen, have left a mark in their industries, but did not succeed in keeping their wealth beyond a single generation.

For each generation of a wealthy family, whether it be the first or the twenty-first, the preservation of wealth in its own generation through proper investment, spending, structuring, and distribution practices is a first priority.

PRESERVATION OF CAPITAL INTO THE NEXT GENERATION

While there are a few examples of families preserving their wealth and standing across multiple generations, there are many more tragic stories of families which have fallen from financial grace, losing their financial wealth and the advantage it once endowed, by failing to develop effective inheritance strategies, beginning with the first transfer across generational lines.

The accomplishments of the first generation, and its successors in building wealth, will need to be matched with a different set of skills, equally testing and demanding, to preserve that created wealth and then transfer it successfully to the second and future generations.

PRESERVATION OF CAPITAL ACROSS MULTIPLE GENERATIONS

In the longer term, the challenges to preserve wealth change and require a broader set of actions, principles, practices, and approaches. Some of the most common skills and expertise required are illustrated in Figure 3.1.

Figure 3.1 Family Wealth Preservation

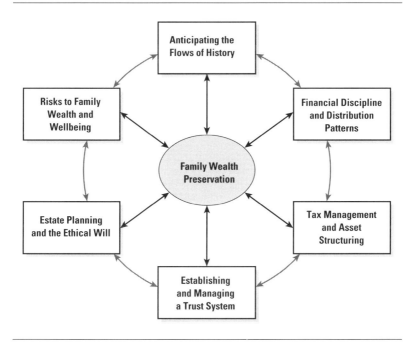

By reviewing the risks and opportunities presented at each and every part of a wealth preservation strategy, wealthy families can address some of the greatest obstacles to ensure that their own family future is one of riches to riches, with family wealth well protected and safely transferred across generations.

ANTICIPATING THE FLOWS OF HISTORY

Many of the worst blows to family fortunes have been struck by external events that no single family, however wealthy or powerful, could have prevented. Throughout history, wars, revolutions, religious persecution, confiscatory tax regimes, outright expropriation, and dramatic political change have caused noble fortunes to be erased and prosperous family businesses to be destroyed.

The Chinese have an unusual curse which states "may you live in interesting times." One of the major challenges of family wealth management *in extremis* is to anticipate these "interesting times" and use the lessons of history to guard against their unwanted impact.

WORLD EVENTS AND FAMILY CONSEQUENCES

The wealth of countless families has been eliminated at one time or another by war, revolution, cataclysmic economic events, and their aftermath, in almost every country in the world. Taking the correct actions with the big picture view in mind may be the saving grace for both family and fortune.

War or armed conflict: Any leader of a family in an area at risk of war or armed conflict of substantial magnitude should be mindful of the right time to dispatch family assets and family members abroad with sufficient foresight that it is not too late to preserve either.

"Not to act is to act."

It is not just bad decisions that can imperil a family's fate and fortune. A failure to act decisively can also be a fatal flaw. As poet, theologian, and anti-Nazi activist Dietrich Bonhoeffer concluded succinctly during the turbulent years prior to his death in April 1945: "Not to act is to act."

Excessive delay can be as decisive in determining the outcome of a family strategy as decisive action consistent with an incorrect premise. The essence of strategy often lies in the timing of actions as much as in the choice of the actions themselves.

Asset bubbles: Like economic cycles and wars, asset bubbles recur with dismaying frequency and bring down many whom they have made wealthy when they burst.

The bursting of asset bubbles is not a new phenomenon. The South Sea Company bubble in the early 1700s, and the tulip craze in the Netherlands in the 1600s, are early examples of what Alan Greenspan, former Chairman of the U.S. Federal Reserve, was later to refer to as the "irrational exuberance" into which capital markets and the investing public can fall with disturbing regularity.

The Dutch tulip craze arose when certain types of selected tulip bulbs rose to extraordinary prices, before collapsing dramatically as the bubble burst. At its peak, the tulip bubble priced some allegedly rare bulbs at a level equal to the price of a normal working farm in the Netherlands.

Not learning the lessons of prices that ran way ahead of values, nineteenth-century Britain saw a wave of asset bubbles swell and then burst, based on financing the infrastructure of canals, railways, and other utilities created by the Industrial Revolution. With excitement-driven demand running well ahead of supply of reliable investment products, especially in an era where stock markets and exchanges were still new and inexperienced, boom-and-bust cycles were a regular part of the investing landscape, with the attendant impact on wealthy families exposed to each succeeding bubble.

America in the 1920s, Japan in the late 1980s, silver in the 1980s, and the media, telecoms and technology sector in "Tech Wreck 2000," as well as the emerging-market crisis (centered in Asia in 1997 and 1998 but expanding outward rapidly) stand as examples of the capital damage and eradication of family fortunes that can take place when market prices run well ahead of sustainable long term asset values.

Confiscatory tax regimes: Although no longer as significant a part of the current economic landscape as they were in the second half of the last century, socialist-inspired confiscatory tax regimes in Europe and elsewhere have led to the economic demise of many families facing exceptionally high rates of income tax (up to 83%),[1] capital gains tax (up to 98%)[2] and inheritance tax (at rates up to 77%).[3]

With a new global mobility of labor and capital, countries tempted to impose such exorbitant taxes are now aware that they are likely to lose scarce human capital and foreign investment in very short order should their tax rates become too far out of line with international norms and the available rates in competing countries.

---

[1] Stuart Adam and Chris Frayne, "A Survey of the US Tax System: Briefing Note No. 9," Table 13: Summary of main reforms, 1979–2001, The Institute of Fiscal Studies, p.17.
[2] Ibid.
[3] Gary Robbins, "Estate Taxes: An Historical Perspective," The Heritage Foundation, Leadership in America, 16 January, 2004, http://www.heritage.org/Research/Taxes/bg1719.cfm.

Nonetheless, with Western European countries and Japan facing dramatic reductions in population, ageing populations, rising state welfare costs, increasing healthcare burdens, and, in the case of the United Kingdom, declining long-term oil revenues, a return to higher rates of tax across the board is not impossible to contemplate in a less advantaged and poorly managed future.

Excessive risk exposure: The Lloyd's of London disasters of the early 1990s, in which wealthy individuals became "names" and participated in syndicates standing behind packaged risks with unlimited personal liability, drove more than 1,500 once-wealthy individuals and families to bankruptcy.

> ...the global derivatives market stood at US$410 trillion by mid-year 2007, seven times larger than the combined GDP of all of the world's nations.

Taking into account Warren Buffett's more recent concerns about derivatives as "weapons of financial mass destruction," many pundits are wondering whether a vast pool of unregulated hedge funds, exceeding US$1 trillion, matched with an unreliable wall of liquidity, inadequate risk pricing and spreading exotic investment vehicles, may yet contain the seeds of the next global risk catastrophe.

A massive derivatives market can only add to global financial volatility. According to the U.K.'s *Daily Telegraph* on July 4, 2007 the global derivatives market stood at US$410 trillion by mid-year 2007, seven times larger than the combined GDP of all of the world's nations.

Nationalization: Russia in 1917; the United Kingdom from 1947 to 1949; China in 1949; Cuba in 1959; France in 1982; Pakistan and India; Zimbabwe; Uganda; Venezuela ... the history of national governments taking over selected private assets, rarely with adequate compensation, is a long tale spun out over many decades and in many countries.

Often predicted or forewarned as a result of larger events, or of political parties running for office with a declared statist agenda, nationalizations have caused many families to lose fortunes, built up over many years and across many generations, if no strategy of international diversification was in place.

Religious and ethnic persecution: Persecution, or even genocide of one people or religious group by another, is a further real risk faced by families in Europe, Asia, and other parts of the world. Jews, Catholics, Protestants, Muslims, Hindus, Armenians, Serbs, Croats, Kurds, Hutus, Tutsis, Palestinians, Tibetans, and other peoples have suffered over the years, or even continue to suffer under the cruel boot of persecution, repression, and occupation.

Preparing to exit, or at least preparing to diversify family affairs before the "tipping point" is reached and events spin out of control, is one of the most important aspects of responsible family leadership and sensible family wealth preservation.

THE TOUGH LESSONS OF HISTORY

From the perspective of family wealth preservation, perhaps the most important history lesson to be learned is that, when the forces of history are about to "cry 'Havoc' and let slip the dogs of war," the best course of action for the wealthy family is to get wealth, and family members, as far away as possible.

Physical security and asset protection are of the utmost importance to any family, and those who are able to avoid the cataclysmic events caused by wars and their aftermath may well be able to survive the longest in a world where big negative events can have a deep impact on a wealthy family.

The second lesson is to ensure that if there is an apparent asset bubble expanding to the point of potential financial catastrophe, wealthy families would be well advised to eliminate, reduce, or hedge their exposure to that bubble in whatever proportion they wish to preserve their money. If in doubt, one rule of thumb is to halve the position, giving away half of the upside on further value appreciation, but also ensuring that, in the worst case, half of the family fortune will still be intact.

A third lesson from these dramatic episodes in history is the value of diversification. If all of the family's golden eggs are in one basket, or exposed to a Lloyd's type risk, then there is a far greater chance for a single risk event to eliminate the entire family fortune. Diversification of investments, financial and operating risks, ownership structures, resident jurisdictions, trustees, currencies, and business (and asset) locations is a relatively low-cost way to take advantage of a wider set of opportunities, to reduce the total tax bill and to reduce a substantial portion of aggregate risk in a portfolio at the same time.

One of the most prescient family leaders in the area of anticipatory action was Mayer Amschel Rothschild. In anticipation of the disasters to come from the nineteenth-century wars in Europe, Mayer sent his five sons to different locations around Europe to build a more diversified business base. Anselm remained with his father in Frankfurt, Solomon was dispatched to Vienna, Nathan to London, Karl to Naples and Jacob to Paris.

With such broad coverage, the Rothschild clan was well positioned to develop business in different parts of Europe, and to ensure that some substantial part of the family's wealth and stature would be likely to withstand any outcome of the looming Napoleonic wars.

EXPECTATION AND ANTICIPATION

Although modern usage of English may tend to create a similarity of meaning between the two words "expectation" and "anticipation," their real meanings are very different. In that difference lies an opportunity to highlight a valuable insight with regard to family management and family wealth preservation. As the Rothschild diaspora shows, there can be a world of difference between the consequences of the two.

"Expectation" is defined in the Merriam-Webster dictionary as the state of mind in which a future event is considered "probable or certain," and linked to words such as "wait" or "stay," underscoring an implied passivity and lack of action.

"Anticipation," on the other hand, carries a sense of action in advance of an expected event or condition. The same dictionary defines anticipation as being "to foresee and deal with in advance…to act before (another), often so as to check or counter."

Family leaders who expect major economic or political events to have a harmful impact on their family wealth, but fail to anticipate that event with action, may well suffer the consequences of their inaction. Failing to act in a timely manner can indeed be an action with grave financial and family consequences.

OPPORTUNITIES IN CRISIS

Although there is great value in avoiding the personal and financial costs of appearing on the wrong side of history, there is also great value in taking advantage of fundamental economic shifts and grand historical changes. The Rothschilds profited enormously by betting on the

"Buy property when there is blood in the streets—even when it is your own."

defeat of Napoleon, lending vast sums of money to his enemies and benefiting from the commissions on the transfer of funds to various armies and European states during the wars.

In a remark attributed to a later Rothschild, a quintessential banking and investment opportunist, the baron advised investors to "Buy property when there is blood in the streets—even when it is your own." This hard-edged advice reflects the fact that crises, properly foreseen and responded to, can contribute to enormous family fortunes at the same time as others are lost.

This perspective is consistent with the Chinese view of cataclysmic events, represented in the dual character for "crisis," *wei ji*. The ideographic representation of the word "crisis" is actually made up of two characters, one symbolizing the adverse content of crisis, and the other signifying the positive value of opportunity.

As we have seen, history can let loose great events that can engulf families and their fortunes. Yet anticipation of those events can, if strategy and timing are right, both reduce risk and create opportunity for substantial family wealth creation.

14. FINANCIAL DISCIPLINE AND DISTRIBUTION PATTERNS

Although anticipating cataclysmic events has played a major role in the preservation of family fortunes over many generations, there are a number of more mundane financial disciplines which can improve the likelihood of a wealthy family beating the odds against successful wealth preservation.

INVESTMENT DISCIPLINE

Bad investment decisions, and bad investment advisors, have ruined many great families, often in a single generation.

By keeping wealth preservation in mind when adopting an investment profile, setting investment objectives and establishing a formal investment process, a wealthy family can give due consideration to the need for the future preservation of capital as well as to the generation of income and increase in capital value.

> "Rule Number One:
>   Don't lose money.
> Rule Number Two:
>   Remember Rule
>   Number One."

After nearly 40 years in value investing, Warren Buffett enunciated his famous "two rules of successful investing," which are well worth remembering when thinking about wealth preservation and risk in a family investment portfolio:

Rule Number One: Don't lose money.
Rule Number Two: Remember Rule Number One.

The required discipline and best proven approaches to ward off a wealth-destroying event are spelled out in the development of Principle 4: Family Wealth Management. While a superior approach to wealth management can increase family financial wealth, the same approach can also play a major role in wealth preservation.

DIVISION AND DEPLETION

A second cause of depletion in a family's fortunes is the increased distribution demands from a growing pool of potential beneficiaries. To take a simple mathematical calculation: if each member of a wealthy family has four children, and each of their children has four children, it is quite possible that, after four generations, there would be nearly 100 potential beneficiaries for the same fortune. Even in a Category II or III family, breaking down family wealth into so many units can be a major source of decline in the collective family's wealth and stature.

SPENDING DISCIPLINE

One of the major reasons why so few families fail to retain their wealth over multiple generations is simply that their members spend more than they contribute to the pool of family assets. Even large family fortunes can be quickly reduced if unsustainable distribution and spending patterns become the norm across generations.

Without the discipline of a sustainable rate of withdrawal, even a large trust or family wealth corpus will be diminished over time, especially in a family with large, growing families at each generation. Even the goose that lays many golden eggs is not infinite in capacity.

A wealthy family that does not have a clear plan for sustainable distributions may well deplete the source of family income so critically

---

The Fall of the House of Vanderbilt

Cornelius Vanderbilt (1794–1877) was one of the wealthiest men in the world in his heyday. Family members dominated the Gilded Age in America, where the super-rich Vanderbilts played a key role in the business, artistic, architectural, social, and sporting events of their time.

Many subsequent Vanderbilts achieved high levels of accomplishment in journalism (Cornelius Vanderbilt IV), sports (notably yachting, where Harold Stirling Vanderbilt won the America's Cup on three occasions) and in other areas. Yet despite this success and a set of stellar family accomplishments, a combination of divorce, extraordinary levels of spending, and family difficulties brought down the family's stature steadily over time.

In 1989, Arthur T. Vanderbilt II published a family history entitled *Fortune's Children: The Fall of the House of Vanderbilt.*

that both distributions and the capital value of the original business asset are substantially threatened.

A sustainable rate of withdrawal: By holding back distributions that would reduce the "real value" of the family's assets (that is, the value of the family's wealth adjusted for inflation), family leaders can ensure that real value will not be impaired.

Since capable money managers can make a substantial gain above the rate of inflation, there should be a defined amount of money for distribution in real terms every year. If wealth management does not yield a surplus above the rate of inflation, then any payout will, *de facto*, reduce the inflation-adjusted value of family wealth.

By the same token, even if investment profits are substantial and well above the rate of inflation, any payout at a rate above the sustainable rate of withdrawal will essentially create a slow liquidation scenario in which the real value of the family assets is on a long-term path to zero.

Example of the calculation: For a family with wealth of US$100 million, earning 2% in after-tax dividends plus 9% in capital gains on its funds (in non-inflation-adjusted terms), the formula works as follows in an environment of 5% inflation:

Sustainable Rate of Withdrawal Calculation	US$
Original wealth	100,000,000
Plus capital appreciation (after tax)	9,000,000
Plus dividends received from investments (after tax)	2,000,000
Minus mandated contribution to charity (for example, 2% of wealth)	(2,000,000)
Equals year-end value of wealth	109,000,000
Amount of surplus above original wealth	9,000,000
Minus impact of inflation (original wealth x inflation rate) (for example, at 5% inflation = US$100,000,000 x 5%)	(5,000,000)
Equals amount available for sustainable distribution to family (that is, to preserve real value of capital)	4,000,000
Wealth post-distribution (equal to original wealth as adjusted for inflation, which becomes the original wealth for following year)	105,000,000

The actual sustainable rate of withdrawal is driven by a number of factors: size of original wealth, investment performance, overall objectives on maintenance or diminution of wealth, the inflation rate, and specific uses of funds for charities or other mandated purposes.

There is no requirement to retain family capital in real terms. Many families simply, and perhaps voluntarily, liquidate their family wealth over time as more and more beneficiaries make greater and greater demands upon a diminishing pool of assets, eventually killing off the goose that lays the golden eggs and realizing, in their own time, the risk of "riches to rags" in a very few generations.

Killing the Golden Goose

One prominent European family, blessed with an exceptionally profitable and renowned family business that has prospered through many generations of private ownership, is now facing a period of difficulty—even the stellar performance of the business is no longer adequate to sustain the distribution claims of an increasingly large and demanding set of family members.

The pattern of this family, by no means unique, emerged as follows: A family business became very profitable and very prominent. Family members, benefiting from a flow of significant distributions without effort, developed expensive and high-profile lifestyles unrelated to business or financial value addition. The high profile that they sought and nurtured created a growing demand for even more funds.

Younger generations, not wishing to live at a standard below that of their parents, grew in number and in their financial expectations as their social prominence expanded. The family business, despite its success, was no longer able to sustain these increasing demands.

The beleaguered senior members of the family are now struggling to adjust a pattern that has grown, by their own reckoning, out of control. Their lament is that it may now be impossible to restore any semblance of orderly distribution in a democratic family environment in which few members of the family are expressing any concern or real understanding about the perilous financial future of succeeding generations.

A LOOMING CRISIS

As for most families in this situation, these prominent Europeans will need to make a clear decision: either to liquidate the business through a long tail of diminishing distributions, or reduce distributions, at least for a while, to ensure that the family reserves are built up and that the financial capital survives to fund future generations.

This is never an easy decision, and this fragmented and fractious family faces many challenges in the coming years to sort out a future that may be enormously different from their past. Unless they change their distribution patterns profoundly, they will be on their way from riches to rags—albeit in eight or nine generations rather than three.

"RECULER POUR MIEUX SAUTER"

This French phrase, which roughly translates as "step back in order to jump higher" can provide useful guidance to families at risk of placing excessive demands on a limited resource pool. By holding back or reducing distributions for a period of time in order to restore the capital base to a sustainable level, family leaders can provide for all their families' needs indefinitely.

The demanding European family mentioned above might have benefited from reviewing the history of Yale University's disciplined investment guru, David Swensen, and his approach to investment and distribution.

Upon taking over as Yale's CIO in 1985 at age 31, Swensen reviewed the investment and distribution history of the university's endowment and determined that the established ratios of investment return, income generation, and distribution would not meet the university's needs and vision into the future. Informing faculty and administration officials of the value of a less conventional approach to investment, and maintaining a conservative approach to distribution, Swensen's model allowed the Yale portfolio of investments to be invested wisely, for distributions to be contained, and for the university's future to be assured.

Yale University's endowment grew from $1.3 billion to $14 billion during the first 20 years of Swensen's stewardship.[1]

By installing a disciplined system of investment and distribution, Yale now has not only more income to spend, it has an appreciating net worth amongst the highest for any university in the world, and an expert investment team dedicated to continuing that success.

If a wealthy family were to adopt a similar approach, the eventual benefits could well justify any short-term sacrifice many times over.

---

[1] Marc Gunther, "Yale's 8 billion man", *Yale Alumni Magazine*, 2005, July/August, Vol.68, No.6 http://www.yalealumnimagazine.com/issues/2005_07/swensen.html.

15. TAX MANAGEMENT AND ASSET STRUCTURING

One of the primary purposes of a structured approach to family asset and wealth management is to minimize taxes wherever possible. This objective, adopted in virtually all countries around the world by wealthy families, may involve both onshore and offshore asset structuring.

Although periodically criticized by governments, politicians, and economists, the world of effective asset structuring is entirely legal, correct, and even blessed by one of the greatest legal minds in the history of American jurisprudence.

Judge Learned Hand specifically encouraged individuals and families to undertake advantageous tax planning in his famous words:

> "…nobody owes any public duty to pay more than the law demands."

Anyone may arrange his affairs so that his taxes shall be as low as possible; he is not bound to choose that pattern which best pays the treasury. There is not even a patriotic duty to increase one's taxes. Over and over again the Courts have said that there is nothing sinister in so arranging affairs as to keep taxes as low as possible. Everyone does it, rich and poor alike and all do right, for nobody owes any public duty to pay more than the law demands.[1]

Taking advantage of all opportunities to manage wealth on an after-tax basis across multiple generations is an essential part of long term wealth preservation for every family in virtually every country.

TYPES OF TAXES

On the tax front, income, gift and capital gains tax (usually based on residence, and occasionally on nationality), inheritance tax or death duties, property taxes, and wealth tax (based on the location of the

---

[1] Marvin A. Chirelstein "Learned Hand's Contribution to the Law of Tax Avoidance," *Yale Law Journal*, Vol. 77, No. 3, January 1968, pp.440–74.

asset in question) can play different roles in tax management based upon the nationality, residence, domicile, and asset profile of the family. Although tax is a complex and specific issue in any national context, a few general points are worth noting:

Income tax: Managing income tax can play a major role in wealth creation and preservation by addressing the location, form, and timing of income and other payments received.

Dividends, in some countries, are taxed as income and, in others, not at all. The relevant treatment of dividends may thus require separate consideration—or may simply be embedded in the strategies to minimize income or corporate tax.

Capital gains tax: Capital gains tax will vary substantially from one country to another, and may involve treatment of short term capital gains (the profits on the sale of an asset held for less than 12 months) in the same manner, and at the same rates, as earned income.

> "In this world nothing can be said to be certain, except death and taxes."

Inheritance tax and death duties: In many families, one of the major considerations in managing family financial wealth is avoiding, to the extent possible, inheritance tax (IHT) and death duties. In some U.S. state jurisdictions, for example, there is an obligation to pay both. As Benjamin Franklin famously pointed out: "In this world nothing can be said to be certain, except death and taxes." Often, unfortuantely, they come together.

The amounts of potential IHT can be so large for a wealthy family that some may contemplate moving out of their home countries to avoid incurring heavy future tax burdens for their families.

However, despite the substantial inheritance tax rates and death duties, many people prefer to die in their home countries—dying alone in a foreign country may be too great a human cost to absorb, no matter how significant the tax savings.

There are many ways to manage asset structures to reduce or avoid IHT and death duties altogether, although any such strategy must comply with the relevant tax codes. In addition to the demands of structuring trusts correctly, time may also be on your side. In most jurisdictions, to be valid for IHT reduction or elimination purposes, any trust needs to have been in effect five or seven years before the death of the testator to be valid.

In addition to creating generation-skipping trusts, taking out large offsetting insurance policies, and rolling forward tax obligations, other opportunities which involve more complex approaches to asset structuring can shape the ownership and management of family wealth.

In the United Kingdom, for example, the terms of the Business Property Relief exemptions to inheritance tax mean that some enterprises, so long as they are not publicly quoted, can pass tax-free from one generation to the next. The same can be true of forestry and agricultural properties.

Gift tax: To prevent wealthy families giving away their money before estate tax falls due, many countries levy a tax on either the donor or recipient of the gift. The treatment and rates vary by tax jurisdiction.

In most cases, there are prescribed amounts that can be gifted to a spouse or child without incurring a gift tax, on either an annual or cumulative basis. These amounts, although potentially small in the context of a wealthy family, may be worth building into a plan that takes advantage of every possible tax management opportunity.

Wealth tax: In some countries (France and Spain, for example), a wealth tax has become a part of the fiscal landscape. Such taxes are based on taxing asset wealth in addition to income. Usually based on net asset values, wealth taxes can be managed in some cases by taking on strategic debt (thereby reducing the net value of the property, business or other asset exposed to the tax), shifting ownership to offshore jurisdictions and implementing other effective programs.

Corporate taxes: Where there is an operating business or where corporate vehicles are used for personal tax purposes, then the full array of corporate tax management approaches need to be embedded in the overall tax strategy and implementation plans.

Other taxes: Other taxes may need to be considered as part of the family's asset structuring and wealth management activities. The 2007 U.K. tax on the establishment of trusts, the taxes levied on deemed interest from loans, or a potential "exit tax" on assets paid upon dropping a nationality, can play a central role in current or multi-generational tax strategies.

AVOIDANCE VS. EVASION

Judge Learned Hand affirmed the propriety of avoiding tax by structuring and other legal means to reduce taxes to the minimal level allowed by the law. He obviously did not condone evading taxes which are properly due. Tax avoidance is entirely legal—tax evasion is illegal and can lead to hefty fines and even jail sentences in some countries.

To date, most tax authorities have focused on reducing tax evasion. Now, in some jurisdictions, historically accepted structures for avoidance are also under attack. Anticipating such changes in regulations could be a key part of an effective tax management strategy.

TAX AMERICANA

The degree to which many wealthy families have contact with the United States makes it worth outlining its unique tax regime for illustrative purposes.

Regardless of current domicile or duration of stay outside the United States, anyone who holds a U.S. passport or green card is obliged to pay taxes to the U.S. government at standard U.S. tax rates for worldwide income, dividends, capital gains, gifts, and inheritance. There are allowances for foreign taxes and some relief for expatriate status, depending, in part, upon the country of foreign residence, but there is no escaping the long arm of the IRS.

Current U.S. inheritance tax rates can be as high as 46% of the value of all global assets over US$2 million.[2] This compares with a U.K. IHT rate of 40% (above a nil-rate band of £285,000),[3] and a zero rate in many countries, including India, Australia, Canada, and Switzerland. Of the 50 countries included in a recent PricewaterhouseCoopers survey, only South Korea (50%) and Japan (at a staggering 70%) have a higher "death tax" rate than the U.S.[4]

---

[2] Internal Revenue Service, United States Department of the Treasury, "Estates and Gift Taxes," http://www.irs.gov/businesses/small/article/0,,id=98968,00.html.

[3] HM Revenue & Customs, "Rates and Allowances—Inheritance Tax," http://www.hmrc.gov.uk/rates/inheritance.htm

[4] American Council for Capital Formation (ACCF) Special Report (July 2005), "New International Survey Shows U.S. Death Tax Rates Among Highest," refers to source data from survey by PricewaterhouseCoopers, LLP. http://www.accf.org/pdf/death-tax-survey.pdf.

A similar tax rate is levied on the donor of gifts, with certain narrowly defined exceptions and small annual exclusions.

Even if a wealthy U.S. citizen, defined as someone with a net worth exceeding US$2 million (or paying a prescribed amount of tax over a five year period), were to give up citizenship, there is still a 10-year period following the cessation of citizenship during which any U.S.-related income or capital gains are taxed as if that person were still a citizen. There is also a proposal on the table for an "exit tax" of 15% to be levied on all assets, not just unrealized capital gain, for citizens abandoning their nationality and its future tax burdens.

CHANGING NATIONALITY, DOMICILE, AND RESIDENCE

Very broadly, your residence (where you live and work) defines the country in which income taxes are paid. Your domicile (the country in which you have an "indefinite intent to remain") will dictate where you pay estate or death duties. The qualification for domicile varies between countries—in the United States, possession of a U.S. passport or green card automatically confers domicile status. In the United Kingdom, residence for 17 out of the past 20 years will currently create a status of "deemed domicile" for non-U.K. citizens.

In some countries, citizens and domiciled non-citizens only pay estate duty on assets within the host country. In the United States, United Kingdom, and other countries, the government will levy an inheritance tax on all assets on a worldwide basis, regardless of how much time an individual has spent outside the country. In yet other countries, becoming non-resident for a number of years can create an opportunity to shed a domicile status and establish, or resettle, family trusts with little or no tax consequence.

> Most wise tax planners will counsel their wealthy clients to determine how and where they wish to live, and then plan their taxes accordingly.

The tax and estate planning benefits to be gained by changing nationality, domicile, or residence can make such options well worth considering for some wealthy families, particularly those in the higher categories of wealth. Many have decamped to places—notably Switzerland, Monaco, Dubai, and the Caribbean—where tax rates are more attractive, bank secrecy standards are high and disclosure obligations are low. Such a tax haven is known to the French as a *paradis fiscal.*

Needless to say, these major changes demand that a much broader set of issues are considered before decisions are made: the lack of proximity to friends and family, the loss of national identity, isolation from various communities, and other lifestyle changes all need to be balanced and evaluated realistially.

Most wise tax planners will counsel their wealthy clients to determine how and where they wish to live, and then plan their taxes accordingly.

ASSET STRUCTURING

Although minimizing taxes is one of the major purposes of family asset structuring, it is not the only one. The list of potential threats to a family's wealth extends beyond the taxman, and may include litigation, marital disputes, profligate or incapable heirs, family discord, economic upheaval, and even expropriation due to political or other unforeseen events.

Using some of the vehicles mentioned below in a defined order and form can ensure that capable administration, equitable distribution, transparent information, and appropriate voting rights are all achieved for a family's wealth, successfully protected and preserved across many generations.

While not all risks and disasters can be anticipated and managed, a sound approach to the structuring and administration of family assets can provide protection from many of the established patterns and risks that have brought down wealthy families over time.

In some ways, developing and building an asset-structuring approach to family wealth is like designing and constructing a family house. There is a need for a central architecture, a vision and a plan that achieves the purpose established by the owner within the prescribed local and international regulations. Within that central architecture are the independent materials and building blocks, the legal and administrative structures that can be assembled by a supporting cast of characters in the proper order and with the proper relationships and operating principles to achieve the overall objectives. Protective walls need to be erected to shelter the family from fiscal and economic storms, and foundations need to be firm enough to support the family through many generations of evolution, testing and change.

Every exercise of this kind is, to some extent, a balancing act. The need to respect the intentions of the original architecture has to be balanced with reasonable future flexibility on behalf of the beneficiaries of trusts or other tax avoidance vehicles.

Referring back to Einstein's theory that problems cannot be solved at the level at which they arise, solutions intended to endure across multiple generations need to be put in place with an anticipatory and long-term view in mind. Long before a potentially wealth-dissipating Next Generation inherits control of family assets, wiser (and usually older) members of the family should have designed and implemented actions to offset any foreseeable future risks.

Some of the vehicles and tools used, the building blocks whose shape, size, and roles are determined by the overall asset structuring architecture, are as follows:

TRUSTS

Essentially, trusts can be thought of as three-way contracts which regulate the relationships between the settler, the trustee, and the beneficiary.

One of the mainstays of Anglo-Saxon tax and estate planning, the trust is a highly controlled legal entity which has a set life and which operates to a set of general principles and specific documents, usually including a deed of settlement and a letter of wishes, establishing the trust and guiding its operation.

Trusts are legal vehicles which can be used to transfer wealth tax-effectively, define the policy on future distributions of funds, delay the transfer of funds if certain conditions are not met, and achieve a whole host of tax and other objectives. A typical trust with multiple objectives could, for example, transfer funds to an intended beneficiary only upon that person reaching the age of 21 and completing a degree from an accredited university.

Trusts can take many forms. They can be onshore, offshore, contingent, special purpose, foreign grantor, revocable (allowing the settler to cancel the trust at his or her discretion), or irrevocable. Many favorable tax treatments require a trust to be irrevocable to qualify for tax exemptions.

There are other variations on the theme: contingent trusts, incentive trusts, charitable trusts, blind trusts (within which the beneficiaries have no detailed knowledge of investments, nor any control over fund management), a rabbi trust (which has been used to defer U.S. taxation under certain circumstances), and a freezer trust (which specifies a preset maximum value of assets, beyond which another vehicle is required to capture any excess value), and other creative approaches.

Generation skipping: One of the major purposes of a trust structure is to provide vehicles to skip ownership of assets in every other generation in order to avoid IHT liabilities. For example, by leaving his assets to a grandchild, a grandfather can avoid one generation of death duties or trust restructuring costs.

Treatment of generation skipping varies enormously from one country to another. In the U.S., for example, transfers into a trust are subject to a gift tax, and any subsequent generation skipping may be subject to a "generation-skipping tax"—a very costly double-whammy.

An example of a traditional trust structure, with a master trust and subsidiary individual trusts, can look as shown in Figure 3.2.

Figure 3.2 Traditional Trust Structure

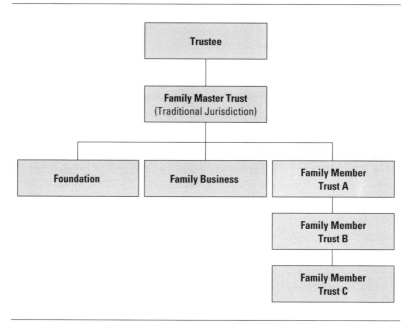

The rule against perpetuities and perpetual trusts: In English property law, there is a long-established rule, The Rule Against Perpetuities, which limits the amount of time that property assets can be tied up in a trust to the duration of a "life in being" (that is, someone who is already alive, but not necessarily the beneficiary) plus 21 years.

Dating from a 1681 case involving the Earl of Arundel,[5] the purpose of this rule was to avoid excessive concentration of property in the hands of a few wealthy families and to limit the risk of tying up great chunks of national assets forever in potentially unproductive protective vehicles.

Over time, some jurisdictions have overturned this judicially created rule by specific legislation which allows testators to establish 100-year trusts, and even 100-year trusts capable of renewal, making them the same kind of virtually perpetual trusts that the old rules were meant to abolish.

A personal view against virtual perpetuities: As stated in the section on the dark side of wealth, in addition to the policy and economic reasons for limiting perpetual trusts, there are potential psychological costs to these trusts as well. Such unwanted effects as distribution dependence, the existence of unproductive adult "trust babies" and the lack of effective redeployment of assets, can have a harmful impact on any family if such a situation endures for too long.

While recognizing the good intentions of such long lock-ups, the potential for dependence on distributions, the potential for dysfunctional resentment that can arise if future beneficiaries feel that the trust established is coercive and disrespectful of their individual wishes and capabilities, and the risk of assets stagnating under external trustee care militate against the perpetual lock-up of assets.

An eventual release of capital to a pre-defined future generation, if tax effective, is but one approach to overcome the risks of a family's suffering from passive distribution dependence for too long.

ANSTALTS, STIFTUNGS AND FOUNDATIONS

In many ways the Germanic speaking countries' equivalent of the Anglo-Saxon trust, these vehicles function on behalf of families in much the same way as a trust, but are regulated by different bodies

---

[5] The Law Commission Item 7 of the Sixth Programme of Law Reform: The Law of Trusts The rules Against Perpetuities and Excessive Accumulations To the Right Honourable the Lord Irvine of Lairg, Lord High Chancellor of Great Britain http://www.lawcom.gov.uk/docs/lc251.pdf.

and according to rules specific to the low-tax jurisdictions adopting these structures.

Although particularly disadvantageous for American citizens, these vehicles may support the tax objectives of wealthy families of non-U.S. origin.

CORPORATIONS AND COMPANIES

Corporations in various jurisdictions can also play an important role in tax and legal plans for families of substantial worth. Many families will have a corporation in one jurisdiction underneath a trust from another, with a private trust company incorporated in yet another jurisdiction.

Corporations have the advantage of protecting owners against liability and are not constrained by trust deeds and documents. They do have costs and disadvantages, however, including directors having fiduciary duties, and a requirement for audits and disclosures on an annual basis.

PARTNERSHIPS

Partnerships, either general or limited, can also be employed to achieve specific structuring purposes related to tax, liability, and disclosure. Many private equity investments, for example, are structured as partnerships, with the managers being the general partners (GPs) operating the fund, and financial investors being the limited partners (LPs), receiving their economic benefits without the full set of broader rights and responsibilities of the partnership GPs.

LLCS AND LLPS

Limited liability corporations (LLCs), often used in the United States for tax planning and risk management purpose, are legal corporate entities with limited liability and provide for much of the benefit of a corporate entity without the unlimited liability on the part of the directors. Limited liability partnerships (LLPs) have the same liability protection, along with the additional advantages and disadvantages of a partnership vehicle.

OTHER VEHICLES

The list of asset structuring options does not end with these traditional vehicles. Captive insurance companies, segregated portfolio companies, protected cell companies, and other such exotic vehicles may also fit into a family's plans, now or in the future.

As many trust and incorporation jurisdictions are now actively competing for business, offering different supervisory regimes and registration requirements, it is worth shopping around to find the most suitable jurisdictions.

It is also advisable to employ an expert lawyer, accountant, or tax practitioner, as the opportunities and risks of different jurisdictions can change rapidly. The full benefits of such new and attractive opportunities as Singapore and New Zealand trusts, which can come along with embedded private trust companies, may not be fully visible to any but the most up-to-date professionals.

MULTI-JURISDICTIONAL APPROACHES

Although all trusts, corporations, and partnerships are registered and "resident" in a single jurisdiction, most asset structuring approaches for very wealthy families, especially those outside the United States, are multi-jurisdictional in nature.

For families seeking to avoid undue scrutiny and preserve family privacy, a multi-jurisdictional approach has many advantages. In addition to sheltering income and assets from taxes, litigation, and other risks, a multi-layered approach can make it very difficult for corporate rivals, journalists, or other unauthorized parties to discover the extent and nature of a family's wealth and operating approach.

Rule of Three: Within the sphere of offshore multi-jurisdictional structuring, there is a long-standing view that structures of three levels or more are virtually impenetrable for outside parties seeking information, damages, or encumbrances against assets. The so-called "Rule of Three" means that any combination of trusts and corporations, with at least three stacked up, one on top of another, would provide an effective barrier against most creditors and litigants, even without the need to change trusts and corporate entities during any litigation or other asset-threatening dispute.

DIVERSIFICATION

In setting up an international asset structure, or even a complex domestic approach, members of wealthy families would be well-advised to think through the benefits of a more diversified approach to asset structuring and trustee or director roles. Although setting up more than one system of interlocking companies and structures is more expensive and cumbersome than working under a single structure and trustee, the longer term benefits may well be worth the incremental set-up and operating costs.

There are benefits to operating under a single master trust or consolidating entity—for example, when it comes to balancing the values of different trusts or setting distribution and ownership rights across different generations—but a weighing of the pros and cons of a single entity as opposed to a more diversified set of trust and corporation jurisdictions should be an essential part of any sound asset structuring review.

A more diversified approach to a wealthy family's affairs could look as shown in Figure 3.3.

Figure 3.3 Diversified Family Trust Structure

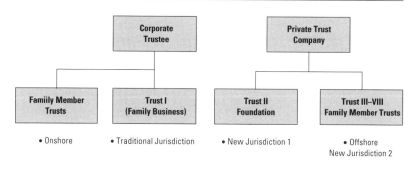

- Onshore
- Traditional Jurisdiction
- New Jurisdiction 1
- Offshore
  New Jurisdiction 2

MARITAL ISSUES

While hopefully leading to a happy expansion of the family, marriages can provide a great source of discord and threat to family wealth and wellbeing if they do not work out. With national divorce rates surpassing 40% in some European countries and in the United

States, family leaders would be well advised to think through in advance the various options available to protect family wealth from any future marital complications.

Even if there is no divorce or difficulty in a marriage, the addition of in-laws can be, for some families, a great source of aggravation and difficulty.

DIVORCE

Some of the most sensitive and complex asset protection issues for a wealthy family are those related to marital disharmony, separation, and divorce. The complexity stems from the fact that national laws on divorce, which can override any specific agreement between partners to a dissolving marriage, are evolving rapidly and unpredictably in many countries, creating a situation where unknown policies and legislation may determine the impact of a future divorce on family wealth.

The impact of a divorce can range from insignificant to enormous, depending upon the couple involved, the nature of the divorce, the quantum and structure of family wealth, and the jurisdiction involved.

In the United States and other countries, there are communal property jurisdictions in which, if a long marriage results in divorce, family assets are assembled and divided equally between the divorcing couple. In some cases inherited property, or even potentially inherited property on one side of the couple, can be taken into account as an asset for consideration in the settlement.

In the United Kingdom, increasingly the jurisdiction of choice for divorce from a spouse's perspective (where either party is a U.K. resident), there are principles that can be applied to Category I wealth in particular, in which the husband loses virtually all of his rights to family wealth, and even a substantial portion of his future income, to his former spouse. As of 2007, pre-nuptial contracts may be considered by a U.K. court but are not yet legally binding.

Should a divorce become necessary, the prior asset structures and the initial selection of jurisdiction, often heavily influenced by the first filing by the petitioner, may have a substantial impact on the final outcome of a litigated action or agreed settlement.

Anticipatory action: To minimize financial loss and to clarify financial responsibilities in the unfortunate instance of divorce or separation, a couple may enter into pre- or post-nuptial agreements. It is to be hoped, of course, that the terms of such agreements would never need to be implemented—however, as at least one strategy guru has pointed out, hope is not a strategy.

- *Pre-nuptial agreements:* Such agreements vary in their effectiveness according to legal jurisdiction. Some jurisdictions require that full disclosure of all assets on both sides be made prior to the signing of a pre-nuptial agreement, and that the agreement be notarized. Others may regard such an agreement as a contract between two willing adult parties without the need for an exhaustive disclosure of private family matters.

> Hope is not a strategy.

While some jurisdictions will do their best to honor the terms contained in pre-nuptial agreements, in others prior agreements between the parties will have no legal weight whatsoever.

If such an agreement is to be put in place, it is very important that it is fully endorsed by both parties and that the issue is raised well in advance of a marriage in a manner consistent with a commitment to a long and loving marriage.

If not pursued in a timely and thoughtful manner, pre- and post-nuptial agreements could damage the relationship, making the couple feel as if they are being forced to pre-negotiate their divorce before their marriage has even begun.

- *Post-nuptial agreements:* Post-nuptial agreements, which are negotiated after a marriage has been consummated, have also emerged as documents with some (albeit limited) reference value in divorce or separation procedures.

- *Trusts:* One leading U.K. family wealth specialist has long advocated the use of trusts established well in advance of any matrimonial dispute, asserting that "an established trust beats a pre-nup any day." If it is in place long enough before the marriage or divorce—usually a two- or five-year period after settlement, depending upon the jurisdiction—courts will allow the protective nature of a trust to be respected.

If the trust is settled shortly before a marriage or divorce, then the court may, at its discretion and consistent with applicable law, set it aside as an attempt to hide from the financial obligations related to the dissolution of the marriage.

NOT JUST DIVORCE

While divorce may be the greatest single threat to family wealth, other issues may arise that also merit prior consideration. Outsiders can also sow the seeds of expensive discord, whether leading to outright division or from fanning the flames of differences in a family setting.

In order to avoid the major risks to their family fortune from outsiders, especially through divorce and the fomenting of division, one multi-billion-dollar European family systematically reviewed the history of dissipation of family wealth over many years. Their conclusion was that two of the greatest risks to family fortunes, even to one as substantial as theirs, were excessively broad shareholdings in a family business and, simply put, difficult sons-in-law.

As a result of their analysis, that family now limit the number of shareholders in the family business to a very small number and allow only a very carefully circumscribed role to be played in their family affairs by in-laws.

On the other hand, historical analysis of many wealthy families will also show that it may be the outsiders who enter a wealthy family through marriage or adoption who can enhance the family's fortunes. In the case of the German Krupps, for example, women who married into the family played a major role in protecting and expanding the family fortunes at critical points in its history.

INTEGRITY AND INTEGRATION

The key to success in any asset structuring exercise is to take a fully informed view of the system as it is set up, and as it evolves, to ensure that it achieves its original purpose and that it has evolved to take into account any important regulatory or testamentary changes along the way.

The principles of operation and the structures selected have to work in harmony, without placing any undue burden on future trustees, beneficiaries, and settlers.

16. ESTABLISHING AND MANAGING
A TRUST SYSTEM

While apparently complex, an effective trust and asset structuring approach can be quickly understood and can operate smoothly, but only if it is properly set up in the first place.

Establishing a trust, or a multi-tiered structure that involves trusts and corporations, requires that certain documents are filed with the relevant authorities. These will probably include a trust deed or declaration, a company's shareholders' agreement, articles of incorporation, governance procedures, and other such documents necessary for the smooth functioning of the legal entities involved.

In addition to the formal incorporation or registration documentation, a side letter or non-binding "letter of wishes" from the settler to the trustee providing guidance on the trust's distribution policy, investment guidelines, and communications policy with beneficiaries may be attached. Examples of these documents are provided in the "Principles in Action" section at the end of this book.

Regardless of the exact vehicles, jurisdictions and structures selected, there can be many entities, processes, and principles operating within the system that require attention.

There are issues related to the registration and operation of asset structuring vehicles, both onshore and offshore, and associated bank accounts. There are annual fees, filings, audits, and other regulatory obligations. Trustees, directors, administrators, custodians, accountants, and tax advisors will be needed to operate and adapt the system to meet its stated objectives.

If there is a private trust company involved, there may be enforcers as well as trustees and directors to appoint, and, if necessary, remove and replace.

KYC and AML: In the post-9/11 world, there are stringent standards for disclosure of the names and identities of the sources of funds and the ultimate beneficiaries of the trust vehicles being established.

The KYC and AML rules described earlier apply in all legitimate jurisdictions as an important part of the registration and settlement process, as well as a key step in setting up bank or brokerage accounts for the trust entities created.

Letter of wishes: A letter of wishes is a non-binding, and usually not too prescriptive, set of standards and principles which a settler, grantor, or testator communicates in written form to guide the investment and distribution decisions of the trustee. The usual points addressed in such a missive may include:

- A personal ethos and set of values.

- Criteria for the use of trust funds—capital and income—to benefit a defined set of beneficiaries.

- Definitions of reasonable lifestyle expectations for beneficiaries, expenditure limits and acceptable uses of funds. These need to be made specific for: income and dividend distributions; capital withdrawals and loans; the influence of a spouse's wishes with regard to income and capital distributions to self, children and others; and the effect a spouse's remarriage will have on the level of income or capital (s)he receives.

- A view as to the appropriate risk level to be adopted in investment strategy.

- Encouraging the financial education, independence, and charitable activities of family members, with specific attention to the adoption by beneficiaries of a "work-ethic" lifestyle.

- Philanthropic objectives and use of funds.

- How remaining funds are to be distributed in the event that a spouse dies without children and there are no living relatives to be selected as beneficiaries.

AN ALTERNATIVE APPROACH

As always, advisors on issues relating to structuring and operating trusts and estates need to remain fully up to date. The need for this is highlighted, for example, by the evolution of the position with regard to letters of wishes in the U.K.

In a first wave of cautionary approaches, some testators were encouraged to avoid letters of wishes on the grounds that they might lend weight to the idea that the testator had not, in fact, relinquished full control of the assets, and thus might put at risk the tax benefits for which the trust was set up.

In a second approach, letters of wishes did not seem to create such a risk, and hence became acceptable practice for all but the most conservative.

However, some experts are now recommending that grantors avoid letters of wishes again, not for the tax implications this time, but because of a court decision which allowed letters of wishes to be included in beneficiary litigation. To avoid creating evidence which could increase the likelihood of litigation, or unfavorably influence the outcome of any litigation, some experts now recommend that a trustee memorandum be prepared and retained by the trustee, a document which is not, at this point, discoverable in litigation over trust or trustee matters.

CHOOSING A TRUSTEE

As the trust is being established, settlers will be faced with the vexing question of who to select to take over legal ownership of the family's assets. This selection is extremely important as the trustee may become the legal owner of the family's assets on an irrevocable basis.

It is extremely important to select the best possible trustee for the family's wealth, as difficulties with trustees, as explained below, can have unintended and grave long term consequences for generations to come. Individuals, professional "corporate" trustees, and private trust companies are all options available for consideration.

ONE TRUST OR MANY?

One of the constant refrains throughout this book is the value of systematic diversification for purposes of both risk management and performance enhancement. This principle applies very directly in the areas of trust and trustee selection.

Establishing more than one trust, with different trustees (and types of trustees) in more than one jurisdiction (especially for non-U.S. families), can create extra complexity and some incremental cost, but may yield great returns in an unknown future.

For a family's current leaders and advisors, thinking forward across multiple generations, the diversification of trusts, jurisdictions, trustees, and investment managers can be a major step toward clear and decisive long-term management of family wealth.

Global race for trust and wealth management business: Over recent years, the long-standing battle between offshore jurisdictions to attract and retain clients forming trusts and establishing companies has heated up, creating newer and better-designed vehicles for wealthy families.

For many years, the world was divided into two segments of offshore jurisdictions for trust formation or company registration: the high-quality, more demanding and more expensive jurisdictions, and a fast-growing set of lower quality, less expensive and less demanding jurisdictions such as those found in Caribbean and Pacific islands, and in the smaller countries in Central America. Many of these jurisdictions were tiny and remote island nations with little, if any, regulation or oversight and little or no business base other than tourism and the offshore incorporation of trusts and corporate entities.

Some of the best known of the higher quality jurisdictions were Bermuda, the Channel Islands (Jersey and Guernsey, in particular), Luxembourg, Hong Kong, the Netherlands, Switzerland (which does not have its own trust system but can provide alternatives), and other such countries with more balanced economies and a greater interest in preservation of a national reputation for clean dealings.

Recent events have shaken up this old order to some extent, albeit with the same jurisdictions continuing to provide the vast bulk of the business for corporate and trust business. A combination of increased scrutiny in the wake of the events of 9/11, greater intrusion into the Swiss banking system through the European Union's withholding tax directive, the increased tax burden on trusts for UK residents, and increased intranational competition for private wealth management business, have made room for emerging high-quality jurisdictions outside of the traditional regions. Among these, four emerging jurisdictions are of particular current interest: Dubai, New Zealand, Mauritius and Singapore.

Dubai, the newest entry, is strategically located within the enormously wealthy Gulf region and provides a convenient location for many Saudi, South Asian and other Family Offices. It offers very low-tax corporate and trust structures as well. It is still early days, but this small emirate with big ambitions may well emerge as a jurisdiction of some presence in the future.

New Zealand has a very competitive combination of a low-tax offshore trust structure with an embedded private trust company. There is a zero tax obligation if the beneficial ownership and all assets are kept out of New Zealand. Although reporting and administration costs may be a bit higher than in many smaller nations, the national reputation and modern terms of the trust structure may make New Zealand a surprising jurisdiction of choice for some years to come.

> Singapore effected a number of comprehensive changes to make it a top global contender for wealthy family asset management.

Mauritius, of particular note as a gateway country for tax-efficient investments into India, has recently updated its offshore structures and become an emerging global player for asset structuring outside of the India-Mauritius corridor.

As a result of the work of a national Economic Review Committee in 2002, Singapore effected a number of comprehensive changes to make it a top global contender for wealthy family asset management.

The Private Wealth Management Initiative (founded and chaired by this author) highlighted the need for a more modern set of rules and regulations governing trusts and trust companies, and provided an opportunity to update and reinforce Singapore's historical pre-eminence as the financial center of Southeast Asia.

One of the longer-term objectives of that initiative was to move the country to the top of the global list of responsible jurisdictions from which wealthy Europeans, Asians, and other nationalities could book (that is, place in a legally registered account) and manage their financial assets. In addition to the newly amended trust rules, which complemented existing rules in the corporate sphere, Singapore's government went even further to develop the country's capabilities and private wealth management eco-system at the recommendation of the Private Wealth Management Initiative team.

A Wealth Management Institute was created; private banks were encouraged to move their training and international operations headquarters to the country; income tax on domestic interest was waived; stringent banking secrecy laws, even tougher than Switzerland's, were confirmed; a large secure depository for art objects was established in a location convenient for linking up private and commercial flights; a new banking license status for offshore private banks was created; a bilateral tax treaty was negotiated to make Singapore competitive with Mauritius for inward investment into India; and other sensible steps were taken to offer an attractive world class wealth management location for wealthy families of all nationalities.

AMERICAN OPTIONS

Within the United States, there is a similar increase in the level of competition between the states for domestic trust businesses. Delaware, long the most advanced and traditional state of choice for American trusts and company incorporations, is now experiencing competition from a growing list of states competing for the lucrative trust administration business.

As Professors Robert H. Sitkoff and Max M. Schanzenbach noted in 2005: "Our perpetuities findings imply that roughly $100 billion in trust funds have moved to take advantage of the abolition of the [Perpetuities] Rule...In spite of the lack of direct tax revenue from attracting trust business, the jurisdictional competition for trust funds is patently real and intense."[10]

For example, in order to allow donors to exploit a loophole in the federal estate tax, The Rule Against Perpetuities, as applied to interests in trust, has not applied in many states since 1986. From 1997, in order to allow individuals to shield assets from creditors, some states have created legislation approving self-settled asset protection trusts, echoing some of the same protective concepts and terms used in the Cook Islands and other offshore jurisdictions.

Wealthy families can improve the terms, costs, and protections afforded by the competitive battle between relevant jurisdictions if they shop carefully when looking for the best jurisdiction in which to create a trust or other asset structuring vehicle.

PRIVATE TRUST COMPANIES

A private trust company (PTC) is usually a corporate entity, controlled by the family of the testator or beneficiary, which can operate as the trustee of a family trust. The mechanism by which the family controls the company is through the nomination of "Enforcers," who

---

[10] Robert H. Sitkoff and Max M. Schanzenbach "Jurisdictional Competition for Trust Funds: An Empirical Analysis of Perpetuities and Taxes," *Yale Law Journal* 2005 Vol. 115, p.356

have the right to remove and replace the directors of the company. Originally used by some of America's most established wealthy families, PTCs are becoming increasingly popular in offshore jurisdictions as well.

PTCs in various jurisdictions, while subject to varying degrees of reporting and regulation, are increasingly affordable and available and may now provide a useful option to families of all wealth categories.

In some highly competitive offshore trust jurisdictions, such as Singapore or New Zealand, trusts may come with an "embedded PTC," a dedicated private trust company set up at the same time as the offshore trust. This combination of trust and PTC can be a very convenient approach to private asset structuring and can be particularly useful for a wealthy family seeking an integrated approach to offshore structuring and protections for its assets.

ALLOCATING ASSETS TO TRUSTS

After establishing a trust or other asset structuring vehicle, the assets appropriate for that vehicle's overall purpose need to be selected and the transfers made on a tax-efficient basis into the chosen vehicle.

For example, assets allocated to a trust whose income is to be distributed to elderly members of the family who are seeking income on a regular basis, could include fixed income or other products which are income-generating and low risk. On the other hand, assets bearing higher risk and with a greater potential for long term capital growth— and lesser expectations for short term income generation—could be better placed into a trust for a second or third generation.

By thus allocating different types of assets to trusts with different purposes, capital can accumulate on an efficient basis over many years in the latter case, while paying out as needed in the former.

STRATEGIC DEBT

The use of debt in a family wealth plan is not limited to the use of leverage to enhance financial returns in a portfolio or to extend the reach of an operating business. It can also be used to shift values between family trusts and other asset structuring vehicles. In this role, strategic debt can shift economic value away from any entity which may be exposed to litigation, wealth or inheritance tax.

In addition, strategic debt can be used to fund diversification in a family's business and financial asset holdings. Leveraging a family business holding, without burdening that debt with excessive covenants, can lead to a position where the family has some debt, but also has more assets in trust which can grow and protect family wealth in the most tax-effective manner.

"TAGGING" ASSETS THROUGH MULTIPLE OWNERSHIP

Another kind of financial structuring which can affect wealth preservation is to share ownership of an asset between multiple family members. This "tagging" of assets as family property can be particularly valuable to protect them from consideration as a marital asset in case of divorce or other marital dispute.

In some cases, strategic debt and asset-tagging can work together to create a double layer of protection for attractive physical family assets such as property, artwork, or other tangible assets. By dividing ownership between family members and attaching debt, the equity value of the asset can drop substantially, thereby reducing its attractiveness in a marital or legal dispute, possibly attracting less wealth tax and reducing the likelihood that the asset would be lost in any dispute.

THE TRUSTEE ROLE AND RELATIONSHIP

Every trust is administered by a trustee—either in the form of a company (often managed by a professional or corporate trustee) or an individual charged with the administration of the trust. The trustee, in addition to complying with the terms and conditions of the trust documents, also needs to act in full compliance with the rules and regulations of the local trust jurisdiction, and to respect fiduciary obligations to act in the best interests of the beneficiaries at all times. Trustees usually give full consideration to, although are not legally bound by, the settler's letter of wishes as well.

Some of the key roles that trustees can play are formal and defined by trusts and estates legislation and legal precedent. These may include prudent investment guidelines, transparent reporting obligations, fiduciary obligations, keeping separate accounts, and other requirements for good administrative performance. In discharging the obligations of the role of trustee, an individual must ensure that all of these basic functions are performed efficiently and correctly.

The relationships between trustees and beneficiaries are shaped by the personalities of the individuals concerned, the history of their relationship, the relationship of their predecessors, and by the terms and conditions of the trusts and letters of wishes.

Although each is unique, there are a number of common categories into which trustee–beneficiary relationships can fall.

In some cases, the trustee may be a revered older figure who has been with the family for many years and acts as a mentor to the beneficiary. The trustee may be a trusted general advisor who provides the necessary impartial support and advice as a respected equal. Or the dealings between beneficiary and trustee may be on a more professional basis, with the latter providing informed advice and support to the beneficiary and trust alike. One step down from this role as engaged trustee is the effective administrator, whose role it is to simply ensure that the trust is administered in accordance with the original intent and on a timely basis without any other, more personal, contact with the trustee.

In some cases, relations may be even less amicable and the trustee is merely tolerated as a bureaucrat with whom the beneficiary may not have a warm or successful relationship. In an even more negative scenario, differences of opinion between trustee and beneficiary may even lead to open conflict. Such adversarial relationships, which often descend into litigation, can be damaging to both parties and may reflect a failing on both sides to foster a proper approach to the effective administration of the trust.

THE GOOD TRUSTEE

Apart from pursuing best practice in fund management, decision-making and distribution policy, a good trustee is someone with the ability and willingness to build the trustee-beneficiary relationship by educating the beneficiaries on their rights and responsibilities under the trust through regular and open communication. The trustee will ensure that he (or she) and the beneficiaries keep up to date on developments that may affect their respective roles. They will plan succession in these roles and can even help to prepare beneficiaries in any coming future generations.

TYRANNY OF THE TRUSTEE

Trustees have an enormous amount of power. Often, beneficiaries do not. Given the human potential for discord between any two individuals and the risk of a trustee acting in an arbitrary fashion, it may be advisable to select more than one trustee in more than one jurisdiction to oversee the family's financial affairs, particularly when the funds in trust are substantial.

It is also essential to ensure that the relevant mechanisms are in place (and recorded within documents) to remove trustees if future beneficiaries are, with cause, dissatisfied with the trustee's performance. Not only does this remove the risk of a single trustee creating a difficult relationship with members of the family, it allows both trustees and family members to compare different approaches. This, in turn, increases the knowledge and performance of all concerned. By sharing experience between a diversified set of trustees, the family remain more at the heart of any trust issues and become more expert in their management.

OVERLY DEMANDING BENEFICIARIES

Problems in the trustee–beneficiary relationship can come from either side of the table. Just as an overly punctilious or domineering trustee can create difficulties, a beneficiary who is too demanding, unaware of the risks and obligations placed on a trustee, or ignorant of, and indifferent to, the precise instructions to the trustee from the settler's documentation, can also create substantial problems.

This may be particularly pertinent if the trustee becomes a focus for rebellion and poor behavior on the part of a beneficiary.

THE GOOD BENEFICIARY

All elements of a family strategy will need to underline the importance of understanding how to be a "good" beneficiary, just as trustees need to understand what is required of a "good" trustee.

A good beneficiary's approach will include having a clear understanding of the trustee's obligations and liabilities, the rules of income distribution and access to capital, and of all relevant documentation. There will be frequent communication and regular meetings with the trustee. The beneficiary will take all steps to avoid conflict, knowing the mutual benefits that will accrue from a constructive relationship.

CONSTANT VIGILANCE

Once the individual components of a tax management and asset structuring approach have been set up, the functioning of the whole system needs to be tested under different operating assumptions. The impact of a divorce, family discord, a change in tax laws, and other potentially wealth-threatening situations need to be tested to ensure that the current system is as robust and effective as possible.

BE PREPARED

One test that should be performed at the outset, and reviewed annually for any required amendment, is the potential response to a tax audit by fiscal authorities.

Most wealthy families, and particularly those in the higher wealth categories, make inviting targets for revenue authorities looking for a good return on the investigative resources invested. From this simple perspective, the larger the family wealth, the larger also is the potential for any tax settlement.

Families should be constantly vigilant to ensure that there is no breaching of trust and corporate status, and that there are no documents drafted or retained which would lead to even the smallest room for suspicion that the necessary trust disciplines are not being maintained.

17. ESTATE PLANNING AND THE ETHICAL WILL

By all accounts, the wealth passing from one generation to another in coming years will be unprecedented in scale. Some estimates place the amount at up to US$40 trillion over the first half of this century. This wave of inheritance will take place in almost every part of the world, with many large entrepreneurial businesses established in the wake of the Second World War, the oil shock of 1973, or the collapse of the USSR in 1989, coming up for transfer, as the founding generation dies out or retires from active management.

Overseeing the successful transfer of this gigantic new wave of wealth will be an unfamiliar challenge for many newly wealthy families, who may have little or no precedent to guide them. In addition, a substantial portion of this wealth will soon be passing into the hands of a third generation of the family, often the critical generation in determining the family's long-term wealth stature.

Wealthy families have very good reason to be concerned about this challenge. Research conducted by Roy Williams and Vic Preisser shows that a high proportion of wealth transfers fail to achieve their objectives.

Only 15% of these failures are attributed to poor estate and tax planning, or incompetent investment advice. A further 60% are the result of family disputes and breakdowns. The remaining 25% have been accounted for by a lack of preparation of heirs for the responsibility of inheritance.[1]

PREPARING TO GIVE AND TO RECEIVE

Being fully organized for an inter-generational transfer means far more than just having a current will. Full preparation requires assembling all relevant documents, ensuring sufficient liquidity to address all relevant claims, loan payments and taxes, and, most importantly, fully preparing the individuals to inherit the wealth that will be theirs, directly or indirectly.

---

[1] Roy Williams and Vic Preisser, *Preparing Heirs: Five Steps to a Successful Transition of Family Wealth and Values*, Robert D. Reed Publishers, 2003.

Wealth transfer across multiple generations brings with it separate challenges for both the grantors and the beneficiaries involved in the process. For the granting generation, there is a challenge of trust and estate planning, of wealth management, and the laying of a foundation of values that can provide sufficient strength to support and carry forward family wealth without harming or unduly burdening the lives of their beneficiaries.

At the same time, the heir or heiress has a different challenge—to develop the specific skills necessary to inherit wealth and also to develop the individual attributes necessary to live a privileged life in a manner consistent with the long term preservation and enhancement of family values which they must learn and, in turn, pass on to their own children.

Preparation of affairs beyond the will: In every country there is a prescribed legal process to be followed after a death. This process, called "probate" in many English-speaking countries, is the process through which the court ensures that all rules are observed, all debts and taxes are paid in the correct order, and that all local laws have been followed with regard to the winding up of the deceased's economic affairs.

One important step in facilitating an executor's role is to assemble, in one place, all of the relevant documents regarding the ownership and transfer of family wealth. A copy of each document should also be kept in a separate, secure location.

The wills, trust deeds, share ownership certificates, bank statements, property deeds, mortgage documents, life insurance documents, birth certificates, business records, loan documents, tax filings, contracts, agreements, and other documents of importance should be indexed, filed and easily retrievable as soon as they are needed. Included in these agreements should be any contracts and nomination forms for executors and other individuals concerned in the winding up of the deceased's affairs.

Any specific requests for funeral arrangements, communications, letters, and an ethical will, if one has been prepared, should be included in the documents and the relevant parties informed of their whereabouts.

These documents should be kept in a safe place or in a deposit box or fire-proof safe in the office of a trusted advisor or lawyer. It is also essential that the location of the key to any deposit box is made known to a number of family members!

A Tale of Lost Wealth

One British entrepreneur in Asia built a fortune through ownership of land and palm oil refineries in Malaysia and Indonesia after the Second World War. Upon his death, his family was unable to locate any of the documents relating to the purchase of his substantial Indonesian holdings.

These documents had, quite possibly, been stored carefully by the entrepreneur in a protected location no one else had been made aware of. As a result, a fortune which would, by now, be worth many, many millions of dollars, has never been found.

Necessary liquidity: There may be specific costs associated with death which could best be prepared in advance: life insurance policies may be required to cover death duties, outstanding loans may need to be paid off, and trusts resettled or equalized with cash payments.

A wealthy family should do its best to ensure, in advance of the death of a family member, that these costs are minimized and are covered to the maximum extent possible with liquid funds.

ADVANCE PLANNING

As we have already seen, the amount of tax taken by the government as a death duty or as a gift tax varies enormously from country to country, and even from one time period to another within the same country. Rates can vary from zero to more than 50%. Hefty estate duties or gift taxes, imposed on two successive generational transfers, can reduce a large fortune to a small fraction of its original size.

Two cross-generational transfers at a 50% tax rate can, by simple mathematics, reduce a family fortune by 75% before any investment gains or income distributions are taken into account.

In addition, in some countries, death duties can vary enormously based upon the relationship of the beneficiary to the benefactor. Death duties on property passing from parent to child may be taxed at a small fraction of the rate levied when money or property is left to an unrelated beneficiary.

Management of these sensitive and important events—asset transfer, death, and succession plans—will benefit, legally and financially, from thoughtful preparation long in advance of a family member's reaching old age. Some trusts, for example, will attract death duty unless settled at least five or seven years in advance of the death of the settler.

NO PREDICTABLE TIMING

It is essential that a wealthy family be prepared for the potential death of family members, which can come at any time. The lack of predictability of the timing of death, along with the high tax costs of imperfect preparation, requires planning to begin as soon as possible.

> If it be not now, yet it will come: the readiness is all.
>
> William Shakespeare, *Hamlet*

An unanticipated death can have a major impact on family wealth if tax-efficient inheritance structures are not fully in place, succession plans have not been developed, death duties are not readily funded by an insurance settlement or available liquidity, and if assets are incapable of being divided efficiently between individuals or generations.

Very few people are fully prepared for the business of death, in part because it is easy to defer or to deny through an unwillingness to face up to the inevitable, and to the indefinite.

Many philosophers have pondered over the impact on human lives if we knew in advance exactly when and where we would die. What difference would it make to the way we live and the decisions we make during our lifetimes? For most of us, it might well have a positive impact on our preparation for an already inevitable end.

Perhaps it would be a valuable exercise to initiate a test to see how prepared a family would be for a death in the family today, or in six months' time. Would the appropriate trusts, wills, ethical wills, instructions, and preparations for succession be ready? Are the individuals who would benefit financially from the death fully prepared for their inheritance?

NO PREDICTABLE ORDER

There is no guarantee that the eldest family member, or even a member of the eldest generation, will die first. Accidents and disease can strike the young as unexpectedly as the old.

The chances that a child may die before its parents are sufficiently high to recommend that every member of every generation should have a will to reflect this possibility, as it should take into account the possibility of a married couple dying together.

A final self-evident observation is that it is those left behind after a death who suffer the most, emotionally and financially, and who will bear the consequences of the preparations—or lack thereof—of the deceased.

The burden of dealing with a badly prepared estate could be particularly painful and difficult at a time when family members are already coping with the emotional sadness associated with the loss of a loved member of the family.

> A man's dying is more the survivors' affair than his own.
>
> Thomas Mann, *The Magic Mountain*

THE ETHICAL WILL

Consistent with the notion of wealth extending beyond the purely material, the ethical will is a document which transfers family history, wisdom, values, and experience across generational boundaries.

Ethical wills have no prescribed form or content but, very often, the expressions of love, comfort, and concern can be more precious than gold to the children and grandchildren of the testator.

COMPLETION AND CLOSURE

Making a statement at the end of a life which summarizes and underscores the meaning of that life is gaining momentum in Western circles and gives individuals a chance to turn their inevitable deaths into more meaningful experiences for the living.

Reflecting on their lives, the writers of ethical wills may find a great degree of peace and happiness in the experience of drafting such a document, reaching a final understanding of relationships, seeing the meaning of repeated historical patterns in the family and reliving positive life experiences. This reflection and understanding can lead to the satisfactory closure—for both the author and the audience—of issues that might otherwise have been left unresolved or incomplete.

In the past, the content of an ethical will was captured in letters to be sent or read out after death, or embedded in the testamentary documents themselves. These days, some people also choose to leave ethical wills and messages through video, CD, or other formats.

LIFE AFTER DEATH

The reading or viewing of an ethical will can have an enormous impact on those caught up in the emotions of death and change in the family. A statement of values, memories, and hopes from beyond the grave can have an enormous beneficial impact on the living, perhaps lasting an entire lifetime, and even across many generations.

A LONG TRADITION

In many parts of the world, death has always presented the opportunity to sum up a life in a way which creates meaning, influence, and insight for others long after the funeral ceremonies are over. Ethical wills are thus no more than a new Western version of traditions that extend back many thousands of years in other cultures and in other places. The Jewish *Zevaoth* reflects this long tradition. Among the better-known examples is the following, by Judah ben Saul ibn Tibbon, in 1190:

> Avoid bad society, make thy books thy companions, let thy book-cases and shelves be thy gardens and pleasure-grounds. Pluck the fruit that grows therein, gather the roses, the spices and the myrrh. If thy soul be

satiate and weary, change from garden to garden, from furrow to furrow, from sight to sight. Then will thy desire renew itself, and thy soul be satisfied with delight.[2]

In medieval Japan, well-educated scholars, samurai warriors, and aristocrats would prepare a death poem, a kind of ethical will which captured, in a few brief words the essence of the life concluded, and the essence of human life itself, as a final message to those left behind.

By passing on experience, insights, family histories, and personal memories through such documents, individual family members can contribute substantially to the depth and quality of the lives of their own descendants.

NO SET FORM

There is no set form for an ethical will. Some are brief, handwritten epistles containing only distilled individual experience or the most important of private messages and citing the most esteemed of personal values. Others are entire volumes long and contain a detailed recounting of family history, address in depth individual perspectives on life, death, truth, and religion, and may contain messages for specific members of the family.

Some individuals prepare more than one such will, preferring to customize messages for different audiences—for the family itself, a family business, or a charitable foundation—to guide the future of the different institutions and relevant individuals. In some cases, these wishes and approaches can be incorporated into the legal will or guiding trust documentation as well.

For those employing a video or other visually recorded format, drafters may prefer to prepare an ethical will when they are in the prime of life, to be remembered as they were at their physical best, rather than waiting for their last days to cement a memory in future generations of them as they are aged, ill, or dying.

---

[2] M. a. Israel Abrahams, *Chapters on Jewish Literature*, IndyPublish.com, March 2005.

NO PRESCRIBED TIME OF DELIVERY

There is also no set time as to when an ethical will should be drafted or delivered. Many are drafted towards the end of life, as part of the process of closure and completion for the dying. Others seek to capture their thoughts when they are still in the prime of life, or at significant moments such as marriage, the birth of a child or grandchild, or at retirement.

Ethical wills can also be read or viewed at different times: some before the testator's death; others at the funeral or at other family gatherings. Some families may choose to read an ethical will on more than one occasion—the anniversary of a death, the ascendancy of a family member to a full-time position in a family business, marriage, the hiring of a new member of a family business or foundation—to share and reinforce family histories, values, and memories.

RULES OF THE GAME

Whatever the form, length, or timing of delivery of an ethical will, a few rules of the game are worth noting with regard to its content:

Stay positive: Vindictive or critical messages can create embarrassment, sadness, or anger that can endure across generation. All of us have much that is valuable to share; critical messages or encumbering demands can obscure or stain that positive legacy, leaving behind only bitter memories. When a positive message would be for more appropriate.

Make your medium last: If an ethical will is to last across generations, the preparation of a written document may require considerable thought. If the will is to be handwritten, the paper should be of high quality, acid-free, and, if possible, placed in a protective binder. Perhaps to mark the occasion, a special fountain pen can be used which can be passed on to future generations. It should contain indelible ink, and, needless to say, the handwriting should be as neat and legible as possible.

Put yourself in the place of the audience: It may be useful for the testator to review the ethical will from the perspective of its intended recipients. Has it included sufficient explanation of the testator's background, history, and views? Is it written or delivered in clear and simple language? Will it have the desired impact on its intended audience, both now and in the future?

Address the most important issues: Much of what an individual has learned in life and can usefully leave behind is the knowledge gained in adverse circumstances. It has been said that we learn the most from our worst experiences, as the best experiences only confirm what we already knew. By addressing the deepest issues, the drafters of an ethical will can ensure that individual and family wisdom, painfully acquired, can be transferred to those who can most benefit from its application.

THE INTEGRATED WILL

Unlike a traditional legal will, which only specifies the distribution of material assets after death, an integrated will combines the content of three documents—the traditional will, the ethical will, and the living will-in a single, comprehensive approach.

The living will addresses the decisions to be made and actions taken in the case of incapacitation, severe brain injury, or other extreme physical condition before death. It also addresses the issue of organ donation and other aspects of dealing with the physical body after death not addressed in the other two documents.

Integrating these wills into a single document ensures that the individual and the family will be well served, no matter how and when death or incapacitation arrives.

18. RISKS TO FAMILY WEALTH AND WELLBEING

Much of any strategy is about reducing risks and taking advantage of opportunities. In many cases, the two are present at the same time in the same idea, event or interaction.

By separating out the idea of risk management, and by designing and implementing a thoughtful approach to risk management across the individual elements of strategy, the long term value of the overall strategy will be much improved. A structured and consistent approach to risk management can enable the wealthy family to identify priority issues and address them long before they ripen into real and costly disasters.

By understanding and applying the principles of risk management to each of the specific principles of strategy for a wealthy family, the likelihood of preserving future family wealth and wellbeing is far greater.

IDENTIFICATION OF RISKS

In the 2007 Family Office Exchange survey of 40 ultra-high-net-worth families referred to in Chapter 1, ten priority risk concerns were highlighted. In order of importance to the families interviewed, these concerns were:

- family legacy
- family governance and decision-making
- family relationships
- investment performance
- family business leadership
- fiduciary exposure
- family dynamics in business
- family reputation
- personal ownership responsibilities
- legal exposure.

Other risks identified in the survey included asset diversification, financial leverage, personal security and privacy, personal health and wellness, physical asset protection, and public equity concentration.

Any one of these risks is enough to destroy family wealth or family unity, with worst-case examples taking down both at the same time.

In Singapore, one prominent wealthy family fulfilled the "riches to rags in three generations" scenario as a result of bitter and protracted public wrangling. Not only did the legal fees from its protracted squabbling amount to several millions of dollars, the many business assets also suffered, causing the eventual break-up of the family and substantial diminution in the asset base of the remaining independent units.

Just as the true definition of family wealth extends beyond the purely financial to areas of family and individual wellbeing, the risks against which a family needs to be protected include those threatening more than just the financial assets of the family.

RISKS TO FAMILY UNITY AND INDIVIDUAL FAMILY RELATIONSHIPS

The greatest risks to the preservation of family wealth often arise from dispute and discord within the family itself. Family schisms can destroy a family, both financially and psychologically; litigation, forced asset sales, lack of cooperation in investment and business operations, and the break-up of family businesses can add financial loss to the emotional misery of a family's internal discord.

Risks of particular concern to wealthy families can also include disagreements and division between family members or family units over the long term direction and financial plans for the family as a whole.

In the absence of a strong and cohering family vision, agreed set of values, and strong leadership, a whole array of personal, professional, and financial disputes can arise that can tear apart even the oldest and best-intentioned of families.

PERSONAL RISK

Substantial family wealth can increase the need for investment in personal security—whether desired or not—especially if the family finds itself mentioned on a local or international "rich list." The inevitable (and usually unwanted) media attention that comes with

---

The Gucci family—grand discord *a l'Italiano*

The glamour and prestige of more than one fashion house masks a turbulent set of family and professional relationships. Although the movie *The Devil Wears Prada* depicted a high-fashion world of intrigue and back-stabbing, the reality of the Gucci saga is even more dramatic than any fictional account could ever reasonably represent.

Following the development of the famous brand from its establishment in 1923 by Guccio Gucci, the business entered two generations of discord and infighting. Guccio's children, and their children, fell into such disarray that there were numerous lawsuits, reports of tax evasion to tax authorities resulting in the jailing of one family member, corporate intrigue, and, eventually, the murder of Maurizio Gucci, onetime head of the family enterprise, in a plot that involved his wife's astrologer.

As a result of family chaos, the famous business rose and fell through numerous dramatic swings in fortune, before passing out of family control; first into the hands of Investcorp, a private equity business based in London and the Gulf, and then on to the public markets before becoming part of the business empire of Francois Pinault in France. Along the way, it made billions of dollars, but very little of the money made ever found its way into the founding family's coffers.

---

such celebrity will increase the family's exposure to robbery, kidnapping, burglary, extortion, and other related crimes.

At the peak of his playing career, Michael Jordan, whose private wealth from his stellar athletic career and related product endorsements is estimated to be several hundred million dollars, was reportedly not able to remain in a public place for more than 30 minutes before gathering crowds could create security issues in his immediate vicinity.

Without necessarily succumbing to paranoia over the issue, a high quality program addressing physical security can be a major contributor toward the minimization of risk and the maximization of family health and happiness—and hence enhancing family wealth in the broadest sense.

The scope and scale of personal risks will vary enormously from one country to another, and from one family to another. Life in Russia, Colombia, Brazil, the Philippines, or Italy for a high profile wealthy family will be very different from a life in Switzerland, Singapore, or Sweden for a quiet family staying out of the headlines.

One of the world's leading security firms has recommended to its wealthy clients to be attentive to a list of essential areas:

Road travel: Every year, more than one million people die, and a further 50 million are injured, in road accidents, many of which could be avoided. Some 85% of these accidents take place in developing countries where there is poor, if any, emergency medical assistance available.

Simple precautions with regard to traveling safely on the roads, particularly in emerging markets, can reduce one of the greatest risks to family safety. Ensuring that cars and drivers used in foreign lands or unknown cities are of an acceptable standard is both important and sensible. The deaths of Princess Diana and Dodi Al-Fayed in Paris in 1997 are but one example of the tragedy that can be avoided by simple actions such as the careful selection of drivers and the use of safety belts.

Drivers employed by the family, as well as family members themselves, can undertake defensive driver training that will prepare them to avoid the single-car or multiple-vehicle accidents that can happen to anyone at any time.

Safety of family residences and other premises: Annual security reviews of the residences, offices, garages, and other physical premises frequented by family members can also be a key part of a family's risk management policy. CCTV systems, burglar and intruder alarms, front door identification procedures, lighting, and other aspects of risk reduction should be considered.

As well as the infrastructure, practices and habits of family members also need to be reviewed. For a single woman living alone, for example, something as simple as having keys ready in hand rather than having to rummage for them in a handbag at the front door can reduce the risk of an unwanted incident.

The use of private security firms; the installation of high quality 24-hour security systems; living in gated communities or in properties well shielded from intruders by walls and other protective barriers; even keeping a large dog at home can help to protect the wealthy family from many of the risks attached to substantial wealth.

Another option available to wealthy families is insurance cover which includes kidnapping and ransom policies to provide advice, ransom payments in cash if needed, and support for the police in any negotiation and recovery effort.

Country risk analysis: The range of country-specific risks should be assessed before traveling or investing abroad. Kidnapping, for example, is a greater concern in the Philippines, Latin America, and Italy than it is in the United Kingdom, United States or Switzerland. Murder rates are much higher in Russia or Colombia than they are in Austria, Switzerland, and Scandinavia.

Back-up systems: In some well-organized wealthy families, every family member is provided with a contact number in case of emergency anywhere in the world. Support systems such as emergency healthcare, medical evacuation, and legal representation need to be considered to ensure that the unwanted and unforeseen can be dealt with as quickly and efficiently as possible, even in the most harrowing circumstances.

DATA SECURITY

The area of data security embraces both privacy and financial security measures. The details of family wealth and its distribution, the issues of tax and inheritance planning and other details of a wealthy family's private life may require an extra layer of security.

In addition to ensuring that its electronic security measures are fully up to date and that passwords are changed regularly, the family may well need to consider the security of physical data and documents as well. The use of safety deposit boxes, the fireproof storage of critical documents, data and correspondence retention policies, and other such measures should be reviewed and updated on a regular basis.

Expert security firms can provide "penetration testing" and advice on data security, virus protection, business continuity, and back-up and server procedures as needed.

A HISTORY OF CONFLICT: THE HAVES AND HAVE NOTS

Across the world, and at all levels, the gap between the rich and the poor is widening to increasingly dangerous proportions. In a world where the top 1% of the population controls nearly half of the world's wealth and resources, two billion people live on less than US$2 per day.

Over the centuries, there have been many rebellions against the wealthy classes by the poor, from the Peasants' Revolt in England in 1381, to the French Revolution in the eighteenth century, to race riots against affluent Chinese in Indonesia in 1998.

In India in 2007, villagers who were unable to irrigate their fields for lack of water attacked wealthy families who had swimming pools and other visible symbols of wealth and privilege. In China, too, there have been many demonstrations and acts of civil disobedience in protest against the widening gap between the rich and the poor in that booming economy.

While not a significant problem for wealthy families in most countries at present, the longer term risk created by this wealth disparity may well create financial, physical and psychological risk for the wealthy family in the future.

PROTECTING PRIVACY

Even in the absence of a single high profile event that focuses the media's attention, outside interest in the affairs of a wealthy family can create an unpleasant atmosphere within and around the family.

Oprah Winfrey is well known for her insistence on strict lifetime confidentiality agreements with employees, as are royal families and high profile musicians. One famous English popular musician even had privacy clauses built into the draft agreements of his purchase of his residential property in order to cut off, in advance, any reference to its location, its price, and any other personal affairs that might have surfaced during the negotiation and purchase.

It may well be worthwhile for the leaders of a very wealthy family listing a business, or appearing on a rich list for the first time, to appoint a high-quality PR firm on a small retainer to advise on how best to deal with unwanted media coverage once the initial interest has subsided.

One wealthy Asian family, "caught" by the *Forbes* magazine team as a result of the public flotation of a formerly low key privately owned business, hired a PR firm to deflect the flurry of interest from journalists, bankers, and brokers and enable the family to resume, as quickly as possible, its previous low profile existence.

HIGH VALUE OF A LOW PROFILE

However, although these specific approaches to reduce personal risk can be necessary, the most valuable response to personal security risk may simply be to maintain a low profile, reducing awareness of the family and diminishing the likelihood of any of its members becoming a target for media or criminal interest.

Even the employment of bodyguards, ostensibly an investment in risk reduction, can actually increase risk by raising the family's profile. While necessary for some wealthy families living in high risk countries, in most geographies the presence of bodyguards may be more likely to highlight wealthy families as valuable targets than to provide protection.

PRIORITIZATION AND FOCUS

Not all risks are of equal magnitude at any given point, and the greatest risks a family faces will change over time. As with any strategy in which resource allocation is one of the most critical activities, the identification of priorities is the first step toward effective risk management.

> "You cannot put out a house on fire with a cup of water."

In ensuring that a family has taken the right decisions in a few, very high priority areas, family leaders will be able to develop and implement approaches to eliminate the greatest dangers, or at least to mitigate substantially any potential damage.

The thought, effort, time, and external resource applied to the problem must be sufficient to achieve the desired result. As the Chinese saying goes: "You cannot put out a house on fire with a cup of water."

ANTICIPATION

By seeing future risks as clearly as possible, and acting with that view in mind, far-sighted family leaders will be able to react quickly and effectively to reduce the likelihood of a risk turning into a disaster, or to develop and implement an effective response once an unavoidable risk event has occurred.

Of course, not all risks can be anticipated. Marcus Aurelius once described life as being "more like the wrestler's art than the dancer's"; having to respond to challenges—expected and otherwise—as and when they arise, rather than following a series of predetermined and neatly choreographed steps.

Even if specific risks and challenges cannot be foreseen, individuals, advisors, and systems can be prepared to deal with crises yet to emerge. For example, a structured approach to family organization and leadership, with a specific dispute resolution process, will reduce the risks of divisions, disputes, and discord within the family, particularly as that family grows and diversifies across generations.

HIGH QUALITY PEOPLE

As with business, investment, organization, and the family itself, the human element is always a constant source of high accomplishment, or of great concern, in a family's future.

> "You cannot soar like an eagle, if you fly with turkeys."

One of the greatest sources of risk in a family wealth strategy, or in any part of the family's eco-system, is the quality of the individuals involved in the effort. By constantly striving to attract, inform, inspire, and retain good people, the entire family eco-system will improve substantially the odds of the family becoming successfully wealthy over future generations. As the saying goes: "You cannot soar like an eagle, if you fly with turkeys."

Careful selection and integration: Finding good people is always a challenge. By spending the extra time to find the best possible individuals, to define the correct role, to ensure smooth integration, to address performance issues and take care of important individual and systemic issues on a timely basis, families can create a team which will, by the very nature of its individual and collective quality, achieve far more and fall prey to far fewer risks.

Before bringing any new person into the family organization or business, a very thorough check on the individual's background is advisable and can be one of those small investments that pay off enormously by avoiding the heavy financial and personal costs involved in hiring, and then removing, the wrong person.

CLEAR ALLOCATION OF RESPONSIBILITIES

Once a path to risk reduction has been identified, allocating responsibilities to implement the chosen strategy, and following up to ensure the selected actions have had the desired effect, is required. Without accountability, and a timeline to match, even the best of ideas will have no real value.

DIVERSIFICATION

By diversifying activities, families can reduce the risk of excessive reliance on the advice of a single manager, can reduce the possible damage from a concentrated asset base, and can put in place a conservative approach to multi-generational ownership (and stewardship) of family assets. Such an approach to risk diversification across the board will decrease very substantially the likelihood of any single cataclysmic event destroying family wealth.

APPLICATION OF BEST PRACTICE AND LESSONS LEARNED

Many of the most important insights of risk management are captured in such simple homespun homilies as "an ounce of prevention is worth a pound of cure" and "don't put all your eggs in one basket."

Whether reflected in splitting a family into five parts and sending different sons to different parts of Europe, or trimming a large concentrated single-stock position, or in employing more than one investment manager or trustee, wise family leaders will be taking and implementing decisions for their family future with the proven wisdom of the past firmly in mind.

"ARMAGEDDON" RISK MANAGEMENT

In addition to the specific actions mentioned above, some Category III and IV families are taking steps to ensure that they, and some proportion of their wealth, are safe in every possible scenario. Such measures can include the preparation of a "bolt hole" which is agriculturally self-sustaining, well equipped with fresh drinking water, safe from a mass influx of refugees, and reachable within 24 hours of travel. For some, this may include access to a landing strip for a private aircraft.

These preparations may also include having liquid funds or gold in one or more locations for use in a possible meltdown of global financial systems.

At a less critical phase, a small proportion of family wealth may be allocated to a dedicated "safety trust" which is invested in risk-free or low risk, income-generating investments, assuring the family's wellbeing no matter what happens in the larger and riskier portfolio investments, and even in the world's financial markets.

REDUCING FAMILY RISK

There is perhaps no greater response to the full array of risks to family wealth and wellbeing than good family values and a clear family strategy. The benefits of strong family values, careful preparation of the next generation, and an attention to risk management in all of its various forms, can lay the groundwork for a long history of successful family wealth preservation, growth and enjoyment.

As stated at the beginning of this chapter, many families fail to preserve their wealth simply because they fail to address the issues related to wealth preservation in a careful and systematic fashion. By addressing these issues directly, one of the greatest risks to wealth preservation has already been removed and the likelihood of remaining successfully wealthy greatly enhanced.

FAMILY WEALTH MANAGEMENT

Diversify assets and access the best investments and investment managers through a formal process of asset allocation and wealth management

19. THE WEALTH MANAGEMENT PROCESS

At the heart of any strategy to protect and grow family wealth lies a need to invest the family's financial assets in a careful, disciplined and profitable manner.

While organizing the family and putting in place the structures and practices to protect wealth are important contributions to a long-term wealth strategy, without a successful approach to financial investment these approaches, in themselves, are not enough to preserve family wealth across generations.

In setting out an approach to the successful management of financial assets, there is much to be learned from successfully wealthy families, and also from the endowments, institutions, and managers who have demonstrated a multi-decade record of successful investment.

These more broadly sourced lessons and best-practice examples reflect aspects of a model for successful investing which is set out in Figure 4.1.

Figure 4.1 Family Wealth Management

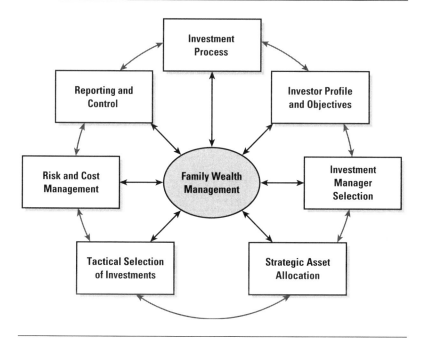

Creating wealth does not need to stop at the first generation, nor does it end with the sale of a family business or other major asset.

The creation of wealth can be a seamless process, eliding from the ownership and management of operating assets or property to the ownership and management of a fully diversified portfolio of attractive financial holdings.

For many wealthy families, the creation of a second fortune through the successful management of the wealth once created, adding substantially to the pool of family financial assets, is an opportunity to write another act in the family's economic history, building a new fortune on the foundations of the old. For the very gifted at money management, this second act may result in wealth creation which surpasses even that created by the family patriarch or founder of the family business.

Yet staying rich, and growing financial wealth successfully over an extended timeframe, is no easy task. The skills needed to manage a diverse pool of financial assets are different from those required to manage or sell a family business or other significant concentrated asset.

Managing money is a complex task which will require mastery of a process that begins with an understanding of the investor's personal profile and the overall investment objectives and ends with a tight reporting and control approach which ensures that the original objectives are being met throughout all stages of that process.

Successful family wealth management requires an understanding of all asset classes and the addressing of a whole set of integrated elements.

Pursuit of a pre-determined set of investment goals, within the policies and parameters established by the family, can best take place in a framework (see Figure 4.1) which systematically addresses every stage of the investment process—and keeps the process on track to accomplish its original objectives.

THE INVESTMENT PROCESS

It is a common saying in the legal profession that "good process makes good law." While there is no sure path to great riches from each and every investment, good investment process can go a long way toward eliminating risk, capturing opportunity, and combining analysis and judgment for the best possible investment decisions in a defined sector or within a defined portfolio.

Virtually every successful investor or fund manager, be it pension, endowment, private equity, fund of funds, broker, or wealthy family, focuses a high degree of effort on defining and refining the best possible investment process. Over time, a well-defined and well-disciplined investment process is far more likely to lead to a good result than a random, intuitive, or relationship-driven approach.

There are many approaches to investment process adopted by different institutions and wealth managers, although all of them will require the presentation of information—financial, strategic, and organizational—in a disciplined format. In addition, a due-diligence review to verify and better understand the information presented, and a formal review and decision-making process will also be included.

> A well-defined and well-disciplined investment process is far more likely to lead to a good result than a random, intuitive or relationship-driven approach.

THE BEST-PRACTICE PROCESS

The key to following best practices starts with having a formal process. Far too often, investment decisions are made on a loosely defined, *ad hoc* basis, with heavy influence from sell-side investment brokers and banks, personal relationships, and a high degree of investor subjectivity.

A well-conceived investment process should include excellent strategy, high-quality governance, and fully informed decision-making. The result should be an investment process that is phased, analytical, systematically skeptical, and, importantly, subject to the discipline of documentation.

Each step needs to be subjected to an ultimate decision test: "What is best for the portfolio, given the strategic framework?" Answers will require comprehensive analysis, a determination of fit with the portfolio strategy, and careful monitoring through post-investment reporting tools.

The basic framework can be tailored to family needs, but without losing anything in the customization, an additional process which should add to, not detract from, the best-practice approach adopted as part of the central strategy.

TAILORED TO THE FAMILY'S NEEDS

There is no "right" approach to wealth management. One size does not fit all. Yet whatever process is adopted, it should, in every case, meet the family's objectives and ensure that as much intellectual rigor and business judgment as possible are brought to bear on investment decisions. The selected investment process must be clearly specified and have full family support.

Tailoring an investment process to suit a family's situation may require changing the resources allocated, balancing the mix of direct and indirect (through fund managers) investments, and involving members of different generations in understanding the family's investment strategies.

In all cases, the investment process must be tailored to meet the family's unique financial and psychological situation. The risks taken with family money, the managers chosen, the reporting formats, and individual family roles in the investment process can all create either additional unity or unwanted discord.

THE INVESTMENT GUIDE

One sign of an organized wealth management process within a Family Office or a family itself is the existence of an investment guide or fully fledged investment manual which describes how the process works. That investment guide will spell out each step of the investment process, from initial statement of profile and objectives through to final investment decision-making and follow-up.

Such a guide will usually set out the following step-by-step approach describing the objectives for each stage and providing templates for each:

- family vision and values
- investment profile and objectives
- investment process
- investment parameters
- first-stage filter and scorecard
- second-stage filter and scorecard
- due diligence procedures (tailored for the type of investment)
- final decision-making procedures
- follow-up reporting and control
- criteria for sale or liquidation.

At each step, the guide will provide an example for reference and highlight the requirements to move from one step to the next.

Obviously, the more high-quality opportunities there are to assess, the more likely it is that the quality of the final investments will be exceptional in their performance over time. At large Elite Family Investment Management firm Capricorn LLC, for example, the team reviewed over 3,000 funds in order to find the 60 that best fit their demanding investment criteria.

PRINCIPLES OF PRINCIPLED INVESTMENT

Whatever the investment criteria chosen, there is a need to align the family vision, values, and mission with the approach taken to investment. If the family's values statement lists adherence to sustainable investment practices or corporate responsibility as core family beliefs, then the investment strategies need to be aligned with those beliefs.

> Whatever the investment criteria chosen, there is a need to align the family vision, values, and mission with the approach taken to investment.

If, on the other hand, the family places the highest priority on financial returns from investment and chooses to address societal issues elsewhere, then the investment models would be implemented in a purely economic environment.

Whether the family wishes to develop only a focused portfolio of businesses it manages itself, or to assemble a highly diversified liquid portfolio managed by professional managers, the investment principles and processes need to be fully aligned with the chosen approach.

DOCUMENTATION

Although it may be counter-cultural to document investment proposals and final investment decisions, the discipline of capturing, in written form, the summary analysis, expected performance, risk factors, risk-mitigating actions (for example, a hedging investment, target sale price, monetization plan, or underpinning floor sell price), and other aspects of the decision can provide useful information for review and response to any environmental changes.

The use of standardized templates for investment proposals can help to streamline the decision-making process and provide an easy summary for the Investment Committee, or other family decision-makers, to compare investment opportunities and to proceed efficiently.

However, it is important to recognize that "military style" discipline must leave room for qualitative decision-making elements and a full consideration of entrepreneurialism which may not be fully quantifiable. A check-the-box, mechanistic investment process will not produce the best results.

DUE DILIGENCE AND REVIEW PROCESS

A thorough investment analysis goes beyond understanding history, estimating economic cycles, and forecasting the future investment environment to spot mega-trends, risks, and opportunities. Successful investing also involves a thorough review for each shortlisted proposal of past results, the chosen business model, competitive performance, industry regulatory environment, asset backing, team dynamics, environmental liabilities, forecast results, and other measures relevant for the kind of investment proposed.

The price, financing alternatives and timing aspects also need to be considered as part of the overall diligence process, including looking beyond the detailed sell-side presentations and investment documentation, into a more systematic view of the proposed investment and the quality of the thinking underpinning the investment thesis. It is critical for the investor to probe deeply into the underlying companies and assets under consideration, rather than simply allocating the capital at hand.

The most advanced portfolio managers inculcate a high level of investor "acumen" into their cultures and ensure that, regardless of the opportunity under review, it is first and foremost reviewed as an investment and not merely as an allocation of capital. This is a fine but critical distinction that leads to far better investment decisions.

Figure 4.2 Seven Principles for Investment Evaluation: The Seven 'Ps'

- Performance and financial history
- People and team
- Philosophy (investment thesis)
- Price and terms
- Process of investment (if a fund) and principles of evaluation
- Partners—strategic, operating, and financial
- Post-investment policies, including reporting, control, management, and follow-up

Figure 4.2 shows a useful checklist for due diligence and investment review. The seven categories shown above, based upon the approach taken by Stan Miranda of Partners Capital Investment Group, address the critical factors in investment success and can be applied to investments in a fund or standalone business.

Developing high-quality due diligence is essential for a best-practice investment process, but is only part of the overall picture; the review and negotiation phases also add great value.

Individual and team due diligence: Due diligence on the people involved in the management or ownership of a potential business investment may merit a special review of each key person's background. This may involve taking references, checking backgrounds, and even using a security firm to verify character and CVs.

Far too often, investors spend all their time and due diligence resources on the business and its industrial environment. Allocating sufficient effort to understand and assess the people involved can be a valuable part of the approach to any investment analysis.

THE INVESTMENT COMMITTEE

An investment committee can benefit the wealthy family in many ways, and can be one of the most valuable elements in a good investment process, no matter how large or small the pool of funds for investment. It can add an element of professionalism and can serve as a check against family members pursuing pet projects or responding positively to friends pushing unattractive schemes.

> An investment committee can be one of the most valuable elements in a good investment process.

The establishment of an investment committee can also make it easier to review and agree an asset allocation model, to select managers or investments on a dispassionate basis, to track performance, to review any follow-on decisions, to exit investments, and to identify good and bad sources of investments.

One cheerful, wealthy investor established his own investment committee as a necessary counterbalance to what he describes as his own "incurable sense of optimism" about the deals anyone places in front of him. As he described himself: "I'm the guy who never met a deal I didn't like. I seem to see how they all might work out and never look to see how they might fail. That's nice, but it is an approach that can get in the way of pursuing deals on a basis of priority and that fit with the investment strategy."

The establishment of an investment committee stood him in good stead, enabling him to balance his positive personal approach with an investment review and a disciplined decision-making process which ensured that only the best transactions were pursued. While the committee took the blame for rejections, he could honestly say to his vast network of contacts that he would listen with an open mind to any interesting proposal.

Most leading investment advisors are vociferous proponents of investment governance, with one even proposing that a large portfolio may need more than one layer of ideas and guidance to ensure optimal returns.

Obviously, establishing and staffing an investment committee requires considerable thought as it can have a significant impact on the future value of the family's investment portfolio.

"Dr No"

Saying no to inappropriate ideas is a key function in investment management. More than one high-quality advisor has been dubbed "Dr No" for the number of times they decline an opportunity to become involved with an apparently strategic investment proposed by a broker, friend, or enthusiastic family member.

In fact, some advisors have a formal process for what are called "special handling opportunities" to protect the family from inappropriate investment proposals. This protection only works if there is an organizational structure in place with real teeth to ward off inappropriate ideas, whatever their source.

POST-INVESTMENT MANAGEMENT

Good investment processes do not stop with the investment decision. Follow-up, monitoring, rebalancing, topping up, and withdrawal can all result from an effective post-investment phase of the investment process.

One experienced U.S.-based family investment advisor expects that approximately 5% of funds are to be managed out of a large portfolio of managed funds on a rolling basis each year. These changes arise from the emergence of new funds, portfolio evolution and the changing scale of assets under management. He summarized the role this way:

> It's like managing a world-class soccer team: each and every week, the players need to be world class as individuals and as part of the fabric of their team. One needs to be aggressive and creative about the role and contribution of each team member, both as individual players and as part of the overall team. These players and the team need to be managed as a coherent whole which, in some ways, is a talent management role.[1]

A COMPREHENSIVE AND INTEGRATED APPROACH

The overall approach to investment this same advisor advocates for Category IV clients contains the steps described above in Fig. 4.2, with the addition of a more detailed (and far more labor-intensive) approach to forward-looking views, active prioritization of risks and opportunities, and the establishment of highly sophisticated strategies between and within asset classes. The more complete investment process could unfold as follows:

- Set investor profile and investment objectives.
- Agree likely forward macro-economic scenarios, short- and long-term (and in the context of long-term history).
- Identify the most dangerous risks and most attractive opportunities.
- Define asset allocation model by, and a strategy within, each asset category.
- Perform detailed due diligence and review findings on short-listed investment options.
- Make tactical investment decisions around the policy target with appropriate discipline, implementation, and structure.
- Monitor and adjust investments as appropriate.
- Ensure comprehensive and timely reporting, exposure, and risk analysis, linking results with strategy and actions.

---

[1] In private conversation with author.

The common element to all of these stages is an attention to detail, a thorough understanding of the facts and relevant principles at each stage of the process, and a clear sense of what practical policies, processes, and principles need to be applied to ensure that only the very best and most appropriate investments are made.

DISCIPLINES AND STRATEGIES

The process defined above is particularly striking in its proactive and forward-looking approach to investments. In the second and third steps, the team actively seek out to "see the future," identifying how the overall economic framework will evolve, and how that evolution will create or reinforce mega-themes of economic interest.

In addition to understanding the macro-environment and economic cycles as best it can, a wealthy family could also consider the validity of long-term trends that unfold over many years and across many short-term economic fluctuations. These long-term, non-cyclical trends, called "secular" trends by the investment experts, can also be predicted to some extent and may create successful investment opportunities.

Among the many secular themes and opportunities that could be pointed out, the following list of forward-thinking investment ideas may help wealthy families to review future opportunities:

- Acquisitions from industry consolidation and private equity fund deals.
- The rise of the emerging markets, with particular reference to China and India.
- Rising demand for selected commodities.
- Increasing demand for energy, agricultural and natural resources, and the concentration of supply under governments and regions that are unstable.
- A shortage of clean water around the world.
- Increased demand for environmental controls in vehicles and buildings.
- The increase in use of alternative fuels and carbon offsets.

- Concerns about food quality.
- The rise of convenience foods and healthy lifestyles.
- Rising healthcare costs and the demographics of ageing populations.
- Increased concerns about security.

By considering such investment themes in the context of a disciplined and creative process, any family investor can set out on the firm pathway to the achievement of *consistently* superior returns over time and across many economic cycles.

20. INVESTOR PROFILE AND OBJECTIVES

Each wealthy family will have a different history, asset base, investment profile, set of investment objectives, and approach to the investment process.

The investor profile, comprising attitudes toward risk, return targets, geographic markets, classes of assets, liquidity needs, and investment horizon, will vary substantially between families, even if these families are of the same wealth category and have similar experience with inherited wealth.

Each wealthy family will have unique investment objectives. Some may need income to support a family foundation. Others may be seeking long-term capital gains through a second set of investment and inheritance vehicles with low income-generating characteristics.

Some family trusts may also contain specific investment proscriptions or mandate a set category of assets in which the trustees are allowed to invest. Some trusts may accumulate all value and income, while others may require a defined approach to the distribution of dividends, income, or sales proceeds.

INFLUENCE OF THE SCALE OF WEALTH

The scale of family wealth may influence the investor profile and investor objectives to a great degree. In the higher categories of family wealth, new investment strategies may sub-divide the portfolio into a set of differing strategic portfolios with differing profiles, objectives, and managers; at the lower end of the wealth categories, there may be a single portfolio with a single profile and set of objectives.

INVESTOR PROFILE

Every investor is different, and every investment program begins with an understanding of the profile and approach to investment selected by that investor.

Many questions could be posed to help to clarify the profile of any investor:

- Is that investor a long-term investor, or short-term in outlook?
- Is the investor going to need cash on short notice or is the "liquidity preference" low?
- Is the appetite for risk high or low? Indeed, how does the investor define risk?
- Is the investor an active, sophisticated investor, capable of making many complex investment decisions over time?
- Does the investor have a particular need for dividends or cash on a pre-set schedule?
- Are there other assets and holdings in the portfolio that would influence investments?
- Are there any constraints on investment as stipulated by trust documents, trustee policies, or other relevant parameters?

DETERMINING AN INVESTMENT PROFILE

The answers to these, and other, questions will capture the key variables that make up an investor profile.

Traditionally, there are three key factors in making up a portfolio: the **timeframe** over which an investor wishes to invest; the **liquidity preference**; and the **attitude to risk**. To these can be added four other elements that apply more directly to the needs and uses of wealthy families: the **financial sophistication** of the family; its specific **needs for distribution or capital growth** (addressed below as part of investor objectives); other elements of its **total wealth portfolio**; and any **trust terms or other limitations** that might restrict certain investment options

Investment time frame: The length of time over which investments are held. This is very important in selecting investments and in managing returns, which are usually correlated to the timeframe available for investment. Long-term investments in, say, a private equity fund or development property may pay off better than overnight or other short-term investments such as money market certificates or seven-day certificates of deposit.

However, a long-term private equity investment involves higher risk and may not satisfy the investor's shorter term liquidity needs, as it is often difficult to sell on an investment that may have an as yet unproven return and carry substantial fees and future capital commitments.

Liquidity preference: An investor's preference for the capability to buy or sell an investment quickly will also affect potential returns. The liquidity preference can be high, medium, or low, and the ability to avoid short-term needs for cash can have a broadening effect on the investments available and a positive impact on long-term returns.

Attitude to risk: There is no gain without risk. Without risk, there is also no potential for a loss of capital and income. An investor's appetite for real risk (and not just for potential gains) is one of the major determinants of the portfolio's construction and its potential returns. An investor's interest in exposing the portfolio to varying degrees of risk will have a major influence on the category of investment, the potential return, and the potential for permanent capital loss through an investment that goes bad.

Although a catastrophic investment in a portfolio can significantly dampen returns, higher risks, properly managed, also produce higher returns over time.

There is a hierarchy of risk between asset classes. Junk bonds, some speculative hedge funds, highly levered private equity transactions, portfolios of derivatives, and highly levered property deals can lead to a high return or to a total loss of capital invested. The same is true for direct investments into businesses, especially those just starting up or in their early stages.

Unmanaged risk can have very harmful results. In the Lloyd's syndicate disasters of the past, many wealthy investors took on unlimited personal liability—and eventually lost everything—for a seemingly attractive investment that carried an apparently limited personal wealth risk.

At the other end of the scale, there are virtually risk-free and highly liquid instruments in the form of U.S. government bonds, and near risk-free assets such as federally guaranteed deposits in healthy banks. The return on these lower risk assets will, of course, be far lower than the potential return on more speculative and higher-risk investments.

What is risk? Many wealthy families have difficulty defining "risk" in its precise form. Each family's subjective definition and its willingness and ability to tolerate risk may vary dramatically in the unfolding of a real risk event.

When the principal of one of America's wealthiest families was asked by the CIO of his Family Office to define his high-level goals for "risk and return," he replied: "I don't know. You are the expert; how do you do that?"

In the course of the conversation, he ultimately concluded that he didn't want "material permanent losses of capital"—his definition of investment risk. This is a more tangible version than the one proffered by most of the investment world, where fuzzy, unreliable terms such as "volatility," "value-at-risk," "Sharpe Ratio," and other academic and imposing phrases are bandied about.

It may be far more useful to have simple answers to basic questions. One very direct Category III family head simply asked each potential investment manager: "Just how much of my money can you lose?"

> "How much risk do you want to take with your money?"

For the professional investor, volatility, efficient frontier calculations, and the like are useful concepts and data points to consider, as they reveal something about the potential for capital loss; yet they may not be so useful in answering such practical questions as "How much risk do you want to take with your money?"

Any lack of precision in definition and answer to this question can be costly for even the most sophisticated investor if the portfolio is not structured to take into account the actual amount of risk as understood by the investor.

Financial sophistication: There are varying degrees of financial sophistication demonstrated by wealthy families and their representatives. Some simply invest only in high-quality corporate and government bonds, avoiding risk, investing for the short term and preferring to have a high degree of liquidity (and freedom from concern) at all times.

Others are highly sophisticated, investing across all asset classes in many currencies and geographies, achieving far higher returns, and remaining comfortable with managing the risk that comes with a more complex but higher-performance portfolio.

Improving the level of sophistication and the investment capability may be an important part of a family's forward strategy, as most wealthy families, sooner or later, end up with a substantial portfolio of investments to manage either alongside, or coming from the sale of, a family operating business.

Total wealth portfolio: In shaping the portfolio, the investment profile should also reflect all important holdings in the family's total asset pool. If the family has an extensive holding in a European consumer goods business, for example, it may wish to avoid investments in similar retail sectors and other customer demand-sensitive businesses in the same geographical area.

The investment program should incorporate such assets and exposures (while not necessarily managing them) to get a better understanding of the family's "total balance sheet" and plan future investments accordingly.

Trust terms or other limitations: Regardless of an individual family member's personal investor profile, trusts and other wealth management vehicles might confine investments to a narrow range of low-risk (and potentially low-return) investments such as government and municipal bonds or triple-A-rated corporate bonds.

At the other end of the trust spectrum, "high octane" trust vehicles can be set up which specifically mandate trustees to pursue investments in higher-risk asset classes such as levered property, hedge funds, private equity funds, or direct business investments.

Some family trusts may carry prohibitions against excessive concentration in any one holding or under the control of any one manager. Since diversification is one of the many answers to risk management in a portfolio, such prohibitions need to be understood to determine the best approach consistent with the documented limitations.

INVESTOR OBJECTIVES

Having determined the vision, values, profile, history, limitations, and philosophy of investment, it is then possible to set out a precise set of investment objectives for the family.

Again a set of pertinent questions can quickly highlight the family's investment objectives:

- Is the priority on capital preservation or capital growth, income generation or some form of balanced return?

- Is there a specified rate of return target to be met for distributions to be made?

- Does the family want to invest for some specific purpose; for example, providing liquidity for family members who wish to opt out of family business ownership?

- Do the decision-makers want to take the risks required to double their family wealth within a set time frame? If so, do they recognize that doing so in, say, five years requires a very ambitious 15% per year return and high levels of investment risk?

- Are there different portfolios or portfolio objectives (a charity that requires income, or a long-term capital gain preference for future generations) which need to be managed separately?

- Are there different family groups, perhaps representing different generations, that require a separate set of investment objectives for their investments?

- Are there specific requirements regarding risks, timeframes or objectives that need special consideration?

For most wealthy families, objectives may vary across different portfolios, or across different parts of a single investment portfolio.

> Family investments are usually required to serve a multiplicity of purposes.

Family investments are usually required to serve a multiplicity of purposes: providing cash for short-term distribution, preserving some portion of family wealth in lower-risk growth instruments, taking some higher-risk investments to pursue capital growth for the next generation, funding a clearly defined charitable program, and, with a minority of funds, setting aside the financial assets necessary to respond to unforeseen contingencies and family emergencies.

INVESTMENT MANAGER SELECTION

In Principle 2, which describes the players in the eco-system surrounding the wealthy family, the various options for a central investment manager are set out in some detail.

The investment manager could be a private bank, a broker, Family Office, Multi-Family Office, Elite Family Investment Manager, or a trusted family advisor.

The choice of manager will vary with the scale of the family wealth, the vision, the investment profile, the financial objectives of the family, and its investment sophistication.

In all cases, it is critical to separate the roles of the central investment manager, who selects fund managers, and the management of funds. By maintaining a clear and effective separation of the two roles, conflict of interest can be avoided and the financial interests of the family best represented.

ALIGNMENT OF ALL ASPECTS

All aspects of investment activity, from manager selection to philosophy, strategy, and tactics, need to be fully specified and aligned to ensure that a family's investment objectives are met with the greatest efficiency—generating the greatest possible returns with the least risk and at the lowest cost.

21. STRATEGIC ASSET ALLOCATION

Given the rise in choice and great variation in role and performance of the asset classes described in the next section, one of the most important parts of a sophisticated approach to investment for a wealthy family is a carefully defined asset allocation model: a framework for investment which sets out in advance the desired spread of investments by asset class, by category of investment within the asset class, by geography, and by currency.

Getting this model right is critical. Analysis shows that up to 90% of relative portfolio performance over time depends upon the asset classes selected, not the timing of the investments made.

CLASSIC ALLOCATION MODELS

Classic asset allocation models, heavily influenced and promulgated by such investment gurus as David Swensen of the Yale University endowment, set out asset class allocation targets based upon a detailed risk/reward analysis. The Yale and Harvard endowment portfolios, reflecting returns exceeding 15% over two decades, include the full range of conventional assets (stocks, bonds, property, cash instruments, and so on) and alternative assets (private equity, hedge funds, timber, commodities, distressed debt funds, and so on).

Over the past 10 years, the degree to which families have participated in alternative asset classes with leading managers has been a main driver of portfolio performance above most public equity and sector benchmarks.

Asset allocation models are traditionally driven by three major conceptual elements—portfolio theory, scientific asset allocation, and the efficient frontier—which combine to provide the foundation for modern asset allocation.

Portfolio theory: The first element of an asset allocation model is the perspective that a portfolio of different asset classes will perform better than any individual asset class. A blend of asset classes can weather inevitable storms better and protect the creation of long-term value in the overall family investment portfolio.

Scientific asset allocation: Once an investor has decided to invest across more than one asset class, the question arises as to how best to allocate capital between so many "classes" of investment.

Asset allocation will be driven, in great part, by the family's scale of wealth, investor profile, and investment objectives. The final model will reflect a unique family appetite for risk and preferences for liquidity, term of investment, currency strategy, and other factors.

No one portfolio approach will serve all masters equally well, but a scientific, data-driven approach to investment allocation is a common element in almost every high-performing portfolio.

The efficient frontier: Within portfolio theory, this is a concept—appearing as a line on a risk/return graph—which will provide guidance on the optimal mix of investment assets within a portfolio. The concept is related to the famed Sharpe Ratio, first calculated by Professor William Sharpe at Stanford (who became a Nobel Prize winner in 1990 for his work on modern portfolio management), which provides a simple way of looking at the risk-adjusted return on investments.

The Sharpe Ratio provides insight into how different investments perform on a risk-adjusted basis, taking into account the volatility of the investment and the risk-free rate underlying the market. The intent behind the calculation is to allow portfolio managers to determine, with mathematical precision, how much of their investment return is driven by excess portfolio risk.

IVY LEAGUE LESSONS

Over recent years, much of the more refined science and practice of asset allocation has come from the Chief Investment Officers of Ivy League university endowment portfolios. Their models have a number of attributes which mark significant departures from past models, most notably a dramatic increase in the use of alternative asset classes, minimal cash holdings, a greater exposure to equities in emerging markets, and more creative financing schemes.

Their balanced approach has led to portfolios which are relatively equally split (in 2005 and 2006, at any rate) between equities, fixed income, timber, commodities, private equity, hedge funds, property, and some cash/liquidity positions. As one would expect, the managers selected within these asset class allocations are of the highest caliber available.

IMPLICATION OF THE NEW RULES OF THE GAME

Family asset allocation will, in future, need to consider some evolution in the rules of the game. The best fund managers are oversubscribed, creating a scarcity of access which needs to be taken into account when determining asset allocation within a portfolio.

To some extent, access to "high alpha" managers (those who significantly outperform the markets in which they invest) can influence the overall allocation model for families of all categories of wealth. Some wealthy families now only indicate broad ranges of potential investment by asset class, with the actual numbers determined by the ability to place investments with selected top-performing asset managers.

Additionally, the use of historic "static" return, volatility, and correlation measurements, embedded in Modern Portfolio Theory and its economic brethren, does not factor-in some potential macroeconomic scenarios such as war or terrorism, deep recessions, and a return to stagflation. Using a more active, forward-looking approach to portfolio allocation, described in greater detail below, extra dimensions to portfolio modeling, asset allocation, and response to market volatility can be added.

Typically, the dataset used in efficient frontier analyses does not include such event risk and "fat tail" (a technical reference to an event with a low likelihood of occurrence, but with a significant impact on the financial markets should it occur) situations; accordingly, capital is not allocated to perform well should such environments present themselves. This risk and potentially significant impact, especially in a world where risk premia have been at all-time—and potentially unsustainable—lows, has led to the increased use of scenario-based planning, augmented by Modern Portfolio Theory, to better understand capital allocations across a wider spectrum of investment environments.

The addition of a more forward-thinking perspective, and one more attuned to the deeper implications of "fat tails" and a more comprehensive view of risk, can have a major impact on the value of financial investments for a wealthy family. Anticipating significant historical events, as we have seen, can play a major role in securing, or even enhancing, future family fortunes in times of economic turbulence.

The growing emerging markets (in both public and private investments), new and smaller fund managers, new classes of investments and other more pronounced elements of a forward-thinking approach to asset allocation will need to be considered by families looking for higher returns—albeit with greater risk—than those afforded by traditional markets.

HOLISTIC AND ACTIVE PORTFOLIO MANAGEMENT

It is important to understand each individual asset class selection and the investments within it. It is equally, if not more, important to understand how a family's investment portfolio will behave in different economic environments. This will require stress-testing and risk-management assessments to provide an understanding of how a particular portfolio will behave if interest rates, energy prices, consumer demand, or a particular currency or stock market rises or falls within the investment horizon.

One investment guru in the United States described a portfolio as being like a cake, where individual ingredients, such as butter, sugar, flour, and eggs, behave very differently when combined together in different proportions under different thermal conditions.

BEWARE FACILE ALLOCATION MODELS

In an attempt to repackage their in-house products in a more "custom tailored" fashion, and in part to justify larger management fees, many brokers and bankers send out young and inexperienced staff members to develop an asset allocation model for their customers.

These models, while appearing sound and adapted for an individual client's needs, are often nothing more than a very superficial allocation of stocks, bonds, cash, and, maybe, property. In addition to some cash holdings, these "cookie-cutter" portfolios often consist simply of "high risk" versions (70% equities, 30% bonds and other), "medium risk" alternatives (50–50), and "low risk" portfolios (30% equities, 70% other).

Another, more amusing, model which has more variety than these pre-packaged new "solutions" is the old stockbroker's rule that the percentage of equities in a wealthy individual's private investment portfolio should be 100 minus the investor's age. Thus a 50-year-old member of a wealthy family would have 50% equities and a 75-year-old patriarch only 25%. Far from scientific, this old rule may be of greater value than the more limited—and less customized—mass-market allocation models that serve primarily to boost product sales in a higher margin "asset allocation model" wrap.

INSIGHTS AND CREATIVE ALTERNATIVES

In addition to the traditional elements and principles of portfolio theory, wealth management for the more innovative wealthy family could include some insights and adopted practices from areas not covered by the standard models, structures, and operating principles of modern portfolio theory. These may be described as new rules of the game, observations that can play an important role in defining the best pathway forward for a wealthy family to achieve its investment objectives.

ALLOCATION, ALPHA, ACCESS, AND ABSOLUTE RETURN

Those new rules of the allocation game can, in part, be captured by considering four new variables in addition to the more traditional inputs. Ideal allocation is a necessary first element to consider, but is now also joined by consideration of alpha (manager performance above the rate of return in the overall market or relevant subsegment), access to top managers and absolute return.

Gaining access to a high-alpha manager in a selected sector may require the commitment of an amount of funds which exceeds that recommended by a pure allocation model. Similarly, lack of access to high-performance managers in another sector may reduce the allocation on a commensurate basis.

Absolute return is the actual rate of return achieved independent of benchmark or market performance overall. Thus absolute return is the percentage return on invested funds, regardless of how a market has done overall.

Increasingly, with the easy availability of hedging strategies and instruments, any net loss or negative absolute return in a portfolio is cause for alarm if the portfolio is meant to be structured to achieve a consistently positive absolute return.

Absolute return is an important measure in wealth management strategies, especially in a declining market. Beating a negative benchmark may not be acceptable. No family ever created its second fortune by losing less money than the market.

Over the past two decades, accessing and allocating capital to the highest-alpha managers was a proven model for high returns adopted by many wealthy families, university endowments, and enlightened pensions in Europe and the United States.

Now, however, there are a number of dynamic factors that mitigate in favor of considering other models. Essentially, the best managers are now so heavily subscribed that access is a closed shop, with existing investors taking up most of the available limited partnership (or its equivalent in a corporate structure) investment slots.

A second issue is the fact that there has been so much liquidity pouring into hedge funds (more than US$1 trillion to date) and private equity funds (many now exceed US$10 billion) that returns may be "dumbed down" as there may be insufficient opportunities to provide attractive returns for all of this money.

A secondary consideration in the area of potential "dumbing down" of future returns is the enormous fees that will be earned by managers of these mega-funds, even before the receipt of carry or profit sharing. There is a common fear expressed by many sophisticated investors that the millions of dollars of fees may sate the financial needs of fund managers and dull their appetite for the extra capital returns to be shared with investors. Fees paid out to managers can include a management fee (historically 2% of total commitments), transaction fees, closing fees, marketing fees, director's fees, and other transfers of profit from the investor to the managers of a fund, in addition to any share of the profits.

Whether the opportunities available at the larger scale and the hunger for the highest possible returns will be as attractive to investors as in the past remains to be seen.

THE "INVESTMENT S-CURVE"

One interesting approach to future asset allocation is captured in an investment S-curve, which provides a simple model of asset allocation along a risk/reward profile. Often used to chart market, product, or technology evolution, an S-curve pattern provides a useful background against which a multi-variable approach to investment can be developed.

The investment S-curve (illustrated in Figure 4.3) plots investment alternatives on an upward sloping curve, with low-risk, low-return investments in the developed markets in the lower left, and higher risk, higher return opportunities in emerging markets, emerging sectors, emerging managers, direct investments, highly levered transactions and other similar areas of potentially attractive inefficiency in the upper right.

Figure 4.3 The "Investment S-curve"

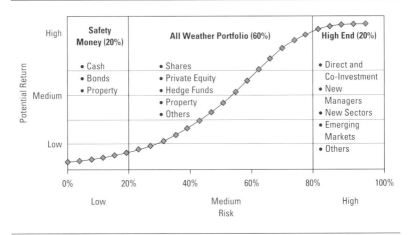

One of the purposes of the S-curve is to highlight the nature of a total portfolio's allocated exposure to risk and potential return, which serves as an easily understood visual supplement to the traditional asset class allocations driven by the efficient frontier displays of modern portfolio theory. A second purpose of the S-curve is to highlight the allocation of funds to the most interesting (and highest-risk) investments in the high end of the S-curve, or "the innovative end of the market" as described by one U.K.-based billionaire.

An overall S-curve strategy in today's markets would allocate the right amount of capital to seek out and profit from undiscovered opportunities ahead of the market, defining and executing an investment and organizational strategy to be successful at all stages of the S-curve through investments in different asset classes. A complete S-curve strategy would include investments of all types of asset classes at various points along the curve, from proven and safe "low end" investments to protect wealth to speculative and risky "high end" opportunities which, if they pay off, can add substantially to the creation or enhancement of family wealth.

This allocation process would also be set to balance high-return investments in higher risk areas (direct equity, emerging markets, new managers, and other areas of inefficient market pricing) with efficient market investments (for example, U.K. and U.S. equity-market indices, proven investment managers, and so on).

The S-curve focuses first on risk-and-return objectives and only then looks to pursue those objectives by strategic selection of asset classes and tactical selection of funds, products, and managers within the defined segments of the S-curve model.

Timing participation in different S-curve segments is critical; one of the pathways to the highest returns is to select investments in emerging areas before a period of rapid growth in global interest and investment, and hence growth in sector prices, takes place.

Investing ahead of an economic "tipping point" can achieve exceptionally high returns through all growth phases of an asset class or sector opportunity. The dotted lines segmenting the overall S-curve in Figure 4.3 indicate the different risk/reward allocations for one family.

Implicit in any S-curve investment strategy is the consideration of multiple markets, currencies, and geographies, and a need for a highly sophisticated understanding of markets, asset classes, global events, and the management skills of professional fund managers.

It is advisable to determine precisely which strategy is being selected within the broad sectors of the S-curve. In each area there is an opportunity to identify and pursue a strategy which can suit a family's own investment profile and investment objectives.

EMERGING MARKETS, EMERGING MANAGERS

One of the implications of investing at the higher end of the S-curve is a need to review and define which new managers, new markets, and new strategies will most likely win out in future markets.

Not entirely subject to historical analysis, the smaller and more talented new managers may still be eager for investments of a smaller order of magnitude; positions that may have a larger long-term return than the huge positions taken by pensions and endowments in established funds.

While it may take more work to uncover and evaluate these emerging funds and emerging fund managers, such opportunities may provide part of the next wave of rapid wealth creation for the successfully wealthy family.

CREATIVE CURRENCY CONCEPTS

One of the critical issues for any wealthy family investor is to decide in which currency to develop the family wealth. For many Category I families, the answer is simple. Since most have built their wealth in a single location, their assets, income, retirement pensions, and future needs are all likely to remain in the currency of that location.

As wealth grows, the range of potential currency options also increases. A family with legacy wealth may have residences in the United States, Europe, and elsewhere. Wealth may therefore need to be divided into a basket of currencies, constructed to match the family's future spending patterns and locations.

At the very highest level of global wealth, unless a family is extraordinarily profligate in its spending, only a small fraction of its capital will ever be needed to fund lifestyle, education, healthcare, or retirement expenses.

One self-made Category IV entrepreneur estimated that 2% of his wealth would easily take care of all of his family's needs for the coming three generations, without any increase in capital over that period.

Many of these exceptionally wealthy families, therefore, want to invest across a spectrum of assets and currencies to maximize their income and assets so as to be able to convert their wealth into a high value in any currency in the future.

Essentially, there are at least four approaches to currency strategy for a wealthy family's portfolio:

Hedge back exposure to a single home currency: A common position would be to hedge back all currency exposures via a rolling set of options to a home currency. This approach would protect the investor in the home currency against any downsides, while retaining the upside should the options not need to be exercised. Depending on investment volatility, relative interest rates, and current currency positions, this can be an expensive proposition, although it does achieve the purpose of wealth protection in a single home currency.

Invest in multiple currencies without hedging: A second approach would be to invest in multiple currencies with a single reporting currency, with each investment calculated as both a standalone investment and as a currency play. French shares are thus seen as both a play on the Paris stock market and a euro exposure. The same would be true for Thai shares and Eastern European property. Hedging could also be selectively employed as part of the overall investment strategy, but on a case-by-case, rather than systematic, basis.

This double aspect of investment requires a sophisticated analysis in each case and an ability to predict currency trends, a gift few people possess over any extended timeframe.

Invest in a surrogate "world currency": A third approach is to create a kind of global currency, made up of a pre-set balance of existing currencies in their current proportion of global GDP. This concept is broadly captured in the Special Drawing Right (SDR) of the International Monetary Fund. The SDR is essentially a synthetic currency unit, currently made up of the U.S. dollar (44%), the euro (34%), the pound sterling (11%), and the Japanese yen (11%).[1] By matching asset allocation to this basket of currencies, a "world currency" position could be established in an investment portfolio that would be buffered, to some extent, from shocks in any one currency.

The SDR is reset every five years, most recently at the end of 2005, and hence is a self-adjusting current reflection of the world's economy.

Estimate future content of the world's currency basket: A final, and perhaps more sophisticated, model would be to use an estimate of the world's future currency basket, a kind of predicted SDR, to allocate current capital. The future world currency unit, set to reflect the growing importance of markets such as China, Russia, India, and Brazil, would add exposure to markets and currencies not currently reflected in the SDR. This model does not mandate what kind of investment to make, nor does it mandate the timing or tactics of portfolio management, but it does add a forward-looking currency perspective which can contribute to a longer term high rate of investment growth.

A SIMPLE SURROGATE

As a quick surrogate for those who are not inclined to review the details of the current IMF Special Drawing Rights allocations or to extrapolate a potential future currency allocation model, a simple surrogate may work almost as well.

---

[1] IMF Press Release No. 05/265.

That simple surrogate would say that one-third of a portfolio should be in U.S. dollars, one-third in pounds sterling/euros, and one-third in other currencies, including emerging markets (primarily Asian) currencies and the yen.

Implementation of this forward-thinking model needs to be overseen with some care since many emerging market currencies are weaker than the growth rate of their economies might suggest. Selecting currencies within the emerging market and Asian sectors will take substantial analysis and experience.

In addition, it should be remembered that the currencies of many emerging markets—China, Hong Kong, and Malaysia, for example—are currently, or have recently been, pegged to the U.S. dollar or trade in a narrow band around an officially determined U.S. dollar exchange rate. Timing their abandoning of the peg, or at least widening the band of potential fluctuation around the U.S. dollar, will be a major source of value if anticipated correctly.

SEEING TOMORROW—FUTURE SCENARIO BUILDING

It is not possible for a wealthy family to navigate efficiently toward the most profitable future using only a rear-view mirror for reference. The proven past is not always a prologue to a predictable future.

The best investors use a very detailed understanding of the past as part of their investment analysis, but combine that with a forward view of the environment and expected risks and opportunities within that future environment.

Far too many families approach asset allocation in a simplistic or purely mechanical manner, often relying primarily on Modern Portfolio Theory (MPT) models that incorporate static return, risk, and correlation data. The purpose of an MPT model is to combine assets with a view primarily to lower volatility, which is used as the sole measure of risk, in the overall portfolio. While MPT can be an important part of any thorough asset allocation process, it is important to go beyond this to include more creative scenario-based forecasting techniques and a forward-looking model in which capital will be deployed in order to see, and act upon, expected changes in the economic landscape.

In particular, the ability to anticipate large changes or "discontinuities" in the future economy can both reduce portfolio risk and create the potential for substantial profit.

The resulting blended approach, taking the best of past data and combining it with an informed perspective on the future, provides an in-depth view of the history of a company, share, bond, fund, property, or other investment opportunity, plus a forward view of how that past might change, for better or worse, in a dynamic future investment world.

> "Risk is a measure of the potential changes in value that will be experienced in a portfolio as a result of differences in the environment between now and some future point."

Some have referred to this as the true "all weather" portfolio, which incorporates both historical and forward-looking environmental perspectives, which is best set to control risk profiles and optimize return.

Ron Dembo and Andrew Freeman underscored the value of a forward-looking risk perspective in investment in their seminal work *Seeing Tomorrow: Rewriting the Rules of Risk*[2] when they concluded: "Risk is a measure of the potential changes in value that will be experienced in a portfolio as a result of differences in the environment between now and some future point."

And in their elaboration of the core essence of risk, they highlighted the need for a forward view to understand "the main elements required for forward-looking risk management," as follows:

- *Time horizon:* Over what period of time are we concerned to consider our exposure to risk?

- *Scenarios:* What events could unfold in the future and how would they affect the value of our investments?

- *Risk measure:* What is the unit we are using to gauge our exposure to risk?

- *Benchmarks:* What are the points of comparison against which we can measure our performance?[3]

---

[2] Ron Dembo and Andrew Freeman, *Seeing Tomorrow: Rewriting the Rules of Risk*, John Wiley & Sons, Inc. 1998.
[3] Ibid, p.36

In order to understand risk and its attendant opportunities, it is important to be able to foresee the potential changes that can affect the risk, and future value, of a family's investment portfolio.

Of particular interest in Dembo and Freeman's summary is the point on the measurement of risk. Many investment professionals believe that risk and volatility are the same, while in truth there are many other measures of risk in any world—financial or otherwise—than can be captured in a pure volatility calculation.

Volatility is perhaps best seen as temporary swings in asset value. Smart investors attempt to use downside volatility as an investment opportunity rather than purely as a point of concern and attention. Investors who over-react to temporary volatility run the risk of turning a price swing into a permanent capital loss.

Volatility measures only one aspect of risk, calculating the relative rate at which prices of an item move up or down in a short period of time. If an investment or investment category moves up and down dramatically over a short period, then it is said to be volatile. If an investment or investment category does not move up or down much over an extended timeframe, perhaps in relation to a pre-determined benchmark, it is said to be not volatile.

This measure, while useful, does not take into account a broader definition of investment risk, which can include such elements as counterparty risk, event risk, geo-political risk, accumulated portfolio risk, concentration risk, future event and environmental change risk and other significant risk-related exposures that can affect portfolio value in the short and long term.

TIMING THE MARKETS

It is heretical, in a world of analytical portfolio managers, to posit that any investor can or should attempt to time the markets. Decades of portfolio analysis says that one of the biggest mistakes made by novice investors is to try to time the entry point on any geographic market, asset class or specific investment. Having a long-term allocation model and an implementation plan built around it helps to curb this natural human tendency.

Sensible investment policy targets can allow for some tactical flexibility to time investment exits and entries when there are clear over- and under-valuations within certain asset classes. Of course, such tactical ranges should allow for reasonable flexibility around the policy target, but not so much as to render the portfolio policy irrelevant.

> Tactical ranges should allow for reasonable flexibility around the policy target, but not so much as to render the portfolio policy irrelevant.

Despite the risk of charges of heresy, some successful investment advisors, particularly those with large family portfolios to manage, state that timing markets is essential in managing a broad portfolio of assets. Many elements of the macro-economic environment are subject to informed forecasting, while others can be predicted within a range of possible outcomes.

PREDICTABILITY AND PRINCIPLES OF INVESTMENT

Once perceived accurately, likely future changes can lead to profitable investment behavior. Whether seen as risk or opportunity, dynamic future markets create the possibility to profit from intelligent anticipation of expected change.

Some tough-minded principles to investment can come into play in this context. Investment in a distressed debt fund or secondary private equity fund can be made at attractive prices when an economic cycle devastates overleveraged private equity portfolios, creating opportunities to buy attractive assets at cheaper prices.

Similarly, overbuilding in a hot property market may create a great time to sell in advance of a crash, and then wait until the market collapses before buying assets at more attractive prices.

By incorporating a well-conceived investment strategy, a disciplined approach to the investment process and decision-making framework, and an allocation model which balances historical guides and sensible forward-looking risk-and-return perspectives into a coherent approach to investment, a wealthy family can navigate along a firm path to continued and growing riches.

22. TACTICAL SELECTION OF INVESTMENTS

There are far more investment choices available to the wealthy family today for tactical selection within an overall strategic model than for any preceding generation. It is important to understand this "endless buffet," as one investor has dubbed it, and to pick very carefully—and at the right time—only the items that fit the family's overall strategy and add specific value to the portfolio.

Over time, and in particular over the past decades, the number of asset classes open to family investors has grown dramatically. What was once a limited offering from a limited set of advisors and institutions has become an enormous selection of investments proffered by a wide range of investment advisors, bankers, brokers, fund managers, management teams, and other suppliers, as Figure 4.4 clearly illustrates.

Figure 4.4　Asset Classes for Consideration

Traditional Asset Classes	Hybrid Asset Classes	Alternative Asset Classes
• Cash and Equivalents • Fixed Income (Bonds) 　– government 　– corporate • Equity Shares 　– large caps 　– small caps 　– others • Real Assets 　– property 　– energy and commodities	• Mutual Funds 　– shares 　– bonds • Foreign Currency • Index Funds/ ETFs • Derivatives • Hard Tradable Assets (e.g. gold) • Structured Products • Co-investment Vehicles	• Private Equity • Mezzanine Funds • Hedge Funds • Pre-Levered Multi-Asset Class Products • Islamic Products • Collectibles 　– art 　– antiques 　– wine 　– furniture 　– other assets • Principled Investments

TRADITIONAL ASSET CLASSES

Three main categories of traditional asset classes—shares, fixed income, and cash—make up, along with property, a large share of many investment portfolios assembled by brokers and private bankers.

Over the past two decades, performance in these three categories has lagged behind the performance of many alternative asset classes (although equities have done quite well in the five-year period 2002–2007), with families in the higher wealth categories with broader investment portfolios benefiting from higher returns from investments in private equity and hedge funds.

Low income generation and low capital gains from equities and U.S.-dollar investments (especially in a low interest rate environment) have led many wealthy families to balance their traditional positions in these markets with more complex and innovative positions in other asset classes and geographic sectors.

Cash and Equivalents

Most families and endowments keep some portion of their funds in overnight or short-term cash deposits in their native currency. The broad strategy in holding cash is to seek stable income with little or no risk to principal. This easily available liquidity is accessible for capital calls, opportunistic investment, lifestyle expenses, and as a general safety net. Overall, for a long-term diversified investment portfolio, the cash levels would normally be very low compared to other asset classes for a high category family.

Leverage and 'liquid hedge' substitutes: Some sophisticated investing families keep virtually no cash in their portfolios on a long-term basis, and even leverage their portfolios to avoid having low-yielding cash on hand whenever possible.

They put their funds into "liquid hedge" funds which yield more than cash and can be managed on a short-term, highly liquid basis, so any decline in capital value can swiftly be addressed. Their argument is that there are low-risk, highly liquid hedge funds (often with a high-quality corporate bond base) that can function as cash, but yield more than double the rates banks have paid in recent years.

Since cash is only negative debt, these investors are comfortable with the risk exposure of short-term hedge funds traded off against the value of the higher yields. The key to such a strategy is to understand and control the level of principal risk (especially the equity correlation) in the cash substitutes which will all carry some form of principal risk.

In a low-interest-rate, low-volatility environment, short-term cash needs are met through low-cost borrowings, an approach which also adds to the disciplines on spending if a family stays fully invested and only borrowed funds are available for unbudgeted expenditure.

> Cash is only negative debt.

In periods of higher volatility and higher interest rates, portfolios may shift to hold a greater percentage of assets in low-risk cash reserves to wait for opportunistic investments and avoid downside risk.

Low-interest-rate "cash and carry" opportunities, which involve borrowing in one currency to invest in another with a higher yield, may also be part of a cash and debt strategy, especially if the currency mismatch is able to be hedged at a reasonable rate.

Cash and foreign currency—risk or opportunity? While there may be substantial portfolio issues to manage in the area of foreign currency risks and exposures, cash held in various currencies (which may be hedged or unhedged) can present some exchange rate risk which is only partially offset by the higher yields that may be available in different currencies. Outside of known near-term cash needs within the currency mix, most investors use simple foreign exchange forward contracts to manage to a preferred currency allocation.

Historically, many families, measuring their performance in local currency terms, saw foreign currency exposure as more of a risk to be actively managed out of a global portfolio than as an opportunity for positive investment returns.

Increasingly, wealthy families are now starting to see foreign currency instruments as an opportunity as

> Increasingly, wealthy families are now starting to see foreign currency instruments as an opportunity as much as a risk within a portfolio.

much as a risk within a portfolio. As an investment opportunity, foreign currency can be considered as an emerging hybrid asset class to be considered alongside other asset classes, with its own risk-and-return characteristics.

Whether viewed as an asset class in which the family is a risk taker, or as an underlying portfolio characteristic to which the family is risk averse, the role of foreign currency will require a specific strategy in every large global portfolio.

Fixed income (bonds)

The strategy most wealthy families pursue in bonds is to seek incremental return potential over cash and equivalents, while maintaining a controlled risk to the family's principal.

There is an entire spectrum of investment opportunities in fixed income instruments and bonds, including, but not limited to, sovereigns, municipals, emerging market, agencies, corporates, high yield, mezzanine, distressed and structured securities.

There are as many ways to invest in bonds as there are to invest in shares. A family can buy an individual bond or a bond mutual fund, or can select from many derivatives and other variations on the theme. Overall, bonds can also act as a counterbalancing force to other risk exposures.

In prolonged bull markets, historical analysis shows that investors tend to reduce their bond exposures below the optimal level. When risk corrects and the equity market sells off, the bond allocations (representing safety) usually rise, creating an opportunity to sell bonds and buy risk at a lower price.

There is a spectrum of investment strategies for bond portfolios, ranging from a passive, laddered portfolio, generally of an average duration of three to five years, to a highly actively managed strategy. Given the highly efficient nature of sovereign and high-grade bonds in particular, most savvy investment offices don't spend a lot of time and resources seeking outperformance in bonds.

Beyond the "core bond" allocations—the safest form of fixed income investing—global strategies, high yield, convertibles, and other equity-linked fixed income strategies can be employed to provide additional return and diversification to a portfolio.

Equity shares

Over the long run, shares have offered investors a return superior to cash, bonds, or other less volatile investments. But to benefit from that return, investors had to endure the anxiety of some swings in the stock market along the way. This is the temporary loss of capital, or volatility, which can provide both risk and opportunity.

The events of 2000 and 2001 provide still-painful memories of what damage a catastrophic decline in shares can do. Many technology companies never recovered from "Tech Wreck 2000"; the overall NYSE index took nearly five years to recover to pre-crash highs. The impact in the travel and leisure sector following 9/11 was also deep and prolonged.

> The strategy of the most forward-thinking families is to develop, implement and manage long-term value strategies, while seeking to avoid losses along the way.

The sophistication and segmentation of the equity markets makes it relatively easy to align investment objectives with equity investments. Shares of public listed companies are usually divided into large cap and small cap, and "growth," "yield," "value" and "blend" categories to fulfill different investment objectives. Growth shares are those which provide growth in revenues, profits, and capital value. They may not pay much of a dividend, since cash is needed by the company to fuel its growth plans.

A yield share is one which is purchased for a relatively large dividend, usually paid out once or twice a year, which provides a high cash return to the investor. A value share is one which is undervalued by the market, but has sound operating characteristics and is seen to have a good chance of future price increases.

The strategy of the most forward-thinking families is to develop, implement and manage long-term value strategies, while seeking to avoid losses along the way. They seek to provide consistent positive returns on invested capital with minimal, and perhaps actively managed, risk.

The dangerous psychology of equity investment: One of the biggest sources of the loss of family fortunes is the overconfidence demonstrated by family investors. Studies have shown that one of the greatest psychological traps for investors worldwide is to hold on to losing positions too long, and even to double up on bad investments on the false assumption that what goes down must come up. All too often this tragic pattern can be very publicly charted in the public share markets.

Given the predilection for overconfidence, perhaps engendered or inflated by growing up in a wealthy family and among the symbols of prolonged economic success, many sons of successful businessmen have lost what their fathers built by making a large, bad investment and then sticking to it—or even raising the stakes—as the value of the investment plummeted.

Warren Buffett, the master of value investing and renowned sage of Omaha, has built up one of the largest family fortunes in the world through shrewd equity investment over an extended timeframe.

Through disciplined investing, he drove the value of Berkshire Hathaway to such an extent that he created a personal fortune valued in 2007, at US$44 billion.

Buffett's investments reflected a consistent philosophy which included:

- pursue a disciplined approach to asset allocation and investment decision-making
- invest in companies you understand
- make fewer, better, investments
- avoid losses in the portfolio
- look for strong cash flow and a strong management team
- hold for the long term
- understand, and benefit from, the psychology of markets.

There is a lovely practicality to what Buffett has done consistently and successfully over a long time. It relates to anticipating how human beings react to the concept of risk. Most people instinctively seek to protect assets against further downside when the investment environment causes assets to fall. Top investors are programmed differently in how they approach rising and falling asset valuations.

The real challenge in family wealth management is that buying when everything is falling is very hard, and selling when markets are

rising is also difficult. However, as
Buffet has remarked, when the sky is
thundering and lightning is striking is
when you want to buy, and when the
sky is clear blue you want to consider

"Be greedy when others
are fearful."

selling. His advice to investors was clear and succinct: "Be greedy when
others are fearful."

These tactical aspects of successful investment may be more
palatable if a comprehensive strategic framework, a sensible process
and a decision-making committee are in place. Then, the wealthy
family, fully informed, is prepared to use downside volatility as an
opportunity to buy and upside volatility as a time to sell.

Real Assets

The real assets spectrum incorporates a broad range of traditional
real estate, energy, and natural resources. Because such investments
carry tax advantages as well as returns specific to the investment,
they have been popular with American and other families of all
wealth categories for many years.

Property investment, in all of its forms, plays a major role in
most wealthy family portfolios in all parts of the world. On the
other hand, the role and track record in other real assets has been
less stellar.

Very few families have had the same success in energy, commodities, and natural resources, although many are rushing to allocate
greater funds to sectors which may or may not pay out as envisioned.

Property: The scarcity of land, general economic growth, the
increasing wealth of individuals and the easy availability of home
mortgages has made the property market attractive to many
investors. In particular, the boom in property prices in the world's
"super cities"—notably London and New York—has been seen by
some economists as a trend that is more secular than cyclical, creating the possibility of long-term appreciation, even if the macro-economic situation passes through the traditional cyclical ups and
downs on a global basis.

The opportunities to invest in property, although constrained
for foreign investors by regulation in some countries, cover a wide

spectrum of opportunities: raw land, development projects, existing residential, rental, commercial, office, retail, leisure, industrial, and other assets can be bought through direct acquisition, shares in companies, funds, and Real Estate Investment Trusts. Indirect property investments can be made through acquiring shares in construction companies, building materials suppliers, architectural or engineering firms, and other property-linked enterprises.

The American author and humorist Mark Twain once said: "Land is a great investment because they aren't making any more of it." While there is a great deal of truth in these words, and property can be attractive on a cyclical basis, it is important that investors don't apply them too literally, because raw land within a portfolio often doesn't produce significant income and may be both illiquid and subject to significant local market value fluctuations.

Another mistake wealthy property investors have made in the past was to bundle their individual properties together, using one property as collateral for another. Failure in one investment brought down whole portfolios where, but for this cross-collateralization, many of the property investments would have survived independent and intact.

Energy and Commodities: In 2006, the trading volume of the world's top 35 commodities exceeded US$2.2 trillion, which exceeds the entire GDP (in PPP terms) of the United Kingdom.

After many years of relatively low investment by private investors, commodities have become a more active element in the portfolios of wealthy families as increases in the prices of energy, alternative fuel inputs, and rising gold and metal prices have re-ignited interest in the category. This has been helped too by analysts describing a new "super-cycle" predicted to lift the prices of commodities for a multi-decade bull run.

In particular, the rise of China and India, combined with a long positive phase of overall global growth, has fueled demand for almost every category of commodities, hard and soft.

Categories of commodities: Commodities fall into two categories: "soft" or renewable, and "hard" or non-renewable. Each has different dynamics, competitors, and investment characteristics.

Renewables are products which can be replaced as they are consumed and include grain crops, livestock, coffee, cocoa, dairy products, and other agricultural products. Prices vary with each crop season and with long-term supply-and-demand trends.

Non-renewables are "hard" commodities such as gold, natural gas, oil, coal, iron ore, aluminum, and other products, many of which are extracted from the earth and are not dependant upon weather cycles.

The energy sector makes up 75% of commodity market volumes. Recently, expected demand for some renewable energy sources, such as maize and other alternatives, has pushed up their prices in line with traditional, non-renewable energy sources, for which they are now becoming a substitute. The emergence of the two giant markets of China and India has also contributed to competition for locking up the sources of oil and gas, and for open-market purchases of the same commodities.

While these mega-trends will affect the price of commodities in which a family may consider investing, it is critical to think of them only as part of a globally diversified portfolio. Energy, soft and hard commodities, and natural resources can, over the long haul, provide both important diversifying and return-generating benefits to a portfolio and a defensive counterbalance to high inflation and shifts in geopolitical forces. But they are always highly volatile assets and must be fully understood as individual investments before being integrated into a portfolio strategy.

Negative correlation: One additional characteristic of an investment in commodities is that, historically, they have provided a natural hedge against financial markets and the U.S. dollar. Since commodities are traded globally, the fact that they are quoted in U.S. dollars should not mask the fact that they can hedge, to some extent, against a decline in the value of the dollar itself, and can counterbalance the cyclical nature of other asset classes.

HYBRID ASSET CLASSES

Between traditional assets and alternative assets, there are some types of investments which do not fall neatly into either category, and may share some involvement and history with both. Either because they are collective investment vehicles or derivative product sets, some classes of assets can be described as "hybrid" asset classes, sharing some elements with the traditional asset classes and other elements with the more modern (in part) sets of alternative assets

Mutual Funds

There are now more mutual funds—a US$10 trillion industry—than listed stocks on the New York Stock Exchange. Mutual funds (or unit trusts, a similar product operating within a different legal structure) are seen by many families to be a relatively hassle-free way of taking a diversified position or a themed focus in the stock market, without going through the laborious process of sorting out the individual shares or bonds which could make up a diversified position around a common investment theme or sector.

As a result of the great number of funds available, and the limited number of attractive stocks within each sector, many funds hold shares of the same company. As a rule of thumb, if a family holds more than eight or 10 mutual funds, unless very different in focus, they may develop a significant exposure to the same companies through different vehicles—and may lose some of the value of diversification in the underlying assets while continuing to bear the full costs of diversification.

As the markets have risen over many years, most mutual funds are becoming increasingly like asset gathering machines and thus are less focused on, and less successful at, providing high performance, measured as "net-of-fee alpha over benchmark." As a result, mutual funds may be decreasingly attractive to sophisticated family investors who can benefit from the rise of ETFs to provide cheap, passive market exposure (at one end of the spectrum) and can also take positions created by the rise of hedge funds and their alternatives to provide more efficient models to take market or themed risk positions and generate alpha for their portfolios.

Foreign Currency

As described above, foreign currency exposure can be seen as either a risk to be hedged out of a portfolio or cash position, or as an asset class opportunity for capital gain.

Over recent years, the number of currencies available for speculative trading has reduced dramatically. The elimination of the deutschmark, the lira, the franc, the peseta, and other European currencies as a result of the arrival of the euro has wiped out a high degree of market variety. The linking of many other national currencies to the U.S. dollar has also reduced the risk or opportunity of fluctuations in currency value.

Foreign currencies can play many roles in a portfolio: diversification, speculation, hedge, or scorecard in building wealth to match future lifestyle expenses.

If a wealthy family is considering or planning for an international life, it may make sense to look into building at least a part of its net worth in the currency most relevant for its future needs.

Index Funds and Exchange Traded Funds

A new trend in family investment is provided by the explosion of index vehicles, known as Exchange Traded Funds (ETFs), which allow index-like (that is, general market risk) exposure for investors to equity markets at low fees. As these are investment products, the details are important and should be analyzed carefully to understand the nature of the underlying holdings, fees, and liquidity limitations.

ETFs have generated enormous interest and provided portfolio managers with the ability to allocate capital to market segments, regions, industries, and even commodities via a publicly listed security. To gain simple market exposure, the most sophisticated family and high-net-worth investors are increasingly using ETFs and passive strategies, to capture "beta" or market performance, while focusing their active "alpha" strategies on differentiated opportunities and top managers.

For the experienced investor, it is important not to pay high fees for simple market exposure, and to allocate funds and fees carefully to only those managers who consistently outperform the market.

Derivatives

Derivatives do not confer ownership of an asset, but are priced in relation to the value of the asset to which they refer. As the value of the underlying asset (or liability) changes, options and derivatives can be highly volatile investments with the potential for a permanent, and sometimes rapid, loss of capital. At the same time, there is as much upside as downside in many contracts, and sophisticated family investors can use such instruments to offset risk, gain exposure to markets (in particular, via leveraged options), and profit from well-timed interventions in the market.

The risks of speculation in derivatives are high. Huge losses are possible; hence Warren Buffett's description of the entire pile of derivatives worldwide as "weapons of mass financial destruction." His warning is not without reason.

Orange County, California, for example, once lost US$1.7 billion speculating on interest rate derivatives. In Singapore, Nick Leeson is well known as the man who single-handedly broke the Barings bank in 1995, when he lost more than US$1.4 billion on derivatives positions. Sumitomo's chief copper trader lost US$3 billion for his company trading in derivatives in the mid 1990s.

In the Barings case, one of the best-known U.K. banking families, wealthy for centuries, lost its major asset in a very short time in an entirely unexpected derivatives-related crisis.

"Do I fully understand what I am buying?"

As with all investments, a simple rule of asking "Do I fully understand what I am buying?" can go a long way. Often, the many purveyors of derivatives products themselves do not understand the exposures, the deltas (changes in relation to the underlying asset), or the contractual and counterparty complexities of some of the products they are selling.

In particular, it is important to keep in mind that most derivative products are a one-to-one counterparty transaction. Thus the ability to pay at settlement is critical; smart family investment offices that do use these instruments approach them carefully, involving their lawyers and experienced advisors in the process to get a complete understanding of the potential consequences of each individual investment.

Ultimately, in a well-diversified portfolio spread carefully across asset classes and managers, derivatives should be used only sparingly.

Hard Tradable Assets (e.g. Gold)

Although it has long played a prominent role in the portfolios of kings and tycoons, gold as a material is not abundant. Although it has been used as an international medium of exchange for thousands of years, only around 32,000 tonnes of gold are now in existence at central banks. Current annual production, at only 2,600 tonnes per year, is lagging behind demand.

Stored quietly in Swiss banks, or in diversified locations around the world, gold is seen as the natural global currency which will retain its value through any political crisis or collapse of the world's financial system.

After going in and out of fashion as a safe-harbor investment, gold has now returned and is playing a visible role in the portfolios of many wealthy families, particularly those residing outside of the United States. Gold also has the attractive defensive characteristic of a "fear hedge," which appreciates in value as geo-political risk increases, and as a hedge against inflation. For some families, a safety allocation in gold bars or coins may be set somewhere below 1% of total portfolio value, reflecting the low (but not zero) likelihood of a major global financial meltdown scenario.

Investment opportunities in gold can be found in the physical substance itself, in the shares of gold mining companies, in financial futures, and in index funds.

Structured Products

The category of structured products is a broad catch-all for combinations of derivatives, bonds, shares, and other instruments to create a specific combination of risk-and-return characteristics.

Often very profitable for their creators, structured products may play a role in the portfolio of a wealthy family to offset or take risk in a specific situation or within a specified investment thesis.

Capital-guaranteed products: This has been one of the more disappointing areas of investment within the structured products arena. Often no more than a zero coupon bond with a set of expensively priced derivative and option combinations on top, in some markets capital-guaranteed products have not returned much more to investors than a guaranteed bank deposit. The typical lack of liquidity in such products (some have a five-year life linked to the term of the underlying zero coupon bond, and a big break fee to get out of the obligation) has made this generally an unattractive option for more sophisticated investing families.

Co-Investment Vehicles

Increasingly, investors in private equity funds are likely to co-invest alongside their investees, often free of fees and carry. The result is a direct investment position in a business (a traditional asset) alongside a private equity fund investment (an alternative asset class), creating a two-pronged approach to hybrid investment.

ALTERNATIVE ASSET CLASSES

Much of the superior performance in investment portfolios and endowments over the past two decades has come from participation in alternative asset classes. For years, these asset classes were open only to ultra-high-net-worth individuals and sophisticated institutional investors. Not well known to the outside world, for many years, private equity, mezzanine, and hedge funds contributed high returns compared to public market alternatives.

These assets provide an alternative to the more traditional classes of cash, shares, bonds, and other products freely traded on the major capital exchanges of the world.

Private Equity

High risk and illiquid, private equity funds have played an increasingly large role in some of the world's most sophisticated and successful institutional portfolios over recent decades, such as those administered for the endowments of Harvard and Yale universities in the United States.

Historically, good private equity funds managed by top-quality fund managers such as KKR, Blackstone, Bain Capital, Carlyle, Golden Gate, TPG, Kleiner Perkins, and others have systematically outperformed the public markets by quite dramatic margins.

There are two major characteristics that need to be taken into consideration when selecting private equity as an investment. The first is that private equity is a cyclical business, with most funds raised during peak years of public stock market performance yielding returns that are far less than satisfactory. Timing this market is essential to achieving good returns.

Second, the family should be aware that private equity, while performing as a category better than public equity markets over many years, is, in fact, a two-tier market. The top quartile make high returns, while most others, and the majority of the market, make returns below public equities benchmarks and charge significant fees to do so.

If a family is seeking diversification by investing in a number of private equity funds that are not in the top quartile, they may well find themselves paying high fees for an illiquid investment with high volatility and low, or even negative, returns.

There is a wide range of private equity funds available, including venture capital, growth capital, leveraged buyout, distressed asset funds, secondary funds (which buy investments from existing or defunct funds), themed funds (technology, energy, and so on), and a whole host of other investment strategies.

The new player in this asset class is the mega-fund, global or regional private equity funds topping US$10 billion in value, either hunting alone or combining with other private equity players to hunt as a pack to acquire far larger companies than was ever possible before.

One should approach such huge new funds with a bit more caution—and perhaps a good deal more skepticism—than past funds under the control of leading managers; while the private equity market may have become more efficient and more competitive in recent years, it has also become far more reliant upon relatively inexpensive debt financing to drive recapitalizations and exits for these funds.

It is not yet clear how these funds will perform, given potential changes in interest rates, market prices, global liquidity, and risk pricing in the future.

Mezzanine Funds

Mezzanine capital, which sits between equity and debt, may be an alternative to pure private equity or pure corporate bond investments.

Mezzanine funds have been of variable interest in recent years as private equity and hedge funds provide more classes of capital to their transactions, including mezzanine, from their own resources. In addition, given the substantial tightening of credit spreads and the general availability of debt via structured and syndicated products, it is critical to assess the risk-versus-reward calculus in any mezzanine fund investment.

Hedge Funds

Traditionally, hedge funds were quiet pools of money, raised from endowments, institutions and wealthy families, which traded to achieve the specific investment objectives of their investors. The few hedge funds that did hit the headlines were the "arb funds," arbitrage investors who took aggressive positions in mergers and acquisitions transactions, or global currencies, to make substantial, and highly visible, short-term gains with their investors' funds.

Now, hedge funds (along with the larger private equity funds) are regular front-page news, having raised, and now deploying, funds exceeding US$1 trillion. These funds have now spread their ambit of activity to cover emerging markets and a full range of asset classes. Including an estimate of leverage levels, broadly speaking, hedge funds now oversee in the range of US$2–3 trillion in gross available capital.

Many still focus on the traditional model of reducing downsides within a portfolio through technical hedging strategies, while leaving the upsides intact, or even enhancing upside return.

Very broadly, hedge funds fall into two overall categories: market-neutral and opportunistic.

The former include fixed income, event-driven (including distressed assets), and market-neutral multi-strategy. Opportunistic strategies include equity long/short, sector long/short, macro-funds, directional multi-strategy, and market-neutral multi-strategy.

Under these broad headings, hedge funds are playing very broad roles, including some roles historically more the province of private equity than hedge fund investment.

> "Work with the best-in-class global investment managers to create absolute returns and capital growth with low correlations to the more traditional asset classes."

One clearly stated strategy for a large Family Office in the United States with regard to hedge funds is to: "Work with the best-in-class global investment managers to create absolute returns and capital growth with low correlations to the more traditional asset classes."

However, it also recognizes that hedge funds are essentially opportunistic funds and will generally orient their capital toward the greatest perceived risk/reward profile in their markets. Nearly all hedge funds have some element of equity market "beta" and correlation, so it is important to appreciate that hedge fund portfolios are not fixed income, safe instruments but opportunistic, growth-oriented, and, hopefully, diversifying exposures.

Focus and timing are critical to successful hedge fund investment. By the year 2007, the sophisticated Family Office quoted above was targeting its resources only on "long-short equity, arbitrage, event-driven, pure absolute return and macro- and multi-strategies across the equities, fixed income and commodities spectrum."

Hedge funds, like private equity, are not for the faint of heart, nor for the amateur investor. The collapse of Long Term Capital Management (LTCM) almost dragged a large portion of the world's financial system down with it. In 1998, after four years of successful operation, the fund lost US$4.6 billion in four months. The fund closed in 2000.

More recently, the well-known and once highly regarded Amaranth hedge fund lost US$6 billion in one week, rolling forward a losing position in natural gas prices. As a multi-strategy firm, it had moved into energy and commodities trading only a few years before it collapsed to take advantage of increased liquidity flows, volatility, and attractive fundamentals.

However, although the dust is still settling on Amaranth's collapse, experts have opined that it may have lacked the experience, long-term perspective, and risk management tools to prevent what became a firm-ending directional bet (the wrong way) on natural gas prices.

It would not be unreasonable to attribute the failures of both LTCM and Amaranth to their "wandering off the farm" and venturing into areas in which they lacked experience and accumulated excessive risk exposure. The dramatic and unexpected reversal of fortunes of these hedge funds reflects that hedge fund investment risk is, indeed, about far more than calculating and anticipating liquid stock volatility.

New Worlds and Rules of Alternative Investment: Given the vast wave of liquidity looking for high returns in an alternative assets world of limited quality managers, many of the old equations are shifting and evolving.

In the past, even the best private equity funds put substantial efforts into raising funds. Placement agents, firms dedicated to raising funds for private equity and hedge funds, could charge as much as 4% commission for their successful fundraising efforts. Prominent families could pick and choose when and where to participate, and often would be able to negotiate to reduce or share management fees, obtain a small piece of the carried interest and pre-book a place in subsequent funds.

Today, however, the tables are reversed. Large high-performing private equity funds have been heavily oversubscribed, in some cases by many billions of dollars, which reduces substantially the negotiating leverage of all but the largest and most prestigious of families, endowments, and institutions.

Family Offices may now need to focus on smaller funds and newer managers in which a substantial family investment (but an amount which may be considered negligible or below minimum threshold for one of the larger funds) can gain access. A small investment in a new fund may even justify the family's negotiating a share of the management company, thus accessing a portion of the carry and management fee.

This new world of excess demand for proven funds, and opportunity with newer (and hence higher risk) funds, may require families to rethink their asset allocation models, investment policies and Family Office staffing strategies. Families may choose to become more actively engaged in discovering promising new managers and emerging opportunities, and may need to increase their resources to search for promising new investments away from the now over-crowded traditional sources of return.

Pre-Levered Multi-Asset Class Products

In order to make allocation easier, and to provide access to multiple classes of assets at lower entry scale, a number of investment managers have created products which embrace a wide range of alternative asset classes in different risk/reward combinations.

Known as "all-weather" investment products, these products combine debt instruments, equities, property, private equity, and hedge funds in a proportion the manager feels is optimal for a target investor group. The same manager then adds in some leverage to optimize product performance, given the forecast of a number of distinct variables in differing combinations.

This testing phase, usually consisting of a Monte Carlo simulation (which runs thousands of different scenarios with different variables to predict potential outcomes) seeks to find the optimal mix of asset products and leverage within the portfolio under a wide range of different scenarios. The resulting product includes a multi-asset class combination of investments with portfolio leverage to optimize overall performance in a "most likely outcome" scenario.

Multi-asset class products serve many purposes. First, they allow a diversified approach to investment to be taken with little need for individual fund selection and leverage analysis by the investor. Second, they may provide multi-market and multi-currency balancing in a portfolio.

Finally, they can provide a substantial risk management approach by spreading investments across multiple asset classes. Prolonged and deep recessions, some lasting more than a decade, have been seen in single asset classes such as commodities and shares. The New York Stock Exchange and NASDAQ, for example, took more than five years to recover from the major declines they experienced in 2000 and 2001. The price of an ounce of silver only recovered in the years 2006 and 2007 to match its peak prices from nearly a quarter-century earlier.

As multi-asset class recessions are relatively rare, shallow in depth, and short in duration, a multi-asset class portfolio or product can play a valuable role in both creating and protecting wealth for a family.

Also, as a result of their liquidity and lower entry point, Category I families may use these kinds of investments to take a pre-managed exposure to a broad set of asset classes on a consolidated basis.

Islamic (and other Religious) Products

Although the Islamic products market is still in its early days of development and global expansion, it is already a US$900 billion market that is growing rapidly as a result of the boom in oil prices and consequent rise in Middle Eastern wealth. Islamic bonds in particular are a new area that is proving particularly attractive to Middle Eastern and Asian Islamic families.

The growth in Islamic finance is not contained solely to these investors, however. Malaysia, striving to be an Islamic financial center, had nearly US$40 billion of Islamic assets under management in 2006, which accounted for 12% of total national bank assets that year. Not all of these assets were tied to Islamic customers.

Even primarily Chinese Singapore, a small and newly emerging center of Islamic banking products, had over US$1 billion in Sharia-compliant property funds, and US$300 million of Islamic insurance funds under management in 2006.

According to the Islamic Financial Services Board, global assets managed under Islamic principles are expected to almost triple by 2015, to just under US$3 trillion.

At a much smaller scale, Judaic, Christian and other principles have been used to establish and invest funds in other countries. One of the best-performing funds in Israel in 2006 was a Judaic fund which focused its investments on companies that observed the Sabbath and other principles of Jewish life.

Collectibles

One of the great benefits of accumulating wealth is the ability to acquire and enjoy assets that are both aesthetically pleasing and increasing in value at the same time.

Some of the great fortunes of history have been associated with the collection of art and antiques. John Pierpont Morgan and The Getty Foundation in the United States, the baronial Thyssen-Bornemiszas of Europe, and the ruling family of the Principality of Liechtenstein were or are great collectors of art whose collections have skyrocketed in value over time. The addition of hedge funds, along with newly wealthy Asian families, as active investors in collectibles is accelerating the increase in value in many sectors.

Given the recent interest in art investments by some investors not interested in the operations and infrastructure required to buy and store individual pieces, art funds have been created to allow easier investment in the overall art market, or in specific national or period segments.

Similarly, with the increased interest in wine as a financial investment, wine funds have also been launched which are managed by professionals who oversee acquisition, storage, insurance, and sale of selected pieces of this literally liquid asset class.

If a family wants to take physical possession of an object or collection, the correct storage or display conditions will be needed to protect the investment from theft or damage and it will need to be insured against all risks.

Steve Wynn, a famed gaming impresario from Las Vegas, recently demonstrated this point rather graphically when he accidentally put his elbow through a US$139 million Picasso he was putting up for sale, causing $135,000 of damage, and, no doubt, no little worry until the damage was repaired.

For purposes of security and safe-keeping, both Switzerland and Singapore have dedicated high-security facilities for the storage of valuable art objects of all sorts.

Toys: Although not usually considered as investments, yachts, jets, private island resorts, helicopters, limousines, and even private submarines may find their way into a wealthy family's portfolio. Their management usually falls under the responsibility of a Family Office or Multi-Family Office, many of which have specialist departments to assist in such matters.

These days, given the explosion of interest in private aviation, a new range of options has emerged to access private aircraft. These options include fractional ownership, purchase of a preset number of hours from a provider such as NetJets, club ownership, and private charter.

Even in a world of greater choice and diminishing costs, wealthy families may want to consider the old and amusingly succinct summary of the best ownership strategy for planes and yachts: "If it flies or floats, rent it…"

Principled Investments

A number of Family Offices have been paving the way at a global level on investment policies that are both financially oriented and have a sustainable impact on the environment or local community. The uniquely personal nature of family investment and family organizations, coupled with a natural longer-term concern for future generations rather than a fixation on the next quarter's earnings or annual investment performance, has led to the development and implementation of sustainable investment strategies by some of the more insightful wealthy families and their Family Office organizations.

Historically, the approaches to a more sensitive program of investment have embraced *sustainability*, usually related to environmental impact; *responsibility*, usually related to the practices of a business in its markets; and *ethical* investment, limited to a defined set of sectors and specifically precluding investment in others.

Although a number of labels are available to describe such an approach, the term which captures best the sentiment underlying active investment which reflects a sound commercial approach plus good business ethics, corporate governance, environmental standards, and community impact is "principled investment."

Negative screens: One of the more consistent approaches to principled investing has been to respect a "negative screen" that automatically excludes investment in sectors considered harmful for the environment, damaging to the community, or dangerous to the consumers of a particular product. The usual exclusions include tobacco, firearms, alcohol, gaming, environmentally damaging extraction or manufacturing businesses, and those businesses dependent upon child or enforced labor, or those oppressive to indigenous people.

The standard adopted for private sector investment by the International Finance Corporation, part of the World Bank organization, provides one set of comprehensive standards, adapted for each industrial sector, which are available for viewing in their current form at the **ifc.org** website.

Ironically, nuclear energy, once a bugbear of NGOs and environmentalists, is now considered by some to be a "clean" energy alternative and an attractive destination for some environmentally sensitive investing families.

In any family, the range of exclusions and standards on investment will be a personal one; actual approaches vary from full and unfettered *laissez faire* capitalism, to an intermediate "do no harm" policy which excludes only a few sectors, to a robust "green and sustainable" approach which embraces stringent standards on sustainability and responsibility in every phase of investment and operation.

Green portfolios: There are many businesses springing up to take advantage of the opportunities presented by global problems in the environment and regulations related to environmental protection.

Opportunities arise for investment in environmental engineering firms that can clean up some of the messes of the past, along with technology businesses and infrastructure projects which can profit from addressing the major environmental risk issues of the future.

Broadly, sustainable investment can be divided into two sectors. The first is the technology and service area, populated by companies operating from a lower capital base and profiting from demand for consulting services, filter and other technologies, clean air and water products, and other such high-growth items.

The second area encompasses the large infrastructure projects such as municipal water treatment systems, land reclamation and clean-up efforts, steel, chemical, automotive and power plant refitting, and similar major capital-intensive activities.

Carbon credits: As a direct consequence of the awareness of the dangers of global climate change, one of the newer areas of potential investment is trading and participating in the carbon credit exchanges, which have been in operation since 2005. Based on successful sulfur dioxide emissions trading schemes arising from concerns over the impact of acid rain, which have been in place in the United States for over a decade, the carbon credit system puts a tangible value (or cost) on carbon emissions and forces polluters to purchase carbon credits for any carbon emissions generated above and beyond the "cap" they have been granted by national authorities.

The "cap and trade" system, created in countries which are signatories to the Kyoto protocol, grants energy, power, chemical and other manufacturing companies a set level of emissions—the "cap"—beyond which they must pay for—the "trade"—further pollution.

Carbon credits are available from companies which have invested in energy-efficient technologies to reduce their emissions below their caps, and by environmentally friendly companies generating credits by developing solar, wind, reforestation, and other assets. These credits, generated by activities under the Clean Development Mechanism, can be traded on the carbon exchanges now operating in Europe and emerging in other jurisdictions.

Going carbon neutral: Some Family Offices active in the sustainable area are going one step further to become "carbon neutral," offsetting their "carbon footprint" with actions taken through commercial service providers such as **climatecare.org** and **carbonfund.org**.

In the higher categories of wealth, a few families are even taking direct initiatives such as purchasing substantial tracts of land in South America to protect them from deforestation, or purchasing large pieces of land in other parts of the world (usually tropical) and planting them with the most attractive species of trees from a climate management perspective.

Funding green funds: There are more green funds springing up every day. From the early Swiss-based water funds offered by Pictet in Geneva and Sustainable Asset Management in Zurich, and a host of U.S.-based environmental funds, a whole array of investment vehicles has appeared to capture investment opportunities in water and other areas in both the public and private sectors.

While many green operating businesses have had a mixed track record from a financial perspective, the additional opportunities, rising demand, more developed industry, and private equity rigors are expected to improve future returns in the sector.

23. RISK AND COST MANAGEMENT

Without making the conscious decision to do so, the under-informed family investor can stack risk on top of risk and fees on top of fees, creating an investment portfolio with unattractive portfolio risk characteristics and low net-of-fees performance, about which the investor may be entirely unaware until a negative event precipitates awareness of the issues.

In order to avoid the accumulation of undue costs, risk, and unnecessary economic inefficiency, investors would be well advised to review their portfolios on a "see-through" basis, taking into account all of the potential cost and risk characteristics of both individual investments and of the overall portfolio.

One of the salient characteristics of modern diversified investing is the multiplicity of risks that can arise in a complex portfolio. Leverage, sector exposure, counterparty risk, and other risk elements need to be uncovered and managed in order to maximize long-term, risk-adjusted performance.

DEBT RISK

The risks inherent in a multi-asset-class portfolio may not all be visible to the investor unless specific reviews are undertaken. Especially as hedge funds, themselves traditionally open to leveraged investment by an investor, broaden their ambit of operation and undertake highly leveraged transactions themselves in private-equity-style LBOs, investors may be adding leverage to leverage, increasing their risks without conscious choice.

A wealthy family may be investing in a company through its position in a hedge fund. The company itself may have initial debt of, say, 50%, which means that its operations are exposed to the risk of leverage on the balance sheet, and its operating income encumbered by the interest it must pay on this debt.

The company could have more debt put onto its balance sheet by the fund through the initial acquisition finance package. This increased debt means that there is, in fact, a much smaller margin of error and a much greater exposure to interest rate risk and business cycles than might first appear when the business was looked at from an historical operating perspective.

Subsequent financial engineering can further increase debt and reduce the asset backing of the balance sheet through sale and leaseback of properties, and through leveraged recapitalizations of the business, in which the company takes on debt to pay dividends to its investors.

This growing burden of leverage not only magnifies interest rate risk, it can be strategically encumbering for the investee operating company—the ultimate creator of value for investors through the entire stack of investments—as companies with more cash and capital are those which may be the most successful at a strategic level over the long term. In periods of economic downturn, in particular, companies with less debt and more available capital are more capable of investing to gain market share, to hire better colleagues and staff members, to compete on price, to invest in marketing and brand building, and to make acquisitions to strengthen long-term strategic position than their more heavily debt-encumbered rivals.

This risk is not purely theoretical. In the United States in the late 1980s and early 1990s, many large and formerly successful companies were saddled with substantial debt burdens after leveraged buy-outs or defensive leveraged recapitalizations, which was at that time an attractive tactic deployed by some companies to take large amounts of debt onto their balance sheets. They then paid out the money taken on to shareholders in special dividends, to avoid the clutches of raiders who would have used the relatively debt-free balance sheets to finance their own acquisitions.

Although the defensive recapitalization may have helped companies escape the raiders, many were left unable to compete in the marketplace as effectively as their less debt-burdened rivals when the raiders departed the scene.

"SEE-THROUGH" PORTFOLIO RISK

In addition to the transactional and multi-layered debt risks described above, there are also invisible risks which may accumulate in a portfolio. A wealthy family, perhaps delegating its investment management function to a Family Office, Multi-Family Office, private bank or other financial intermediary, may unconsciously be accumulating different types of risk in the portfolio.

A wealthy family could develop an excessive exposure to interest rates (through investments in financial institutions, property, and fixed income portfolios) or to consumer spending in one country (through investments in consumer goods companies, retail, and leisure properties), or to energy prices (through the automotive, transportation, or specialty chemical sectors).

If the family does not have a "see-through" view to the companies in which it is investing, directly or through fund managers, it is impossible to determine whether there is excess collective or portfolio risk exposure to such factors as oil price, interest rates, macroeconomic cycles, stock market indices, geo-political risk, currency risk, consumer demand, or many other similar risks which may not be relevant for individual fund managers to consider.

The most sophisticated of private equity funds, funds of funds, financial intermediaries, and other advisors, along with high-quality hedge funds and other collective investment vehicles, will have a robust risk monitoring and management system which can identify and police risk factors throughout an entire portfolio, setting a worthy example for the wealthy family.

COUNTERPARTY RISK

Although the risks of an investment going bad through the willful or illegal actions of a bank or high-quality intermediary are low, there is always a risk that a broker, intermediary, or manager will not follow the highest ethical policies in the management of investor funds.

As ever, dealing with honorable individuals and financially sound institutions is a form of insurance that may well be worth the incremental costs involved. Diversification, which limits the potential damage of any one approach, also provides relatively inexpensive immunization against a concentrated counterparty risk.

At a transactional level, as pointed out above, counterparty risk will need to be considered to ensure that options, derivatives, swaps, and other such investments will be able to be paid out as expected.

PORTFOLIO COSTS

In addition to the accumulating debt and other risk factors highlighted above, there is a risk that costs, carry, and commissions can build up in a portfolio in a manner that substantially reduces the investor's eventual net-of-fees-and-carry return.

For example, it is possible for a family to make an investment through a private bank which, in turn, invests through a fund of funds which, in turn, invests through a fund which, in turn, invests into an individual company. At each level of this stack of participants there are fees to be paid, along with the potential accumulation of inefficient information, excess leverage, and other risks.

The total fee stack can look as shown in Figure 4.5.

Figure 4.5 Accumulated Fees for a Private Equity Investment

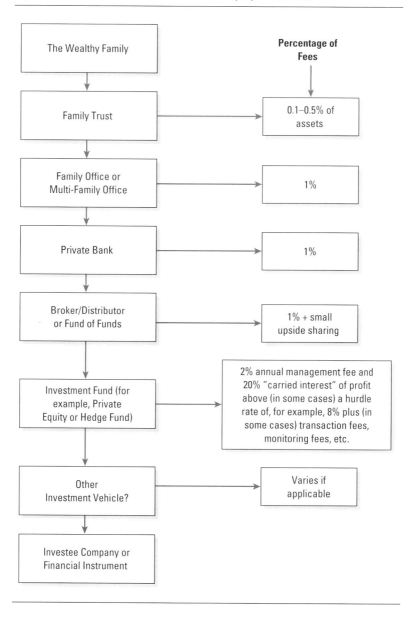

One of the great disappointments to many families, particularly those investing in alternative assets for the first time, is that the checks finally received are far less impressive than expected as a result of the long chain of participants to be paid before distributions are made.

As with risk, the cumulative effect of fees due may not be clear at the outset to those responsible for making the investment decisions.

Individual funds: In most cases, the managers of a private equity or hedge fund, known as General Partner (GPs), will receive a management fee equal to 2% of the assets committed by the investors, known as Limited Partners (LPs). This approach prevails in most funds, even if the fund vehicle is corporate in form rather than operating as a partnership.

In addition, the GP receives a percentage of the profits earned above a set rate of return to investors. The minimum rate that the LPs receive before calculating any carried interest is known as the "hurdle rate," or minimum rate of return. The hurdle rate of, say, an annual rate of 8% is earned by the LP investors before any profit-sharing with the GP is calculated.

Thus, assuming LPs have no interest in the GP itself, an LP investor will get a return of capital plus a rate of return equal to the hurdle rate before the GP gets any carried interest.

The share of profits above the hurdle rate to be shared with the GP managers, usually 20% of those profits, is called the carried interest or "carry"; this amount, which can be substantial, is the major incentive for most private equity and hedge fund managers. The interests of the partners and staff of the GP are thus aligned with those of the LPs in that a return on fund investments significantly superior to the hurdle rate will be targeted to generate a substantial amount of carry for the GPs and capital gain for the LP investors.

In most cases, "losers" are also netted off against "winners" in the portfolio before any carried interest is paid to the GP. This assures that GPs will not take profits on the good transactions and leave their investors alone to face the losses of the unsuccessful investments.

In addition, the GP may take management fees, transaction fees, special management fees, restructuring fees, syndication fees, director's fees, closing fees, and other expenses out of their investee companies which are not shared with investors.

Funds of funds: Funds of funds are collective investment opportunities, usually confined to a set asset class such as hedge funds, private equity funds, and property funds, which contain a collection of alternative asset fund investments, thus providing asset class access, diversification, due diligence, fund selection, and fund management on behalf of their investors.

Funds of funds may charge, say, 1% of assets under management in order to select and monitor the private equity funds in which investments are made, plus 5–10% of profits above a predetermined hurdle rate or, in the case of the best-performing funds, 1% of committed assets and 10% of profits without any hurdle rate. Funds of funds justify their fees by performing detailed due diligence, spreading risk between managers, sectors, and geographies, and negotiating tougher terms with the funds in which they invest than would individual investors.

Channel and transaction costs: If the investment is made through a private bank, broker, or other institution, there is yet another layer of costs to be paid to that intermediary.

A private bank, investment bank, broker, or other intermediary may charge a placement fee of 1–2% on the investment to cover its own marketing costs. This means that an additional one-time commission of 1–2% may be paid to the institution which brings the investment to the investee, plus any ongoing fees due from any asset-based account charges. While not usually requiring the payment of carry, the commission fee to the distribution company will, again, eat into ultimate investor profits, albeit perhaps only on a one-time placement basis.

Private banking fees: It is always important to be aware of the full set of fees charged by private banks. In many cases, these recur on an annual basis as a proportion of total assets under management. Other hidden charges may be embedded in various products and services provided by the bank.

Some fees and profits earned by the bank on in-house products sold through relationship managers, for example, do not show up on monthly statements and are not easily open to negotiation. In particular, investors and families who have turned over their funds to a private bank on a discretionary asset management basis (in which the private bank makes the decisions as well as executing its own investment recommendations) may pay commission fees on an actively traded account, which can build up to a surprisingly high percentage of portfolio profits.

Family Office costs: As we have seen, the costs of running a Family Office can exceed 1% of assets. While not all of that cost can be attributed to the investment function, some of it will need to be allocated to wealth management functions, further reducing the net portfolio return.

Trust and administration fees: Operating through a trust overseen by a corporate trustee may also attract trust fees. In many cases, high-quality trust services may be obtained relatively cheaply. In other cases, trust and administration fees can grow out of proportion and provide little in the way of incremental financial value to the family or much in the way of return to the trustee responsible for the investment.

AN AGGREGATE VIEW

Each of the players in the chain can play an important role in bringing attractive investment opportunities to a wealthy family. Gaining access to a high-performance hedge fund or private equity investments can cover all of the expenses in this long chain and still provide a substantial margin of return above public equity markets. However, since the average return in a good private equity portfolio may only be 5–10% above public benchmarks, the fee stack can, in some circumstances, eat up much of the investor's risk return.

Ultimately, wealthy families will need to understand how much of the risk benefit they are taking in any one investment is going to be eaten up by the costs and fees paid to intermediaries along the way.

In the search for absolute return in a world of risk and complexity, removing as much cost from a family's investment system, while retaining the return and avoiding excess risk, may require families to adopt a different strategy with regard to intermediaries.

Many of the world's wealthiest families are now looking to skip many layers in this chain, going into direct and co-investment with other wealthy families to bypass the fee-and-carry stack altogether.

REPORTING AND CONTROL

One of the most important elements of a high-quality approach to wealth management is a clear, accurate and usable set of plans and performance reports. Each month (at least), and in greater detail each quarter, the family should receive a summary report on its net worth and investment performance by asset class, manager, and individual investment.

That report, based on a pre-set plan and allocation model, should cover:

- current and historic performance summary
- variance analysis against target and historic performance
- current allocation against target ranges
- absolute return for the current and recent past periods (for total portfolio, asset class, and each individual investment)
- return against benchmark (with performance net of fees)
- any proposed additions to or exits from the portfolio
- upcoming investments, disposals, or potential investments (based on pre-set templates and following procedures outlined in Chapter 18).

Without this kind of strategic monitoring and control, information is inadequate for portfolio management and no remedial actions can be taken. Further information of a more detailed nature can be requested for strategic allocation adjustments or tactical decisions as necessary.

Accurate information can perform many valuable functions: it can guide the review of asset allocation adjustments, inform specific investment decisions, and highlight the accumulation of risks and costs on a total portfolio basis.

Most importantly, high-quality reporting and control can make a substantial contribution to the achievement of overall investment objectives. With accurate and timely information, wealth managers will be far more able to make the right decisions to keep a portfolio of investments on the track to long-term prosperity.

CONTRADICTING FITZGERALD

F. Scott Fitzgerald, famous novelist and attentive observer of the wealthy classes in the United States, once famously said: "There are no second acts in American lives."

While perhaps true in some individual cases, there is no reason why wealthy families, properly guided, cannot extend their wealth far beyond its original dimensions and long into the future, writing a second act of great family wealth creation and individual success beyond the original script handed down from previous generations.

Whether the investor is a fifth-generation multi-billionaire, a new self-made millionaire, or somewhere in between, the successful management of financial assets can be the source of further accomplishment, a new and positive chapter in a family history—and a critical element of any family wealth strategy.

THE FAMILY
BUSINESS

*Clarify and integrate family business
strategy with long-term family wealth plans*

24. THE IMPORTANCE AND PERFORMANCE OF FAMILY BUSINESSES

It is difficult to overestimate the impact of family business on the world's economy. In virtually every country, developed and developing, the heart of the business community is made up of family businesses.

DEFINITION

Perhaps the most succinct definition of a family business is that provided by *BusinessWeek*, as: "those in which the founders or their families maintain a presence in senior management, on the board or as significant shareholders."[1]

There is a range of businesses captured under this broad heading. At the purest end are privately owned businesses which have been held in their entirety by a single family across multiple generations.

At the opposite end of the scale are those businesses which have a public shareholding and are subject to all of the disciplines, advantages, and disadvantages of being a publicly listed corporate entity, but still have a controlling, or highly influential, family ownership stake.

THE ECONOMIC IMPORTANCE OF FAMILY ENTERPRISE

More than two-thirds of the world's companies are privately held by families, or controlled through a major family stakeholding. In Western Europe, family business makes up 65% of the GDP. More than 50% of the Paris and Frankfurt stock exchanges are made up of family businesses.

In the United States, more than 50% of GDP and more than one-third of the Fortune 500 are made up of companies with a strong family affiliation.

---

[1] Joseph Weber, Louis Lavelle, Tom Lowry, Wendy Zellner, Amy Barrett, "Family, Inc. Surprise! One-third of the S&P 500 companies have founding families involved in management. And those are usually the best performers," *BusinessWeek*, 10 November, 2003.

In emerging Asia, the percentages are even higher, as broad share ownership, stock exchanges, and other avenues to broader public participation are still in the early stages of development.

As a result of the dominance of family businesses in economies new and old, those businesses play a disproportionately large role in providing jobs, paying taxes, serving customer needs, training and developing staff, developing suppliers and distribution systems, accelerating the application and knowledge base of IT, expanding the scale and application of intellectual property, and fulfilling other important development and economic functions. In addition, family business owners make substantial contributions to other businesses in the community, may be active in philanthropy or charitable activities, and play other informal roles in supporting the development of the countries, communities, industries, and business networks in which they participate.

IMPORTANCE TO THE FAMILY

A family business, if one exists, can play an equally important role within the wealthy family. A family business can play a central role in a family's historic legacy, economic fortunes, community stature, business careers, philanthropic funding, social contacts, and the individual lives of its members.

A family business can contribute substantially to the identity and common experience of the family, as well as creating significant opportunities for wealth creation (or destruction). While many of the standard elements of business strategy will also apply to the family business, there are additional complexities to consider, including family business history, values, ownership, governance and management, succession planning, professionalization, and policies to opt out or sell out entirely from ownership in a family enterprise.

> More than one family head has had to ask: Is the family keeping the business together or, in fact, is it the business that is keeping the family together?

In fact, the family business can be such an influence that it is the central force that keeps a family together across generations. More than one family head has had to ask: Is the family keeping the business together or, in fact, is it the business that is keeping the family together?

Although challenging and multi-dimensional, family business ownership can lead to a continuing economic success story, and contribute enormously to the preservation and growth of family wealth across multiple generations.

The oldest businesses in the world, not surprisingly, are family businesses which have been passed down for extraordinary periods of time to create interesting and lively modern businesses. This shows the resilience and potential for future duration of a family enterprise, if properly managed within and across generations.

THE WORLD'S OLDEST PROFESSIONAL FAMILIES

Perhaps the longest enduring family business in the world was the Kongo Gumi Business, which, until its closure in 2006, had been responsible for the construction of many notable temples and religious buildings across the 14 centuries of its single family-owned and managed existence.

A number of European businesses in the agricultural and hospitality sectors have also been in existence for 1,000 years or more. One such business, based around a French castle, continues to provide and oversee the production of wine, host social functions, and house a rare butterfly collection and museum.

The well-known Barone Ricasoli wine and olive oil business in Siena, Italy, was founded in the year 1141. Wine production and olive farming are still pursued on the 3,000 acre (1,210 hectare) estate, with the produce marketed worldwide under the highly respected family name.

Other well-known businesses, such as the Antinori business in Florence and the Barovier & Toso glass-making business in Murano, have produced some 20 succeeding generations of owner-managers from the same family.

Even the United States—whose entire existence as an independent nation spans only one-fifth that of the oldest Japanese business—is still home to many successful family businesses that have been handed down through generations.

Cargill, for example, a family business founded in 1865, now has revenues exceeding US$50 billion and employs nearly 100,000 employees around the world. For the most part, the descendents of the founder, now in their fourth or fifth generation, have run the family business throughout its life. The Hearst media empire, founded in 1887, and the Weyerhaeuser business, founded in 1900, are other outstanding examples of successful multi-generational family businesses.

One of the most successful consumer product businesses in America, Anheuser-Busch, was founded in 1860 and holds a strong position in the U.S. beer market, with an approximate 50% share. Although the family now only controls 6% of the stock of the company, it continues to provide leadership to a business that has built and reshaped itself over many generations.

HISTORIC AND FUTURE PERFORMANCE

The performance of older family companies, particularly those listed on American, European or Asian stock exchanges, has shown that family ownership can lead to superior business performance across generations. A comparison by *BusinessWeek* magazine between family businesses and non-family businesses revealed that the former systematically outperformed the latter in annual shareholder return (15.6% to 11.2%) and in return on assets (5.4% to 4.1%). The same study showed that in annual revenue and business profit growth, family businesses outperformed by 23.4% to 10.8% and 21.1% to 12.6%, respectively.[2]

CORPORATE RICHES TO TATTERED PERFORMANCE IN THREE GENERATIONS

Despite the good news on performance, deeper analysis will show that some family corporate performance, as with family fortunes, could be captured by the same aphorism of "riches to rags in three generations."

A more detailed analysis of the businesses listed above showed that there were very different performance groupings, depending on the generation of family management in control.

---

[2] Ibid.

First-generation family businesses, in which the founder was still actively involved, had the highest levels of performance in the categories of shareholder return, revenue growth, and income growth. These companies, which include Dell, eBay, Microsoft, Starbucks, and Nike, have been among the best-performing businesses in the Fortune 500 for many years.

The dynamism and success of these first-generation families may set a standard which following generations find hard to match. This is confirmed by the analysis, which showed that companies in which the second generation played a significant role outperformed on only one dimension, return on assets, but they were within a point or two of non-family companies in the performance of the other categories listed above.[3] However, second-generation family businesses are, on the whole, only slightly above average when all elements of performance are considered.

Unfortunately, when family businesses are handed down to a third generation, or beyond, they traditionally encounter difficulties in performance and, all too often, they end up in the hands of more experienced professionals with a mandate for change and a board directive to restore the high performance levels of the past. Even Wrigley's, which had a rare fourth-generation family member as CEO until 2006, elected to bring in an outsider to head the company after nearly 100 years of family leadership.

> It is clear that family enterprises, properly focused and motivated, can achieve leading performance along every dimension.

Other family businesses which have experienced substantial performance challenges when passing down management from one generation to another include McGraw Hill, Comcast, Chintas, Motorola, AMD, Dillards, Campbell's Soup, and others.

Although only one in seven family companies survives into the third generation, according to a comprehensive study of 10,000 family companies over 12 years by Professor Randel Carlock,[4] by looking at the potential for cost leadership, customer service excellence and other critical dimensions of business success, it is clear

---

[3] Ibid.

[4] As cited by Lorna Tan, "Only 1 in 7 family firms makes it to the 3rd generation," *The Straits Times*, 13 February, 2006.

that family enterprises, properly focused and motivated, can achieve leading performance along every dimension.

WINNING FAMILY BUSINESSES ALONG EVERY DIMENSION

Along each key strategic dimension can be found many examples of privately owned and successful family enterprises pushing the borders of what is commercially—and competitively—possible.

Costs: Ryan Air, Air Deccan, Kingfisher, Virgin, and a new generation of family-owned value carriers around the world have reset the bar on cost-efficient air travel. By pursuing every opportunity to streamline operations, to harmonize fleet configurations, and to minimize the cost of service, these new low-cost competitors are often the profitable victors in an industry where the total cumulative historical profits of the entire industry, from the Wright brothers to the present day, would add up to less than zero.

A second group of companies driven by cost arbitrage against entrenched competitors are the new businesses arising in China and India. Great chunks of the world's manufacturing businesses are now passing into the hands of successful Chinese manufacturing operations. High-cost Western companies are also increasingly shifting to outsource expensive IT and other business processes to lower cost, higher quality, and, often, entrepreneur-run or family-controlled companies in India such as Wipro, Infosys, and Tata Consultancy.

Customers: Few companies have as clearly differentiated a strategy with regard to customer understanding as long-established private banks LGT, Julius Baer, Pictet, Lombard Odier Darier Hentsch, and the like. The clearly distinguished customer selection criteria and high levels of service offered by these private banks have been adopted as a hallmark in other industries. The plethora of "private banks" within large universal banks only confirms the value of a high-end customer focus. Imitation is indeed the highest form of flattery.

Competitors: Perhaps no companies more exemplify the spirit of hard-nosed competition and successful global operation than

Cargill, Microsoft, and Bechtel. Each of these underscores a culture of intense competition, as their executives not only compete against rival companies but are exhorted to battle constantly against internal inefficiency as well.

Capital: Over recent decades, the providers of private capital—including buy-out funds, hedge funds, intermediate capital providers, and venture capital firms—have added an extra edge to the capital efficiency of the industries in which they compete or in which they are seen to be considering investment. KKR, The Carlyle Group, Investcorp, 3i, the Texas Pacific Group, Blackstone, Bain Capital, and the private equity arms of such banks as Morgan Stanley and Goldman Sachs have redefined the ownership and operating landscape of American and global business.

In some ways, the entire industrial landscape of the United States was restructured by the appearance and actions of a few highly capable individuals at the top of a very few private equity houses and privately dominated businesses. With a constant focus on asset efficiency and the pursuit of value arbitrage opportunities, the private equity houses have shown that there are powerful lessons and great benefits to be harvested from a focus on the capital element of strategy for all companies, private and public alike.

Capabilities: The Tata Group, India's largest and most successful conglomerate, is currently in its fifth generation of family leadership, under chairman Ratan Tata. The Group currently covers seven major business sectors, with 96 operating businesses. With sales exceeding US$20 billion, and a combined market capitalization exceeding US$50 billion (with just 28 of the 96 entities listed), the Group is now expanding rapidly with its investments in consulting, consumer products, and other areas of operation.

Operating in more than 40 countries, and selling products in 100 more, the business stands as a testament to the potential to develop a winning capability in many sectors and profitable growth over many generations of the same family.

Context: While focused on serving the logistical and product needs of modern multinational food and industrial companies in the United States, Europe, and Asia, Singapore-headquartered Olam has ridden a global wave of deregulation in the origin markets of its key product areas. Following the decertification of commodity boards in numerous origin markets, Olam, initially sponsored by the 150-year-old family-owned Kewalram Chanrai group, was able to capitalize swiftly on the opportunity created by the change of context and to develop highly profitable businesses and top global competitive positions in most of its product areas.

By providing a low-cost and highly reliable supply-chain service "from farm gate to factory gate" in 39 jurisdictions, Olam has been able to convert change in the public regulatory system into a great success story in the private sector and has created a business with a multi-billion-dollar equity market capitalization in the process.

A Wiley Success Story

One of the most fascinating and enduring of successful family businesses is John Wiley & Sons, the family-led media business which has published this book.

Founded in 1807, during the presidency of Thomas Jefferson, the Wiley publishing business is now in its seventh generation of family leadership. Qualifying as a "publicly listed private business," Wiley is a global leader in the publishing and distribution of books and other high quality media products.

Peter Wiley, current chairman of the Group, attributes the family's business success to six guiding principles:

- Commitment to the mission of creating a special company
- Family commitment and engagement
- Treating people with dignity and respect
- Taking a long view
- Being flexible, adaptive, and entrepreneurial in pursuing "creative opportunism"
- Thinking and acting globally

Consistent with many of the themes developed in this book on both strategy and leadership, the long history and great success of the Wiley family business shows that it can indeed be done.

---

25. FAMILY ISSUES IN BUSINESS STRATEGY

The field of family business, and family business strategy, has long been a fertile source of analysis and insight for advisors, managers and owners of family enterprises of all sorts. Recently, however, the topic seems to have gained enormous currency in the academic, investment banking, and consulting fields. New academic centers focused on family business have been springing up all over the world, from Wharton in the United States to INSEAD and IMD in Europe to the Indian Institute of Management (Bangalore and Ahmedabad) in India.

In these centers, and in the body of knowledge to which they are contributing, new insights and ideas are emerging which can help to guide the entrepreneur, family business owner, or member of a wealthy business-owning family. Without attempting to summarize even a small fraction of the information available on family businesses, it may be worth noting that there are very different combinations of types of families and types of family businesses which can contribute to an understanding of the best pathway forward in any individual case.

Just as there are many different types of family businesses, there are also many different types of business families, embracing operating business families, investing families and hybrid families, which can include both activities in varying forms.

The Imerman Turn

A family business need not be confined to a single operating entity, nor even to any one geography. South African-born Vivian Imerman, a successful international businessman and owner in the past of both Del Monte International and Whyte & Mackay, a leading Scotch whisky company, has shown that a family business can in fact be the business of buying, operating, and selling other businesses—and that a family fortune can be built on a series of successful investments rather than dependent upon any one single legacy entity.

PUBLICLY LISTED PRIVATE COMPANIES

Located halfway between a purely private or completely public company lies what could be known as a "publicly listed private company." This form of business may be particularly important for families in the upper categories of wealth as their wealth may have been created by the partial flotation of a private business, an event which would both create substantial liquid wealth and a continuing role of great importance in the family enterprise.

These companies, which are listed on a stock exchange but have a controlling or dominant shareholder or shareholding family, are characterized by different rules, expectations, and behaviors from companies which are purely public or purely private in nature.

Although publicly listed, and perhaps even without the presence in management or on the board of any member of the founding family, some of these public companies still retain the culture and reputation of a family business.

UNIQUE ADVANTAGES OF A FAMILY BUSINESS

While strategy, ownership, governance, and management of a family business present a unique set of challenges, there are also a unique set of advantages which can improve the odds of success for all family businesses and which may not be available to their public market brethren.

Unique Family Business Advantages

- Longer term view and commitment
- Greater preparation time for succession
- A more sophisticated appetite for risk
- Higher degrees of speed and flexibility
- Personal nature of corporate and social responsibility
- Natural diversification through family members
- More limited reporting and disclosure burdens
- Higher degree of confidentiality and discretion
- Greater and enduring commitment

Longer term view and commitment: Taking a longer term view can be extremely important when developing a brand with enduring positive values. In France, for example, Jean-Louis Dumas-Hermès, the esteemed *président directeur general* of the 4,000-strong company Hermès, and great-great grandson of its founder, has limited the growth of stores to only a few per year and to products which are manufactured only in France.

By exercising care and a controlled rate of growth in its selection of outlets and being conservative in its production strategies, avoiding the short-term growth and profit pressures forced upon more broadly held competitors, Hermès has managed to preserve and extend its aspirational brand values, and, by association, the prosperous future of the family business.

Greater preparation time for succession: Among the many advantages to be had from a family succession within a business are a higher likelihood of a sufficient understanding of the business, a natural long-term commitment, the potential for targeted and relevant external preparatory placements, relevant core business experience, and the ability to adapt a position to a well-known individual's strengths and weaknesses. The addition of a family member to a more senior position also creates a potential business asset with customers, lenders, and employees. Individual limitations may be balanced by external experience and development programs, and by careful appointments of non-family managers and non-executive directors.

Even with carefully structured succession plans, the potential costs of limiting business leadership positions to family members need to be fully explored. The first cost is the loss of potential management talent due to the fact that many of the most ambitious and most capable individuals could refrain from taking up employment in a business in which the most important positions will never be open to them. A second cost is the risk that an individual born into a leadership role may not have the skills and capabilities of his or her predecessors, adding to business risk and the potential for lost opportunities for many years.

As one family member stated, upon making the decision to professionalize all aspects of the family business: "Do Brazil think they can win the World Cup every four years if they're only allowed to select Pelé's kids and grandkids as team captain?"

> "Do Brazil think they can win the World Cup every four years if they're only allowed to select Pelé's kids and grandkids as team captain?"

A more sophisticated appetite for risk: An understanding of risk, particularly of high-risk and potentially high-return opportunities, can allow a private company to undertake investments that a public company might find untenable because of the risk of outright failure and a subsequent career risk for senior management.

Just as a private portfolio investor may be able to select investments with a higher volatility and higher potential return than an endowment or public institutional investor, private companies may well undertake venture capital opportunities, initiatives in unproven competitive spaces and "Blue Ocean Strategies" which open up whole new market opportunities which public company managers may feel are too risky—either for the business or for their own careers.

Higher degrees of speed and flexibility: Having concentrated decision-making processes gives private companies the ability to act with more speed and greater flexibility than their publicly listed competitors. Time is of the essence in developing competitive advantage. As strategic cycles get shorter, the combination of greater speed and flexibility can contribute substantially to a family enterprise.

Although rushed decisions are rarely good decisions, a privately owned or controlled entity can move much faster to review all aspects of shareholder value. More than one prominent family has described the great benefit of a decision-making process where a board of directors and group of owners meet every night at the dinner table.

Personal nature of corporate and social responsibility: Many wealthy families may feel themselves duty-bound to pursue a path of greater responsibility in the communities in which their businesses operate. Their family and personal reputations can be burnished by being recognized as leading a highly responsible and engaged model of business.

By adopting a more enlightened attitude toward corporate and social responsibility, and seeing it as a core element of strategy rather than as an isolated set of public relations activities, forward-thinking family business leaders can create opportunities to motivate staff, give a greater purpose to the enterprise, and build a network of beneficial relationships outside the walls of the corporation.

Bill Ford, current chairman of the Ford Motor Company (still 40% owned by the Ford family), captured this concept in his description of a great company: "A good [company] delivers excellent products and services; a great one delivers excellent products and services and strives to make the world a better place."[1]

Natural diversification through family members: One way in which many families diversify risk is to allocate responsibilities to develop new business and new markets between family members or between generations.

A new generation or senior family member may logically focus on a particular area of expansion—a new business line, distribution channel (such as an online activity), or consumer market, or extending a supplier line through new opportunities opened up by globalized logistics.

> "A good [company] delivers excellent products and services and strives to make the world a better place."

One European family, long tied to a traditional industry sector, backed a young family member who was passionate about alternative energy. The result: within a decade, 40% of the revenue, and a far greater proportion of family wealth, was made up by this new initiative.

More limited reporting and disclosure burdens: Privately owned companies have a much greater degree of freedom when it comes to reporting and disclosure. Listed entities, particularly in the United States, are subject to demanding reporting requirements and the constant fear of potentially costly litigation arising from their corporate statements.

Although not burdened by these obligations and concerns, it would be a mistake for private companies to become complacent and limit reporting to a mere comparison of current and past results. In doing so, they would miss out on the benefits of best-practice reporting delivered by such practices as benchmarking, comparable company analysis, calculation of financial ratios of all kinds, and other analytical techniques used by expert analysts when assessing the performance of a publicly listed entity.

The best private companies will calculate these ratios, investigate relative performance, and take the same corrective actions as leading public companies, even if so doing requires a greater investment in internal training and systems analysis to ensure that the best possible

---

[1] In Annual Report Letter, March 1999.

information is delivered to those who can best use it to drive effective change.

Higher degree of confidentiality and discretion: Preserving the confidentiality of trade secrets, advantageous financing structures, investment plans, and business and brand development initiatives are other sources of potential advantage for a family enterprise.

Many publicly listed companies issue lengthy statements about their strategies and financial progress, thus highlighting interesting investment opportunities for competitors. Many also open themselves to scrutiny by equity analysts, and, hoping for positive recommendations, give away information which could create greater advantage if not made quite so publicly visible.

Greater and enduring commitment: In a job market where talented managers job-hop to build a personal resume and seek out increasingly well-paid senior positions, engaged members of a family-owned business are far more likely to stay with the same business for an extended time, bringing to bear an extra dimension of experience and dedication to the long-term success of the enterprise.

THE BALANCING ACT

Leadership and successful strategy in a family business is a constant balancing act between the unique demands of the family and those of a competitive market indifferent to the family's ownership and management objectives.

To be successful, leaders of family enterprises need to be expert at elements of the business mix which are primarily market-driven, those which are likely to contain a greater element of family-related issues, and those that fall somewhere between the two.

These challenges evolve over time and as the role of the family in the business changes. The diagrams in Chapter 4 (Figures 1.2–1.8) reflect this changing role of the family in ownership, management, and governance as a business passes through different generations.

At any point in time, the unique attributes—good and bad—need to be considered for both the current and following generations in order to gain the full benefit of family ownership and influence on a business.

Figure 5.1   Family Business Strategy—The Balancing Act

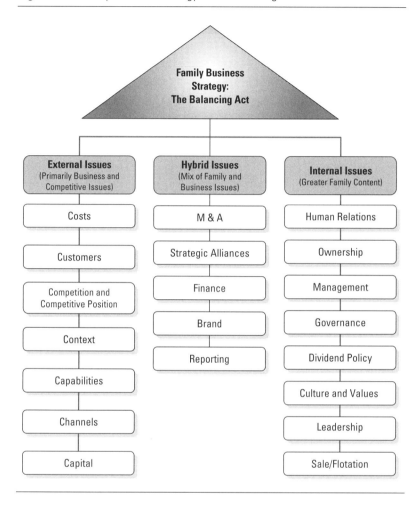

Examples of the three types of strategic and operating variables are shown in Figure 5.1.

A few of the variables contained in this diagram merit special mention as differing the most between a family enterprise and a non-family business venture, but in which private companies must also learn to excel if they are to outperform their publicly listed competitors.

Human relations: Problems regarding compensation, promotion, reward, and social differences are just some of a whole host of people-related issues that can arise within an organization from family ownership or the presence of family owner-managers. All require specific policies and approaches.

Success in a family business is not determined simply by establishing the correct structures and procedures for family members to enter the business; nor is it limited to the selection, management, and appropriate compensation for the best talent in an industry. The balanced management of all human resource issues is a highly sensitive and important area to get right.

Leading analysts would agree that promotion, succession, communication, performance review, and other business operation procedures should be established and run equally for all staff, so that members of the controlling family who are active in the business are treated as equals with the rest of the management team. The creation of a two-tier system, in which family members are subject to less scrutiny and given privileges and greater leeway in their behavior, could well lead to problems in staff quality, motivation, and overall business performance.

Succession: Some experts believe that the best approach to family business is to professionalize in the second or third generation and allow subsequent generations to focus on business ownership, philanthropy, and family matters. While this may be the best course for families wishing to maximize commercial success in their business, there could be greater benefits to family succession in the family business, as discussed above, if the right individuals and family business opportunities can be combined.

Compensation: The level and structure of compensation for professionals within the family business can have a substantial impact on business performance. All too often, family members believe that there should be a special discount to market compensation for the privilege of working for a well-known and wealthy family's enterprise, which can translate into lower-than-average market compensation for employees. This, in turn, attracts executives who are more interested in stature or security than in performance, or perhaps are unable to get a better-paid job elsewhere.

While there is a special premium for loyalty to a family enterprise, particularly where discretion is required about family affairs, paying below market rates for management talent is rarely a recipe for competitive or commercial success.

Finance: Finance options may be more limited for a family business than for publicly listed entities. Equity market options may be constrained or non-existent, and bank loans more expensive. Trusts can prove problematic if the business moves contrary to the settler's letter of wishes or the terms of key documents.

Dividend policies and capital payouts may also be the subject of influences not found in a publicly owned enterprise.

Dividend policy: In many families, there is a constant tension between the desire for dividend distribution and an implicit expectation that the business will act as a golden goose for future generations as well.

It is a very exceptional business that will grow at a sufficiently rapid rate to provide the same real annual dividend to each member of an enlarged family across multiple generations while preserving the real value of the family's net worth. Excessive dividend demands and inadequate reinvestment in the business asset base are two related reasons for the failure of many family businesses.

Many European and Asian businesses founded after the Second World War are now moving into a third generation, where this tension is reaching a critical dimension. Even successful businesses are beginning to feel the strain of dividend payouts to increasing numbers of family members at a time when the pressures of globalization, consolidation, and technology are increasing investment demands on scarce capital resources as well.

26. STRATEGIC SUCCESS FOR A FAMILY BUSINESS

While there are many challenges to managing a business successfully across multiple generations, beating the odds is not impossible. A number of very successful family businesses in many countries prove that it is indeed possible to balance the three variables of family business strategy discussed in the previous chapter, and create and sustain positive results across generations.

STRATEGIC SUCCESS IN A FAMILY BUSINESS

From a selected set of long-term successful companies, and from the combined analyses of the INSEAD Business School and corporate strategy specialists Bain & Company, nine key characteristics for strategic success in an individual family enterprise can be highlighted, as follows:

Nine Characteristics for Strategic Success in a Family Business

- Ownership commitment
- Strong family relationships
- Strong values of work and stewardship
- Clear succession plans
- Ability to redefine strategy and renew the business
- Entrepreneurship
- Effective shareholder structure and processes
- Resilience in hard times
- Clear and explicit rules for ownership, management, and governance

---

Ensuring that a family business reflects as many of these characteristics as possible will add to the chances of any one business emerging as a rare victor in the battle for survival and long-term family and business prosperity.

Ownership commitment: A family fully committed to ownership will attract better staff, create the energy for change and innovation, and reassure colleagues that the business is in safe hands.

Strong family relationships: Divisions, discord, and differences of opinion, especially if played out in public, can all create confusion, greater risk, counterproductive behavior, or, at a minimum, substantial operating inefficiencies.

Strong values of work and stewardship: Great wealth does not always lead to a great work ethic or an understanding of the actions and attitudes that make a good owner or manager. The most successful family businesses demand, and receive, adherence to the highest standards of effort, attainment, and stewardship of family assets from all generations.

Clear succession plans: In a world where there may be limited room for outsiders to rise to top positions, clear succession plans will need to be worked out well in advance of any actual transition. However, one of the unique advantages of family business is the luxury of multi-year and multi-generational succession planning.

Ability to redefine strategy and renew the business: At times, the need for change runs so deep that only a fundamental change in the business model can preserve the business and prepare it for continuing prosperity. Although revolution does not often start with the monarch, profound change may need to be initiated and supported by the leaders and owners to survive big changes in the environment.

> Revolution does not often start with the monarch…

Entrepreneurship: Whether from within the family or from selected colleagues brought in from the outside, entrepreneurship is a major virtue which can be applied to existing and new business opportunities alike.

Effective shareholder structure and processes: The private or family-controlled business leadership team needs to set and achieve the highest standards of ownership and board processes.

Resilience in hard times: Every business passes through cycles, good and bad. INSEAD Business School research shows that only one in seven family businesses makes it to the third generation.[1] One of the major differentiators separating the quick and the dead is an ability to ride out hard times, to adapt business models, reinvent companies, implement painful decisions, and place the survival of the family business above all other commercial goals.

> Only one in seven family businesses makes it to the third generation.

Clear and explicit rules for ownership, management, and governance: These three roles are fundamentally different, requiring different skills, styles, and capabilities. A failure to separate the three increases the risk of an expensive failure in one or more of these critical activities.

PRIVATE EQUITY PRINCIPLES APPLIED

The rise of private equity as a major force in the capital markets and as a major source of value addition may provide valuable insights to owners of private family businesses, even though their timeframes for ownership may be different.

Analyzing the family business from a value-maximizing perspective, restructuring the balance sheet, selling unproductive divisions, closing unproductive facilities, outsourcing low-value operations, and other similar changes can all help the family to exploit the full benefits of private ownership.

SELLING OUT, OPTING OUT, AND KEEPING IT IN THE FAMILY

One of the toughest disciplines of a high-quality private equity firm brought to bear on a diversified holding is the policy that everything in the portfolio is for sale to someone willing to pay a higher price than the current value of the business to the owner. The discipline of maximizing value, through operations or sale, is a valuable approach which many private businesses could adopt to their advantage.

---

[1] As noted in Chapter 24, note 4.

Unlike a private equity fund, however, whose business is buying and selling businesses on a dispassionate basis, family owners must consider a broader array of issues before adopting such a policy. For most families, ownership considerations go far beyond the purely economic, and include the extent to which the business contributes to family identity and cohesion. It may be that a sense of family is more valuable than incremental pecuniary funds.

Selling out: A key question for any family considering the sale of the family business is as cited earlier: Is your family keeping the business together or is the business keeping your family together?

The family may be widely dispersed and pursuing very different interests in very different parts of the world. In this case, an annual family business meeting can act as the mortar that binds the family together.

In considering the broader definitions of family wealth posited in the first part of this book, the role of the family business can assume even greater importance in shaping the lives of family members. The vision, values, purpose, influence, and opportunities open to family members can vary enormously depending upon whether or not a family business forms part of the family's traditions and economic activities.

In each generation, numerous opportunities may arise to sell all or part of the family business. Even major charitable owners of businesses may find it appropriate to sell down their major holding at the right point in time. In 1986, the Wellcome Trust did just that, selling a 25% stake of its once family-owned pharmaceutical business to the public.

In choosing the sale option, families and trustees will need to consider not only the business and financial logic of a sale, but will also need to consider all aspects of the family dynamic involved.

Opting out: Many wealthy business families that have endured across generations have a mechanism through which individual members can sell their share in the family business. The price, consequences, and options available vary dramatically—from paying full market value on demand to providing nothing but a handshake and good wishes for the departing member's independent and unsupported future.

In one wealthy international family based in Geneva, members who decide to leave the business take no financial assets with them. This family is centered on its business, and members who are no longer involved become very marginal in the determination of family issues of any consequence.

In another family of equal wealth and standing, individuals who wish to opt out of the family business are given a payout over three years which is as close to the market value of their shares as possible. These individuals, providing they do not leave with ill will between themselves and other family members, remain very much a part of the larger family regardless of their diminished equity shareholding in the family enterprise.

Buying out: It is not impossible for a small subset of family members to buy out the economic interests of other family members. Such a consolidation of ownership may be necessary in order to get full and focused support for a business, or to resolve conflicting ownership objectives of a broader ownership cohort.

The Singapore-based Eu Yan Sang family business has manufactured traditional Chinese medicines for more than a century. After some years of cross-generational fragmentation in the ownership of the business in the large Eu family, a new generation, led by former investment banker Richard Eu, led a buyout and concentrated ownership in a smaller group of family shareholders.

Following the buyout, the business was cured of many of the ills that had beset it, became publicly listed and has now progressed in such a manner that its business portfolio has been expanded to include clinics and other creative and financially successful add-ons to the traditional medicine business.

Cutting out: Some prominent European families, including the Oetker family in Germany, have established a process which deliberately cuts out many potential family shareholders in favor of a concentrated group of family members.

The large Dr. Oetker bakery, food, shipping, and services conglomerate underpins a family fortune worth an estimated US$8 billion. In its 2005 Annual Report, the company spelled out its policy on business in no uncertain terms, asserting: "The interests of the company have priority over those of the family." In line with this statement, following the death of family patriarch Dr. Rudolf August Oetker in 2007, ownership of the business was passed on to a select group of only eight family shareholders. Family decision-makers had decided that an equal distribution across all family members would lead to an excessively broad shareholder base in the family and would be likely to be sub-optimal from both a business and family perspective.

Established as a means to protect a family business from excessive fragmentation of ownership, cutting out now joins opting out and selling out as an important operating approach to be considered by family leaders.

Vendor's remorse: According to such experts as Professor J. William Petty of Baylor University in the United States, many vendors of family businesses come to regret their decisions, even on the same day as the sale is completed.[2]

Their remorse arises from the lack of a replacement activity for themselves, a missing forum to bring the family together, dismay at the way purchasers manage the business and the people within it, loss of their position in the local and larger community, and a feeling that the next generation have missed out on the opportunity to develop or maintain something unique and significant.

Keeping it in the family: One European family, to avoid being forced into a position of having to go public to finance the buyback of a departing member's shares, has developed a sophisticated mechanism by which these shares are offered at a set price, in the following sequence:

1. To members within that individual's Family Unit.

2. To existing family shareholders in other Family Units on a pro rata basis.

3. To the Company.

4. To outside purchasers, but with the express proviso that no shares can be sold outside the scope of this mechanism without the express permission of the Family Council.

The aim of this approach was to ensure that all opportunities to keep the family business in family hands were fully considered, and that the entire process was both fair and transparent. Given the importance of a family enterprise to this—and other—families, careful consideration of any sale transaction, and an appropriate process, needs to be established in order to avoid unnecessary loss of control of the enterprise.

---

[2] podcast: http://www.baylor.edu/content/services/document.php/24692.mp3

27. MANAGING THE FAMILY IN A FAMILY BUSINESS

Diagnosing, designing, and implementing strategies which take into account the nine key characteristics outlined in the previous chapter will align the strategic orientation of a business with the directions most likely to lead to long-term success.

There are also proven, enduring principles for success in running a family business on a day-to-day basis to help beat the odds against that business reaching the third generation which also merit consideration by family and family business leaders.

Among the many operating principles which differentiate between successful and unsuccessful approaches in managing a family business, 10 imperatives stand out:

Family Business Management Imperatives

- Separate family and business issues
- Ensure freedom of decision-making
- Insist on equal career opportunities within the business
- Value external business experience
- Do not assume automatic employment, compensation, or promotion for family members
- Insist on equal behavior
- Actively involve independent advisors and directors
- Ignore the coincidence of age
- Pay market compensation for market performance
- Observe the four tests

Separate family and business issues: This can have the most fundamental impact on a business. Bringing family issues—especially divisions, discord, or divorce—into a family business can never be good for the smooth functioning of that business.

A decision to professionalize the management of a business (perhaps thereby excluding all family members from active management positions in the future) can be the right decision from both a family membership and business ownership perspective, as well as from a management perspective. While this may be difficult to accept for family members aspiring to management positions, the fact that such a decision is consistent with the higher order needs of the family over the longer term may outweigh any immediate individual expectations.

As Professor Randel Carlock summed up so eloquently: "It is far better to be a good owner than a bad manager."[1]

Ensure freedom of decision-making: There must be the same freedom of decision-making within the business for family and non-family members. Just as professionals should be left to make their own decisions within an organization, family members should not be handicapped by the need to have the Family Council review independent decisions, which may slow down or perhaps contradict their own sound judgments.

> "It is far better to be a good owner than a bad manager."

Insist on equal career opportunities within the business: There should be consistent and equal criteria for the review process, compensation structures, and promotion opportunities for family and non-family members alike.

Many families, particularly those from emerging markets, may have preferences for male leadership in business matters. However, such an approach could rule out 50% of potential leaders where management selection may already be severely constrained by being open only to family members.

Value external business experience: External experience must be weighted properly; sitting on other boards, pursuing alternative careers, and seeking continued education should all be valued and supported appropriately for family members as for non-family members. In particular, sitting on the boards of other family businesses or, preferably, of publicly listed entities can provide valuable knowledge and parallel experience for application to family business matters.

In order to offset the risks of underperformance and lack of fresh experience, many families have installed a three-tier system of preparation to ensure that the management of the family enterprise is as

---

[1] As noted in Chapter 24, note 4.

strong as possible: a rigorous development program; a professional assessment of the suitability of family members to enter the business using real market criteria; and a requirement that family members each spend a minimum time (from two to 10 years) in an outside enterprise before coming into the family business.

Do not assume automatic employment, compensation, or promotion for family members: Parents or children of the family with an entitlement mentality can bring a significantly reduced edge to the performance and experience base of a family business, demotivating colleagues in the process. This is in no one's interest.

It is only the most insightful of families which can build in a desire for success, an objective set of standards for employment, compensation, and reward, and an appropriate (but not stifling) fear of failure which can push individuals and family groups to maintain excellence in performance across generations.

Valuing Independent Experience

A prominent European family, with a policy of a minimum 10-year period of outside experience before joining the management of the family enterprise, was encountering serious difficulties in the operation of the business. One of the younger family members, concerned about the future of the business, offered to cut short his period of development in the external business world to help out.

The Family Council demurred on the issue, insisting that it was important for all members of the family to commit to the established rule in order to overcome future challenges and difficulties.

The business recovered from the difficult period and welcomed the younger family member at the requisite time, when his outside experiences could prove very useful in moving the business forward and, in particular, should a similar crisis arise in the future.

Insist on equal behavior: When members of the family are allowed to behave in ways that would not be tolerated in others employed in the business, this can only lead to the great disadvantage of business culture and performance.

Actively involve independent advisors and directors: The process of professionalization of boards and governance procedures, even if leaving family management in place, can be a substantial step forward in building the value and capabilities of a family organization. It may be instructive to pursue this on a step-by-step basis, starting with one independent director or advisor and using that experience, good and bad, to build toward a new order which could incorporate different types of outsiders at different generational levels in the business.

Ignore the coincidence of age: Drawing on aristocratic and regal traditions from Europe and elsewhere, many family businesses limit the chairmanship to the eldest son in each generation, even when the eldest is not the best suited for the leadership position. A process which selects and develops only the best management talent from within the family, and places that talent in the most appropriate positions, may well be the key to long-term success.

Leadership positions may even best be filled by skipping an entire generation of less-qualified or less-capable family members. While this may be painful when first put into effect, especially in families where the eldest son has always held sway simply by virtue of birth order, both the family and the family business may be much healthier in the long term if a more meritocratic process is adopted, managed carefully, and communicated fully.

Pay market compensation for market performance: Salary base and bonus, along with phantom stock options and other elements of compensation, need to be considered and set for family members and outside professionals alike to ensure all interests and motivations are aligned. Salary and bonus for all staff, including family members, should be as close as possible to market compensation for market-level performance. Even for the very rich, a relatively small bonus reflecting excellent individual performance may be more personally satisfying than a large distribution payment received through an inherited ownership position.

Observe the four tests: As strategy guru Chris Zook has pointed out in many public speeches, winning organizations in turbulent environments across all industry sectors demonstrate the same characteristics; they are long-term in their orientation; fast and flexible; externally focused; and dissatisfied with the status quo.

Every family business may benefit from applying these testing standards to its own success—whether or not the business is in a turbulent period—and investing time and effort to ensure it passes every test every time.

28. FAMILY BUSINESS ROLE IN FAMILY WEALTH MANAGEMENT

The importance of a family business to a wealthy family does not extend only to the career paths, governance systems, and operating consequences of the business enterprise itself. It can also play a central role in the family's wealth management plans.

The business may provide the bulk of a family's income, asset value growth, dividends, capital gain, funds for distribution from leveraged recapitalizations, financial engineering, and other commercial or financial activity. As such, the business, publicly listed or not, requires consideration from a wealth management perspective as well as playing an important role in a family's heritage and community presence.

A substantial operating business also carries with it a set of related risks discussed in earlier chapters which may require active management. These can include all forms of competitive and operating risk, interest rate risk, cyclical exposure, and geographic risk. If in an emerging market, the asset may carry with it unique risks of expropriation, political, fiscal or regulatory interference, or economic, political or currency swings.

While insurance policies can cover some of these risks, a broader approach to business risk management may be in order as part of a sound approach to overall family wealth management.

Managing single-stock concentration risk: The holding of a major position in a single stock, listed or not, will require strategies to manage the risks and opportunities created by that holding.

One obvious (but possibly inappropriate) strategy would be to sell all or part of an ownership position, reducing exposure and investing the funds into a diversified portfolio of investments. It should be remembered, though, that investment banks, private banks, and other advisors can now offer a whole range of new products and services to help manage single-stock concentration risk without necessarily selling off part of the ownership stake.

Lending against shares, even of unquoted stocks, and investing the loan proceeds in diversified areas, is another traditional approach to taking the risk out of a single concentrated holding.

Derivatives and more complex combinations of structured products can also be put together to manage a family business holding. Pioneered by Goldman Sachs and other leading wealth managers, puts, calls, "collars" (a combined approach which locks in a limited value range for a period of time by capping upside opportunity and limiting downside risk), "synthetic puts" (which can be a put or short position against a basket of similar stocks), and other approaches can be used to ensure that an overall asset portfolio has all of the performance and protective characteristics sought by the family.

One of the advantages of employing an Elite Family Investment Manager as discussed earlier is that it can provide a sophisticated approach to single-stock concentration risk as part of an overall customized approach to family wealth management.

The Painful Cost of Unmanaged Concentration Risk

More than one Asian entrepreneur discovered the real cost of unmanaged concentration risk during the Asian Economic Crisis of 1998. One Thai entrepreneur, publicly acclaimed as the creator of a Category III fortune, lost everything he had built up over 12 years in less than 12 months.

His mistake was to leave all his wealth in the shares of his own company. Resisting family urging to diversify, his wealth plummeted to below Category I as the regional economic earthquake caused his business to collapse.

Five years after the dust had settled on the events of 1998, he was quoted as ruing his lack of diversification, noting that his new total net worth was less than his former annual contributions to charity.

Many business families, following the sale of their major operating business, swing to the opposite end of the investment range and develop some of the most highly diversified investment portfolios in the market. It is rare indeed that a family will pass from one concentrated portfolio to another without diverting at least some of its funds into other, more secure and more diverse, investments.

THREE PARALLEL STRATEGIC STREAMS

Although there are many elements of business strategy which are "pure business" issues, such as cost position and product or service delivery, there are a number of unique features related to family businesses which require an integrated family review and action.

One such feature is the parallel process required to address three main interrelated elements of a family wealth strategy: the family itself, the family business, and family wealth management. All three of these parallel streams need to be addressed simultaneously, with a shared family vision and set of values in mind. In more generous families, philanthropy may play such an important role that it requires integrating as a fourth stream of activity.

The family: all aspects of the family need to be considered and thought through from a multi-generational perspective. Individual roles and responsibilities will need to be considered, given a realistic assessment of the capabilities and experience available in the current and following generation.

Family business strategy: Where a family business exists, its future and that of the family are inextricably intertwined. Individual career plans, family business finances, potential sale or merger, family governance, philanthropy, and wealth management all need to be decided upon together in a manner which optimizes the entire mix of interrelated considerations.

The strategy for the family business will need to be addressed across the full set of issues specific to both the business and the family's role in the ownership, governance, and management of the enterprise.

Family wealth management: Preserving family wealth across generations means understanding the role of the business in the family's overall wealth portfolio, seeing wealth management as a separate activity in itself, and making decisions with regard to family and non-family roles and assets on a consolidated basis.

An integrated and harmonized approach to all three streams of strategy will be required to ensure that the best possible outcome is achieved in each area for the family, the family business, and family wealth in the largest sense of the term.

.

PRINCIPLE 6

EFFECTIVE PHILANTHROPY

Share wealth in a manner that unites the family and gives it meaning

29. THE HISTORY OF GENEROSITY

Generosity, sharing, and charity are valued as essential elements of a worthy life by almost every religion and culture in the world.

While philanthropy is generally associated with the idea of large-scale financial contributions to charitable causes, this interpretation is far from the original meaning of the word. Philanthropy is actually a word formed by a combination of two Greek words: *philos*, meaning love, and *anthropos*, meaning mankind. Quite literally, philanthropy means the love of mankind.

The virtues of giving, and the impact such generosity can have on a family's stature, sense of common purpose, unity and wellbeing, make philanthropy an essential part of a comprehensive strategy for a wealthy family.

The usual questions of who, what, when, where, why, and how can usefully be posed in the contemplation of making a one-off gift or setting up a long-term institution such as a family foundation or separate trust. Every answer to every question will be entirely unique, and asking the *who* should give question gives rise to its natural corollary *to whom*.

> Quite literally, philanthropy means the love of mankind.

Finding and following up on good philanthropic initiatives is no easy task. It is often difficult to ascertain the impact of proposed investments in social causes, to determine how efficient or effective are the administrators and what impact can be expected on both the family and the recipients of its generosity.

By considering all of the elements of effective philanthropy in the broader context of family strategy, a wealthy family may be able to achieve a far greater impact in the areas selected for charitable grants or activity—and ensure that the impact on the family is as deep, long-lasting, and as positive as possible.

As Marcus Aurelius said, "The only true wealth we have is that which we give away." The fundamental idea of philanthropy—which can be defined as charity on a grander scale—is one which extends back across thousands of years to the beginning of recorded history.

The earliest recorded moments of generosity have been found in records over 4,000 years old and relate to gifts from the wealthy to the poor in Egyptian tombs. The *Li Ki*, the Chinese "Book of Rites" also expounded on the concept of charity 3,000 years ago.

Over time, traditions of alms-giving, tithes, and donations of family wealth played out in different forms and to different themes. English giving in the eighteenth and nineteenth centuries, for example, focused in great part on the Church, the poor, and education. Generosity in other parts of the world has focused on religious institutions, orphans, the sick, local communities, art, music, and other causes deemed worthy of support by rich benefactors.

Although varying in focus and scale, the history of human generosity is one which runs deep in the traditions of the wealthy family in virtually every recorded civilization. The impact is two-fold, making an enormous difference to those benefiting from the donations, and adding enormously to the quality of life and the personal legacy of generous benefactors.

Acts of generosity can engage all members of a family in a meaningful pursuit and unite them across many generations.

SPIRITUAL FOUNDATIONS

Religion and spirituality often play a large role, directly or indirectly, in shaping the charitable actions of a wealthy family. Most systems of religious belief make specific mention of the value and virtue of the wealthy practicing generosity towards the less fortunate.

- The Christian religion exalts faith, hope, and charity as supreme virtues, with charity the most highly valued. The Book of John (*1 John 3:17–8*) specifically urges Christians to take actions consistent with this Christian notion of charity: "If anyone has material possessions and sees his brother in need but has no pity on him, how can the love of God be in him? Dear children, let us not love with words or tongue but with actions and in truth."

- The Sioux, Native Americans famed as warriors and as one of the great North American indigenous cultures, held the four supreme virtues of bravery, fortitude, wisdom, and generosity as the cornerstones of belief and action.

- The practice of generosity, *zakat,* is one of the five pillars of Islam.

- Charity is one of the transcendent virtues in Buddhism.

- Of the eight endeavors from the principles of Jainism, helping others is among the first mentioned.

- Among the divine qualities, the *Daivi-Sampat*, of Hinduism is alms-giving.

ISLAMIC PRINCIPLES

In the sacred Koran and in the traditions of Islam, there are specific requirements for individuals to share their wealth with others in need of support.

In addition to the *zakat*, an obligatory share of income and capital given to the poor by the wealthy as a religious observance, the Koran itself spells out the benefit of charitable giving in this lifetime: "But they are righteous…who donate goods and money for love of God to relatives and orphans, and to the poor and the wayfarer, and to the needy, and for freeing slaves; And who are constant in prayer and gives alms for welfare…"[1]

A DEEP TRADITION OF JEWISH CHARITY

Judaism, too, exhorts the same spirit of generous giving. *Tzedakah*, the Hebrew word most closely related to the word "charity," incorporates the idea of giving aid to the poor and needy and to other worthy causes. Yet, while the Hebrew and English words are similar in the actions they promote, *tzedakah* carries a greater sense of duty on the part of the giver, a sense of fulfilling righteous obligations, universal in their application, which are part of an ordered system of socially and religiously sanctioned justice and fairness.

The idea of charity developed in the Talmud was later expounded upon by Maimonides to identify eight different levels of giving, from which even the poor are not exempt. The *pushke*, a box for collecting money for the poor, found in many Jewish homes, serves both to collect coins and to remind members of the household of their obligations

In every part of the world and in every culture, acts of generosity are likely to be part of the religious and ethical fabric of every rich family's history.

---

[1] The Koran, Chapter 2 Verse 177.

AN AGE OF INDUSTRY AND GENEROSITY

Many great philanthropists emerged from the entrepreneurs, financiers, and investors who achieved prominence in Europe and the United States during the Industrial Age, the period roughly from the end of the American Civil War in 1865 to the outbreak of the First World War in 1914.

Such iconic philanthropists as John D. Rockefeller, Louis Harkness, Henry Ford, John Pierpont Morgan, and Andrew Carnegie set new standards for their era in giving away significant percentages of their hard-earned assets. The impact of their investments in philanthropy is still being felt today.

The Generosity of Andrew Carnegie

Despite his intensely commercial approach to business, Andrew Carnegie eventually became one of the great heroes of global corporate philanthropy, declaring that it was "a sin to live poor or to die rich."

Carnegie put great effort into addressing "the problem of our age", which he defined as "the proper administration of wealth, so that the ties of brotherhood may still bind together the rich and poor in harmonious relationship."[2]

True to his word, Andrew Carnegie dedicated his fortune to a number of social causes, ranging from world peace to education to public parks. Carnegie's greatest gift may be the building of a network of more than 2,500 free lending libraries around the English-speaking world. The first of these was built in Carnegie's home town of Dunfermline in Scotland, in 1883. The last library grant was made in 1919, toward the end of the golden era of library building in America.

At the time of the last grant, there were more than 3,500 libraries in America; more than half of them had been built with Carnegie money. Contrary to common perception, the Carnegie name did not appear on any of the library buildings he funded. Rather, Carnegie had inscribed over the entrance the simple motto "Let there be light."

A self-made man who had been the beneficiary of access to the books in personal libraries in Scotland, Carnegie founded an empire of learning and giving, helping poor people to become independent and achieve their own ambitions.

---

[2] Andrew Carnegie, "Wealth," *The North American Review*, June 1889.

AMERICAN GENEROSITY

Americans have long been noted for their generosity and community spirit. As a result of America's unique religious and economic history (and, no doubt, aided as well by the fiscal system), the number of donors to charity, the percentage of the population involved, and the absolute amount of giving are among the highest in the world.

Some of America's wealthiest families have converted a substantial quantity of their wealth into dedicated philanthropic foundations. At least 10 families have created foundations which, by the middle of 2006, amounted to more than US$5 billion each in endowment funds.[3]

Other families of varying categories of wealth, varying degrees of prominence, and with varying degrees of public exposure, have made substantial contributions to many charities, communities and worthwhile causes, gifts which serve both to improve the lot of recipients and enhance the legacy of the donors themselves.

GATES AND BUFFETT—A LEAGUE APART

Bill Gates, the world's wealthiest individual, may have blunted the edge of his reputation as a hard-nosed capitalist by his highly publicized activities in Africa and elsewhere with the Bill & Melinda Gates Foundation.

The combined contributions to charity of friends and chess mates Bill Gates and Warren Buffett now total nearly US$65 billion. Buffet's contribution to various charities of shares worth US$37 billion, out of a total personal fortune of US$44 billion, included a staggering US$31 billion bequest to the Gates Foundation.

Although Buffett and Gates may be entrepreneurs and philanthropists on an extraordinary scale, they are not alone in America as generous benefactors of charity. Nearly 90% of American households make some contribution to charity each year, with a large number

---

[3] In order of size and market value of assets, these funds were the Bill & Melinda Gates Foundation, the Ford Foundation, the J. Paul Getty Trust, the Robert Wood Johnson Foundation, Lilly Endowment Inc., the William and Flora Hewlett Foundation, W. K. Kellogg Foundation, David and Lucille Packard Foundation, the Andrew W. Mellon Foundation, and the John D. and Catherine T. Macarthur Foundation.

contributing time and effort, as well as funds, to local, national, and, increasingly, international charities.

EUROPEAN COUSINS

The grand American philanthropists of the Industrial Age were matched in spirit and largesse by a number of European entrepreneurs and their families, many of whom left substantial ownership stakes and, in some cases, total ownership of their businesses to foundations set up to benefit their companies' workers and other defined social causes.[4]

THE THIRD SON

Asia is still, primarily, a collection of developing economies in which charity is focused on family, clan, and community. With the great rise in wealth in the region, and a growing sensitivity to the value of charitable contributions, Asian philanthropy is showing many of the signs of similar development as its Western counterparts.

Hong Kong entrepreneur Li Ka-Shing, in donating one-third of his billions of dollars of personal wealth to charities, said that he was making the contribution to his "third son." For some Asians, historically sensitive to future generations of male heirs, thinking of philanthropy as an additional "son" is an interesting way to explain the sense of obligation and apportion investment in a brighter future for society.

A model approach: At least one other young family, inspired by this model, has decided to add one "child" to its own estate-planning approach. Should they have two children, like the Li family, then they would leave one-third to charity. Should they have four children, then they have resolved to give 20% to charity.

---

[4] Among the 10 largest European Foundations are many bearing the names of their founding families. In order of endowment, these foundations include the Wellcome Trust, Fondazione Hans Wilsdorf (Montres ROLEX) Geneve, Robert Bosch Stiftung, Bertelsmann Stiftung, Sandoz Fondation de Famille, and the Calouste Gulbenkian Foundation. All are multi-billion-dollar bequests, with the Wellcome Trust alone exceeding US$15 billion in value.

The addition of the charitable "child" to any family may make the assessment of an equitable portion of giving to charitable causes an easy and comfortable calculation.

UNSUNG HEROES

There are many unsung heroes of modern philanthropy in the developing world whose good works merit far more coverage than they receive in the world's media. The Rangoonwala Foundation is one such example.

Primarily endowed by successful Memon entrepreneur Mohamed Ali Rangoonwala and carried on today under the direction of three of his children—Asif, Tariq, and Khalid—the Rangoonwala Foundation operates in many countries to promote the welfare of various poor communities, with a focus on the education and training of women to become economically more self-sufficient.

With students and course attendees now exceeding 200,000 per year at their centers, this laudable and low-profile wealthy family has put into practice the Islamic virtue of generosity through a practical, modern approach to education, infrastructure development, and training.

CREATIVITY AND IMPACT

Not all giving is traditional and straightforward. Many of the philanthropic gifts that have had the greatest impact were, in their time, speculative ventures by creative families with no certainty as to their outcome. The Nobel Prize is one such institution. At its founding in 1901, Alfred Bernhard Nobel remarked: "I intend to leave after my death a large fund for the promotion of the peace idea, but I am skeptical as to its results."

Ten years earlier, Leland Stanford, a California tycoon and former State Governor, decided that the West Coast needed an educational institution to rival Harvard and Yale. As a result, the excellent university which bears his name today was established.

Carnegie-Mellon University, the Said Business School at Oxford University, and other institutions of higher learning were all generously endowed by wealthy families as a means to influence the future for the better.

Today, modern philanthropists are searching for new approaches which will have an impact as far reaching as their predecessors to improve the state of the world in ways which are creative, innovative, and untested. The measurement of success for this type of creative effort may be felt only in generations to come, but will be a direct result of investments made today to shift the attitudes and consciousness of a large number of people toward critical social issues.

30. NEW PHILOSOPHY AND APPROACHES TO PHILANTHROPY

For many generations and in many wealthy families, philanthropy was pursued as a hobby, or was seen as an activity in which the details were a distraction. There was no systematic approach or strategy involved.

The result was a series of disconnected acts which comprised, primarily, writing a series of checks for charities whose operations and impact were neither quantified nor audited by independent experts.

THE END OF "CHECKBOOK PHILANTHROPY"

The era of "checkbook philanthropy" is fading fast, with the new breed of philanthropists and wealthy families far more concerned about the process, dispensation, and impact of their charitable contributions.

By applying strict selection criteria, or perhaps giving money on an outcome-determined basis (for example, contributing a set amount of money for each cataract operation completed, rather than a general contribution to a national or regional eye-care program), many wealthy families aim to ensure the maximum impact from their charitable contributions.

There is a saying that "new philanthropy is big philanthropy." While this may be true for the wealthiest families, there is also a new spirit of philanthropy spreading across all categories of wealth, stemming from a generation of baby boomers who have made substantial amounts of money at relatively early ages. New philanthropy is also smart philanthropy.

This new spirit is both large and widespread in its sources of contribution, and focused on the achievement of ambitious social agendae. It is characterized by a hard-headed approach to the creation of tangible value for the money "invested"; as such it provides very clear answers to the how and where questions of philanthropic activity.

New philanthropy is effective philanthropy. Many modern entrepreneurs, profiting commercially from a focused approach to investment and a results-orientation to operations, have imported the central aspects of that culture to the business of generosity.

A whole new vocabulary has arisen with regard to the role of the "social entrepreneur." Labels include the "philanthropreneur" and the "social venture capitalist"—vocabulary created to bridge the worlds of commerce and giving.

RANGE OF APPROACHES TO PHILANTHROPY

The approaches of wealthy families to philanthropic contributions and activities range from the highly organized to the highly individualized, each with different implications for the family concerned.

Random personal contributions: In this traditional and relationship-driven model of giving, individuals make contributions to charities of their choice, with little forethought and without any common strategy or plan. Money may go towards art galleries, schools, women's rights groups, and all kind of charitable institutions which, while perhaps good in themselves, do not follow any common patterns, are not characterized by any sharing of understanding or assessment of impact, and donors may miss out on the opportunity to consolidate effort and understanding to increase the impact of the well-intended contributions.

Considered allocation: At another level, prior thought is given to the family's charitable activities. This planned approach will very likely lead to a greater commonality of donations and a greater collective understanding of the impact of the donation. Any audit of this approach will focus purely on ensuring that the funds are in fact allocated to the prescribed activities and in accordance with the wishes of those who established the gifts.

Meeting targets: Going one step further, there are families who require that reviews be performed on the organizations to which they make contributions to ensure that their donation eventually ends up as far as possible in the hands of their intended beneficiaries, rather than being spent on the organizational overheads of the charities themselves. In some cases, expenses associated with fundraising activities, audit, overhead, and travel expenses can consume up to 50% of every charitable dollar contributed. Even three-star charities in the United States can use more than 10% of contributed funds on administrative and overhead expenses.

Achieving impact: A new impact-specific or outcome-specific approach targets philanthropic investment to achieve the maximum impact from the donation. Taking the previous approaches one step further, it is concerned not just with ensuring that the money arrives at the target destination, but with the impact that money achieves. In the case of a charity focusing on cataract reduction in the Himalayas, for example, the measure of impact is not how many dollars arrive in Bhutan, Nepal, China, or India, but on how many operations are performed, and how many individuals regain their sight as a result.

This businesslike approach to outcome-specific programs may link results achieved to future contributions. This results focus is increasingly being taken up by wealthy families as a way of ensuring that charitable contributions achieve the maximum intended impact.

Charitable funds integrated with business goals: In some cases, reflecting the understanding that charitable contributions can be beneficial to the strategic success of a business, families integrate their philanthropic activities with their family business activities. This may be particularly true in an emerging market where a small amount of philanthropic money can have a substantial community impact, thereby improving relations with local communities and national governments alike who can support the development of that business.

Businesses may well operate to high standards of corporate responsibility, assuring compliance in areas of workplace safety, corporate governance, environmental cleanliness, diversity, customer safety, product quality, and all of the other attributes of good business, but some go even further by actively donating a portion of profits, or sales, to worthy causes not directly involved with their commercial business system.

These contributions may be coordinated through a Family Office which is engaged in other philanthropic activities in areas outside the immediate business-related investments.

It should be noted that business-related philanthropy is not limited to the emerging markets. For many decades, support of opera, art galleries, educational institutions, and other worthy social causes in the developed world has been linked to positive benefits for wealthy families and their family businesses.

SEPARATE FOUNDATION

For families in the higher net worth brackets, a formal foundation may be established to set aside capital, as well as income, to make annual or longer term contributions to a defined set of charitable causes. For both tax and other reasons, some families will have a separate endowment, foundation, or philanthropic board which oversees philanthropic activity.

Setting up a dedicated family foundation as a separate legal entity may be a strategy to achieve one of many objectives. In the first instance, the allocation of funds to charitable activities can guarantee that the benefits of the family's generosity will long be felt.

By allocating and transferring funds to a separate legal entity, usually in the form of a charitable trust or its equivalent, a wealthy family can ensure that its philanthropic objectives are pursued, no matter what the later fortunes of the commercial and family wealth outside of the designated charitable trust funds.

A second objective of establishing an independent vehicle to hold and manage trust monies is the ability to identify and implement a proper wealth management strategy for the philanthropic funds allocated by the family. It may well not be appropriate for such a charitable trust to take high risk investment decisions or make illiquid investments which will only pay out over the long term if the needs of the charity are to make a defined annual contribution to cover operating costs of an orphanage, art gallery, educational institution, or other charitable purpose in need of a constant flow of income.

A third purpose of establishing a foundation is to ensure proper governance and a dedicated management team are put in place to pursue the foundation's objectives on a low-cost, high-impact basis; and also to ensure that any allocated capital is well and properly managed.

Investing foundation funds: Just as in the case of the best investment approach for a wealthy family, the processes, objectives, and reporting obligations for a foundation should be formal and disciplined. A separate investor profile and set of investment objectives should be established. In all likelihood, the need for a reliable income stream may be higher and the need for capital preservation may rise up the list of wealth management priorities.

The net result of a new investor profile and set of objectives may be a lower appetite for risk, a more conservative policy with regard to growth and volatility, and a tighter control on the set of fund managers selected for investment management mandates in defined sectors.

HIDDEN BENEFITS

One of the hidden benefits of a professional approach to the management of foundation endowment funds is the example it sets for the allocation of those funds to various charities. If there is a highly professional approach taken to fund management, with excellence in allocation, manager selection, and follow-up reporting, these same disciplines are more likely to flow through to the other side of the organization, maximizing the social return on funds "invested" and supporting an effective and efficient outcome that benefits everyone involved in the process.

31. PRACTICALITIES AND BENEFITS OF FAMILY GIVING

There is, of course, no set answer to the questions of *when* to give, *how much* to give, *to whom* and *how* one can give, and even *why* to give.

In part, the answers are driven by the category of wealth, the availability of funds, the disposition and number of individual family members involved, and other factors specific to each individual family.

> There is, of course, no set answer to the questions of *when* to give, *how much* to give, *to whom* and *how* one can give, and even *why* to give.

WHEN?

Many wealthy families make simple annual contributions to philanthropic causes; others take a more *ad hoc* approach, making generous contributions on a less systematic basis, with the timing, destination, and type of charitable contribution varying with the attitudes, interests, and economic vicissitudes of the family and its individual members.

Some major gifts may be made at a time of major events in the family's history—the sale of a business, the passing of leadership to a new generation, or the establishment of a separate legal foundation.

While the form and efficiency of giving will vary, one point mentioned by some of the bolder philanthropists, often in a rueful tone, is to avoid giving away money that is not yet tangibly in hand. More than one intended bequest has had to be reversed or reduced as a result of unexpected financial or family events which occurred after the original generous promise was made. It may be better for all concerned if only fully available money is pledged.

HOW MUCH?

As we saw earlier, almost every religion encourages or requires acts of generosity, yet there is no agreement on the amount that any individual or family should give. The Mormon Church requires tithes of 10% of after-tax income; the Church of England encourages its members to give between 1% and 5% of their income to charitable causes; Islam specifies 2.5% of savings and valuables as an appropriate level of charitable donation; the Jewish tradition of *tzedakah* recommends a 10–20% donation of after-tax income, depending on the wealth of the individual and with a balance between contributions for religious purposes and contributions to the poor.

However, even with this solid foundation of spiritual and religious beliefs and practices, philanthropy still remains a limited concept for many wealthy families. A few facts from research quoted in *More than Money*[1] bear this out:

- Only 20% of rich people make charitable bequests.

- Households in the United States earning in excess of US$100,000 a year give a lower percentage of their income (2.5%) than those who earn US$10,000 a year (3.6%).

- Estimates are that the lifetime giving of the more than 2,500 households in America with a net worth exceeding US$100 million, totals less than 0.5% of net worth.

With such low levels of considered giving, any family which actively sets out to establish an alternative family model, leading to a more philanthropic family legacy, will already be differentiated from the vast majority of its economically advantaged brethren.

The 10% solution: If one were forced to set a target of generous donation, based on a range of experiences and situations, 10% (of annual income or one-time capital grant) would seem to be a common number appearing in the history of many wealthy families and in many learned, moral and spiritual tracts on philanthropy.

One endorsement for a 10% target comes from the Reverend Thomas Binney, who wrote in his 1865 collection of sermons: "If anyone lays down for himself the rule of devoting a tenth of his income to God, he does well… It is to be remembered, however, that for some, a tenth of their income would be too much, while for others it would be far too little."[2]

---

[1] "Lessons from Wingspread: A Report of Recommended Strategies for Prompting Philanthropy" (Boston: Philanthropic Initiative), quoted in *More than Money*, No.9 (Autumn 1995).
[2] Thomas Binney, *Money: A Popular Exposition*, Jackson, Walford and Hodder.

Many go far beyond this target, with Warren Buffett the most generous of a large number of benefactors who have given the bulk of their enormous family wealth to charity.

TO WHOM AND HOW?

The selection of the causes, organizations, and forms of charitable donation (gift, loan, transfer of stock, income interest, capital interest, foundation, trust, insurance settlement, and other structures relating to the form of gift) are entirely the province of the family and its members.

Family history, future vision, values, personal experience, or the results of an objective analysis of need and potential impact of a gift can all contribute to the determination of a worthy case for a family's philanthropy.

While different in kind, the process of allocating charitable contributions and that of allocating financial assets have many structural elements in common:

- *A vision* needs to be set.
- *The scale, type, and timing of gifts* and funds to be invested have to be specified, along with the investment manager (in the case of a capital grant), and after taking the advice of tax and other advisors.
- An *"investment process"* is determined, with neutral advisors helping to oversee the entire process, along with an organization or individual capable of overseeing the process.
- An *"investment" profile* is determined to establish what sort of charitable contributions are to be considered and with what type of anticipated return.
- *An allocation model* is prepared, which sets out the overall allocation of resources across different class and type of "investment."
- *Tactical allocation decisions* are made within the selected categories and programs with an eye to maximize the impact at the lowest possible cost.
- *A reporting and control system* with a clear accounting for administrative costs needs to be set up.

By following this best-practice approach from the highly experienced world of investment management, wealthy families can act as social entrepreneurs who magnify their impact on selected causes.

Long-term view: Some philanthropic families are now looking to develop programs designed to have the highest impact at the lowest possible cost over the longest possible time. This type of engagement, which goes beyond contributing funds and auditing results, requires a deeper engagement by members of the family, and, possibly, professional advisors in developing the most effective mechanisms for creating and measuring long-term, beneficial social change.

WHY?

Perhaps the most difficult of all the questions relating to philanthropic activity is the *why* question. Why should a family, even one in the higher categories of wealth, give away money to people it will probably never know?

Moral and philosophical reasons: The first chapter of this section looks at the virtue and spiritual value of charitable acts, including some cultures for whom charitable contributions are part of a system of obligations which righteous men and women are expected to uphold.

Each family has to decide for itself what it stands for, what makes it unique and to which set of values it subscribes. Within the context of those wider decisions, the role of charity can be more precisely defined: if a family's sole purpose on this earth is to maximize its income at any cost and spend that money lavishly on its members, then there is no role for charitable engagement.

On the other hand, if a family wishes to pursue a more balanced and complete way of life, then it will need to consider the best way to integrate chosen philanthropic activities within its own larger strategy and set of family activities.

Philanthropy legacy and family unity: A structured set of charitable activities can enhance a family's legacy and bind families together, particularly those which have no substantial family business to create a sense of common interest and common cause. It can give them a sense of purpose for the future by creating a platform of philanthropic and associated wealth management activities that can extend forward across many future generations.

The result will be a more unified family acting on a firm set of values, focused on a laudable set of common initiatives, enhancing respect, and establishing institutions and practices which can endure long after the sale or dissolution of a family business.

Potential impact: The importance of engaging the wealthy and their families in this way is perhaps spelt out most eloquently by Jessie H. O'Neill:

> Although problems of poverty far outweigh problems of affluence, we cannot solve the enormous social problems we are facing without the financial resources, skills and knowledge of the rich. That is why the healing of the wealthy plays a vital part in healing our society. If empathy and understanding [of the wealthy, by the poor] can begin to grow where there has been only hatred and fear, we may yet find a way to save our country from financial and spiritual bankruptcy.[3]

Prominent development economist Jeffrey Sachs, seen by many to be a future Nobel Prize candidate for his work in developing economies, has stated that the world's rich could do more than the G-8 grouping of the world's most developed economies to eliminate poverty in the world.[4]

Joining such wealthy celebrities as Bono, Bob Geldof, Angelina Jolie, Richard Gere, and others, a raft of wealthy families and individuals are changing the face of charity, and influencing the future of the world as a result.

NO OTHER SOURCE OF SOLUTIONS

At a very high level, there is no alternative to the wealthy of the world stepping in where the old system of community, church, and state have failed to provide the resources and the know-how to solve society's problems. There are far more opportunities for improvements in society than there are government programs and existing charitable resources.

---

[3] Jessie H. O'Neill, *The Golden Ghetto: The Psychology of Affluence*, The Affluenza Project, 1997.

[4] Leyla Boulton and James Lamont, "Philanthropy 'can eclipse G8' on poverty," *Financial Times*, 8 April, 2007.

With opportunities to prevent avoidable deaths and to provide improved education, clean water, vaccinations for needy children, healthcare for the elderly, and a vast array of other beneficial causes, the lack of any alternative funding is a reason in itself to step up to a more active role in philanthropic contribution.

FAMILY PHILANTHROPY AND INDIVIDUAL PURPOSE

> "What is the use of living, if it be not to strive for noble causes and to make this muddled world a better place for those who will live in it after we are gone?"

Although Winston Churchill is often attributed with one of the most famous lines about philanthropy— "We make a living by what we get, but we make a life by what we give"[5]—the words are apparently not his. What he did say, though, with perhaps even more elegance is: "What is the use of living, if it be not to strive for noble causes and to make this muddled world a better place for those who will live in it after we are gone?"[6]

In addition to the practical benefits of philanthropic engagement, there is also a very personal benefit to sharing family wealth, which goes to the heart of who we are as human beings, and what we do to create meaning and value in our individual lives.

By sharing what we have and by thinking about others, we create a different relationship with the greater world and add an extra dimension to our own lives. As the greater forces of the universe create opportunities, the choices we make and the actions we pursue will define who and what we are within a far larger context.

> "A hero is someone who does what he can."

If we choose to act in a manner consistent with the higher values we set for ourselves, we will be contributing both to the memory and stature of our families and to our own personal legacies.

As Romain Rolland so aptly put it: "A hero is someone who does what he can."[7]

---

[5] See The Churchill Centre, www.winstonchurchill.org.
[6] In a speech in Dundee, Scotland, 10 October, 1908.
[7] "*Un héros, c'est celui qui fait ce qu'il peut. Les autres ne le font pas.*" Romain Rolland, *Jean Christophe*, Holt Rinehart & Winston, 1927.

LIVING A TRULY WEALTHY LIFE

*Remember the unique nature of individual
family members—including yourself*

32. MASTERING THE INDIVIDUAL CHALLENGES OF FAMILY WEALTH

Perhaps the most important part of any family strategy is the element of individual participation and fulfillment. While a substantial amount of thought and effort needs to go into thinking about the family as a collective unit, any forward plan will need to reflect the fact that any family is also a collection of individuals whose beliefs, attitudes, and behaviors will shape the family's future—and make or break its legacy.

Because of the importance of each individual, extra care must be taken to ensure that each family member is committed to the collective family strategy, and that each feels that his or her individual life plan has been fully considered in the context of that strategy.

Each individual family member might do well to use the following poetic analogy as a guide to compose and perform an entirely personal symphony of his or her own making:

My Symphony

To be content with small means;
to seek elegance rather than luxury, and refinement rather than fashion;
to be worthy, not respectable, and wealthy, not rich;
to study hard, think quietly, talk gently, act frankly;
to listen to stars and birds, to babes and sages, with open heart;
to hear all cheerfully, do all bravely, await occasions, hurry never.
In a word, to let the spiritual, unbidden and unconscious,
grow up through the common.

This is to be my symphony.

William Henry Manning (1810–1884)

INDIVIDUAL LIFE PLAN

Composing and pursuing a personal life plan is a major challenge for any individual. It goes to the very basic belief systems about the private self and the determination of individual purpose, within the family and in the world at large.

There are, of course, a multitude of ideas and approaches that can provide guidance in determining a set of personal beliefs, objectives, and actions. Some of these will be shared with other members of a nation, religious denomination, community, family, or social group. Others will be entirely personal, driven by the individual's unique background, personality, circumstances, experiences, choices, and relationships.

> "No man is an island, entire of itself..."

Each individual life is also deeply and broadly interconnected with others in a kind of individual eco-system which influences, and is influenced by, the individual concerned, a state summed up in John Donne's famous phrase: "No man is an island, entire of itself..."[1]

In determining the best pathway forward, the isolated nature of the individual self needs to be considered, as does the complementary view of humankind as one great interconnected family.

While there are no right answers to the issues of individual purpose, and no correct selection of a personal pathway that applies to everyone, there are a few essential questions that might begin to provide help in this regard.

ASKING THE RIGHT QUESTIONS

> By asking the right questions, we are far more likely to get better, if not perfect, answers.

By asking the right questions, we are far more likely to get better, if not perfect, answers. Conversely, if we ask the wrong questions, we are very unlikely ever to get the right answers.

In order to prompt an individual set of answers, the following general questions may serve as a useful guide:

---

[1] From *Devotions upon Emergent Occasions*, Meditation XVII.

WHO AM I?

All informed action begins with self-awareness. Knowing who and where we are is a first step in determining what we can, and should, do in the future. Background, individual character, personal strengths and weaknesses, values, accomplishments, failures, aspirations, fears, goals, place in the family, important relationships, place in the community, and other elements that contribute to the making of the unique individual and collective self need to be understood. The individual needs to take stock of the path followed to date and its attendant results, as well as the feelings he or she has about the current and past phases of life.

By clarifying the current point of departure, we will be far better placed to move toward the desired point of arrival, perhaps unencumbered by the baggage with which we began.

WHAT IS IMPORTANT TO ME?

A second question individual family members must ask themselves relates to the values, achievements, relationships, emotions, spiritual and material attributes, and other aspects of life they value most highly. These can then serve as possible beacons to guide future decisions. This process will prompt further questions: What makes me happy? What makes me sad or upset? Why? Is there a need to change any decisions and directions to align my life more closely with what I most value?

The answers to these questions can lead to an understanding of true priorities and can identify future standards and principles by which to live.

WHAT DO I WANT TO DO?

What we do is not merely a choice of career. The choice of a profession or vocation is one of the most important decisions we make, but what we do and how we do it embraces all of the actions we take to pursue a set of life goals, and to respond to the challenges and opportunities we face along the way.

We are, to a great extent, what we do.

As Andre Malraux pointed out in his many novels and erudite essays, we are, to a great extent, what we do. Our actions define our existence and speak louder than any words to reflect our true beliefs, values, and character. In consciously selecting the things we do, and the things we will not do, we give shape and meaning to our lives and destinies.

It may also be worth remembering that the quantum of accomplishment and quality of result may vary in direct proportion to the energy applied.

WHAT DO I WANT TO BE?

While action and accomplishment contribute greatly to our personal legacies, there is a greater state of being which is important to consider. Being a good parent, a successful business person, a spiritual or artistic individual, a teacher or student (or both), a widely traveled citizen of the world, or an embedded member of a small local community are differing states of being toward which an individual can orient both decisions and actions.

In many ways, the answer to this question will establish a personal statement of vision and values similar to that which is essential to the overall family strategy.

WHAT PRACTICAL OPTIONS DO I HAVE TO PURSUE MY CHOSEN PATH?

Physical, financial, familial, ethnic, historical, geographical, and a whole host of other factors which are not of our choice influence who we are. Within this context, each of us has, or can create, alternative pathways and different life options from which to choose.

By broadening the list of options, and in clarifying the full set of opportunities, each of us will have an opportunity to consider different life patterns and determine the quality of an individual life in the future.

HOW CAN I BEST SELECT BETWEEN THE AVAILABLE OPTIONS?

Setting out the options is a large step forward, but does not provide a final answer. Choosing between the different pathways, relationships, belief systems, professions, communities, families, roles, value systems, and supporting actions are among the most important decisions we face as human beings; the choices we make determine, in great part, who we are and what we become over the course of an entire lifetime.

The answers to the big choices in life will have an enormous impact on individual fulfillment, personal happiness, and family fortunes. The answers to these biggest questions can only be determined with full consideration given to the most personal matters of the mind, heart, and soul.

Needless to say, there is no one point at which life choices end. Life is indeed a journey and not a destination. There are constant opportunities from the beginning of a life to the end to give that life meaning, value, identity, and purpose. Even in death there is an opportunity to create meaning for future lives, as ethical wills, dispensation of earthly goods and other actions can add value to the lives of those left behind, or even to those not yet born.

Solon the Wise, a sixth-century B.C. Athenian aristocrat considered by the ancient Greeks to be one of the Seven Wise Men, said that no life could be judged until it was over. In fact, one could take an even longer view and state that no life could be judged until its full consequences have been played out over time, which could well be many family generations forward.

Perhaps a better view of assessing the events of time and history was presented by a former foreign minister of China, Chou En-Lai, when he was asked to give his judgment on the effects of the French Revolution, which had taken place 200 years earlier: "I'm not sure," he responded; "It is still too early to tell."

HOW CAN I BEST FOLLOW THE PATH I HAVE CHOSEN?

Once a particular pathway is chosen, there will be countless opportunities to confirm or change direction, and to determine the quality and content of the journey along the way. *How* one chooses to live will be as important as *what* one chooses to do.

There is no set of answers that can guide every action over time. Circumstances change. Influences evolve with experience, shifts in the personal and family eco-system, and changes in individual beliefs and attitudes.

Sources of guidance: Different systems of belief, traditions, and insights from the past can illuminate the pathway forward and provide guidance. Each religion, community, association, philosophy, family, and individual will have its own views on how best to navigate ahead.

The Principles of the Unitarian Universalist Association sum up what many, irrespective of their different religious and philosophical backgrounds, would agree to be some of the important principles to respect in life:

- The inherent worth and dignity of every person.
- Justice, equity, and compassion in human relations.
- Acceptance of one another and encouragement to spiritual growth in our congregations.
- A free and responsible search for truth and meaning.
- The right of conscience and the use of the democratic process within our congregations and society at large.
- The goal of world community with peace, liberty, and justice for all.
- Respect for the interdependent web of all existence of which we are part.

Aspiring to live in a manner consistent with such principles can provide orientation and guidance for many of the decisions that will shape the history of an individual life, and which will contribute substantially to a family's longer term legacy.

Living a life consistent with a constant awareness of higher value, purpose, effort, and standards is never easy. Often it makes for periods of loneliness, difficulty, and turbulence. Yet, as described by so many philosophers and *savants* over the centuries, the high road is often the more difficult pathway to follow, but it always leads to a better place.

In setting out on a forward-looking personal plan, ensuring that the most valuable sources of guidance and inspiration from the past are not forgotten can be an essential part of determining the best direction and quality of a future existence.

> The high road is often the more difficult pathway to follow, but it always leads to a better place.

THE FOUR NOBLE PURSUITS

One example of a larger set of aspirational attributes and accomplishments is the four-element system captured in the Indian ideal of the four worthy purposes and pursuits of an earthly life. These four *purusarthas*, or goals of life, are captured in the Sanskrit terms *artha*, *dharma*, *kama*, and *moksa*.

Artha, the pursuit of wealth, is to be understood as encompassing not solely material assets, but as including all kinds of intangible wealth such as knowledge, friendship, and love.

Although a worthy pursuit in itself, *artha* only finds its full value in being integrated with the other three pursuits: *dharma*, meaning societal responsibility and engagement in those things that sustain the social world; *kama*, meaning personal happiness at an individual level; and *moksa*, which adds the internal and eternal dimensions of spiritual fulfillment.

By living in a manner which combines and respects the value of each of these four individual elements, and which reflects a greater value of the integrated whole, any human life can be given meaning, purpose and direction.

TRUE FAMILY WEALTH

Perhaps a return to the fundamental idea of true family wealth, introduced at the beginning of this book, can provide another framework for individual understanding, planning, and action in the context of a broader family strategy.

By addressing the elements of a truly wealthy life in the broader sense of the term, both individuals and families will have an

---

The Content of True Family Wealth

- Financial wealth
- Integrity
- Accomplishment
- Physical security, health, and fitness
- Knowledge, wisdom, and spiritual growth
- Family harmony
- Individual happiness

---

opportunity to discover and address many of the most influential issues that relate to the family's future strategy and the plans of its individual members.

Financial wealth: In the end, when contemplating a full definition of family wealth, money counts. Money is a kind of energy with the potential to create the type of life, security, and freedom we seek for ourselves and our families. If not pursued as a sole goal, or to excess, the creation of material wealth is an aspiration admired in almost every civilization known to man.

Integrity: By setting out firm moral borders and by determining the virtues by which to guide our lives, we can create a platform of integrity and a substantial accumulation of ethical capital which can endure across many generations and a whole gamut of wealth-creating activities.

Accomplishment: As Malraux asserted, we are, in great part, what we do in pursuit of our life goals. The goals we set, the values we live by and the achievements we record all contribute to our personal history and individual legacy. By reaching higher, and accomplishing more, we expand the borders on what we do and who we are. The greater the accomplishments and the deeper the experience, the more complete and satisfying any individual life can be.

Physical security, health, and fitness: In the homespun wisdom of many countries, aspiring to a life which is healthy, wealthy, and wise begins with a hope for physical and mental wellbeing. By keeping a family healthy and safe, other goals can be pursued within a less physically and emotionally stressful environment.

Knowledge, wisdom, and spiritual growth: Developing a healthy mind and a wealth of useful knowledge is an important part of a full and wealthy family life. This goes beyond mere education or schooling; wisdom and knowledge are to be pursued throughout life through effort, curiosity, experience, and reflection.

In virtually every civilization, the pursuit of man's relation to God and the divine, seeking an understanding of purpose and greater order in the universe, is another essential part of the human condition. Whether that pursuit is through independent spiritual search, active participation in an established religion or the practice of pure meditation (which some Asian *gurus* have described as "listening to God," as opposed to Western prayer, which is seen as "talking to God"), finding one's way forward on a chosen spiritual pathway can be one of the most important contributions to a complete personal existence and a fulfillment of a unique personal destiny.

Family harmony: For almost every family member, harmony in the immediate, surrounding family and greater family is an important element in individual happiness. Discord, disagreement, and divisions can be enormously disturbing and disruptive to both the family and the individuals within it.

Individual happiness: In a world in which billions of individuals struggle to survive on a couple of dollars a day or even less, it may be hard to conceive of the fact that very few of the now more than eight million millionaires fully enjoy their wealth.

For many, great financial wealth can become a burden and source of constant stress, rather than a source of endless pleasure. The truly wealthy life, fully lived and fully enjoyed, is an elusive goal for many members of financially privileged families.

There is an enormous amount of information available on the link between money and happiness. Some studies have shown that, after a basic level of physical security is achieved, there is no correlation between having more money and finding more happiness. Others show that once income surpasses US$10–20,000, there is little correlation between incremental increases in income and incremental increases in happiness.

There is no correlation between wealthy nations and national happiness, with some poorer countries in Latin America and Asia scoring well above their more prosperous nations in surveys related to individual and national happiness.

On the other hand, studies have also shown that individuals do value money and enjoy the stature and pleasures it can bring. In one striking neurological study completed in 2006, it was shown that making money, at least for traders in an investment banking environment, stimulates the pleasure centers in the brain associated with sexual excitement. For this population, at least, making money is a stimulating and exciting experience which can be pursued with great energy and satisfaction.

A MIDDLE WAY

Ultimately, what constitutes family and individual wealth—and happiness—is always a blend of factors coming together in a comfortable middle way between two polar extremes.

For almost everyone, family wealth includes a substantial consideration of financial wealth, but also takes into account in different ways a loving relationship with a spouse and family members, family harmony, community participation, a contribution to the greater world, the values and rewards of maintaining an ethical way of doing business, the virtues of honesty and integrity, religious belief and practice, spiritual belief and practice, and the overall physical and emotional states of affairs of a given family.

CLOSING THE CIRCLE

Although it is focused on the content of true *family* wealth in the earlier part of this book, the list of seven elements on the previous page also goes a long way toward identifying the constituent parts of true *individual* wealth. However, in a search for the deepest sources of individual happiness, even this list is incomplete.

In any human life, the conditions necessary for complete happiness are the great emotions and exalted spiritual states of being that can only be partially discovered in the pursuit of family wealth and material wellbeing. While striving to pursue all of these elements in the strategy for a wealthy family, one should not lose sight of the supreme importance of love, hope, charity, purpose, meaning, enlightenment, and a realization of the full potential of the human condition.

Much of what will contribute to our ultimate happiness and the fulfillment of the promise of a wealthy life is the pursuit of these higher-order aspirations and the full accomplishment of an individual's private destiny.

REALIZING FULL POTENTIAL, BEATING THE ODDS OF HISTORY

Great strategy is all about realizing the full potential inherent in any situation, no matter how complex the issues and how challenging the legacy of the past appears at the outset.

In understanding the full amplitude of the task, and the full scale of the potential success, the perceived value, investment, and engagement in a strategy exercise may multiply in very quick order. Families can indeed protect their financial wealth over generations; the mechanical elements of a family wealth strategy as laid out in these pages can ensure that happens. But there is much more to the challenge, and the victory, than the mere retention or enhancement of a pre-defined quantum of financial assets over time.

In completing the diagnosis, design, and implementation of your own successful family strategy, you will have contributed enormously to the lives and life choices of those who follow. Like planting a tree that will only reach its full height long after the planter is gone, a family strategy may not come to fruition until long after the members of the family who designed and implemented it have passed away.

ACTS OF LOVE AND CARING

By designing and implementing far-sighted and highly informed strategies that plan forward across generations, actions can be taken today to improve the lives of children not yet born. This caring for unknown future family members reflects the great power of the family as a collective entity, and highlights the love that binds a family together over time and through many challenges. Such a dedicated effort can capture the full "promise and grace" inherent in the situation of any wealthy family.

A family can thus overcome the risks of writing a sad saga of riches to rags in three generations, and can achieve far more in lifting the family, and the individuals within it, to a higher level of accomplishment, a deeper level of understanding, and the realization of the potential for more balanced and meaningful lives which enjoy all aspects of true family wealth.

By observing the seven principles underlying a successful strategy for the wealthy family, individuals and their families can indeed assure that their legacy is one of true riches to riches across generations.

Ultimately, the effort to create a harmonious and wealthy family, in the broadest sense of the words, can be an enduring act of the greatest love and caring imaginable.

PRACTICAL EXAMPLES OF STRATEGY DOCUMENTS FOR THE WEALTHY FAMILY

INTRODUCTION

PRACTICAL EXAMPLES TO SUPPORT THE SEVEN PRINCIPLES OF FAMILY WEALTH STRATEGY

In this final section of *Strategy for the Wealthy Family*, examples of key strategic documents are provided to support each of the seven principles presented throughout this book.

The preparation of clear and carefully worded documentation, as already observed, will help family leaders to focus on their family wealth objectives, clarify the content of their strategy, and communicate correct and consistent messages to all members of the family.

These practical examples, together with the strategic framework described in the text of this book, are designed to tackle the riches-to-rags challenge head on, allowing families to implement a fully integrated strategy which addresses all elements of family wealth on an informed and coordinated basis.

It should be noted that these documents are included purely for illustrative purposes; each family should seek legal or tax advice from its own professional advisors, develop its own strategies, and pursue its own implementation process.

It should also be noted again that the Cuscaden example chosen is entirely fictitious and is not based on any real person, alive or dead, or family by that same, or any similar or different, name.

This list of examples is not exhaustive—tax filings, local regulations and many other obligations could require that a more comprehensive set of documents be drafted and incorporated into a family wealth strategy.

PRINCIPLE	STRATEGIC DOCUMENTS
Principle 1: **A Framework for Family Strategy** Set a family strategy with an objective of multi-generational preservation and growth of family wealth	**Example 1A:** Family Strategy Document for a Category I (US$5 million) Family **Example 1B:** Family Strategy Document (Full Version) for a Category III (US$500 million) Family
Principle 2: **Family Organization and Leadership** Organize the family and manage the surrounding eco-system	**Example 2:** Family Constitution
Principle 3: **Family Wealth Preservation** Structure asset holdings and adopt practices for long-term asset preservation	**Example 3:** Trust Deed and Letter of Wishes
Principle 4: **Family Wealth Management** Diversify assets and access the best investments and investment managers through a formal process of asset allocation and wealth management	**Example 4:** Investment Policy Statement
Principle 5: **The Family Business** Clarify and integrate family business strategy with long-term family wealth plans	**Example 5:** Family Business Strategy: Executive Summary
Principle 6: **Effective Philanthropy** Share wealth in a manner that unites the family and gives it meaning	**Example 6:** Philanthropic Foundation Document
Principle 7: **Living a Truly Wealthy Life** Remember the unique nature of individual family members—including yourself	**Example 7:** Ethical Will

As discussed in Chapter 5: Process and Content of Family Strategy, all families (and family strategies) must evolve and adapt within an ever-changing environment if they are to survive and prosper. It is therefore important that all family strategy documentation is regularly reviewed to meet the evolving needs of the family.

FAMILY STRATEGY DOCUMENT FOR A CATEGORY I (US$5 MILLION) FAMILY

CUSCADEN FAMILY STRATEGY
SUMMARY DOCUMENT
PRIVATE AND CONFIDENTIAL

As we enter a new era, we have decided to develop and implement a forward-thinking strategy for the Cuscaden family which can guide us over the next five years and put in place a framework to ensure continuing family prosperity and harmony across many future generations.

AN INTEGRATED APPROACH TO STRATEGY

The purpose of the current Cuscaden Family Strategy, as summarized in this document, is to translate the family vision described below into concrete achievements in all areas relevant to our family's future. This strategy will address:

- Family vision, values, and organization
- Wealth preservation
- Wealth management
- Effective philanthropy
- Individual plans
- Long term forward planning

These elements of a coordinated vision will require substantial change and sustained effort from all members of our family.

Everything from the family organization to trust structure and documentation (for example, letters of wishes) to investment strategy to eco-system management to philanthropy must be aligned behind the new family vision and supporting objectives.

The specific changes we will pursue include:

FAMILY VISION, VALUES, AND ORGANIZATION

We propose to adopt a family statement of vision, values, and approaches to apply to all areas of family activity which will help us to preserve and enhance our family's wealth across future generations.

We shall establish a Family Council to meet once per quarter to clarify the overall goals, roles, rights, responsibilities, and required actions in the family. By formalizing the vision, values, and approaches we adopt, we hope to establish a model to support family harmony and progress for multiple generations.

The vision statement and family values proposed for discussion and adoption by the Cuscaden family are as follows:

Vision statement

"The Cuscaden family will strive to become one of our region's most highly respected business families, constantly setting and achieving new standards of excellence in family accomplishment, business results, sustainable wealth management, community engagement, philanthropic contribution, and family harmony across generations.

Throughout all of our endeavors we shall respect the highest standards of business ethics and family integrity—building on our historic reputation as 'capitalists with a conscience.'"

Values

In pursuing our Family Vision, we shall adhere to a set of values which lie at the core of our family's history and our unique identity. These values are to be honored in our family and in our business ventures. These values are:

Unity: The family will remain united and strong through all environments and events, no matter how adverse or challenging. This may require individual sacrifice to ensure that the family's interests are maintained and that the harmonious integrity of the Cuscaden family is preserved.

Perseverance and adaptability: We shall foster a strong work ethic in every individual in every generation and build a culture which recognizes that life changes and that we must change with it. Adaptability is the essence of survival and our approach to the family and business matters will reflect this understanding.

Discretion: Our family values and corporate activities require that individual family members avoid excessive personal and corporate coverage in the press and media. To that end, all external communications should be made consistent with the policies and parameters determined by the Family Council.

Social responsibility: We shall always remember the privileges that result from our commercial efforts and endeavor to share the benefits of our activities with those less fortunate than ourselves. Especially in the local markets in which we pursue our business interests, we shall pursue extraordinary opportunities to make a substantial and positive impact on the lives of the many colleagues and individuals who engage with our business systems.

In our approach to business we shall be sensitive to the appropriate standards of socially responsible behavior—in the pursuit of our family philanthropic objectives we shall be generous and thoughtful in improving the lives of other citizens whose needs are far greater than ours.

It is essential that all members of the family function as a single entity. This will require a set of efficient and effective systems and processes, a culture of cooperation and communication, and individuals within the family who are willing to work for our common success as well as their individual achievement.

Improve the quality of the family eco-system

There will be a new structured approach adopted to select and manage a more professional set of advisors. We shall reduce the number of relationships we have with outside financial advisors and select and work only with the most accomplished and most responsive to our needs. In order to broaden our coverage of information and opportunities, we will undertake to rationalize our approach to the private banks, brokers, fund managers, and other advisors with whom we do business.

We shall start by employing an advisors' matrix model, which will identify the high-priority changes needed.

In order to ensure we are working toward that goal, we shall add a discussion item on each quarterly session of the Family Council on progress in building a best-in-class family eco-system for a family of our scale and ambition.

WEALTH PRESERVATION

We shall adopt a more sophisticated approach to financial investment, asset structuring (that is, trust strategy) and risk management.

Financial investment will be pursued through an allocation model which is scenario-based, comprehensive, and which takes into account the family's financial security and wellbeing under any national economic scenario.

Asset structuring will reflect a more sophisticated approach to trust management. We shall, in the near future, establish separate trusts for the Next Generation members of the family, with specific letters of wishes to guide the corporate trustees.

Risk management will take into account the financial aspects of risk and the personal aspects of risk which could have a significant impact on the happiness and wellbeing of individual family members and the family as a whole.

The strategy to preserve family wealth will be twofold: to structure assets in a more effective manner and to undertake a formal risk-management process which addresses all relevant family risks.

Financial objectives and asset allocation model

The financial investment strategy is focused on pursuing an objective to double Cuscaden family net worth in seven years, after all distributions. The target of "2x in 7" implies an average after-tax growth rate in investments of 10% per year, which we believe is a reasonable objective. This will be accomplished through careful asset allocation, top-decile manager selection, and an active S-curve approach to investment which allocates funds to the following categories:

- *Safety money* which is available under any circumstances to ensure family security and support a reasonable family lifestyle. This will be a minimum of 20% of family funds.

- *All-weather money* which is invested across a broad set of asset classes with a mix of capital growth and income returns, specifically tailored for each trust's specific needs. We shall actively access opportunities and diversify risks through the selective use of investments in funds and funds of funds. Our overall allocation will be split equally between fixed income, public equities, private equity, and property. This total should average around 70% of family investment funds.

- *"High end of the S-curve" money* put at risk with the expectation that the funds invested may provide an exceptionally high return, but may also be lost in their entirety. This will be a maximum of 10% of family funds.

Currency: As all of our expected future costs and obligations are in our home country currency, we shall only make investments in that currency to avoid the risks of capital loss through adverse foreign currency movements.

Simplify reporting: The historic reporting formats were too fragmented, lacked any consolidating summaries, and could not be tied back to any meaningful strategy. As a result, a new approach to reporting has been proposed which will:

- *Provide a clear investment and investment performance summary,* including a consolidated report by asset class, investment manager, and by currency.

- *Summarize* and describe investment performance vs. objectives and vs. benchmarks by asset class and type of manager.

- *Specify* a strategic plan and track progress against major action items and targets.

Asset structuring

An essential element of the current trust strategy is to protect what has already been accumulated from tax, capital, investment, litigation, marital, or other potential loss.

This will now require, *inter alia*, a review of all existing trust structures and associated letters of wishes, along with the establishment of a new trust for the members of the Next Generation.

Risk management

A comprehensive review of risks to our family wealth and wellbeing has been undertaken for the first time and a new approach agreed.

- *Manager diversification is needed to ensure* no one manager handles more than 50% of total family assets.

- *Restructure asset ownership approach with all managers to ensure* assets are held under direct trust ownership arrangements.

- *Insurance in place* needs to be increased for key family figures to cover potential death duty and IHT obligations.

- *Rigorous and regular reporting* on investments needs to be put in place, with an early alert on any performance, individual, or other risk.

- *Other risks* and future marital issues to the trust corpus may need to be considered as trust structures, investment, and staffing policies evolve.

Family health and security: In addition to the initiatives mentioned above, key risks have been identified and responses put in place to reduce risks as follows:

- *Personal:* annual health screens and appropriate plans for lifestyle improvements to be made for each individual member of the family.

- *Family:* security review to be undertaken of premises, offices and habits of key family members by a qualified security company.

WEALTH MANAGEMENT

The primary objective is to improve the risk-adjusted return of the investment portfolio in the coming five years, which are expected to be more difficult than the past five. The entire strategy, with all of its attendant financial and other costs, is meant to further the objectives set out below and to yield a return on investment well above cost.

A *secondary objective* of building such a solid approach is to make the overall approach to financial wealth management understandable, manageable, and controllable for future generations who may have less interest or capability in wealth management than the current entrepreneurial generation.

One of the objectives of the approach taken is that it could be driven "like a Ferrari" by the current family leadership team, but is also capable of being put into "automatic transmission" mode and operated comfortably and safely with far less need for expert input and control from family members responsible for the family's future financial legacy.

EFFECTIVE PHILANTHROPY

A new and more formal approach to fund disbursement will be adopted which measures and rewards the highest impact philanthropic endeavors within the areas selected by the Cuscaden Foundation.

In addition to existing family philanthropic activities, a new approach to establish a dedicated philanthropic trust will be pursued, with 10% of income being paid into the trust on an annual basis. The philanthropic trust will be funded with an initial gift of $500,000, 10% of our investible net worth.

INDIVIDUAL PLANS

Personal aspirations and development plans should be provided by each member of the family over the age of 18. These personal plans will be discussed at a meeting of the Family Council or with a named mentor, for review and discussion on a confidential basis.

Those plans should address the personal, professional, spiritual, family, educational, and other elements selected by the individual member which reflect the content of the life that family member wishes to achieve.

Each member of the family will have an opportunity, and be encouraged, to fill out a personal plan addressing all aspects of family wealth for the current period, and consider creating an ethical will in the future, in order to capture what he or she feels is most important to communicate to future generations of the family.

LONG-TERM FORWARD PLANNING

By ensuring that we are thinking about tomorrow as well as today, we hope to put in place actions and ideas that will allow our family to avoid problems, find new areas of harmonious common activity, and establish a platform to assure that our descendants benefit from a happy tradition of riches to riches across generations.

Following the approval of the content of this document, the family leadership team will need to develop an implementation plan which includes:

1. Timetable of Key Action Items
2. Forward Budget and Plans.

FAMILY STRATEGY DOCUMENT (FULL VERSION) FOR A CATEGORY III (US$500 MILLION) FAMILY

CUSCADEN FAMILY STRATEGY
PRIVATE AND CONFIDENTIAL

As we enter a new era, we have decided to develop and implement a forward-thinking strategy for the Cuscaden family which can guide us over the next five years and put in place a framework to ensure continuing family prosperity and harmony across many future generations.

The purpose of the current Cuscaden Family Strategy, as summarized in this document is to translate the family vision described below into concrete achievements in all areas relevant to our family's future. This strategy will address:

A. An integrated approach to all elements of strategy

B. Family organization and support

C. Wealth preservation

D. Wealth management

E. Family business strategy

F. Effective philanthropy

G. Personal plans for individual family members

These seven elements of a coordinated vision will require substantial change and sustained effort from all members of our family.

A: AN INTEGRATED APPROACH TO ALL ELEMENTS OF STRATEGY: EXECUTIVE SUMMARY

Everything from the Family Constitution to trust structure and documentation (for example, letters of wishes) to investment strategy to team constitution to network management needs to be aligned behind the new family vision and supporting objectives.

A summary of the specific changes we shall pursue includes:

Formalize family organization: We propose to adopt a family constitution to clarify the overall goals, roles, rights, and responsibilities in the family. By formalizing the vision, values, and approaches we adopt, we hope to establish a model to support family harmony and progress for multiple generations.

The proposed family organization structure is shown in Figure 1.

Increase resource to support family: The increasing demands from an expanding family require greater supporting resource in the areas of family services, risk management, and wealth management. The specific areas of activity to respond to those needs include:

- *Upgrade family office network and resources:* Add an offshore office in Geneva (100% owned by and dedicated to Cuscaden family trusts), where the organization needs to have a loyal team and resident skills in key areas of trust, tax, fund management, direct investment, and structuring transactions of all kinds.

Figure 1   Family Organization Chart

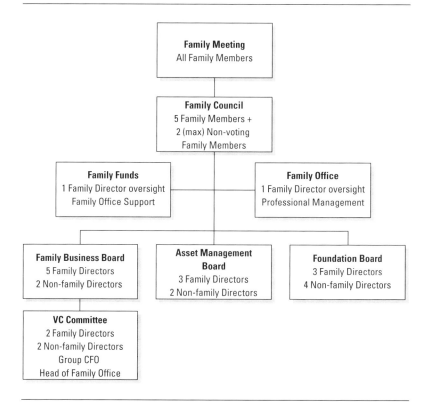

- *Establish strategic platforms* with partners in Russia, Indonesia, and in the energy sector, including alternative energy investments.

Improve the quality of the family eco-system: There will be a new structured approach and resident skills added in the organization to select, monitor, and manage outside advisors. In particular, the selected set of outside managers will need to be more closely managed by Cuscaden Family Office team members, building direct relationships with key funds and fund management teams.

Wealth preservation: We shall adopt a more sophisticated approach to financial investment, asset structuring (that is, trust and trustee strategy), and risk management.

- *Financial investment* will be pursued through an allocation model which is scenario-based, comprehensive, and takes into account the family's financial security and wellbeing under any global scenario.

- *Asset structuring* will reflect a more diversified approach to trust jurisdiction and trustee diversification. We shall also, in the future, be setting up a private trust company in Bermuda to focus solely on Cuscaden family affairs.

- *Risk management* will take into account the financial aspects of risk and the personal aspects of risk which could have a significant impact on the happiness and wellbeing of individual family members and the family as a whole.

Wealth management: This is focused on pursuing a strategy to double Cuscaden family net worth in seven years, after all distributions. The target of "2x in 7" implies an average after-tax growth rate in investments of 10% per year, after distribution, which we believe is a reasonable objective. This will be accomplished through careful asset allocation, top-decile manager selection, and an active S-curve approach to investment which allocates funds to the following categories:

- *Safety money* which is available under any circumstances to ensure family security and support a reasonable family lifestyle.

- *"Family endowment" money* which is invested across all asset classes by the world's best Elite Family Investment Managers with a mix of capital growth and income-return objectives specifically tailored for each trust's specific needs.

- *"High end of the S-curve" money* put at risk with the expectation that the funds invested may provide an exceptionally high return, but may also be lost in their entirety.

Family business strategy: A new, and more focused, approach to business strategy is recommended, along with the addition of a non-family CEO, to improve business performance and value.

Effective philanthropy: A new and more formal approach to fund disbursement will be adopted which measures and rewards the highest-impact philanthropic endeavors within the areas selected by the Cuscaden Foundation.

Personal engagement and motivation for family members: Each member of the family serving in the family businesses, and each family member drawing from family funds, and any other family member over the age of 18 who wishes to do so, will submit a personal development plan to be reviewed and discussed in confidence with the Family Council, addressing his or her role within the family and business activities, and addressing all elements of family vision, values, and individual definitions of a successful life.

These are very ambitious goals and will require substantial and simultaneous change on many fronts.

Family leadership roles: The roles played by the family leaders will be critical to the whole process. It is essential that family leaders assess their priority activity areas, take responsibility for selected initiatives, and allocate their time and family resources accordingly.

Current and desired family leader time allocation is shown in Figure 2.

Immediate next steps: Without delay, actions will include identifying and negotiating lease contracts for suitable office space in Geneva, staffing the new office in Geneva and increasing staff at our Family Headquarters Office (including working with two separate executive

Figure 2 Family Leadership Time Allocation

Area of Activity	Current Time Allocation	Desired Time Allocation (%)	Needed Change
Family Organization and Governance	5	10	New Constitution needs to be finalized
Family Eco-system	10	15	Need to add Geneva FO Expand network
Wealth Preservation	10	15	New Trust Structure needed
Wealth Management	5	20	Establishment of Asset Management Board
Family Business Strategy	65	25	Strategy to focus portfolio Non-family CEO
Effective Philanthropy	3	5	Need to move to new outcome-specific model
Next Generation	2	10	Specific personal plans and strategy needed

search firms to find suitable investment professionals), and working with a design consultant on office layout for the expanded Family Headquarters Office and the new Geneva office.

In addition, investment and tax strategies need to be formalized within each strategic platform.

Continued momentum: Looking forward, it is important to continue the momentum developed during this year of review and redirection. Building on the learning from the strategic review and design phase, a forward schedule will include an annual three-day strategy review session in Bermuda (perhaps spread over a five-day week with breaks in between for informal team building and relaxation), a mid-year full-day review and two quarterly half-day review sessions. These meetings could coincide with Investment Committee meetings and would include advisors as well. A weekly control meeting led by the Head of the Family Office will track performance on a regular basis.

All meetings will be offshore, most likely in Bermuda and Geneva, with the possibility of one quarterly session in Asia or Latin America as well.

An integrated approach to family strategy is illustrated in Figures 3, 4, and 5.

Figure 3 An Integrated Approach

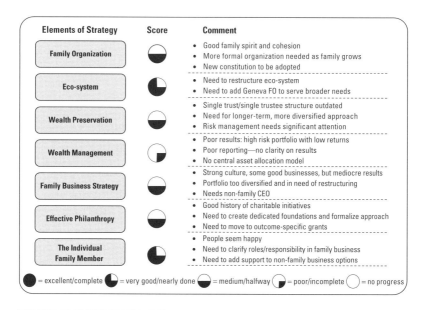

Figure 4 Family Plan – An Integrated Approach

Stop	Start	Continue
• Sub-market compensation in family business	• Extended Annual Family Meetings (formal)	• Family (informal) summer holidays
• Confusion about roles in family leadership	• Family newsletter (monthly)	• Open spirit
• *Ad hoc* rules and principles approach	• Drafting Family Constitution	• Having fun as a family
	• Succession planning in family and family eco-system roles	

Figure 5 True Family Wealth

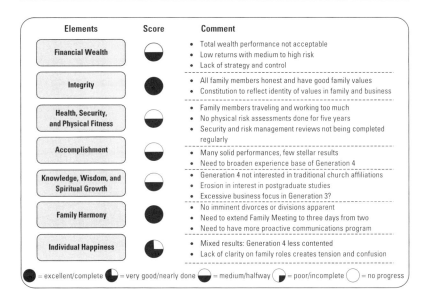

Elements	Score	Comment
Financial Wealth		• Total wealth performance not acceptable • Low returns with medium to high risk • Lack of strategy and control
Integrity		• All family members honest and have good family values • Constitution to reflect identity of values in family and business
Health, Security, and Physical Fitness		• Family members traveling and working too much • No physical risk assessments done for five years • Security and risk management reviews not being completed regularly
Accomplishment		• Many solid performances, few stellar results • Need to broaden experience base of Generation 4
Knowledge, Wisdom, and Spiritual Growth		• Generation 4 not interested in traditional church affiliations • Erosion in interest in postgraduate studies • Excessive business focus in Generation 3?
Family Harmony		• No imminent divorces or divisions apparent • Need to extend Family Meeting to three days from two • Need to have more proactive communications program
Individual Happiness		• Mixed results: Generation 4 less contented • Lack of clarity on family roles creates tension and confusion

= excellent/complete   = very good/nearly done   = medium/halfway   = poor/incomplete   = no progress

B: FAMILY ORGANIZATION AND SUPPORT

The overall approach is to create a combination of owned offices in Bermuda (Headquarters, now with PTC added), Geneva (new), and a set of partially owned strategic platforms (Russia, Indonesia, environmental technology, property, and philanthropy (healthcare and education)) which can access and process the most attractive global investment and philanthropic opportunities while serving the tax and personal objectives of family members.

In addition, a special initiative will be taken to review and restructure the family's financial eco-system of advisors beyond our dedicated offices and partially owned platforms.

While no family member is planning a full-time move to offshore residence in the near term, the structure should be capable of supporting such a move as smoothly as possible should any Cuscaden family member decide to do so.

DEDICATED FAMILY OFFICES

The expanded family office structure and strategic platform approach is shown in Figure 6.

Figure 6 Proposed Family Office Structure

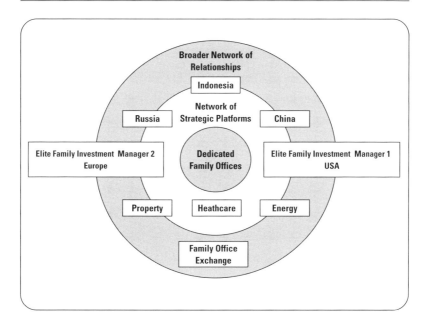

The Family Headquarters Office in Bermuda will continue to focus on Cuscaden family service needs, family business and operating entities, fund management, direct equity, environmental technology, sustainable investment, philanthropy, and networking with UK and US funds, banks, advisors, entrepreneurs, and other creative sources of ideas and investments.

This office will cover US and Latin American fund management, co-investment, direct equity support, and Family Office networking across North and South America.

The new Geneva Office will cover continental and emerging market (especially Asia and Africa) fund management, direct equity support, energy and strategic platform coordination, International Advisory Board support, and Family Office networking across all of Europe and Asia.

Stability and continuity beyond the current generation: Quality succession and continuity planning will require that the family has an experienced and tested team in place for the Next Generation by adding advisory and Family Office team members aged 40 or below. We also need to provide long-term succession plans for all key members of family, as well as for Family Office and advisory team members.

Team and culture: It will be essential that individual roles are well defined in the new structure, and that the team spirit and traditionally selfless Cuscaden Family Office ethos is carried forward into the larger organization.

An example of a family office score sheet is shown in Figure 7.

Figure 7 Family Office Score Sheet

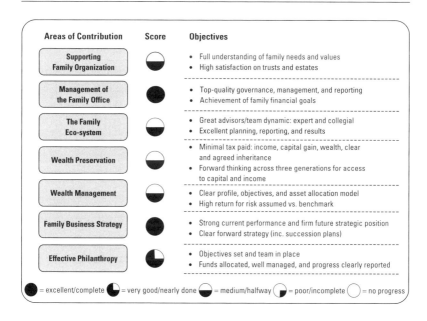

STRATEGIC PLATFORMS

Specific legal entities will be set up with partners to harness world-class expertise and access the best investment opportunities in the selected areas of energy, clean energy, property, Russia, and Indonesia.

Each strategic platform will be jointly owned and operated with a proven world-class partner in the area of interest. The specific objectives, strategies, costs, and staffing plans will be agreed with all parties on a three-year forward rolling basis.

BROADER NETWORK AND FAMILY ECO-SYSTEM

In order to broaden our coverage of information and opportunities, we shall undertake to rationalize our approach to the private banks, fund managers, and other advisors with whom we do business.

The family eco-system, highlighting priority areas of change, is shown in Figure 8.

Figure 8   Family Eco-system

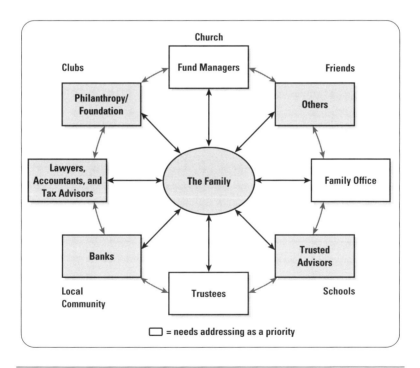

The roles and services offered by professional advisors in the broader network are shown in Figure 9.

Figure 9   Role of Professional Advisors

Family Services (payments, tax filing etc.)	Trusted Advisor	Private Bank	Multi-Family Office	Family Office	Elite Financial Investment Manager	Investment Bank	Specialist Professionals
		☆	★	★			
Wealth preservation	☆	☆	☆	★	☆		★
Tax and estate planning	☆	☆	☆	☆	☆		★
Family issues (Next Generation etc.)	☆	☆	☆	★			
Trusts and trustee management	☆		★	★			★
Risk management	☆	☆	☆	★	☆	★	★
Wealth management	☆	★	★	★	★	☆	
Financial planning	☆	☆	★	★	☆		★
Asset allocation	☆	☆	☆	★	★	★	★
Manager selection		★	★	☆	★	★	
Financial reporting			☆	★	☆		
Family business advice	☆			☆		☆	★
Charitable counseling	★	☆	☆	★			★
Integrated strategic advice	★	☆	☆	★	☆		
Overall performance reporting			☆	★			

★ = primary role   ☆ = offer services

We shall start by employing an advisors' matrix approach, which will identify the high-priority changes needed.

An example of an advisors' matrix, with proposed changes, is shown in Figure 10.

- *Unifying approach:* It is essential that all parts of the global network function as a single entity. This will require a set of efficient and effective systems and processes, a culture of cooperation and communication, and the selection of high-quality

Figure 10 Advisors' Matrix

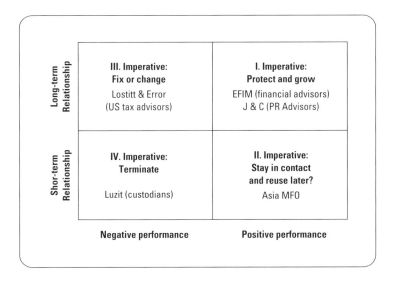

individuals to join the system who are willing to work for the common success as well as individual achievement.

- *In the flow:* It is important for the Family Office teams to be aware of, and up to date with, new ideas and initiatives, new managers, interesting products, and other opportunities. To that end, a specific program of networking with other family offices and identifying future advisors will be added to the management of the family eco-system.

C: WEALTH PRESERVATION

The strategy to preserve family wealth will be twofold: to structure assets in a more diversified manner and to undertake a formal risk-management process which addresses all relevant family risks.

ASSET STRUCTURING

An essential element of the current trust strategy is to protect what has already been accumulated from any risks of loss through problems related to tax, capital, investment, litigation, marital issues, or other areas of potential loss.

This will now require, *inter alia:*

- The diversification of our trust jurisdictions through the establishment of an alternative trust structure in a new jurisdiction under different trustee arrangements. Primary consideration will be given to non-European jurisdictions.

- The addition of a PTC in Bermuda (to operate under the guidance of the Family Office) to improve family control of trust assets in the future.

- A review of all existing trust documents and associated letters of wishes.

Examples of current and proposed trust structures are shown in Figures 11 and 12.

Figure 11   Trust Structure—Current

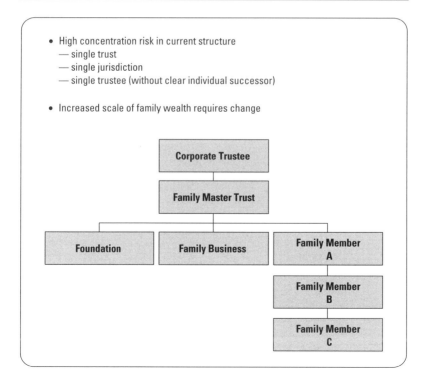

Figure 12 Trust Structure – Proposed

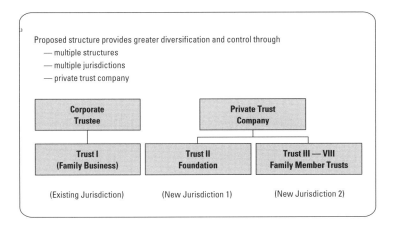

Proposed structure provides greater diversification and control through
— multiple structures
— multiple jurisdictions
— private trust company

Corporate Trustee		Private Trust Company	
Trust I **(Family Business)**	**Trust II** **Foundation**	**Trust III — VIII** **Family Member Trusts**	
(Existing Jurisdiction)	(New Jurisdiction 1)	(New Jurisdiction 2)	

Family trust principles are shown in Figure 13.
(See Example 3 for trust deed and letter of wishes.)

Figure 13 Family Trust Principles: Capital and Income

Generation	Group	Capital Access and Distribution Policy	Income Distribution Policy	Control and Governance
I	Founder(s)	Full Access	10% of business PAT and portfolio profits	Full control No voting— founder's sole discretion
	Broader Family	None		
	Charitable Foundation	None	10% of PAT to fund foundation	
	Allocation of Capital only — No Capital Access in Generations II and III			
II	Direct Descendants	50%	10% of business and investment profits if no more than sustainable rate of withdrawal—distributions in proportion to capital	Board of three (all of founder's children) to retain 100% voting power
	Broader Family	20%		
	Charitable Foundation	25%		
	Other (staff)	5%		

(continued)

Generation	Group	Capital Acess and Distribution Policy	Income Distribution Policy	Control and Governance
III	Direct Descendants	50%	10% of business and investment profits if no more than sustainable rate of withdrawal—distributions in proportion to capital	Board of six (maximum two direct descendants from each child of the founder if they exist) to retain 100% voting power in Charitable Foundation
	Broader Family	20%		
	Charitable Foundation	25%		
	Other (staff)	5%		
	Full Distribution of Capital to groups as per allocation			
IV	Direct Descendants	50%	Sustainable rate of withdrawal in proportion to capital until member reaches 35, then full capital distribution	Charitable Foundation Board of six (maximum)—two from each family group—i.e. descendant of child of founder if they exist) to retain 100% voting power
	Broader Family	20%		
	Charitable Foundation	25%		
	Other (staff)	5%		

RISK MANAGEMENT

A comprehensive review of risks has been undertaken for the first time and a new approach agreed.

- *Manager diversification is needed to ensure* no one manager handles more than 50% of total family assets.

- *Restructure asset ownership approach with all managers to ensure* assets are held under direct trust ownership arrangements.

- *Insurance in place* needs to be monitored and increased as necessary for key family figures to cover potential IHT obligations.

- *Security company review* of potential employees and investing partners.

- *Rigorous and regular reporting* on investments, with an early alert on any performance, individual, or other risk issues.

- *Regular third-party audits* of Cuscaden operations, offices, and charitable foundation.

- *Succession plans:* specific plans for all key individuals.

- *Other risks:* litigation and any other marital issues, and other risks to the trust corpus, are to be considered as trust structure, staffing, investment, and staffing principles evolve.

FAMILY HEALTH AND SECURITY

In addition to the initiatives mentioned above, individual family-member risks have been identified and responses put in place to reduce risks as follows:

- *Personal:* health screens and appropriate plans for lifestyle improvements to be made at individual level.

- *Family:* security review to be done of premises, offices, and habits of key family members and Family Office employees by a qualified security company.

Also to be considered in the coming year are:

- *Key family member going offshore:* Although there is no current intention of any core family member moving offshore, the Chairman may consider such an action (a four-year commitment) in the future, using Bermuda as a primary personal residence.

- *Training manuals to ensure trust-driven processes are respected* in the new Family Office in Geneva and in the strategic platforms.

- *Regular rebasing* of trust asset valuations to reduce any future tax impact.

As mentioned above, all of these individual elements of strategy need to be further broken down into action items and integrated into a coordinated timetable.

Figure 14 Family Risk Management

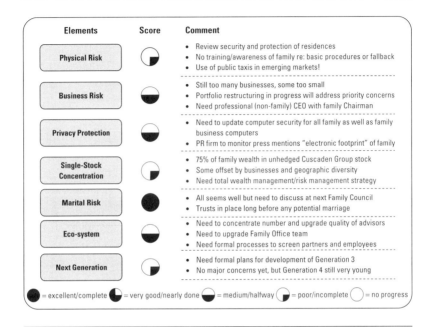

Elements	Score	Comment
Physical Risk		• Review security and protection of residences • No training/awareness of family re: basic procedures or fallback • Use of public taxis in emerging markets!
Business Risk		• Still too many businesses, some too small • Portfolio restructuring in progress will address priority concerns • Need professional (non-family) CEO with family Chairman
Privacy Protection		• Need to update computer security for all family as well as family business computers • PR firm to monitor press mentions "electronic footprint" of family
Single-Stock Concentration		• 75% of family wealth in unhedged Cuscaden Group stock • Some offset by businesses and geographic diversity • Need total wealth management/risk management strategy
Marital Risk		• All seems well but need to discuss at next Family Council • Trusts in place long before any potential marriage
Eco-system		• Need to concentrate number and upgrade quality of advisors • Need to upgrade Family Office team • Need formal processes to screen partners and employees
Next Generation		• Need formal plans for development of Generation 3 • No major concerns yet, but Generation 4 still very young

● = excellent/complete ◕ = very good/nearly done ◑ = medium/halfway ◔ = poor/incomplete ○ = no progress

A family risk-management plan is shown in Figure 14.

D: WEALTH MANAGEMENT

The overall vision is to put in place an approach to Cuscaden family wealth management which is world class in every aspect and which can achieve a set of ambitious and interrelated objectives over the next seven years.

The overall vision is to protect, grow, transfer, and share the Cuscaden family wealth in a high-quality manner across multiple generations. Overall, the financial objective is to double the family net worth over the next seven years while respecting all family values and principles—and making all contributions to the Cuscaden Foundation as envisaged and set out in the appropriate documents.

An example of investor profile and objectives is shown in Figure 15. (See Example 4 for an expanded investment policy statement.)

Figure 15   Investor Profile and Objectives

Investment Profile			
Timeframe	short term	medium term	_long term_
Risk Appetite	low	_medium_	high
Liquidity Preference	high	medium	_low_
Savings Rate	low	medium	_high_
Contingency Needs	high	medium	_low_

Investment Objectives
1. Double value of family financial assets in seven years (after distributions)
2. Distributions below sustainable rate of withdrawal
3. Shift to top-decile managers only, using EFIM
4. Diversification of managers
5. High quality reporting

The primary objective is to improve the risk-adjusted return of the investment portfolio in the coming three to five years, which are expected to be more difficult than the past five. The entire strategy, with all of its attendant financial and other costs, is meant to further the objectives set out below and to yield an incremental return on investment well above any incremental cost.

A secondary objective is to make the overall approach to financial wealth management understandable, manageable, and controllable for future generations who may have less interest or capability in wealth management than the current entrepreneurial generation.

A good analogy for this approach to Cuscaden financial wealth management is that it could be driven "like a Ferrari" by an expert family leadership team, but would also be effective when put into "automatic transmission" to be driven by potentially less highly motivated or less expert family members in the future.

ADVISOR STRATEGY

The financial advisor strategy will be to have three core portfolios, of roughly equal size; one managed in-house and two managed by outside advisors. The Family Office will provide an integrated asset allocation model and define the roles of all outside investment proposals

SIMPLIFY REPORTING

The historic reporting formats were too complicated, lacked summaries and could not be tied back to any meaningful strategy. As a result, a new approach to reporting has been proposed which will:

- *Provide a clear investment and investment performance summary,* including a consolidated report by asset class, investment manager, and by currency.

- *Summarize* and describe investment performance vs. objectives and vs. benchmarks by asset class and type of manager.

- *Specify* a strategic plan and track progress against major action items and targets.

OVERALL ASSET ALLOCATION MODEL

The portfolio of assets (not including Cuscaden family business operating entities) has undergone careful review and discussion. The main focus of the portfolio has been to select an investment model which is spread along the investment S-curve from high to lower risk and is aimed primarily at a balance of capital protection and growth rather than income generation. The portfolio is also selected as a medium-liquidity (relatively little cash and on-demand investment) and medium-risk (low leverage) portfolio.

Strategic asset allocations (current and objective) are shown in Figures 16 and 17.

Figure 16 Strategic Asset Allocation

Asset Class	Current	Objective
Cash and Equivalents	25	10
Fixed Income	50	25
Shares	10	10
Property	10	10
Private Equity	0	20
Hedge Funds	0	5
Derivatives and Options	0	2 (hedge only)
Commodities	0	10
Gold	0	3
Arts and Antiques	5	5

ALLOCATE ASSETS TO MAXIMIZE POTENTIAL RETURN

The overall strategy is to define and execute an investment and organizational strategy to be successful at all stages of the investment S-curve, which reflects the risk/return by category of investment.

The investment strategy is set to balance high-return investments in higher-risk areas (direct equity, emerging markets (geographic and product), new managers, and other areas of inefficient market pricing) with efficient market investments (for example, UK and US equity markets, proven investment managers, and so on).

One of the pathways to high returns is to select investments in emerging areas before a period of rapid growth takes place—an economic "tipping point"—and high returns can be achieved by holding high-return investments through the growth phase.

In addition to asset allocation between different stages, risk is managed by careful selection of investment managers (the top 10% within each category in every case) by a central investment advisor who has no vested interest in promoting any in-house products.

"SAFETY MONEY" STRATEGY

Ten per cent of the total family net worth will be invested in a set of "safe" investments—unlevered and low volatility—which will be held in a new and separate trust structure. The purpose of this is to ensure that the family vision is capable of being pursued and that family lifestyle is maintained in the event of a major financial meltdown or legally encumbering initiative affecting the existing trusts.

"MELTDOWN PROTECTION"—THE ULTIMATE FALLBACK SAFETY OPTION

In addition to the "safety money" allocation, consideration is being given to the creation of an ultimate safety destination which ensures physical safety as well as financial safety in the event of a major economic meltdown. The current thesis is that either Scandinavia or New Zealand would be the safest place to be; opportunities are to be pursued for a large tract of farmland (more than 500 acres with water and self-sustaining agriculture) to be purchased, developed, and kept ready in case of future need.

CURRENCY (EXCLUDING CUSCADEN OPERATING ENTITIES)

The portfolio will be set to balance currency positions to avoid an excessive (and industry-standard) reliance on the US dollar.

Figure 17 Currency Objectives

Currency	Current	Objective
US$	90	40
€	0	30
£	0	10
¥	10	10
Other	0	10

GEOGRAPHY

A final tactical overlay of geographic exposure has also been developed.

This factor of accessing emerging markets through OECD investments has been taken into consideration when selecting investments to achieve the selected geographic and currency balance of one-third each to the U.S., Europe, and Asia/emerging markets. It is worth mentioning that many U.S. investments, and to some extent, European investments, are, in fact, global businesses which happen to be run from the U.S. or Europe. This is true for core large capital holdings and for alternative asset investments and will be taken into account in the allocation model.

E: FAMILY BUSINESS STRATEGY

Appended as a separate document (Example 5) is an executive summary of a family business strategy.

F: EFFECTIVE PHILANTHROPY

(Family philanthropic strategy is shown in Figure 18.)

Figure 18 Philanthropy

Vision:	To make a substantial positive impact in the two areas selected by James and Catriona Cuscaden—healthcare and education—in a manner that creates independence and sustainable change in the poorest areas of the world
Objectives:	• Provide an education to 1,000 girls and young women in selected poor countries • Provide training for 100 healthcare professionals for women's healthcare in emerging markets
Approach:	• Create separate trust and dedicated organization • Adopt outcome-specific standards and selection criteria • Performance audited every year • Select and work with strategic partners where 1+1=3 • Programs which create substantial community impact • Programs which contribute to the longer term independence of all beneficiaries of our programs: "a hand up, not a hand out"
Team:	• Double team size in program locations (not HQ)
Foundation Investment Philosophy:	• Three managers of world-class standing • 50% low risk/high income generation • 50% medium risk/capital gain focus

In addition to existing family philanthropic activities, a new approach to foundation grants and loans will be undertaken to ensure that the maximum impact will be made from each contribution.

This will require a more formalized definition of results targeted, a tighter selection process and more thorough follow up.

In order to achieve these objectives, additional resources and some change of personnel will be required in the foundation team.

(A foundation document is shown in Example 6.)

G: PLANS FOR INDIVIDUAL FAMILY MEMBERS

At the discretion of the individual family member (but required of family members who are active in the family business), those over the age of 18 should submit personal aspiration and development plans to the Family Council (for those active in the business) or to a named mentor (for those not involved in the business) for review and discussion on a confidential basis.

These plans should address the personal, professional, spiritual, family, educational, and other elements selected by the individual member which reflect the full set of life goals that family member wishes to achieve in both the short and long term.

Examples of personal goals, a personal plan, and a summary of issues and actions facing members of the Next Generation are shown in Figures 19, 20 and 21.

Figure 19 Personal Goals: Family Member A

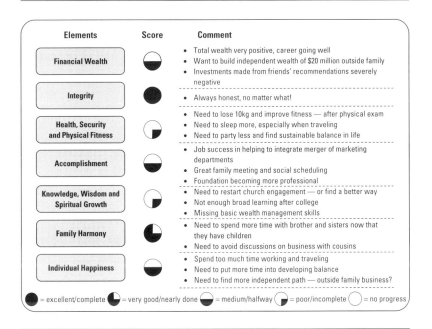

Figure 20 Personal Plan: Family Member A

Stop	Start	Continue
• Drinking for six months	• Education program in wealth management	Family holidays
• Relying on friends for investment ideas	• Yoga and meditation lessons	Role on Foundation board
• Conflictual discussions with cousins about business	• Regular exercise	Helping to organize social events at Family Meetings
	• Sitting in on Investment Committee meetings	

Figure 21 Next Generation Plan: Summary

Individual	Issues	Actions
Ian (Jr.)	• Starting external business experience at Azurlon Pharmaceuticals	• Need to organize training in marketing and finance • Need to obtain work permit (and check tax and residency issues)
Mary	• Taking year off from school next year—wants charity role	• Find substantial role with one of Cuscaden Foundation charities
Robert	• Third-year review in business not good (attitude an issue)	• Assign mentor (James) • Change assignments • Issue warning (James)

Each member of the family will be encouraged to complete an ethical will, which captures what he or she feels is most important for the family to retain over coming generations.

(An example of an ethical will is presented in Example 7.)

LONG-TERM FORWARD PLANNING

By ensuring that we are thinking about tomorrow as well as today, we will initiate actions and ideas that will allow our family to avoid problems, find new areas of harmonious common activity and put in place a platform to assure that our descendants benefit from a happy tradition of riches to riches across generations.

An example of a multi-generational strategy plan is shown in Figure 22.

Figure 22 Strategy Across Generations

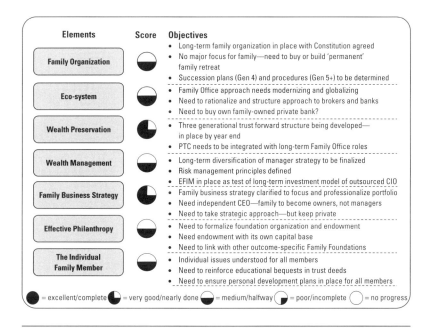

Following approval of the content of this document, the family leadership team will develop an implementation plan which includes:

1. Timetable of Key Action Items
2. Forward Budget Plans.

EXAMPLE 2

FAMILY CONSTITUTION

CUSCADEN FAMILY CONSTITUTION

CONTENTS

I. STATEMENT OF PURPOSE

The purpose of this Family Constitution is to set out an enduring and equitable approach to family matters which will preserve the harmony, integrity, and prosperity of the Cuscaden family through all future events and environments across generations.

To that end, we have set out below the guiding vision, institutions, principles, and procedures to realize this aspiration in each succeeding generation of the family, with an overall objective to provide a structure and framework to guide the decisions and operations of the family and Cuscaden family business in a manner consistent with our identity, history, vision, and values.

II. FAMILY MEMBERSHIP

Membership of the Cuscaden family includes all direct bloodline descendents of James and Catriona Cuscaden. Adopted children of a bloodline descendent and children born out of wedlock to bloodline descendants may be admitted by a majority vote of the Family Council, with such admittance to membership not to be unreasonably withheld.

Family members over the age of 16 may attend and vote on matters arising at the Annual Family Meeting.

By a 75% majority vote of all family members, a family member may be barred from Family Meetings on a permanent or other basis. It is envisioned that this vote will only be taken for behavior significantly at odds with family values, such as criminal activity or behavior aimed at creating deep divisions and discord within the family.

III. FAMILY VISION

A. To secure the future health, education, and financial welfare of all members of the Cuscaden family.

B. To make a valuable contribution in selected areas of philanthropy, in particular in the developing nations in which we operate

C. To create a fair and equitable process to protect, enhance, distribute, and share the Cuscaden family values and family capital—financial, ethical, spiritual, and human—across all future generations of the family.

IV. FAMILY VALUES

In pursuing this vision, we shall adhere to a set of values which lie at the core of our family's history and our unique identity. These values, to be honored in our family and in our business ventures, are:

A. *Unity:* The Cuscaden family will remain united and strong through all environments and events, no matter how adverse or challenging. This may require individual sacrifice to ensure that the family's interests are maintained and that the harmonious integrity of the Cuscaden family is preserved.

B. *Integrity:* We shall always act with the utmost honor and integrity.

C. *Fairness and respect:* We shall treat all family members, business colleagues, government officials, and people who interact with our family with courtesy and respect. We shall listen to their views and consider their thoughts carefully. We shall treat all individuals with dignity and act in a manner which reflects the full set of family values set out in this document.

D. *Excellence:* In our various family business initiatives, and in our individual lives, we shall strive to achieve excellence in all that we do. This will require substantial and continuous effort to ensure that we are achieving all that we can, individually and collectively.

E. *Entrepreneurial spirit:* Our business was built on a foundation of intelligent risk-taking and initiative. Only through the continued application of that initiative and the measured acceptance of risk can we continue to grow and prosper in the future as we have in the past.

F. *Strong work ethic:* We shall foster a strong work ethic in every individual in every generation, whether or not that individual is active in the family business.

G. *Discretion:* We understand the great value to the family of each individual member observing the highest standards of confidentiality with regard to family affairs and the lowest possible profile with regard to public exposure and media coverage. No member of the family may disclose any detail concerning the family, family wealth, family business, or other family matter without express prior permission from the Family Council.

H. *Social responsibility:* We shall always recognize and appreciate the privileges that result from our commercial efforts and endeavor to share the benefits of our commercial activities with those less fortunate than we. Especially in the emerging markets in which we pursue our commercial activities, there will be extraordinary opportunities to make a substantial and beneficial impact on the lives of many colleagues and other citizens whose needs are far greater than ours. In our approach to business we shall be sensitive to the appropriate standards of socially responsible behavior; in the pursuit of our family philanthropic objectives we shall be generous and thoughtful in improving the lives of the recipients of our donations.

I. *Individual commitment:* Each and every member of the Cuscaden family will be asked to commit to the contents of this constitution and its successors. Without the commitment of our individual family members to a greater set of values and goals, we will not be able to realize our vision and achieve the greater aspirations we have established for the family. Each and every member of the family will adhere to these values, whether that member is involved in the family business, is engaged in another commercial enterprise, or is pursuing other goals of a non-commercial nature.

V. FAMILY STRUCTURES AND PROCESSES

It is essential that the structures and processes designed to guide and govern the family and the family's financial interests address both on an integrated basis.

To that end, a governance structure will be established which takes into consideration the family itself, the ownership of our businesses, the governance and management of those businesses, the creation of new family enterprises, the management of family assets which exist outside of the current operating businesses, and a Foundation Board to serve the philanthropic interests of the family.

A. *Cooperative mode of operation:* While each board will have its own members, objectives, and distinct capabilities, each will operate within the context of a united family and an integrated approach to business. As such, the operations of each entity specified within this document will be open, transparent, and fully supportive of the aspirations and operations of other boards and activities within and across the family.

B. *One-family policy:* All structures and operating principles should reinforce the central concept that we are one family with a united approach to business and family matters. Each family member and organizational entity will do all in his/her/its power to preserve the harmony and integrity of the Cuscaden family.

In addition to building a common platform through the development and enforcement of the content of this unifying constitution, the Chairman of the Family Meeting will organize the format, date, and location of the annual Family Meeting.

All family members are strongly encouraged to attend this meeting except under exceptionally adverse or encumbering circumstances.

C. *Common history:* In addition to the activities dedicated to improving current and future family harmony and identity, a special effort will be made to organize the writing and annual updating of the Cuscaden family history. This unique history will be documented to provide a sense of common roots, highlight shared values, and illustrate that each family member has an opportunity to contribute to the successful future of the family.

VI. THE FAMILY MEETING

A. *Overview:* All members of the Cuscaden family over the age of 16 will come together at least once per year at a Family Meeting.

The overarching purpose of the Family Meeting is to unite and harmonize all of the family's various constituencies and interests—generational, family unit-specific, commercial, structural, geographical, and personal. The existence of the Family Meeting legitimizes all delegated activities and promotes the primary goal of unifying the Cuscaden family.

The responsibilities of the Family Meeting will be to review any proposed changes to this Constitution, to review the progress of the Cuscaden businesses, the annual performance of the investment portfolio and asset structuring activities, and any other high-level issues of common interest to the family.

Decisions in these areas will be reserved to the Family Council, but all family members will retain the right to provide input into those decisions at the review sessions held during the Family Meeting.

Decisions with regard to the strategy for family philanthropic activity, presented by the Chair of the Foundation Board, will require approval by a majority vote of the members present at the Family Meeting.

Every member of the Cuscaden family has an equal voice at the Family Meeting. All members will be encouraged by the Family Meeting Chair to put forward their views in a candid and respectful manner. These views will be considered sincerely, with appropriate responses given during the meeting or in a subsequent private session.

B. *Governance:* The Family Meeting shall be organized by a supervisory group consisting of a Family Meeting Chair, four family members and a non-voting secretary. The first Chair will be nominated in this document and hold the position for a three-year term. Subsequent Chairs will be elected by secret ballot by family members at the annual meeting every third year. All family members over the age of 50 are eligible to serve as the Chair of the Family Meeting.

The first Chair will be Ian Cuscaden.

If the position of Family Meeting Chair becomes vacant between annual meetings through resignation, death, or incapacitation, the family will select a new Chair from within its membership by ballot at a special meeting of the Family Meeting called with at least 45 days' notice. Prior to that meeting, the most senior member of the Family Council, defined as the longest-serving member of the Council, will act as interim Family Meeting Chair and will assume responsibility for organizing the election.

Family Meetings will be arranged to coincide with a Family Council and a Cuscaden Foundation Board meeting in order to ensure efficiency of procedures and broad inclusion.

C. *Generational meetings:* During the Family Meeting, in order to develop teamwork and communication within each generation of the family, there will be a separate meeting of each generation arranged to take place within the schedule of the Family

Meeting. It is expected that there will be at least two separate generational meetings: a "Council of Elders" for family members over the age of 60, and a "Next Generation" group for family members under the age of 30.

Subsequent meetings will be chaired by a member of the generational group, with such Chairs to be elected for a one-year term by the members present at that meeting.

D. *Funding:* The cost of the above Family Meeting events will be met by the dedicated Family Fund focused on promoting a One-Family culture. The annual budget for these costs will require approval in advance from the Family Council.

E. *Required attendance:* Unless excused in advance by the Chair, attendance by all members of the Cuscaden family over the age of 16 will be required at the annual Family Meeting.

Failure to attend without prior approval will result in a penalty of 10% of dividends due to the member not attending to be contributed to the Foundation in his or her name.

VII. THE FAMILY COUNCIL

A. *Overview:* The role of the Family Council is to act in a manner similar to a corporate Board of Directors of the family as a whole. All matters not reserved to the Family for discussion at the Family Meeting will be delegated to the Family Council for decision-making and implementation as and when it determines.

The Family Council will serve as the oversight board for all family and family business issues. It will set long-term direction, agree shorter-term plans, review and adjust resource allocations as appropriate, and act to resolve any disputes arising with regard to individual or collective family matters.

B. *Responsibilities:* These will include setting and managing the implementation of short- and long-term goals and strategies for the family, individual family members, the family businesses, family wealth management (including trusts, estates, and tax matters), and philanthropic activities.

The Family Council will nominate and approve changes in the directors of the Business Board, Asset Management Board, the Cuscaden Venture Capital Committee (CVC), and Foundation Board membership. Any changes to other Board structures or committee appointments to the Boards of the Family businesses will require approval of the Family Council upon presentation of recommended names by the Family Business Board.

In addition, the Family Council is charged with the responsibility to think forward across multiple future generations to ensure that a robust platform of values, institutions, and practices is established which can carry forward our family's success for as long as possible into the future.

C. *Developing family wealth:* The Family Council will also be responsible for the fostering of family wealth in all of its forms—financial, ethical, human, and spiritual. This will specifically include the development plans for the family as a whole and for individuals within the family.

D. *Financial structures and planning:* The Family Council will also determine all matters related to the establishment and oversight of trusts, corporate structures and tax planning, business ownership, the membership of the family boards (Business, Asset Management, and Philanthropy), the appointment of non-family members to family boards, and the promotion of family members within family businesses.

The Family Council will also develop and promulgate an annual strategic plan for the family's various interests, including a specific review of asset allocation between and within the business, asset management, and philanthropic areas of investment. The Family Council will also approve all major acquisitions or disposals outside of the approved budget and any major change to the direction or strategic focus of the family business.

E. *Approvals and decisions:* The Family Council will have the right to approve all major business and investment-related decisions, following submission of final recommendations from the Family Business Board.

The Family Council will also approve the annual plan of the Asset Management Board, with specific reference to the risks and expected returns proposed for the portfolio of investments recommended by the Asset Management Board.

F. *Annual distribution and compensation:* The Family Council, taking into consideration all relevant factors, will decide on the annual distribution of capital or income from the family's commercial activities to philanthropic activities and to members of the family as it sees fit. The remuneration to be received by each family member will comprise three elements:

1. a dividend to reflect the individual's ownership stake or beneficial interest in the family business and the funds adjusted by the family Asset Management Board

2. a base salary to reflect time (part-time or full-time) spent in the various family initiatives—in business, philanthropic, family service, or other areas of activity

3. a performance bonus to reflect performance or value added above and beyond the contribution reflected in the base salary

G. *Career management:* The Family Council will be charged with the responsibility and authority to decide on matters related to the employment, promotion, removal, review, and compensation of family members in the family business. Such decisions will be taken after extensive and comprehensive consultation with the Family Business Board. External consultation and advice may also be sought to provide an independent third-party view on capability, performance, and long-term career and personal skill development plans.

The family acknowledges that all family members should be free to pursue whatever career aspirations they may have and should be given the freedom to choose whether or not they wish to work within the family business. The family will endeavor to assist family members to find suitable jobs for interested family members within and outside the family business, based on their individual capabilities, skills, and experience.

H. *Appointments to the family business:* Entry into the business is an opportunity, not a birthright, and high levels of commitment and performance will be expected from any family member joining the business.

It is recognized that the business should only appoint family members into positions of employment if suitable vacancies exist. Family members will not be permitted to work within the family businesses without a defined role, a normal line of accountability, and full participation in performance review and other developmental and assessment systems expected for a non-family employee.

In addition, any member of the family who wishes to enter into the family business must meet two separate criteria as defined below. Completion of these two requirements, creating a combined five-year obligation, does not create a right to become a full-time member of the family business; only the right to be considered for employment within the family business. Other criteria will be applied as determined by the Family Council, which will also determine at its sole discretion how those criteria are to be applied.

The two requirements for consideration are:

1. *External experience:* At least three years must be spent in a successful career in a business outside of the portfolio of businesses owned or controlled by the family, or in which the family has, or is likely to acquire, a stake exceeding 5%. That experience should be deemed to have been successful by the Family Council, which will be apprised of progress and performance (including the submission of any and all written performance evaluations) by the individuals who wish to be considered for full-time participation in the family business. This business may or may not be located in our home country.

2. *Core business experience:* In addition, each member of the family desiring to pursue a career in the family business must spend at least two years outside our home country in a non-English-speaking country and be engaged in a full-time role in the family business there.

MBA exception: If a family member obtains an MBA from a reputable university or business school, he or she is eligible, with the consent of the Family Council, to shorten the requirement for outside experience to only two years, making the total commitment a minimum of four years—two outside our own country and two outside the family business.

I. *Succession planning:* The Family Council has a special obligation to prepare succession plans for its members and for key operating executives within the family business. These plans should prepare for both unexpected succession needs requiring immediate succession and longer-term plans which can address business needs and individual development plans, with an element of succession planning contained therein.

J. *Family Council membership:* As James Cuscaden had four surviving grandchildren, and specifically requested that these direct descendants be treated equally, the direct descendants of each of the four children will be considered to be a Family Unit. To the extent possible and as set out in this document, each succeeding generation of the family will make its best efforts to ensure a full and equal participation of each Family Unit whenever possible

The Family Council will consist of one family member from each Family Unit and a Chair, to be selected from among any Family Unit, by majority vote of the members of the Family Council.

If a Family Council member dies or is incapacitated, a generational peer or following generation family member over 25 years of age from that Family Unit will join the Family Council in the vacated position. This replacement should be identified in the Group succession planning exercise and developed to take over successfully on either a planned or unplanned transfer of the position.

It will be left to the discretion of the individual Family Units to determine the succession plan, selection procedure, and retirement age of their members on the Family Council, with a maximum age of 65 years. Each member will serve a term of four years.

To the extent possible, divisive elections should be avoided; any contending claims or candidacies should be worked out in advance of balloting to avoid undue conflict within the family.

K. *Family Council decision-making process:* It is acknowledged that the Family Council, as well as all boards and committees, will strive at all times to reach consensus on all issues; ballots will only be held in exceptional circumstances.

Where a consensus has not been reached, each Family Council member will hold a deemed proxy for the number of shares which the individual members of his Family Unit hold at the time of the vote.

All proposals to the Family Council on which consensus cannot be reached will be approved provided a majority of votes cast are in agreement.

L. *Special exceptions:* For any decision in conflict with the terms of this document, and for any permanent revision of the terms of this document, a minimum vote of 80% of total votes cast will be required. This exceptional approval will be required, for example, if a family member is proposed to enter the Family Business who does not meet the required criteria outlined above.

M. *Chair election procedures:* The Chair of the Family Council will be selected by the members of the Family Council to serve a four-year term.

In the event of the Chair's sudden death or incapacitation, the surviving members, along with the Family Unit successor to the Chair's seat on the Council, will elect, with a 75% vote required in favor, the succeeding Council Chair, who will complete the unexpired portion of the current four-year term.

N. *Meetings:* The Family Council should meet at least once per quarter, and more often if it so determines, with one meeting set to coincide with a Family Meeting.

O. *Changes in this Constitution:* Any permanent variation in the terms of this constitution can be proposed by any member of the Family Council at any time, and on an annual basis by any family member at the Family Meeting, with such a proposed amendment drafted and circulated at least three months prior to the annual meeting and commented upon by the Family Council.

Any motion proposing a permanent change will require an 80% vote in approval by the Family Council.

VIII. FAMILY BUSINESS BOARD

A. *Overview:* The Family Business Board will address and decide on matters related to business ownership not reserved for the Family Council, including, but not limited to, the performance, development, restructuring, or other operating aspect of any business or group of businesses. The determination of what is reserved for the Family Council will be decided by the Family Council in its sole authority.

The Family Business Board will also address and decide on any issue related to the management of the family's operating businesses—defined as entities in which the family holds either a controlling interest or an equity stake exceeding 10%.

In particular, the Family Business Board will determine the roles, career plans, and development activities of both family members and professional non-family managers within the family business.

The Family Business Board will develop and monitor all strategic plans and operations of the operating businesses with approval by the Family Council. All decisions within the operating businesses, except those specifically requiring the approval of the Family Council, will reside with the Family Business Board. This will expressly include target-setting, compensation schemes, development expenditure approvals, and all such similar strategic elements of each business.

The role of the Family Business Board will also be to develop and sustain a prosperous and ethical business enterprise which will operate consistent with the family values enumerated above. The results of the commercial activities are intended to provide sufficient funds to support an appropriate lifestyle for its current members and create sufficient value to provide equally well for future generations.

B. *Business Board membership:* The Family Business Board will consist of seven members, with at least two being non-executive, non-family members. All external directors will be selected by the Family Council and re-appointed by the Council in groups of one or two on a rolling four-year basis. The Chair of the Family Business Board and at least one other board member should, by preference but not necessity, be a family member appointed for a four-year term as Chair by the members of the Family Council.

It is also preferred, but not required, that the Chair of the Family Business Board also be a member of the Family Council.

Term of Chair: The initial Chair of the Business Board will be appointed and hold this position for a two-year period. Thereafter, appointees will hold the position for terms of four years.

This initial two-year term will ensure that the Chairs of the Family Council and Family Business Council are not co-terminus. If a death or other event occurs which results in the two positions coming up for election in the same year, the term of the Family Business Board will be altered by the Family Council to re-establish the initial staggered schedule.

C. *Family Directors:* It is the responsibility of each Family Director to fully commit his or her time and best efforts to the position and to perform in accordance with the designated role.

If a Family Director holds an executive position in the business, he or she will be prohibited from engaging in any other business ventures outside the Group. This includes financing any business ventures with children unless such a venture is fully disclosed or receives the approval of the Family Business Board and Family Council.

Once a Family Director moves to a non-executive role on the Family Business Board, he or she is free to engage or invest in other business ventures so long as these ventures do not compete with or create a conflict of interest with any family business. If such a conflict exists at the time of the investment or arises subsequently, the Family Council reserves the right to require that the investment be terminated.

Failure to terminate an investment or other business activity within the timeframe determined by the Family

Council will result in the offending family member not receiving dividends for shares on a pro rata annual basis until the breach is corrected, with such dividends being contributed to the Family Philanthropic Foundation.

Family Business Board Directors will be expected to retire by the age of 60. This may be varied by a majority vote of the Family Council on an individual and exceptional basis, if special circumstances so dictate.

Family Directors will be appointed for a period of four years. Subject to retirement, there is no limit to the number of four-year terms a Family Director is able to serve.

Potential future Family Directors, including any potential future Chairs of Boards or Committees, will be formally appraised on an annual basis by the non-family, non-executive directors. The methodology of these appraisals will be agreed upon by the Family Business Board and the non-executive directors. Family Directors will be expected to prepare and present their own professional development plans.

D. *Remuneration of Family Directors:* All Family Directors will receive the amounts established by the Family Council on an annual basis. Remuneration will be in line with the market rate for that position and will be based on merit. In setting these market rate salaries, no account will be taken of dividends or any other amounts paid to them as shareholders, which are to be considered as an entirely separate matter.

Family Directors, along with non-family directors, will be eligible to receive performance-related bonuses based on a bonus pool arrangement set up by the Family Business Board and approved by the Family Council.

E. *Succession plans:* Every Family Director should have in place a succession plan to cover two contingencies: an immediate unanticipated need for replacement, and a planned longer-term transition.

The Family Office is responsible for ensuring that such plans are in place and agreed by the Family Business Board and Family Council.

F. *Other business interests:* Family members who work full time in the business or have received Cuscaden venture capital funding should not have any other business interests or be engaged in other activities which could divert their attention from that of the Group and its related activities.

Passive investments and other business interests not interfering with family business activities and responsibilities will be considered acceptable so long as the demands created are not such as to divert attention from Group responsibilities, and their nature not such as to create a conflict of interest with other current and potential interests of the Group. A register of these passive investments should be maintained by the Family Council to ensure full transparency.

G. *Related party transactions and conflicts of interest:* The Family Council should be notified of any potential conflicts of interest or related transactions between individual family members and the family business.

A register of these potential conflicts and transactions will be maintained by the Family Council, with such a register to be made available for inspection by any family member at any time in order to ensure full transparency.

Family members should never pledge their shares in the Group as security to an outside party or to any other family member without the express advance approval of the Family Council. All relevant documents—shareholders' agreements, articles of incorporation, memoranda, constitutions, and so on—are to be drafted to reflect the obligations incurred under this clause and all other clauses of this Constitution.

H. *Non-family, non-executive directors:* Non-family, non-executive directors should be chosen carefully and future appointments should meet the following basic criteria:

1. They should be wholly independent of other board members.

2. They should have a deep understanding of working with similar-sized, family-owned businesses in similar markets.

3. They should have top-class global business experience and have no conflicts of interest.

Compensation for non-family directors will be based upon market norms within the relevant geographical and industry markets.

I. *Meetings:* The Family Business Board should meet at least once per month, either in person or by phone, to review and direct the activities of the business interests of the family.

Minutes of these meetings should be compiled and transmitted to the Family Council within one week of each meeting.

IX. CUSCADEN VENTURE CAPITAL FUND

A. *Overview:* In the interest of encouraging and developing entrepreneurship within the family, a Cuscaden Venture Capital (CVC) Fund will be established to encourage and provide financial support to family members interested in starting up a new business venture.

B. *CVC Committee membership:* The CVC Committee will consist of the following members:

1. Two Family Directors appointed by the Family Council, one of whom is to serve as Committee Chair

2. At least one non-family, non-executive director appointed by the Family Council who may be, but is not required to be, a member of the Family Business Board

3. The Group Finance Director or other senior non-family financial executive from within the Group

4. The Head of the Family Office.

A Family Director will recuse himself or herself from the review of any proposal if a member of his or her Family Unit is applying for CVC funding. In such a circumstance, another Family Director will be named to join the review process for this specific project, with such director to be nominated by the Chair of the Committee.

The Chair will be elected by the Committee from among the two Family Directors, to serve a four-year term renewable for a maximum of three terms.

C. *Procedures:* The CVC Committee will establish and promulgate the procedures, criteria, terms, and timetable necessary for a successful funding application.

A two-thirds vote of the CVC Committee will be required to approve any CVC funding.

In addition, the CVC Committee will monitor the performance of all investments and set appropriate parameters for continued support, closure, or sale of a CVC business venture. The CVC Fund Committee will prepare and present a report on a quarterly basis to the Family Council and annually to the Family Meeting.

D. *Meetings:* The CVC Committee will meet quarterly or more often as opportunities are ready for presentation and review.

X. ASSET MANAGEMENT BOARD

A. *Overview:* The role of the Asset Management Board will be to invest the non-operating business funds of the Group on an informed basis within the risk/return guidelines established by the Family Council.

Non-operating business funds are defined as publicly quoted investments, fixed-income instruments, alternative assets, liquid funds, and securities representing an interest of less than 10% of any business in which there is no direct operating control.

The Asset Management Board will specify the risk appetite, liquidity preference, investment horizon, and fund manager selection criteria, with a plan submitted to the Family Council for approval on an annual basis.

Over time, the balance between family business operating assets and family financial assets will vary. Noting that the skills and capabilities required to manage liquid funds efficiently and effectively are not the same as those required to run an operating business, the management of the family's financial assets, including those dedicated to fund the philanthropic activities, will require the separate attention of senior family members.

The Asset Management Board will specify each year the full set of objectives and approaches to asset management and will report on a monthly and quarterly (more detailed) basis on performance of the funds under management.

Performance should be targeted at an absolute return target and the risk/return profile set to balance, as appropriate, the family's risk/return profile across the entire set of financial and commercial activities.

Asset management performance shall be compared to peer performance benchmarks on a transparent annual basis and be reported as part of the Family Meeting agenda.

It is expected that the head of the Family Office will also feature as the Chief Investment Officer of the Family Asset Management Board and serve as a director of that Board.

B. *Membership:* The membership of the Asset Management Board will be determined by the Family Council. There will be an initial group of three Family Directors and two non-family directors. The Chair will be a Family Director and appointed by the Family Council. It is expected, but not required, that one of these directors shall be the head of the Family Office if he or she is fulfilling the role of CIO in the asset management area. All members will serve a three-year term, with re-election on a rolling three-year basis.

Should the funds under the management of the Asset Management Board become significant, with significance to be determined by the Family Council, the size of the Asset Management Board will be increased by one additional Family Director and one non-family director by appointment of the Family Council. At the discretion of the Family Council, these additional directors may be appointed as and when appropriate.

C. *Meetings:* The Asset Management Board should meet monthly to review tactical allocations, direct and co-investments and manager selection, making changes as needed to develop and implement an effective investment plan.

XI. FOUNDATION BOARD

A. *Overview:* The role of the Foundation Board is to allocate funds to approved charities within the ambit of the fund's mandate, and to ensure that the funds disbursed are allocated in accordance with the philanthropic terms of reference and consistent with the family's wishes.

B. *Strategic objectives:* The Foundation's primary objective is to focus on the education of children in the emerging markets in which Group businesses operate, with such grants to reflect the relative scale of operating presence by the family business in the market.

C. *Membership:* The Foundation Board will consist of seven members; four from the family (one from each Family Unit) and three from outside the family. The Chair will be chosen by the members of the Foundation Board for a three-year term and will be a member of the Family Council, unless the Council approves with a 75% vote that an alternative family member can serve in that capacity.

    The first family members of the Foundation Board will be the more senior family members in each of the Family Units, who will serve during their lifetimes until incapacitation, to a maximum age of 60, or until they elect to retire from the Board in advance of this maximum age.

    The next four family members will be the elected representatives from within each of the Family Units. The process of nomination and election for each position will be determined by the members of that Family Unit by vote by all family members over the age of 18 within that unit.

    The three non-family members will be appointed by the Family Council for a renewable term, with each Family Unit invited to nominate candidates for inclusion on the Board.

    Any member of any generation is encouraged to become involved with the work of the Foundation should they so wish, with the approval of the Foundation Board and Family Council, whether or not that member is an active member of the Foundation Board.

    Following the retirement of the current family members of the Board, all seven Foundation Directors will serve for a renewable three-year term. There will be no limit on the number of terms which a Foundation Director is able to serve, although the Chair will be limited to two three-year terms and will not be followed by a member of the same Family Unit.

D. *Income and endowment:* The family will make donations to the Foundation from various sources of funds at various times at their full discretion. It is required that the Family Business and Family Asset Management Board contribute 10% of pre-tax profits and capital gains to the Foundation.

E. *Endowment and fund management:* The capital for the endowment of the Foundation will comprise an initial grant by the James and Catriona Cuscaden Trust.

    The Foundation funds, and any subsequent contributions, prior to distribution, will be managed by the Family Asset Management Board and/or at least one other fund manager of impeccable reputation, to be approved by the Foundation Board, the Asset Management Board and the Family Council. No one manager must ever manage more than 50% of Foundation funds or adopt an investment strategy in which there is any but the lowest likelihood of permanent loss of capital.

F. *Meetings:* The Foundation Board should meet every six months to review proposed grants and to review progress against targets for existing investments.

XII. FAMILY OFFICE

A. *Overview:* In order to facilitate the operations of the family and family activities, a Family Office will be established in a location and with a staff to be selected by the Family Council.

    The Family Office will be set up to assist individual family members with the day-to-day management and organization of the family's affairs including, but not limited to, supporting corporate functions, legal, trust and estate planning, share administration, personal tax filing, and other aspects of family financial planning and administration.

B. *Management and oversight of the Family Office:* The Family Office will be managed under the direction of a Family Council member, who will not be the Chair. The member responsible for the Family Office will be selected by the Family Council to serve a four-year term in this role, with a three-term limit.

    The initial member responsible for the Family Office will be Ian Cuscaden.

A non-family administrator will be employed to run the Family Office on a day-to-day basis. The Family Council will be responsible for choosing this individual.

The Family Office, in its first year of operation and in conjunction with the Family Council, will develop a detailed mandate outlining its roles and responsibilities. Included in these roles and responsibilities will be the development and implementation of a long-term strategic plan covering a forward three-year strategic, human capital and financial plan.

This three-year plan must be in full alignment with a three-generational perspective on all aspects of the family's activities, which the Family Office will prepare and review on a triennial basis.

In addition, the Family Office will be responsible for presenting and managing to a detailed annual plan to run concurrent with the financial year of the Family Business.

The Family Office manager will report on its activities to the Family Council on a quarterly basis.

XIII. FAMILY FUNDS

A. *Overview:* Special-purpose funds will be established to provide financial support to the family's overall vision and objectives. These funds will be determined by the Family Council and managed by the Family Office. These funds will cover the following needs:

1. *Family Contingency Fund:* This fund will provide support to cover the costs of unanticipated family emergencies and hardship such as uninsured medical emergencies and medical insurance.

2. *Family Development Fund:* This fund will cover the tuition costs of primary, undergraduate, and graduate education for all family members.

3. *One-Family Policy Fund:* This fund will cover reasonable expenses associated with Family Meetings and other pre-approved activities which strengthen the bonds between family members and Family Units.

The Family Council shall develop guidelines for the Family Funds and distribute these to the Family Meeting for review.

These guidelines will include details on the amount of funding available, individual eligibility, the selection process, monitoring of the proper use of funds, and reporting on progress within the timeframe for which the funds are allocated.

XIV. CUSCADEN GROUP BUSINESS OWNERSHIP

A. *Overview:* All of the Cuscaden businesses will be held under a single legal entity, which will hold all shares in the various family operating businesses, asset management businesses, and any other family property of any value whatsoever. The ownership of that legal entity will be divided into 10,000 shares of equal value and voting rights. Each of the four Family Units will be allotted 2,000 shares of equal value, carrying one voting right per share. These shares will be distributed within each Family Unit as the family members decide in their sole capacity.

The Foundation will also hold 2,000 shares, with voting rights to be exercised by the Chair of the Foundation.

In all succeeding clauses and descriptions, voting rights and economic rights to a dividend, capital distribution or other right and obligation will depend upon the number of shares held by any individual or by the Foundation. Each share carries with it a non-severable individual voting right and, as such, voting rights cannot be separated from economic ownership.

In all cases, the relevant share certificates and other documentation relating to shares and shareholding, and their equivalents, must carry a reference to the terms of this Constitution and make their ownership and transfer subject to the terms herein.

It is the family's wish that the Family Business remains private and principally in the ownership of family members for as long as possible. This requires that shares, or their equivalent, should be held only by the direct descendants of James and Catriona Cuscaden.

The following provisions should be interpreted and implemented to reflect that sentiment.

Whilst the four Family Units currently have equal ownership of the shares, the family acknowledges that the rules that follow include mechanisms which may result in this balance not being maintained in the future.

B. *Inter-family transfers of shares:* Family shareholders agree that they will only gift shares, whether in their lifetime or through their estates on death, to family members. If appropriate, this may be done by means of a trust or other similar vehicle. Shares will only be transferred to family members, as defined above, or to trusts which solely benefit this same set of individuals.

C. *Sale of shares and rights of first refusal:* If any family shareholder on the Foundation Board wishes to sell some or all of their shareholding, they will be required to appoint the Family Council as the agent for the purposes of finding a party willing to acquire those shares. In such circumstances, those shares should be then offered in accordance with the following sequence:

1. To family members within that individual's Family Unit, on a pro rata basis.

2. To existing family shareholders in all other Family Units, on a pro rata basis between and within those Family Units.

3. To the Family Business as a whole.

4. To outside purchasers, but with the express proviso that no shares can be sold outside the above designated potential purchasers without the express prior permission of the Family Council, with such permission not to be unreasonably withheld.

D. *Dividends payable:* It is the responsibility of the Family Council to set the amount of money to be allocated to the Family Funds and to determine the dividend payable to the shareholders of the family business.

XV. FAMILY MEMBER RIGHTS, RESPONSIBILITIES, AND INDIVIDUAL COMMITMENT

A. *Rights:* Members of the Family will have the following rights, with such rights only to be suspended for specific individuals by a 75% vote of the Family Council. These rights are to:

1. Be informed of all important matters relating to the family and to participate in the Family Meeting.

2. Obtain access to any information provided to other family members.

3. Be heard at Family Meetings in accordance with the procedures pertinent thereto.

4. Vote as a member of the family, in proportion to shareholding, on family business matters and as an individual in non-business matters.

5. Be considered for roles in family business governance and management, based on an ability and willingness to fill those positions, subject to meeting the criteria established in this document and as set out separately by the Family Council.

6. Leave the family business without penalty if employed therein, subject to appropriate succession planning, transition, and other actions within the context of business needs.

7. Receive a market rate of compensation if selected for an active management role in the family business.

8. Opt out of ownership at a fair price which allows the family business to remain private and, where possible, owned by family members.

9. Be considered for any role in the family business equally, regardless of gender or age, except as stipulated herein.

10. Participate in the elaboration and implementation of a personal development plan, whether or not an individual is employed in the family business, which includes education, learning beyond school, and personal and professional development.

B. *Responsibilities:* In addition to the specific rights elaborated above, family members at every generational level also agree that there are certain responsibilities that accompany the rights granted which will be equally weighted in importance. These responsibilities include:

1. Learning and understanding the family history.

2. Respecting and living the Family Values specified above.

3. Working hard at school, in employment within and outside the family business to pursue a high level of achievement, and to set an example for family business employees.

4. Pursuing a high-quality education appropriate for the individual's personal and professional aspirations and consistent with the family member's individual capacity.

5. Contributing to family unity and harmony.

6. Working constructively within the family structures and operating principles defined herein.

7. Striving to ensure that family capital of all types is in better shape when passed on than when received.

8. Exercising discretion at all times, keeping a low personal profile and not speaking to the press outside of specific business parameters or on family matters without specific permission of the Family Council.

9. Limiting disclosures of family financials to any non-family member (including spouses) without specific permission of the Family Council.

10. Communicating with spouses and in-laws to ensure that understanding is achieved on the specific rights, roles, and responsibilities reserved only to family members.

11. Respecting the decisions and policies set down by the Family Council.

12. Fostering and contributing to a spirit of excellence and integrity in all that we do.

C. *Individual Commitment:* In order to qualify for any position within the family business, or to take up a role in any of the committees and boards and other entities described above, each member of the Cuscaden family will, at age 18, sign a copy of this document on each page in the presence of the Family Council.

That signature will serve to witness his or her agreement to support the vision, to respect the values, and to adhere to the structures, principles, rights, and responsibilities contained herein. Failure to sign this Constitution will result in the individual's disqualification to hold shares, to receive dividends, or to attend further Family Meetings.

EXAMPLE 3

TRUST DEED AND LETTER OF WISHES

DECLARATION OF TRUST
(SIMPLIFIED)
OFFSHORE JURISDICTION

This document, once recorded in the Central Registry, will establish a Trust known as "Cuscaden Family Trust VII."

THIS DECLARATION OF TRUST is made the 1st day of April 1967 by Mr. James Cuscaden II, who is acting as both Settler and as an initial Trustee.

WHEREAS:

1. It has been resolved to create a Qualified Offshore Trust for the objects hereinafter declared.
2. The Trustee and Settler shall provide an initial sum for the purposes set out below, with said sum to be determined and deposited no later than 1st May 1967, with said sum to be determined solely at the discretion of Mr. James Cuscaden II.
3. Additional initial Trustees shall be Mrs. Jane Cuscaden and Mr. Ian Cuscaden.

NOW THIS DEED WITNESSETH AND IT IS HEREBY AGREED AND DECLARED AS FOLLOWS:

1. NAME OF TRUST

The Qualified Offshore Trust hereby constituted shall be known as Cuscaden Family Trust VII, and referred to hereinafter as "C-VII."

2. THE TRUST FUNDS

The Trustees shall stand possessed of the sum specified above and of all other money and property which may be paid or transferred to them for the said objects and the investments and property from time to time representing the same (hereinafter called "the Trust

Fund") upon trust either to retain or sell the same and invest the proceeds in or upon any investments hereinafter authorized with power from time to time to change such investments for others of a like nature UPON TRUST that both the income and the capital thereof shall be applied at the discretion of the Trustees in pursuance of the said objects as hereinafter declared.

3. OBJECT

The objects of the Trust are to provide equal annual income to the direct descendants of James Craig Cuscaden II. This annual income shall be paid in quarterly installments from the income and capital distributions received by the Trustee on behalf of the beneficiaries specified herein.

The Trustees shall only pay out as income those amounts which are received from investments which are in excess of the annual rate of inflation (as determined by the Central Bank annual reports in our home country), thus preserving 100% of the initial capital on an inflation-adjusted basis for future generations.

Upon the death of any beneficiary, his or her income may be distributed to his or her direct descendants in equal proportion.

Upon the death of the last surviving direct descendant, the Trust capital shall be distributed in equal portion to all children of the initial beneficiaries.

4. POWERS

In furtherance of the said objects but not otherwise the Trustees shall have the following powers:

i. To select financial advisors and fund managers.

ii. To select and pay staff members at current market rates, as necessary.

iii. To file annual registration forms and tax statements (with an expectation that no tax will be due in any jurisdiction on income or capital gain associated with this Trust).

iv. To charge fees in line with trustee Fee Guideline 27-B(i) of this jurisdiction.

5. AMENDMENTS AND INTERPRETATION

The Trustees may amend or interpret the relevant portions of this deed with the exception of Clause 3 (the objects clause) and Clause 13 (the winding-up clause). No amendment or adaptation shall be made which shall create any obligations not envisioned hereunder or shall change the nature and intended object of this Trust in any material manner.

6. INVESTMENT GUIDELINES

In order to provide a reliable flow of income to the beneficiaries of this Trust, and to reduce the risk of impairment or permanent loss of capital, the following guidelines are recommended:

   i. There shall be at least three separate managers appointed to manage the funds of the Trust, with none holding more than 50% of total assets of the Trust and none having less than 20% of Trust assets at any one time.

   ii. All selected managers shall have a minimum of US$5 billion of funds under management from individuals and endowments.

   iii. All investments shall be low to medium risk, with no more than 50% of assets in the latter category.

7. POWER TO DELEGATE

The Trustees shall retain the right to delegate administrative and other activities to outside suppliers provided the fees charged thereupon are reasonable and there is no reduction in the fiduciary obligations of the Trustee, and that the Trustee exercises due care and control over all Trust assets and accounts at all times.

8. PROCEEDINGS

   a. Two of the three Trustees shall form a quorum and are enabled to make all decisions within the ambit of this trust.

b. The Trustees shall elect one of their number as Chair and shall determine the period for which she or he is to hold office.

c. The Chair or two Trustees jointly may, at any time, call a meeting of the Trustees.

d. The Chair shall preside at all meetings of the Trustees save that if at any meeting the Chair is not present within ten minutes after the time appointed for the same the Trustees may choose one of their number present to be Chair of that meeting.

e. Questions arising at any meeting shall be decided by a majority vote, with each Trustee present having one vote.

f. Every notice of a meeting shall state the place, day, and hour of the meeting and the business to be transacted thereat.

9. RECORDS AND ACCOUNTS

The Trustees shall ensure that one of their members shall act as secretary and undertake the responsibility to ensure that accurate and complete minutes are taken and which are entered in a book kept on file at the Offshore Bank; and that record, once approved by the Chairman, shall serve as a complete and sole record of the Trustees' deliberations and decisions.

10. APPOINTMENT AND RETIREMENT OF TRUSTEES

a. A new Trustee may be appointed for a period of three years by a resolution of the Trustees, voted on unanimously by the existing trustees and signed by the new and remaining Trustees in the presence of a witness; such record shall be conclusive evidence of his/her appointment.

b. A Trustee may retire by submitting his or her resignation to the Chairman, with such resignation duly noted at the next meeting of the remaining Trustees.

c. The office of a Trustee shall be vacated if a Trustee becomes ineligible as a result of legal, regulatory, or personal incapacitation reasons; or is absent from three consecutive quarterly meetings and asked to resign by the Chairman and the other Trustee.

d. The number of Trustees shall not be less than three nor more than seven, with a majority of Trustees in any number required to come from the group of descendants of James and Catriona Cuscaden.

11. PAYMENTS

Fees, expenses, indemnifications, and other economic items are as registered in the Master Trust document.

12. INDEMNITY

In the execution of his or her performance as a Trustee, no Trustee shall be liable to pay economic damages from his or her personal resources, and shall not be liable for any costs, settlements, or claims entered against the Trust or Trustee other than for willful and individual fraud or wrongdoing or wrongful omission on the part of the Trustee who is sought to be made liable.

13. WINDING-UP

If the Trustees at any time unanimously decide to discontinue the Trust any assets remaining after the satisfaction of all its debts and liabilities shall be distributed in equal portions to all members of the youngest generation of the Cuscaden family, with such assets to be held in trust by senior family members appointed by the Trustees.

IN WITNESS whereof the parties hereto have executed this Declaration of Trust as a Deed the day and year first before written.

SIGNED AS A DEED

by the said __[*Insert signature*]__
in the presence of   [*Insert witness signature*]__

LETTER OF WISHES

To the Trustees of the Settlement dated the _____ ("the Settlement")

The Settlement gives you wide discretionary powers over capital and income, including the power to distribute either capital or income within a defined class of beneficiaries over a long period of time. I appreciate that I cannot restrict or fetter the exercise by you or your powers and discretions in any way whatsoever. The purpose of this letter is merely to set down in writing my ideas on the subject, which are, of course, not intended to bind you in any way or to constitute any trust.

Points to be addressed:

1. I believe in the value of hard work, education, and sharing family wealth with others less fortunate. I do not believe that heirs and heiresses should allow their inheritance to lead them to a life of indolence or low accomplishment. Any wealth our family has accumulated should be used to support our family members to achieve the careers they desire, and not as a replacement for an independent professional career.

2. The criteria I believe are appropriate to support our family members are:
   a) An annual income supplement, providing the descendant is in credible and reasonable full-time employment or in an accredited graduate school program, for reasonable personal expenditure and family purposes (for example, education for all children, annual family trip abroad, and so on).
   b) A grant at age 30 of sufficient capital to provide a house or apartment in a city of their choice, free of mortgage, with each residence of an equal value to all other residences provided for members of that same family generation.
   c) In the case that I predecease my wife, I would like her to be consulted and her opinion given substantial weight in terms of income/capital distributions to her/the children/others.
   d) Provided our marriage ends with death rather than divorce, there will be no effect, should my spouse remarry, on the level of income/capital she receives.

3. I would recommend for consideration by the Trustees that family trust funds be managed prudently, taking on investments only of a low to medium risk, and managed in a manner similar to that of the larger university endowments.

4. I would like the Trustee to provide guidance, monitoring, and appropriate financial education to assure the independence and commercial awareness of my children.

5. In all cases, prior to distribution of income or capital, I would like the Trustee to assure that there has been a genuine adoption of a work-ethic lifestyle by each member of the family and that each person's livelihood is not dependent on Trust distributions unless that person is engaged in a credible charitable pursuit, or in other exceptional cases to be approved by the Trustee consistent with a work-ethic lifestyle.

6. In the event that my spouse and children die with no remoter issue, all remaining funds should be transferred to the Cuscaden Foundation and used to serve the purposes thereof.

This letter addressed to you as my Trustees is to be treated as a Trust document to be made available to the beneficiaries at your discretion.

Signed …..............…..
Dated …..............……

EXAMPLE 4

INVESTMENT POLICY STATEMENT

ELITE FAMILY INVESTMENT MANAGEMENT, INC.* INVESTMENT POLICY STATEMENT

1. STATEMENT OF PURPOSE

The purpose of this Investment Policy Statement (IPS) is to describe the investment management philosophy, strategy, and policies for the Cuscaden Generation IV (CG IV) Trust and to identify guidelines to be used by Elite Family Investment Management (EFIM) in implementing an investment management program within the CG IV Trust mandate.

It is generally expected that an IPS will be drafted, reviewed, and approved on an annual and as needed basis by the CG IV Trustee and EFIM. It should be noted that, in the process of executing the investment management program, EFIM will utilize the IPS only as a framework and not as a strict set of rules.

2. DEFINITION OF INVESTMENT POLICY STATEMENT SCOPE

Investment entities: CG IV and subsidiary trusts of individual family members who are beneficiaries under the CG IV Trust documentation.

Non-managed assets: All direct property holdings under CG IV Property Trust Ltd and shares in any Cuscaden family companies.

3. INVESTMENT OBJECTIVES AND PRINCIPLES

The Investment objectives of the CG IV Trust for the EFIM-managed portfolios are as follows:

---

entirely fictitious entity

1. Long-term growth of capital
2. Minimization of permanent capital loss at the portfolio level
3. Preservation of purchasing power on a real inflation-adjusted basis.

It is noted that neither liquidity nor income is an objective of the CG IV investment program.

Return

The long-term investment return objectives are generally 10%+ annually on the portfolio in nominal terms, net of all investment management fees and performance incentive payments.

Risk

We recognize that a certain level of investment risk must be assumed in order to achieve the return objectives; however, risk must be properly defined, measured and managed in an effective manner.

We define risk in the portfolio in the following manner.

Permanent capital loss: We will generally seek investments that minimize risks of a permanent loss of capital on the overall portfolio. As part of the risk-management program, we analyze volatility and other metrics to monitor risks. Central to the investment program will be diversification, driven by the CG IV model of targeted investment across asset classes in the context of a long-term investment horizon. Furthermore, assuming the CG IV allocates to co- and direct investments, it is acknowledged that these types of investments increase overall portfolio risk, specifically with regard to possible capital loss. Direct investments carry a high degree of capital loss, at both the investment and portfolio level.

Temporary loss of capital: We are willing to accept a material level of temporary loss of capital, often defined as volatility of returns (and measured by standard deviation); an annualized portfolio volatility in the range of 5–15% (one standard deviation) is acceptable in the investment program, given our return objectives and long-term time horizon. Philosophically, we believe that high-quality investments generally recover from short-term financial volatility and we will seek to use declines in asset class valuations to buy attractive investments.

Time horizon

The time horizon for the investment management program is defined at a minimum of five years, but with a stated perspective of approximately 10 years. It is recognized that for illiquid, drawdown investments, the time horizon is approximately seven to 10 years and such allocations are not liquid until realizations occur.

Rebalancing

Rebalancing is defined as the process of selling a portion of investment assets and, with the proceeds, buying other assets with a general objective of bringing the portfolio weighting into alignment with the strategic policy asset-allocation model. Rebalancing will not bring asset weightings exactly to the policy targets given volatility, liquidity flows, and other factors.

Analysis of the need to rebalance will generally occur on a quarterly basis and as needed. Herein, EFIM is granted the authority to initiate rebalances, in its best judgment, on a quarterly and/or as-needed basis should EFIM believe such rebalancing is appropriate and in line with CG IV Trust investment parameters and policies.

Stock distributions

All stock distributions generated from investment activities will be sold upon receipt of the distribution, unless unique circumstances or policies exist. EFIM is hereby granted the authority and discretion to implement and address all issues related to stock distributions.

Restricted investments

The restricted investments are summarized as follows:

Asset classes: no general restrictions

Strategies: no active trading strategies in stocks or other similar instruments which will create a high level of "churn" in the portfolio

Industries: no tobacco, alcohol, gaming, or firearms

Companies: no business related to or trading with any Cuscaden family enterprise.

On an ongoing basis, EFIM's Capital Commitment Committee may designate additional restricted investments, which will be communicated to the investment team and any relevant parties.

Liquidity

Liquidity is an important part of any investment management program, and can affect a variety of elements of the portfolio.

As an over-arching perspective, the CG IV investment portfolio is intended to be essentially illiquid and targeted for long-term return on capital rather than liquidity.

The CG IV Trustees and EFIM will coordinate liquidity planning matters. The strategic policy model may define a certain portion of the portfolio to be held in illiquid, long-term investments such as private equity, venture capital, real assets, and absolute return opportunities. This illiquidity characteristic also includes direct investment strategies allocations.

It is acknowledged that a three-year lock-up exists on the portfolio and that all drawdown funds are completely illiquid until potential realizations are completed. In addition, it is recognized that, after the lock-up term is exceeded, the portfolio can only be redeemed at two intervals per year, with six months' advance written notice to EFIM.

Taxes

The CG IV trust, depending on its tax domicile, may be subject to certain taxes. EFIM, as the investment manager, takes no responsibility for tax filings and payments for the CG IV Trust, but will work with the CG IV Trustee and tax advisors to minimize taxes as much as possible.

Conflicts of interest

EFIM will abide by the guidelines consistent with standard conflicts-of-interest policies in its activities related to the investment management program.

All EFIM officers, employees, and committee members are expected to uphold high ethical standards, to conduct themselves with professionalism and dignity, and to observe and respect all legal requirements.

Tax, accounting, and legal

Tax and accounting matters will be overseen by accountants appointed by the CG IV Trustees.

Legal matters will be overseen by the CG IV Trustees, with lawyers to be appointed by these Trustees.

It is expected that additional service firms may be used at the discretion of EFIM.

Custodian and record keeping

EFIM currently uses Master Bank and Trust of Manhattan (MBTM) as master record keeper for financial performance reporting. Given the diversity and structure of the portfolio, some investments are custodied externally from MBTM or not custodied at all in the case of most limited partnerships.

4. ASSET ALLOCATION MODEL

The heart of CG IV's asset allocation model is a scenario-based planning approach that takes account of a range of macro-economic and event-risk circumstances; the scenario model will help to guide the asset allocation model.

In addition to this scenario-based analytical framework, we also employ a traditional mean-variance model and various elements of Modern Portfolio Theory (MPT). Ultimately, the strategic policy model is a blend of scenario-based, MPT, and simulation analyses designed to produce an asset allocation framework which considers a variety of investment environments.

Asset allocation policy model

The asset allocation policy model will be approved by the CG IV Trustees and managed by EFIM according to the following framework:

1. Strategic policy model
2. Tactical policy ranges.

It is important to acknowledge that these policy models are only targets and are not expected to be achieved at all times. The proposed model for CG IV is set out in Schedule A below.

We expect to revisit these asset allocation policy models annually, but do not expect major changes unless circumstances or long-term objectives change. The discipline of staying true to the long-term model is an important component of investment success.

5. GOVERNANCE

EFIM believes that clearly defined responsibilities, authorities and accountabilities are critical to a successful investment management program. These elements are reflected in governance and maintenance to the guidelines in this IPS.

EFIM Investment Policy Committee (EIPC)

EFIM's IPC exercises the following basic responsibilities:

1. Provides general strategic investment advice
2. Provides input and oversight on policy-level decisions outside of those determined by CG IV
3. Importantly, the EIPC does not make specific investment decisions (the purview of the ECCC).

EFIM Capital Commitment Committee (ECCC)

The ECCC exercises the following basic responsibilities:

1. Implements the investment management program
2. Reviews, approves, and recommends to the EIPC the selected strategic and tactical policy models
3. Implements all investments and performance.

6. ASSET CLASS DEFINITIONS

The basic guidelines for each asset class are defined as follows and reflected by EFIM's various asset allocations. The types of securities listed are meant to serve as broad descriptions of the characteristics for securities within an asset class. In the course of managing the portfolio, EIPC and ECCC will propose any modification as necessary.

SCHEDULE A

The following asset allocation policy targets have been approved by the CG IV Trustee as of [date] until [date].

Strategic policy model

The strategic policy weights refer to the target allocations to each asset class.

Asset Class	Targets
Core Fixed Income	0
Non-Core Fixed Income	0
U.S. Equities	10
Developed International Equities	5
Emerging Market Equities	10
Absolute Return	10
Private Equity	15
Venture Capital	5
Real Estate & Infrastructure	10
Energy & Commodities	3
Hard Tradable Assets	2
Pan-Asian Strategies	5
Direct Investment Strategies	15
Special Opportunities	2
Foreign Exchange	8
Total	100%

Tactical policy ranges

The tactical policy ranges provide for necessary flexibility in managing the assets in line with the strategic policy model. They provide room for increases or decreases due to investment performance, rebalancing and timing, cash and asset inflows and outflows, investment ramp-up models, and flexibility for opportunities to overweight or underweight a particular asset class or asset sub-class. Such ranges are set at +/– 30% of the weightings in the strategic policy model.

EXAMPLE 5

FAMILY BUSINESS STRATEGY: EXECUTIVE SUMMARY

CUSCADEN FAMILY BUSINESS STRATEGIC DOCUMENT: EXECUTIVE SUMMARY

INTRODUCTION

The Cuscaden Group is at an important transitional moment in our 130-year history.

In North America, Europe, and Asia, our businesses are performing well. Group borrowings have been reduced to 25% of their peak, reflecting the results of our restructuring efforts and creating a more sound financial base for the Group.

With the flotation of our pharmaceutical business and the sale of our steel business, we have eliminated corporate guarantees and all other off-balance-sheet liabilities. We have also created a pool of liquid funds for investment under a new Cuscaden Group asset management business.

In the wake of these major initiatives, we believe it is time to reset vision and strategy to chart the next phase of our family's business development. There are still many elements of the strategy to be confirmed and refined, but we hope the summary below will provide a useful statement of direction for the Cuscaden Group and the aspirations we propose to achieve in the coming five years.

1. VISION

The Cuscaden Group will build on past successes and current capabilities to become one of the most successful and respected large family businesses in the markets and business sectors in which we choose to compete.

We will build a strong portfolio of profitable and growing businesses in which we hold sole or joint control, and will manage these businesses in the most professional manner to build a sustainable commercial platform for the benefit of all stakeholders.

In addition to targeting top-decile results from our operating assets, we will establish a wealth management division to group together and manage the liquid and non-operating assets of our group, aspiring to achieve top-decile results from that division as well.

In pursuit of our commercial objectives, we shall:

- set clear objectives for financial and operating accomplishments for the coming five-year period which will achieve an overall doubling of value every seven years;

- establish a clear measure of business value, employing profit multiples, market valuations, and asset valuations as appropriate between operating entities to achieve a fair view of our accomplishments over the term of the strategy;

- pursue a range of initiatives tailored for each market in Africa, Asia, Europe, and North and South America, which will move us towards our long-term goal of being as big a player in attractive emerging markets as we are in developed markets;

- develop an organization highly capable of achieving the objectives we set for ourselves;

- clarify the role and level of involvement in the business for all members of the family in all generations;

- build a brand to attract and exploit interesting investment opportunities;

- honor values of entrepreneurship, integrity, and loyalty;

- value teamwork and flexibility.

By adhering to these principles and achieving the business objectives we set for ourselves, we will be able to add constructively and positively to the long and proud history of the Cuscaden Group.

2. BUSINESS STRATEGY

The strategy required to achieve this vision can be broken down into seven groupings of key initiatives. Five of these relate to group business activity, here described as "CUSCADEN GROUP I" to "CUSCADEN GROUP V" initiatives. A sixth relates to philanthropic and charitable activities. The last specific strategy will address cross-Group and HQ issues focused on organizational development.

The five business areas for separate strategic approaches can be described as follows:

CUSCADEN GROUP I: CORE BUSINESSES

Strategy: With the exception of our newly listed pharmaceuticals business, these are unlisted businesses with good long-term growth and profit potential in which we hold sole or joint control. We will invest to grow these businesses in selected areas.

All of these businesses are professionally managed and capable of achieving strong growth and returns in the coming years. CUSCADEN GROUP I is the primary area for investment and growth in the five-year period covered by this plan.

Our approach will divide this core business area into five separate strategic business units. A more detailed strategy and timeline will be developed for each of these areas.

CUSCADEN GROUP II: TRADING ASSETS

Strategy: These two operating businesses, warehousing and distribution of automotive components and steel fabrications, are to be listed or sold, prior to which we will retain joint control with management. These investment positions are available to be divested or sold down at the right time and at the right price in coming years to fund new enterprises, or to provide liquidity to family members.

They are not core to our Group business but will remain within the Group until we are able to meet our price objectives.

CUSCADEN GROUP III: NEW INVESTMENTS

Strategy: These are minority positions or controlling investments in start-up business opportunities. We will invest only very selectively in this area, and only in those opportunities which will not demand any guarantees or lead to other significant risks to the Group's balance sheet.

Although we have concluded that this is not an area for primary development for the coming period, due to the need to complete the group restructuring, upgrade the organization and grow the CUSCADEN GROUP I businesses first, we will investigate attractive situations and invest in those which represent truly extraordinary opportunities. While open to attractive opportunities in any sector in any geography, we will set out strict financial criteria to determine what will be the appropriate hurdles for investment.

Those criteria are:

- no guarantees
- no disproportionate risk/return profiles
- no "bet-the-company" transactions
- US$5 million of maximum exposure per deal
- clear exit strategy defined
- active board role.

CUSCADEN GROUP IV: UNDERPERFORMING ASSETS

Strategy: This is a collection of assets that do not have a positive future outlook. We will exit them.

We have already removed most of the underperformers from our portfolio. All that remain to be disposed of are some machinery and associated property holdings from our steel division, most of which are in the process of disposal already. The small real-estate investments that we have in various cities in the northeast United States are also on the block for sale.

CUSCADEN GROUP V: FINANCIAL ASSET MANAGEMENT

Strategy: These are liquid assets capable of being traded on global financial markets. It is our objective in the long term to build up this portfolio to provide liquidity as and when needed for distribution, and also to counterbalance the risk inherent in a family portfolio still weighted towards operating assets in highly competitive markets.

We will divide our current liquid assets into four pools of funds, which will be allocated to the following purposes and in the amounts shown in Figure 1.

All external investment advisors and fund managers will be top-decile and will report monthly and quarterly in a common Cuscaden format.

Figure 1 Liquid Assets Funds

Portfolio	% of assets	Purpose	Manager(s)
1. Conservative	25	Return of 7–10% Low risk. Income for family and philanthropy. Primarily in older generation trusts.	EFIM 1
2. Growth	50	Long-term capital gain, c. 15%. Predominantly in Next Generation trusts.	EFIM 2
3. Safety	20	Low/no-risk funds in Switzerland. Separate trust and trustee.	Private Bank
4. "Bolt hole"	5	New Zealand presence. Gold (in various locations).	Family Office + Private Bank

SUMMARY AND IMPLICATION OF STRATEGY

As a result of implementing the strategy outlined above, the Cuscaden Group will be more clearly oriented to the development and management of a portfolio of profitable, growing businesses with an asset-light flavor and more potential for positive cash generation. The Group would be more focused on distribution and services, some of them in emerging markets, than asset-intensive manufacturing and property holdings.

This shift in portfolio emphasis and business profile will require supporting changes in the organization and individual skill sets of senior managers within the Group.

The overall goals are to double the value of the Cuscaden Family wealth in the upcoming seven-year time frame, implying a 10% growth in value, after tax and distributions, every year.

CHARITABLE ACTIVITIES

The James Cuscaden Neurological Research Center, along with the James and Catriona Cuscaden Memorial Foundation, will remain at the core of our charitable activities.

In addition, we would like to extend and further professionalize our emerging markets initiatives within the terms of the Foundation for the first time, beginning with the poorest countries in Africa and Asia.

In developing and pursuing our philanthropic activities, the following principles are proposed:

1. The Group businesses must be profitable enough to support the chosen activities;

2. The investments benefit our core business and corporate reputation;

3. Each program has substantial and measurable impact;

4. The new program and our involvement must be welcome in the local communities in the emerging markets in which we propose to "invest";

5. Each element of the program has a vision, plan, and objectives approved in advance, which will support the long-term independence and success of all beneficiaries—a hand up, not a hand-out.

ORGANIZATION

Developing and implementing these strategies and charitable plans over the next few years will not be easy. We will need to invest in resources in new countries and in new markets. We will need to support and develop the best people within our organization. This organizational effort will also be the subject of a detailed plan within each business area and co-coordinated as necessary at HQ.

There are a number of potential changes to take into consideration as we put together our organizational plans, with the major items highlighted below.

HQ staff will need to be supplemented. The ambitious growth plans for CUSCADEN GROUP I, the strict review needs and the potential for new business in CUSCADEN GROUP III, and a major new wealth management initiative in CUSCADEN GROUP V will add to the workload in all business groups.

While we are still considering the full implications for an expanded HQ structure, our current plans are to bolster resources by adding the following positions:

1. Non-Family Group CEO

2. CUSCADEN GROUP III Business Development Manager, reporting to Group Finance Director

3. Asian Business Development Manager, reporting to CEO

4. Managing Director of Wealth Management, CUSCADEN GROUP V, reporting to Chairman

5. Group Internal Auditor, reporting to the Group Board

6. Head of Emerging Markets Philanthropic Initiatives, reporting to the Head of the Foundation Board

7. Wealth Management Board members.

NEW GROUP CEO ROLE

The new Group CEO role will evolve on completion of the restructuring phase and the new Group strategy, but will include overall responsibility for the Group's vision, strategy, and the accomplishment of agreed targets.

Particular attention will be paid to:

1. The quality of earnings;

2. Attributes of entrepreneurship;

3. Quality and depth of management, especially related to the ability to execute the agreed growth strategy;

4. Improving market positioning;

5. Identifying and sharpening sources of competitive advantage;

6. Developing the potential of the Group—management, infrastructure, finances, and brand—to develop new products and services and penetrate new markets;

7. Exercising control over systems and communication to ensure the quality, quantity, and timeliness of the flow of information between management and the Board.

Succession: One issue to be still fully addressed is that of longer-term succession at all senior positions. We need to develop succession plans on an emergency basis (if short-term unanticipated change is needed) and for planned succession (on a longer term, pre-managed basis).

The latter issue can be addressed after we have made substantial progress on the plan presented here, and when future leadership needs of the Group and family are clearer.

3. FINANCIAL NEEDS

Unlike past years, where financial demands were putting pressure on our balance sheet, we will have substantial liquid funds for investment going forward.

Those funds will be managed by a combination of highly capable external investment advisors and internal resources.

To the extent necessary, we shall use Group financial resources to obtain any necessary funding at the most advantageous rates and terms.

4. POINT OF ARRIVAL

If successful, the strategy outlined above would change quite substantially the shape and performance of our Group over the coming years.

The Group would have a greater focus on and investment in CUSCADEN GROUP I operating businesses. We could, under the right circumstances, realize further liquidity on an orderly basis from CUSCADEN GROUP II trading assets and CUSCADEN GROUP IV underperforming assets. We would have a greater focus on core activities and "adjacent" growth opportunities, having reduced our less successful CUSCADEN GROUP I and III efforts.

We would have a stronger organization within the remaining business units. We would continue to have a lean headquarters unit, albeit somewhat larger in carefully selected areas, staffed to meet the needs of the business units, perform group functions, and respond to any attractive growth and investment opportunities that arise.

5. IMPLEMENTATION TIMETABLE

Embedded in the strategic plans that have been circulated to you is a precise timetable of expected events and results. After securing your agreement on the full content of this strategic document and the plans, we will put in place measures and steps to secure the agreed outcomes along the scheduled timetables.

Reminder on confidentiality: It is important that we keep this strategy, and comment on its content, strictly to family members only. Some of the content contains market-sensitive information. Other aspects could have a significant impact on morale (and hence value) in our Group companies.

EXAMPLE 6

PHILANTHROPIC FOUNDATION DOCUMENT

CUSCADEN FOUNDATION
SUMMARY DOCUMENT

HISTORY

The James and Catriona Cuscaden Memorial Foundation was established to honor the founders of the Cuscaden Group of companies and ensure that their charitable legacy was protected for all future generations who could benefit from their generosity.

MISSION

The purpose of the Foundation is to support women's healthcare, and primary and secondary school education for both boys and girls in selected poor countries, in particular those where the Cuscaden family businesses have operated for many years.

James Cuscaden himself grew up with little formal education and wanted to ensure that part of his legacy went to provide a good head start in life for those who otherwise might not be able to afford schooling. He further wanted to honor the contributions to his business success made by his mother, Mary, and his wife, Catriona, by providing medical care for women and young girls who otherwise might suffer with treatable illnesses and injuries.

In all cases, the purpose of the Foundation grants will be to help beneficiaries to create and lead independent and productive lives.

ENDOWMENT AND SUPPORT

Funding for the Foundation will come from a one-time lump-sum contribution from the Cuscaden family equal to 20% of the family's net worth, made in the form of transfer of ownership of shares in the various family businesses. Further contributions will come from the various Cuscaden operating entities who have an obligation, so long as the Cuscaden family retains a controlling position in their ownership structure, to contribute 10% of pre-tax income to the Foundation unless there are extraordinary circumstances that would render this obligation either illegal or counter to the interests of the Foundation, or the family business, in the longer term.

Support to the selected causes will be determined by the trustees of the Foundation upon the recommendation of the professional staff of that organization.

Support will be provided in the form of grants, loans, investments, and other forms of financial support to yield the highest possible impact for each dollar spent. The principles and approaches of effective "performance philanthropy," "social entrepreneurship," "outcome-specified" programs, or "philanthropeneurism" will be respected and developed to ensure the largest long-term impact is made in the areas selected for support from funds available.

FOUNDATION VALUES

In pursuing our purpose, and in respecting the rules set down to govern our operations, the following values are highlighted as part of our system of belief and action:

- the highest standards of integrity and honesty
- transparent accounting and accountability
- close liaison with community leaders in the areas of our donation
- pursuit of "high impact" philanthropy, measuring results from each grant or loan
- conservative management of Foundation funds by professional fund managers
- complete independence from family business operations
- avoidance of conflicts of interest
- creating a great place to work and grow for all our colleagues
- cost consciousness in all aspects of our operations
- always focusing on giving a hand up, not a hand-out.

FOUNDATION GOVERNANCE AND COMPLIANCE

The structures and principles of the systems of governance will be world class at all times and in all areas, in compliance with all standards and obligations as set down in the following documents:

1. Charter and Mission Statement

2. Articles of Incorporation and Trust documentation

3. Bylaws of the Foundation

4. Committee Terms of Reference—including Investment Committee policies and procedures

5. Standards of Independence

6. Trustee Compliance Manual and Code of Ethics

7. Staff Compliance Manual and Codes of Conduct and Ethics

8. Investment (grant and loan) Procedures Manual.

THE FOUNDATION TEAM

The Board of Trustees will be made up of seven members, of whom at least three must be direct descendants of James and Catriona Cuscaden, including one who will serve as Chair of the Foundation.

The Trustees, who will all be appointed to a series of staggered three-year terms by the Cuscaden Family Council, will at their sole discretion determine all policies and make all decisions with regard to investment, distribution, management, and operations of the Foundation. No Trustee will be required to resign from the board without a 75% vote of the remaining Trustees.

The dedicated management team will be made up of individuals of the highest available capability and with the highest respect for the values and objectives of the Foundation. Each staff member will serve at the pleasure of the Trustees and no contract longer than three years will be allowed.

Conflicts policy: There will be no activities or investments by the team which could constitute a conflict of interest as outlined in the relevant Foundation documents.

PLANNING AND REPORTING

Each year, the management will present to the Board of Trustees for their approval a long-term strategic plan, an annual operating plan and monthly income/distribution and cost targets. In addition, each month, and on an annual basis in full detail, the management team will be required to provide an audit of the effectiveness of past donations and any lessons learned from those that failed to achieve their initial objectives.

No funds may be disbursed in the absence of a plan agreed by a two-thirds majority of the Trustees.

COST CONTROL

The costs of the Foundation, including all salaries, bonuses, overheads, and out-of-pocket expenses, will be capped at 10% of annual income. An annual audit by a credible accounting firm will be undertaken as part of the standard operation procedure of the Foundation.

EXAMPLE 7

ETHICAL WILL

JAMES CRAIG CUSCADEN III
ETHICAL WILL

To be read at my funeral and on any occasion thereafter so chosen by the members of my family

I, James Craig Cuscaden III, here leave behind some thoughts, memories, principles, and ideas for my children, their children, and any and all family and non-family members who might benefit from these observations.

I have left separate documents for the Cuscaden Family businesses, to be shared with each new employee, and for the James and Catriona Cuscaden Memorial Foundation, to be shared with Board members and employees alike on different occasions.

In hopes that technology does not change so much as to render my efforts useless over time, I have also put together an audio visual version of this ethical will, which has been recorded on a CD and distributed to all of my living siblings, children, and grandchildren.

It is my wish that the audio visual version of this ethical will be shown at my funeral, and on the first anniversary of my death, with any further use to be entirely at the discretion of family members, the leaders of the business and the Foundation.

It is also my hope and wish that my children and other family members produce similar testaments to this ethical will so that future generations will have a broader and deeper understanding of who we are as a family, what we have learned and accomplished, and in what we truly believe.

THE IMPORTANCE OF THE FAMILY

Although most of you will know our family history, I have always been particularly proud of the accomplishments, traditions, and values established by my paternal grandfather, James Cuscaden. His sound practices and approaches to life and business were also carried on in similar measure and with similar dedication by my own father. I send them my thanks, prayers, and best wishes wherever they are. Long may their values, modest standards of living, and deep faith in a greater purpose and divine power in the universe remain a part of our family for generations to come.

By way of thoughts to share with those of you who remain after I have departed, I would like to say that my greatest experiences have all been centered around our family and family life. Meeting and having the great honor to be married to my wife, the birth of our five children, their marriages, and the arrival of their own children have been surpassed by no other experience in my business, public, or private life.

Of all of life's memorable times, loving, sharing, laughing, striving, and working through good times and bad with members of my family have been the most precious of gifts.

SHARING BUSINESS AND PHILANTHROPIC ACTIVITY

I have also enjoyed working with family members and non-family colleagues in the family businesses. We were both fortunate and worked hard for the successes we created, while noting with humility the many mistakes we made along the way. Despite the difficult times and many errors we did make, my generation are pleased that the family business we leave behind is far larger, stronger, and more profitable than when we inherited it from our own parents 24 years ago.

In addition to the business success for which we worked long and hard, I am particularly proud to have developed and grown the family's philanthropic activities to include new programs in Africa and Asia. It is my wish that family members spend some time in these poorer countries, both to assist in the causes to which the Foundation is dedicated, and to grow as people in a world where privilege can buffer us from the difficult experiences which allow us to reach our fullest potential.

REFLECTIONS ON WHAT IS IMPORTANT

While there have been far too many experiences, and far too much valuable learning in my long life to fit into one brief document, I would like to commend the following values and reflections to family members for their own contemplation.

Love and happiness: Of all things to pursue in life, love and happiness are the highest goals. My greatest happiness came from marrying the woman I loved, pursuing the career in business and public service which was my great passion and to which I was always fully committed, and in creating the large family I always wanted; a wonderful family that grew up in a loving and caring environment.

Honor and ethics: Being true to one's word, speaking frankly, and acting with integrity are the bedrock of a life worth living. Without honor and a profound sense of what is right, and acting upon that belief, the quality of any one life is vastly diminished.

It may not be easy taking the high road. There will always be people trying to drag down those who are following the better path, and there is often a personal cost to maintaining a life of integrity. It will always be worth reminding our children and their children that the higher road is often the more difficult pathway to follow, but it always leads to a far better place.

Education and literature: In my life I benefited from a great education that lasted far beyond the end of my schooling. Good books, a constant curiosity and honest discussions with people of depth, wisdom, humor and understanding have made my life much richer, and contributed to an education that I continued until the last day of my life.

Expertise and excellence: I have found, over the years, that it is not what someone does that makes for a full life, but how they do it. That makes all the difference. An attention to quality, a high level of effort, striving to achieve excellence in whatever field of endeavor is chosen and seeking out experience, expertise, and knowledge from those more skilled or capable than I have always made a great contribution to the quality of my own life. I commend this attitude to others and hope that it has the same beneficial effect on your lives that it did on mine.

When I failed to live up to any high standard, the results spoke for themselves in ways I am not happy to remember, but which served as a constant reminder of how much better it is to do a good job in whatever we choose to do.

I would also commend to my children, their children and those beyond, to find a career or profession for which you have a deep passion and in which you can excel, no matter whether that leads to an artistic, medical, military, commercial, religious, educational, or other pathway in life. Find what you are good at and stick to it.

Self awareness: No one is like anyone else. No one in our family, or anywhere else, was put on this earth to live someone else's life. In order to understand what it is that we can do best, in work or in our personal lives, it is important to understand who we really are, what are our strengths and weaknesses (the latter understood in full humility and with a full knowledge of human frailties) and how we can best identify and pursue an individual path that leads to the greatest personal accomplishment, the greatest personal happiness, and the greatest personal development along all the vital dimensions that life has to offer.

Purpose and meaning: Perhaps the greatest observation I can pass on to my children, their children, and anyone else who is following these words, is the importance of a belief in and an understanding of the greater forces of the universe. That understanding can only come about through a lifelong quest for external experience, inner knowledge, and meditation on how the various aspects of human existence—physical, material, emotional, and spiritual—fit together.

In this area, I departed rather substantially from my father and grandfather. They were stalwart members of a Scottish Protestant church with which our family has been associated for many generations. I, on the other hand, have taken more time than they to consider alternatives, to explore Unitarianism, Buddhism, Catholicism, and to question the link (or maybe even the contrast) between religion and spirituality.

While not yet having any firm answers, I can commend to anyone the value of the journey, and the benefits of having an enquiring and open mind.

I would like to end this document where I started, noting that the most important elements of our family wealth are love, family, and sharing life's gifts with those we treasure most.

I am very grateful to have had my wife as my spouse, partner, best friend, and confidante over these past 50 years. For her love and support across half a century I can never say enough.

I am also vastly proud of all of our five children. You are all honest, decent people with good values, a great sense of humor, curiosity about the world, and an apparent desire to lead balanced and productive lives. I thank you also for the many years we had together and the great joy you brought to your mother and myself.

I lived, and I died, a happy man. No one could have asked for more in any one lifetime. I wish that my children, their children, and all generations of the Cuscaden Family beyond, find nothing less in their own lives.

God bless you all and may you all find the joy, the happiness, and the love that you so richly deserve.

BIBLIOGRAPHY

Abrahams, M. a. Israel. *Chapters on Jewish Literature*. IndyPublish.com, March 2005.

Abts III, Henry W. *The Living Trust, The Failproof Way to Pass Along Your Estate to Your Heirs Without Lawyers, Courts, or the Probate System* (Revised and Updated Edition). Contemporary Books, 2003.

Adam, Stuart and Chris Frayne. "A Survey of the US Tax System: Briefing Note No. 9", Table 13: Summary of main reforms, 1979–2001, The Institute of Fiscal Studies, p.17.

American Bar Association. *Guide to Wills and Estates* (Second Edition). Random House Reference, 2004.

American Council for Capital Formation (ACCF) Special Report (July 2005). "New International Survey Shows U.S. Death Tax Rates Among Highest", refers to source data from survey by PricewaterhouseCoopers, LLP. http://www.accf.org/pdf/death-tax-survey.pdf.

Anderson, Jenny and Julie Cresswell. "Top Hedge Fund Managers Earn Over $240 Million", *New York Times*, 24 April 2007.

Aronoff, Craig E. and John L. Ward. *Family Business Compensation*. Family Enterprise Publishers, 1993.

———, *How to Choose and Use Advisors: Getting the Best Professional Family Business Advice*. Family Enterprise Publishers, 1994.

———, *Family Business Ownership: How to Be an Effective Shareholder*. Family Enterprise Publishers, 2002.

———, *Family Meetings: How to Build a Stronger Family and a Stronger Business* (Second Edition). Family Enterprise Publishers, 2002.

———, *Family Business Governance: Maximizing Family and Business Potential*. Family Enterprise Publishers, 1996.

Aronoff, Craig E., Joseph H. Astrachan and John L. Ward. *Developing Family Business Policies: Your Guide to the Future*. Family Enterprise Publishers, 1998.

Aronoff, Craig E. et al. *Making Sibling Teams Work: The Next Generation*. Family Enterprise Publishers, 1997.

Aronoff, Craig E., Stephen L. McClure and John L. Ward. *Family Business Succession: The Final Test of Greatness* (Second Edition). Family Enterprise Publishers, 2003.

Bailey, Becky A. *Easy to Love, Difficult to Discipline The 7 Basic Skills for Turning Conflict into Cooperation*. HarperCollins, 2002.

Baines, Barry K. *The Ethical Will Writing Guide Workbook*. Josaba Limited, 2001.

Bartlett, Christopher A. and Ghosal Sumantra. *Transnational Management Text, Cases & Readings in Cross-Border Management* (Second Edition). The McGraw-Hill Companies Inc., 1995.

Bauman, Zygmunt. *Globalization The Human Consequences*, Polity Press, 1998.

Beinhocker, Eric D. *The Origin of Wealth: Evolution, Complexity, and the Radical Remaking of Economics*. Harvard Business School Press, 2006.

Bennis, Warren, ed. "Leaders on Leadership Interviews with Top Executives", *Harvard Business Review*, 1996.

Bernstein, Peter L. *Against the Gods: The Remarkable Story of Risk*. John Wiley & Sons, Inc., 1998.

———, *The Power of Gold, The History of an Obsession*. John Wiley & Sons, Inc., 2000.

Bernstein, William. *The Intelligent Asset Allocator: How to Build Your Portfolio to Maximize Returns and Minimize Risk*. McGraw-Hill, 2001.

Binney, T. "The Good Man in Trouble" (A Sermon delivered on Sunday Morning, 7 November 1852, at the Weigh House Chapel, Fish Street Hill, London). *Mother's Magazine*, 1853.

———, *Money: A Popular Exposition*. Jackson, Walford and Hodder, 1865.

———, *Sermons Preached in The King's Weigh-house Chapel, London, 1829–1869*. Macmillan & Co., 1869.

———, *The Best of Both Worlds: A Book for Young Men*. Edward Knight, 1895.

Blue, Ron with Jeremy White. *Splitting Heirs: Giving Your Money and Things to Your Children Without Ruining Their Lives*. Northfield Publishing, 2004.

Boston College Social Welfare Research Institute. "Millionaires and the Millennium: New Estimates of the Forthcoming Wealth Transfer and the Prospects for a Golden Age of Philanthropy". Havens, John J. and Paul G. Schervish, October 1999, introduction.

Boulton, Leyla and James Lamont, "Philanthropy 'can eclipse G8' on poverty", *Financial Times*, 8 April 2007.

Brunel, Jean L.P. *Integrated Wealth Management: The New Direction for Portfolio Managers*. Euromoney Institutional Investor Plc., 2002.

Buffone, Gary W. *Choking on the Silver Spoon: Keeping Your Kids Healthy, Wealthy, and Wise in a Land of Plenty*. Simplon Press, 2003.

Carlock, Randel S. and John L. Ward, *Strategic Planning for the Family Business, Parallel Planning to Unify the Family and Business*. Palgrave Macmillan, 2001.

Carnegie, Andrew. "Wealth", *The North American Review*, June 1889.

Cheatham Willis, Thayer. *Navigating the Dark Side of Wealth: A Life Guide for Inheritors.* New Concord Press, 2003.

Chirelstein, Marvin A. "Learned Hand's Contribution to the Law of Tax Avoidance", *Yale Law Journal*, Vol. 77, No. 3, January 1968, pp.440–74.

Churchill, Sir Winston. Speech in Dundee, Scotland, 10 October 1908. The Churchill Centre www.winstonchurchill.org

Cimino, Richard and Don Lattin. *Shopping for Faith: American Religion in the New Millennium.* Jossey-Bass Publishers, 1998.

Commager, Henry Steele. *Jefferson, Nationalism, and the Enlightenment.* George Braziller Inc., 1975.

Condon, Gerald M. and Jeffrey L. Condon. *Beyond the Grave: The Right Way and the Wrong Way of Leaving Money to Your Children and Others.* HarperCollins Publishers Inc., 2001.

Crouch, Holmes F. *Your Trustee Duties* (Second Edition). Allyear Tax Guides, 2004.

Daniell, Mark. *The Elements of Strategy: A Pocket Guide to the Essence of Successful Business Strategy.* Palgrave Macmillan, 2006.

Daniell, Mark Haynes. *World of Risk: Next Generation Strategy for a Volatile Era.* John Wiley & Sons (Asia) Pte Ltd, 2000.

———, *Strategy: A Step-by-Step Approach to the Development and Presentation of World Class Business Strategy.* Palgrave Macmillan, 2004.

Daniell, Mark and Karin Sixl-Daniell. *Wealth Wisdom for Everyone: An Easy-to-Use Guide to Personal Financial Planning and Wealth Creation.* World Scientific Publishing Co. Pte. Ltd., 2006.

Davidson, Mike. *The Transformation of Management.* Butterworth-Heinemann, 1995.

Davis, William. *The Rich: A New Study of the Species.* Icon Books, 2006.

De Geus, Arie. *The Living Company: Habits for Survival in a Turbulent Business Environment.* Harvard Business School Press, 1997.

Dembo, Ron S. and Andrew Freeman. *Seeing Tomorrow: Rewriting the Rules of Risk.* John Wiley & Sons, Inc., 1998.

Donne, John. *Devotions upon Emergent Occasions.* Meditation XVII.

Evensky, Harold R. *Wealth Management: The Financial Advisor's Guide to Investing and Managing Client Assets.* McGraw-Hill, 1997.

Farkas, Charles M. and Philippe De Backer. *Maximum Leadership.* Henry Holt & Company Inc., 1996.

Federal Register/Vol. 72, No. 2/Thursday, 4 January 2007/Proposed Rules. *Part III Securities and Exchange Commission, 17 CFR Parts 230 and 275,* pp.405–6. See www.sec.gov/rules

Federal and State Constitutions Colonial Charters, and Other Organic Laws of the States, Territories, and Colonies Now or Heretofore Forming the United States of America Compiled and Edited Under the Act of Congress of June 30, 1906 by Francis Newton Thorpe, The. Washington, DC : Government Printing Office, 1909.

Fithian, Scott C. *Values-Based Estate Planning: A Step-by-Step Approach to Wealth Transfer for Professional Advisors.* John Wiley & Sons, Inc., 2000.

Fleishman, Joel L. *The Foundation: A Great American Secret.* Public Affairs, 2007.

Fleming, Quentin J. *Keep the Family Baggage out of the Family Business, Avoiding the Seven Deadly Sins that Destroy Family Businesses.* Simon & Schuster, 2000.

Forbes Magazine. "The Top 100 Celebrities", 2006. www.forbes.com/lists/2006/53/T5P9.html

Forbes Magazine Special Report: "The World's Richest People", Kroll, Luisa and Allison Fass, eds. 03.08.07. http://www.forbes.com/2007/03/07/billionaires-worlds-richest_07billionaires_cz_lk_af_0308billie_land.html

Ford, Bill. Ford Motor Company Annual Report Letter, March 1999.

Freed, Rachael. *Women's Lives, Women's Legacies: Passing Your Beliefs and Blessings to Future Generations.* Fairview Press, 2003.

Frey, Bruno S. and Alois Stutzer. *Happiness and Economics.* Princeton University Press, 2002.

George, Bill. *Authentic Leadership: Rediscovering the Secrets to Creating Lasting Value.* Jossey-Bass, 2003.

Gersick, Kelen E. et al, eds. *Generation to Generation, Life Cycles of the Family Business.* Harvard Business School Press, 1997.

Gersick, Kelin E. et al. *Generations of Giving, Leadership and Continuity in Family Foundations.* Lexington Books, 2004.

Gibson, Roger C. *Asset Allocation: Balancing Financial Risk* (Third Edition). McGraw-Hill, 2000.

Godfrey, Joline. *Raising Financially Fit Kids.* Ten Speed Press, 2003.

Godfrey, Neale S. and Carolina Edwards. *Money Doesn't Grow on Trees: A Parent's Guide to Raising Financially Responsible Children.* Simon & Schuster, 1994.

Godfrey, Neale S. *Money Still Doesn't Grow on Trees: A Parent's Guide to Raising Financially Responsible Teenagers and Young Adults.* Rodale, 2004.

Gough, Leo, with the Citibank Asia Wealth Management Team. *The Citibank Guide to Building Personal Wealth.* John Wiley & Sons (Asia) Pte. Ltd., 2005.

Gouillart, Francis J. and James N. Kelly. *Transforming the Organisation.* McGraw-Hill Inc., 1995.

Gould, Michael and Andrew Campbell. *Strategies and Styles: The Role of the Centre in Managing Diversified Corporations.* Blackwell Publishers, 1994.

Gray, Lisa. *The New Family Office: Innovative Strategies for Consulting to the Affluent.* Euromoney Institutional Investor Plc., 2004.

Greenwald, Bruce C. N. et al. *Value Investing, From Graham to Buffett and Beyond.* John Wiley & Sons, Inc., 2001.

Gunther, Marc. "Yale's 8 billion man", *Yale Alumni Magazine*, 2005, July/August, Vol. 68, No. 6.

http://www.yalealumnimagazine.com/issues/2005_07/swensen.html.

Gyatso, Tenzin, His Holiness the Dalai Lama. *Ancient Wisdom, Modern World Ethics for a New Millennium.* Little Brown and Company, 1999.

Hagstrom, Robert G. *The Warren Buffett Portfolio, Mastering the Power of the Focus Investment Strategy.* John Wiley & Sons, Inc., 1999.

Hagstrom, Robert G. *The Essential Buffett, Timeless Principles for the New Economy.* John Wiley & Sons, Inc., 2001.

Hagstrom, Robert G. *The Warren Buffett Way* (Second Edition). John Wiley & Sons, Inc., 2005.

Haman, Edward A. *The Complete Living Will Kit.* Sphinx Publishing, 2006.

Hamel, Gary and C.K. Prahalad. *Competing for the Future.* Harvard Business School Press, 1994.

Hamilton Hird, D. *History of Merrimack and Belknap Counties, New Hampshire.* J.W. Lewis & Co., 1885.

Hamilton, Sara. "Families at Risk", *Worth* (April 2007) Vol. 16, No. 4, pp. 46–8.

Hawthorne, Nathaniel. *The Marble Faun* (First published 1860). Penguin Books, 1990: Ch.5.

Hax, Arnoldo C. and Nicolas Majluf. *Strategic Management.* Prentice-Hall, 1984.

Hayes, Stephen K. *Wisdom from the Ninja Village of the Cold Moon.* Contemporary Books, Inc., 1984.

Hesselbein, Frances, Marshall Goldsmith and Richard Beckhard. *The Leader of the Future.* Jossey-Bass, 1996.

———, *The Organisation of the Future.* Jossey-Bass, 1997.

HM Revenue & Customs, "Rates and Allowances—Inheritance Tax". http://www.hmrc.gov.uk/rates/inheritance.htm

Hoffman, Yoel, compiled by. *Japanese Death Poems—Written by Zen Monks and Haiku Poets on the Verge of Death.* Tuttle Publishing, 1986.

Hughes Jr., James E. *Family Wealth—Keeping It in the Family.* New York: Bloomberg Press, 2004.

Ibbotson, Roger G. and Gary P. Brinson. *Global Investing: The Professional's Guide to the World Capital Markets.* McGraw-Hill, 1993.

IMF Press Release No. 05/265.

Ineichen, Alexander M. *Absolute Returns, The Risk and Opportunities of Hedge Fund Investing.* John Wiley & Sons, Inc., 2003.

Internal Revenue Service, United States Department of the Treasury, "Estates and Gift Taxes", http://www.irs.gov/businesses/small/article/0,,id= 98968,00.html.

Jaeger, Lars, ed. *The New Generation of Risk Management for Hedge Funds and Private Equity Investments.* Euromoney Institutional Investor Plc., 2004.

Jaeger, Lars. *Through the Alpha Smoke Screens: A Guide to Hedge Fund Return Sources.* Euromoney Institutional Investor Plc., 2005.

Kansas, Dave. *The Wall Street Journal: Complete Money & Investing Guidebook.* Three Rivers Press, 2005.

Kaplan, Robert S. and David P. Norton. *The Balanced Scorecard.* Harvard Business School Press, 1996.

Kenny, Bob. "Giving to Children. When Is Too Much Not Enough?" in *More Than Money*, Issue 34. www.morethanmoney.org/magazine/back_issues/mtm34/mtm34_kenny.htm

Kiyosaki, Robert T. with Sharon L. Lechter. *Rich Dad's Guide to Investing.* Warner Business Books, 2000.

Kochis, S. Timothy and Partners and Staff of Kochis Fitz. *Wealth Management: A Concise Guide to Financial Planning and Investment Management for Wealthy Clients.* CCH Incorporated, 2003.

The Koran, Chapter 2, Verse 177.

Lama Surya Das. *Awakening to the Sacred: Creating a Spiritual Life from Scratch.* Broadway Books, 1999.

Landau, Sue. "The very rich pay family retainers to talk to their bankers", *International Herald Tribune*, Business Section, 20 November 2006. www.iht.com/articles/2006/11/19/business/rwmtopbar.php

Lansberg, Ivan. *Succeeding Generations: Realizing the Dream of Families in Business.* Harvard Business School Press, 1999.

Law Commission The. Item 7 of the Sixth Programme of Law Reform: The Law of Trusts.

Levinson, Marc. *The Economist Guide to Financial Markets* (Third Edition). *The Economist* in association with Profile Books, 2000.

Link, E. G. "Jay". *Family Wealth Counseling, Getting to the Heart of the Matter, A Revolution in Estate Planning for Wealthy Families.* Professional Mentoring Program, 1999.

Lipnack, Jessica and Jeffrey Stamps. *The Age of the Network.* John Wiley & Sons, Inc., 1994.

Lucas, Stuart E. *Wealth: Grow it, Protect it, Spend it, and Share it.* Wharton School Publishing, 2006.

Luftman, Jerry N. ed. *Competing in the Information Age: Strategic Alignment in Practice.* Oxford University Press, 1996.

Marxer & Partner, Rechtsanwälte. *Companies and Taxes in Liechtenstein, Selected Topics of Liechtenstein Law* (Eleventh Edition). Liechtenstein Verlag, 2003.

Maude, David. *Global Private Banking and Wealth Management: The New Realities.* John Wiley & Sons Ltd., 2006.

Maxwell, Nicholas. *From Knowledge to Wisdom: A Revolution in the Aims and Methods of Science.* Basil Blackwell, 1984.

McConnell, Carmel. *Make Money, Be Happy.* Pearson Prentice Hall Business, 2005.

McGannon, Michael. *The Urban Warrior's Book of Solutions: Staying Healthy, Fit and Sane in the Business Jungle.* Pitman Publishing, 1996.

McLaughlin, Corrine and Gordon Davidson. *Spiritual Politics: Changing the World from the Inside Out.* Ballantine Books, 1994.

Merrill Lynch–Capgemini. *World Wealth Report 2006*, Figure A. "HNWI Ranks Show 10 Years of Steady Expansion", p.3. www.us.capgemini.com/**worldwealthreport/**

———, *World Wealth Report 2006*, Figure 12. "Sources of HNWI Wealth, 2005", p.19. www.us.capgemini.com/**worldwealthreport/**

Mobius, Mark. *Mutual Funds, An Introduction to the Core Concepts.* John Wiley & Sons (Asia) Pte Ltd., 2007.

Mobius, Mark with Stephen Fenichell. *Passport to Profits, Why the Next Investment Windfalls Will be Found Abroad—and How to Grab Your Share.* Warner Books, 1999.

Montes, Manuel F. and Vladimir V. Popov. *The Asian Crisis Turns Global.* Singapore: Institute of Southeast Asian Studies, 1999.

Morris, Virginia B. and Kenneth M. Morris. *Standard & Poor's Guide to Money & Investing.* Lightbulb Press, 2005.

Murrah, Jeffrey D. "The True Meaning of Wealth", in Pasadena ISD Parent University magazine, www.pasadenaisd.org/ParentUniversity/parent42.htm

Naisbitt, John. *Megatrends: Ten New Directions Transforming our Lives.* USA: Warner Books, 1984.

Naisbitt, John and Patricia Aburdence. *Megatrends 2000: New Directions for Tomorrow.* New York: Avon Books, 1990.

Nash, Laura and Howard Stevenson. *Just Enough: Tools for Creating Success in Your Work and Life.* John Wiley & Sons, Inc., 2004.

O'Neill, Jessie H. *The Golden Ghetto: The Psychology of Affluence.* The Affluenza Project, 1997.

Oechsli, Matt. *The Art of Selling to the Affluent: How to Attract, Service, and Retain Wealthy Customers and Clients for Life.* John Wiley & Sons, Inc., 2005.

Opdyke, Jeff D. *Love & Money: A Life Guide for Financial Success.* John Wiley & Sons, Inc., 2004.

———, *The Wall Street Journal: Complete Personal Finance Book.* Three Rivers Press, 2006.

Owen, David. *The First National Bank of Dad: The Best Way to Teach Kids About Money.* Simon & Schuster, 2003.

Perry, Ann. *The Wise Inheritor: A Guide to Managing, Investing and Enjoying Your Inheritance.* Broadway Books, 2003.

Peters, Thomas J. and Robert H. Waterman Jr. *In Search of Excellence: Lessons from America's Best-Run Companies.* Harper & Row Publishers Inc., 1982.

Phelan, Thomas. *1-2-3 Magic: Effective Discipline for Children 2-12* (Third Revised Edition). US: Child Management Inc., 2003.

Podcast: http://www.baylor.edu/content/services/document.php/24692.mp3

Porter, Michael E. ed. *Competition in Global Industries.* Harvard Business School Press, 1986.

———, *Competitive Strategy Techniques for Analyzing Industries and Competitors.* The Free Press, 1980.

————, *On Competition,* Harvard Business Review, 1996.

Porter, Michael E. and Mark R. Kramer. "The Competitive Advantage of Corporate Philanthropy", *Harvard Business Review,* 80:12 (December 2002), pp.56–68.

Prahalad, C.K. and Yves L. Doz. *The Multi-National Mission: Balancing Local Demands & Global Vision.* The Free Press, 1987.

Reichheld, F. Frederick ed. *The Quest for Loyalty: Creating Value through Partnership.* Harvard Business Review Books, 1996.

Reuters Limited, *USA Today,* www.usatoday.com/money/industries/energy/2007-04-08-oxy-pay_N.htm

Riemer, Jack and Nathaniel Stampfer. *So That Your Values Live On: Ethical Wills and How to Prepare Them.* Jewish Lights Publishing, 1991.

Robbins, Gary. "Estate Taxes: An Historical Perspective", The Heritage Foundation, Leadership in America, 16 January 2004, http://www.heritage.org/Research/Taxes/bg1719.cfm

Rogers, Jim. *Hot Commodities: How Anyone Can Invest Profitably in the World's Best Market.* Random House, 2004.

Rolland, Romain. *Jean Christophe.* Holt Rinehart & Winston, 1927.

Rottenberg, Dan. *The Inheritor's Handbook: A Definitive Guide for Beneficiaries.* Simon & Schuster, 2000.

Rules Against Perpetuities and Excessive Accumulations to the Right Honourable the Lord Irvine of Lairg, The Lord High Chancellor of Great Britain. http://www.lawcom.gov.uk/docs/lc251.pdf.

Schoch, Richard. *The Secrets of Happiness: Three Thousand Years of Searching for the Good Life.* Profile Books, 2006.

Schrecker, Ellen. *The Age of McCarthyism: A Brief History with Documents.* Boston: Bedford Books of St. Martin's Press, 1994, pp.201–2.

Schwab, Charles R. *Charles Schwab's New Guide to Financial Independence.* Three Rivers Press, 2004.

Senge, Peter M. *The Fifth Discipline: The Art and Practice of the Learning Organisation.* Currency Doubleday, 1994.

Shaw, John C. *Corporate Governance & Risk: A Systems Approach.* John Wiley & Sons, Inc., 2003.

Shenkman, Martin M. *The Complete Book of Trusts* (Third Edition). John Wiley & Sons, Inc., 2002.

Shook, R.J. *The Winner's Circle IV: Wealth Management Insights from America's Best Financial Advisors.* Horizon Publishers Group, 2005.

Sitkoff, Robert H. and Max M. Schanzenbach. "Jurisdictional Competition for Trust Funds: An Empirical Analysis of Perpetuities and Taxes", *Yale Law Journal* 2005, Vol. 115, p.356.

Spence, Linda. *Legacy: A Step-by-Step Guide to Writing Personal History.* Swallow Press/Ohio University Press, 1997.

Spender, Stephen. "I Think Continually of Those Who Were Truly Great" (l. 22–26), *Oxford Anthology of English Literature*, Vols. I–II. Kermode, Frank and John Hollander, general eds. Oxford University Press, 1973.

Statistik Austria, *Geborene seit 1998 nach ausgewählten demografischen und edizinischen Merkmalen*, www.statistik.at/web_de/statistiken/bevoelkerung/geburten/022899.html.

Stewart, Thomas A. *Intellectual Capital*. Nicholas Brealey Publishing Limited, 1997.

Stoval, Jim. *Wisdom of the Ages*. Executive Books, 2000.

Swensen, David F. *Pioneering Portfolio Management: An Unconventional Approach to Institutional Investment*. The Free Press, 2000.

Tagiuri, R.and J.A. Davis. "Bivalent attributes of the family form", Working Paper, Harvard Business School, 1982.

Tan, Lorna. "Only 1 in 7 family firms makes it to the 3rd generation", *The Straits Times*, February 13, 2006.

Telegraph the. London. "JK Rowling conjures up $1 billion fortune", James Burleigh. 10 March 2007. http://www.telegraph.co.uk/news/main.jhtml?xml=/news/2007/03/09/nrich09.xml

Templar, Richard. *The Rules of Wealth*. Pearson Prentice Hall Business, 2007. *http://www.yale.edu/lawweb/avalon/amerdoc/mayflower.htm*

Thompson, William Irwin. *At the Edge of History and Passages About Earth: Exploration of the New Planetary Culture*. Lindisfarne Press, 1990.

Train, John and Thomas A. Melfe. *Investing and Managing Trusts Under the New Prudent Investor Rule*. Harvard Business School Press, 1999.

True Happiness Can Be Yours. Singapore Every Home Crusade Co. Ltd., 2005.

Turnbull, Susan B. *The Wealth of Your Life: A Step-by-Step Guide for Creating Your Ethical Will*. Benedict Press, 2005.

Wallace, Alan B. *Genuine Happiness: Meditation as the Path to Fulfillment*. John Wiley & Sons, Inc., 2005.

Ward, John L. *Keeping the Family Business Healthy: How to Plan for Continuing Growth, Profitability and Family Leadership*. Family Enterprise Publishers, 1997.

———, *Perpetuating the Family Business: 50 Lessons Learned from Long-Lasting, Successful Families in Business*. Palgrave Macmillan, 2004.

Weber, Joseph et al. "Family, Inc. Surprise! One-third of the S&P 500 companies have founding families involved in management. And those are usually the best performers", *BusinessWeek*, 10 November 2003.

White, Doug. *Charity on Trial: What You Need to Know Before You Give*. Barricade Books, 2007.

Whittier, John Greenleaf. In *Maud Muller* (1856) St 53 *Familiar Quotations*. John Bartlett Fourteenth edition, Little, Brown and Company, 1968, p.626.

Williams, Roy and Vic Preisser. *Preparing Heirs: Five Steps to a Successful Transition of Family Wealth and Values.* Robert D. Reed Publishers, 2003.
————, *Philanthropy, Heirs and Values: How Successful Families are Using Philanthropy to Prepare Their Heirs for Post-Transition Responsibilities.* Robert D. Reed Publishers, 2005.
Wood, John. *Leaving Microsoft to Change the World.* HarperCollins Publishers, 2006.

INDEX